BLACKBURN WITH DARWEN LIBRARY

B

D0433794

Catherine Parr

FOR SCOTT
'Not a day goes by'

Catherine Parr

Henry VIII's Last Love

SUSAN JAMES

BLACKBURN WITH DARWEN LIBRARY SERVICE	
01400627₆ 0140062766	
Bertrams	10.03.08
9423.052092	£20.00

First published 2008

Tempus Publishing
Cirencester Road, Chalford,
Stroud, Gloucestershire, GL6 8PE
www.thehistorypress.co.uk

Tempus Publishing is an imprint of The History Press

© Susan James, 2008

The right of Susan James to be identified as the Author
of this work has been asserted in accordance with the
Copyrights, Designs and Patents Act 1988.

All rights reserved. No part of this book may be reprinted
or reproduced or utilised in any form or by any electronic,
mechanical or other means, now known or hereafter invented,
including photocopying and recording, or in any information
storage or retrieval system, without the permission in writing
from the Publishers.

British Library Cataloguing in Publication Data.
A catalogue record for this book is available from the British Library.

ISBN 978 0 7524 4591 5

Typesetting and origination by The History Press
Printed in Great Britain by Ashford Colour Press Ltd, Gosport, Hampshire

Contents

The Parrs (1370–1571)

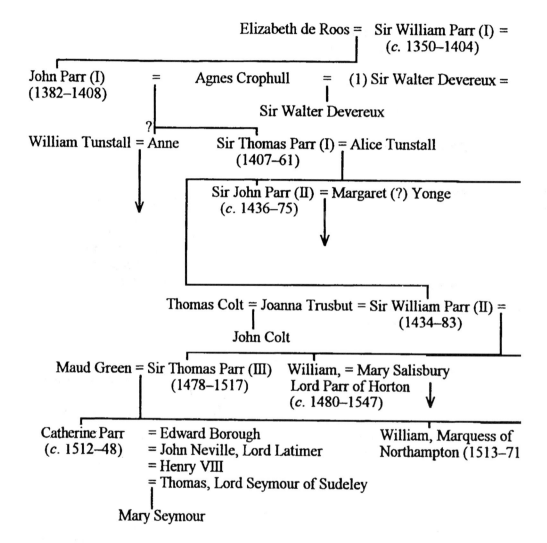

Elizabeth de Roos = Sir William Parr (I) =
(c. 1350–1404)

John Parr (I)   =   Agnes Crophull   =   (1) Sir Walter Devereux =
(1382–1408)

Sir Walter Devereux

William Tunstall = Anne   Sir Thomas Parr (I) = Alice Tunstall
                       (1407–61)

Sir John Parr (II) = Margaret (?) Yonge
(c. 1436–75)

Thomas Colt = Joanna Trusbut = Sir William Parr (II) =
                            (1434–83)
John Colt

Maud Green = Sir Thomas Parr (III)   William, = Mary Salisbury
          (1478–1517)   Lord Parr of Horton
                           (c. 1480–1547)

Catherine Parr   = Edward Borough   William, Marquess of
(c. 1512–48)   = John Neville, Lord Latimer   Northampton (1513–71
              = Henry VIII
              = Thomas, Lord Seymour of Sudeley

Mary Seymour

= Margaret Dutton (widow.)

= (3) Sir John Merbury

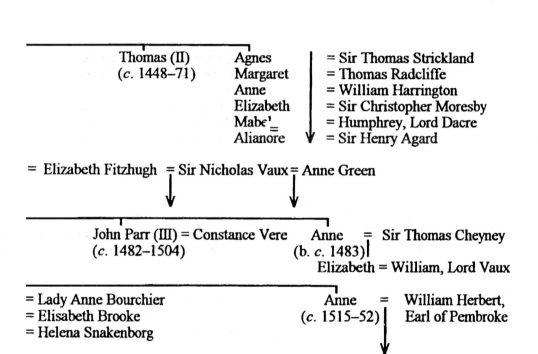

Thomas (II)	Agnes	= Sir Thomas Strickland
(c. 1448–71)	Margaret	= Thomas Radcliffe
	Anne	= William Harrington
	Elizabeth	= Sir Christopher Moresby
	Mabel	= Humphrey, Lord Dacre
	Alianore	= Sir Henry Agard

= Elizabeth Fitzhugh = Sir Nicholas Vaux = Anne Green

John Parr (III) = Constance Vere   Anne   = Sir Thomas Cheyney
(c. 1482–1504)   (b. c. 1483)
Elizabeth = William, Lord Vaux

= Lady Anne Bourchier   Anne   =   William Herbert,
= Elisabeth Brooke   (c. 1515–52)   Earl of Pembroke
= Helena Snakenborg

= descendants

Part One: The Parrs of Kendal

Introduction

Catherine, William and Anne Parr were born within a short four-year span, between the winters of 1511–12 and 1515–16. Close in age, they became emotionally close to each other as children, a bond no doubt strengthened by the early loss of their father. As adults, they continued to rely on each other for emotional support, as well as for more concrete reciprocities. Their lives entertwined in a way that makes it difficult to tell the story of one without the inclusion of the others. The Tudor age particularly was an age of families, great and small, aristocrat, gentry, yeoman and peasant, whose members attempted in a myriad of ways, legal and illegal, moral and immoral, to raise both themselves and the family groups to which they belonged into a higher sphere of property and influence than the one to which they had been born. Even queens were an integral part of this family social system, acting not alone but in concert with the interests of kith and kin. They were, in their own minds as well as those of their subjects, identified by their kinship groups, owing and generally acting upon an allegiance to the higher aspirations of mother, father, brother, sister, uncle, aunt and cousin. Family solidarity could and did raise an entire group by virtue of one successful individual. Men such as William Paget or William Cecil, women such as Jane Seymour or Catherine Parr, pulled in the wake of their rise whole cadres of cousins behind them. Nepotism was not a pernicious anomaly, it was a sacred obligation. By the stroke of a pen on a royal marriage license, Catherine Parr took her family where no Parr had gone before, into the highest strata of court society. That they managed to remain there after her death owed as much to their own talent and shrewdness as to their relationship with a Tudor queen of England.

A true understanding of Catherine Parr as queen comes only with an understanding and assessment of the family from which she sprang and which throughout her life she held in abiding affection. In chess, a game that Catherine played, the queen's gambit is a move which places the queen in jeopardy, or even sacrifices her, to gain a tactical advantage for her side. To a greater or lesser extent, all of the families who provided queens for the uxorial Henry VIII engaged in this move. Henry, himself, sacrificed four queens by divorce or execution to attain a perceived advantage. For Catherine Parr, the queen's gambit not only provided place and patronage for her family, it accelerated the pace of the reformed religion, ensured its continued integrity into the next reign and guaranteed the survival and preparation of her stepdaughter Elizabeth to preside over the glories of the Elizabethan age.

Part One of this book deals with the childhood of Catherine, William and Anne and their adult lives up to 1543. Catherine, who became queen consort of England in that year, had, by virtue both of her position and her character, the most significant impact of any of her family on the history of the last half of the sixteenth century. Part Two discusses her influence on her times and the historical significance of her life. This influence did not end with her death but reverberated through the reign of her stepdaughter, Elizabeth I, who, having observed Catherine's strategies of queenship while growing up, used many of these same strategies to pattern her own approach to power.

Where William and Anne Parr have been generally ignored, Catherine Parr has been marginalized in much of the literature of the period due primarily to a lack of research into her life and activities and a consequent lack of understanding of her seminal importance to the power politics in the final years of Henry VIII's reign. Married by the king solely on the grounds of her nursing abilities, so the popular story goes, romanced by her fourth husband, Thomas Seymour, when he failed in his attempts to attach the affections of the fourteen-year-old Princess Elizabeth, and generally consigned to a role draped in the crepe of religious gloom, Catherine Parr has failed to arouse the imagination of romantics. This is unfortunate, for her life contained all of the elements so beloved of romantic fiction – personal peril, clandestine romance, war, political intrigue, jealous husbands and royal matrimony. Her character, so often misconstrued, was passionate, vital and at times dangerously impulsive. More importantly, the lack of serious, sustained attention to the life and works of Catherine Parr has had the result of burying her real importance in a number of areas behind the hotly debated questions of her birthplace, her capabilities in Latin and her influence on her stepchildren.

This narrow viewpoint has created a distorted picture and afforded only an incomplete account of the politics of the latter half of the sixteenth century. For Catherine Parr was a strong-willed and outspoken woman, a committed player of power politics, an active patron of a multitude of arts taking shape in the emerging English Renaissance, a vigorous contributor to and supporter of the English Reformation and arguably the first Protestant queen of England.[1] She acted as Regent-General for the nation in 1544 and fully expected to be appointed so again at her husband's death when her young stepson ascended the throne as Edward VI. That she was not so appointed had more to do with Henry's vagaries at the end of his life (or perhaps with the post mortem changes to his will by others) than with her own proven abilities. The queen's belief in the moral right of Mary to be included among her father's heirs led Catherine to mount a persistent and ultimately successful campaign to reinstate her eldest stepdaughter in the royal line of succession, an act whose consequences would echo through the critical years following Henry VIII's death.

Catherine's own commitment to the new religion was zealous and absolute but it was not exclusive. Both her compassion for Mary and, just as importantly, her passion for Thomas Seymour caused her to make compromises with her conscience and in the latter case, with her own good sense. Yet in the cause of her religion, Catherine was an energetic advocate. Her involvement with the great translation project of Erasmus' *Paraphrases*, with the *King's Primer*, with the translation of Bishop Fisher's *Psalms or Prayers*, as well as the volumes published under her own name, present a clever woman diligent in her attempts to provide resource materials in the vernacular for the new religion. The list of her ecclesiastic protégés – Matthew Parker, John Parkhurst, Miles Coverdale and Nicholas Ridley – contains most of the architects of the reformed religion. In 1545, she appears to have encouraged Henry VIII to attempt the formation of a Protestant League, a radical political move for a Tudor consort and one in which her personal secretary was employed as secret ambassador to the European Protestant princes.

The increasing radicalization of Catherine's religious and political views, and her willingness despite cultural restrictions on women to vocalize them, brought her enemies like the wily Bishop of Winchester, Stephen Gardiner, who plotted against her life and nearly orchestrated her arrest and execution in 1546. Catherine's sexual infatuation with the mutually enamored Sir Thomas Seymour, which began before her marriage to the king and ultimately led to an ill-advised clandestine marriage just months after Henry's death, further alienated her from her former friends at court and diminished her influence with her royal stepson, Edward VI. Although she outlived Henry VIII by less than twenty months, the actions and events of Catherine's life were to have a ripple effect for the next fifty years.

In the area of the arts, Catherine was a patron *par excellence* of the evolving world of English language literature. She was the first queen of England to write and publish her own books and to become a recognised author during her lifetime and the first Englishwoman to publish a work of prose in the sixteenth century. In education, she encouraged her second husband, Lord Latimer, to found a free school at Well in Yorkshire, was a faithful patron as queen of the college of her Honour of Clare in Suffolk and supported the founding of Trinity College, Cambridge. Recipients of her patronage in the fine arts included such artists as John Bettes, Levina Teerlinc, Lucas Horenboult, Peter Richardson, and Giles Gering, musician and composer Antonio Bassano and his family, playwright and translator Nicholas Udall, as well as men in important collateral fields, such as printer-publishers Thomas Berthelet, Richard Grafton, and Edward Whitchurch, educators John Cheke, Anthony Cooke and Roger Ascham. She was also an enthusiastic patron of the nascent art of the English miniature and of English portrait painting and employed many of the major artists of the day to paint both herself and her royal stepchildren. Her love of music and dancing is well documented by the various foreign ambassadors at the English court during the time that she was queen, and her own privy chamber accounts indicate a woman who loved luxury, beautiful fabrics, stylish clothing and cleverly set jewels. This Renaissance sense of self, combined with her obvious enjoyment of sybaritic splendor, are at odds with Catherine's popular image as a colourless and unimaginative queen.

To a lesser but still significant extent, William Parr, Marquess of Northampton, is an important figure of the age. One of three men who put Lady Jane Grey on the throne of England, a generous patron of the arts, a friend of and donor to Cambridge University, the founder of Guildford Grammar School, and prop of the Duke of Northumberland's political overthrow of the lord protector, Northampton's career has deserved more scholarly interest than it has heretofore received. Yet Northampton's career in the final analysis owes less to his own efforts than to the efforts of the women in his life. Through his marriage to the outspoken and rebellious Lady Anne Bourchier, Northampton achieved the earldom of Essex. Through his sister, Catherine, he achieved the favour of the king. Northampton's second wife, Elisabeth Brooke, suggested the marriage between Lady Jane Grey and Guildford Dudley and became so close to the young Queen Elizabeth that the Earl of Leicester grew jealous. The career of the Marquess of Northampton is an important and neglected one but it also offers a framework for the lives and careers of his three wives, the equally important and neglected Anne Bourchier, Elisabeth Brooke and Helena Snakenborg.

The extant evidence recording the incidents of the life of the third Parr child, Anne, are far more sparse than those of her brother and sister. During Catherine's queenship, Anne acted as her most trusted advisor, while her husband, William Herbert, built a career on his familial connection to the throne. It was Herbert's good fortune to marry Anne Parr, for this marriage secured for him the opportunity to raise himself to the first ranks of the aristocracy. In Anne Parr's descendants, the Herbert Earls of Pembroke, the Parrs produced a fitting legacy of artistic patronage that did honour to the roots from which it sprang.

A Note On Spelling

Spelling during the Tudor period was erratic and idiosyncratic. For the sake of clarity, period quotations have been given a modern English spelling.

I

The Parrs of Kendal

In 1507, a twenty-nine-year-old courtier at the court of Henry VII purchased the wardship and marriage of a fifteen-year-old heiress from Northamptonshire.[1] Having taken his time to weigh up the character of the girl and possibly to give her time to become accustomed to him, he married her a year or so later. Such marriages were commonplace among the gentry in the sixteenth century and the heirs to large or even moderate estates, regardless of sex, were generally married, or at least betrothed, at puberty. It was considered essential to secure the succession of land within a recognized and accepted circle of families and in order to accomplish this, the heir to that land had to be used to dynastic advantage as soon as biologically feasible. Thus a year or so after having purchased the rights to both her person and her property, Thomas Parr of Kendal in Westmorland (1478–1517) wed the teenaged Matilda Green (1492–1531) of Green's Norton.[2] The feelings of the bride on this occasion went unrecorded.

The new Mistress Parr, always known in the family as 'Maud', was the daughter of Sir Thomas Green of Green's Norton in Northamptonshire. Green was the last male heir of a family who had lived at Green's Norton since the middle of the fourteenth century. An exceedingly wealthy man, he had made an advantageous marriage with the granddaughter of Sir John Fogge, treasurer of the royal household under Edward IV. Sir Thomas Green was a man of his times, pugnaciously conservative in religion, quarrelsome, conniving, and given to taking the law into his own hands. He ended his days in the Tower on trumped up charges of treason, dying there in 1506 and leaving two motherless daughters as his heirs. The younger daughter Maud, fourteen at her father's death, was a girl of passionate nature and stubbornness of spirit, who possessed a love of learning and a self-confidence in her own abilities unusual in a woman of her day and age. These qualities were to help determine the course of her life. At the age of fifteen, ten months after her father's death, Maud Green's person and prospects were sold to Thomas Parr, a man nearly twice her age. Having married the teenaged heiress and secured her lands in the following year, he lost no time in getting her with child, thus ensuring that the Green inheritance would stay in the Parr family.

Thomas Parr, father of Catherine,[3] William and Anne Parr, was the descendant of a rough and ready northern gentry clan, the Parrs of Kendal. They had been, after the Crown itself, the most influential presence in southern Westmorland since 1381. The paternal grandfather of the Parr children, Sir William Parr of Kendal (1434–1483)[4], served as comptroller of the household, councillor and friend to the first Yorkist king, Edward IV, whose own grandson Catherine would later marry. When Sir William Parr died in 1483 during the tumultuous reign of Richard III, he left four small children, among them five-year-old Thomas, and a twenty-three-year-old widow – born Elizabeth Fitzhugh. Descended from Edward III and niece of Warwick, the 'Kingmaker', the widowed Lady Parr's natural orbit seems to have revolved around the court. She served as a lady-in-waiting to Richard III's queen and at the fall of the Yorkist dynasty made a second marriage with a protégé of Margaret Beaufort, mother of the new king, Henry VII, which saved the family fortunes.

Elizabeth Fitzhugh's eldest son, Thomas Parr, father of the Parrs, seems to have inherited his easy-going, pleasure-loving disposition from his mother. When the widowed Lady Parr took Sir Nicholas Vaux of Harrowden in Northamptonshire as her second husband, Thomas soon developed close bonds with his stepfather. He grew up in Vaux's household, content to live in the south where he had been raised, and less than eager to change his comfortable Northamptonshire residence for the crumbling stone walls of Kendal Castle, his ancestral home, located an inconvenient distance from court. Thomas, it seems, was a man of singular charm. When the fouteen-year-old Princess Margaret Tudor left England to become the queen of James IV of Scotland in July 1505, she began her journey from her grandmother's house at Colyweston in Northamptonshire where Thomas Parr may have spent part of his youth. When she returned to England ten years later, Thomas was a member of the party who greeted her at Newcastle. By the time the party reached York, 'her grace rode upon a white palfrey behind Sir Thomas Parr, he riding bare head ... and when the said Queen was anenst the said Mayor [of York], the said Sir Thomas Parr advanced the Queen['s] horse toward the said Mayor, saying to her grace – here is the Mayor of this city.' By the time they reached London, almost a month later, Margaret was still clearly desirous of Parr's company and 'her grace did ride behind Sir Thomas Parr through Cheapside about six o'clock, and so to Baynard's Castle ...'[5]

By the time of his marriage, Thomas Parr was thirty years old. Like his mother and grandmother before him, both former royal ladies-in-waiting, he enjoyed the atmosphere of the court. Yet it cannot be said that his king, Henry VII, had proved a particularly good lord to Parr during the last decade of his reign. Between 1499, when he attained his majority, and 1509, the year in which Henry VII died, Parr's chief difficulty with the crown lay in balancing his attempts at personal enrichment against the king's notoriously aggressive policy of royal enrichment through the rigorous prosecution of his feudal prerogative, a policy that was to leave his royal heir with a full treasury at his death. Exorbitant punitive costs were imposed by the state for attaining livery of the Parr lands, for renewing long-held leaseholds, and for attaining title to his wife's inheritance. When Henry VII died in April 1509, Parr was bound to the crown for unpaid sums totaling nearly £9,000.[6] The horrendous size of this financial obligation can be gauged by the fact that the income from the Parr estates was worth roughly £150 a year. In simple arithmetic, then, it would have taken Parr nearly sixty years to pay off the bonds if he invested the entire income from his estates as they were in 1499. Ultimately, Henry VIII cancelled much of this debt to the crown but it was the threat of demanded payment that Henry VII held over Parr's head just as he did over the heads of as many of the English upper classes as it was possible to bring into his web of control. Nor was the king content with merely the threat the bonds represented. Parr was forced to pay off at least a portion of this enormous debt (about 3,000 marks) and when he could not make the payments, various pieces of his estate were confiscated by the crown, reducing the amount of rental fees available for the repayment of the balance. Inheritor not only of his family's lands but of his family's burning ambition for position and title, by 1508 Thomas had nothing to show for his ambitions but a load of debt and an appointment as esquire for the body. Choosing the age-old solution of dissatisfied courtiers everywhere, he began to cultivate a friendship not with the present monarch but with his heir. In 1508 the old king's heir was Henry, Prince of Wales, the future Henry VIII.

Born in 1491, heir to the throne at eleven, Prince Henry was all a Renaissance prince should be – attractive, affable, intelligent, an excellent sportsman and scholar, with pretensions to musical ability. He was known for his looks, his wit and his intellectual understanding. Catherine Parr's future royal husband deplored his father's pinchpenny economies and lacklustre lifestyle. As a young man, Henry Tudor proved to be the true grandson of Edward IV, glittering with possibility and promise. The younger men at court gravitated naturally to the lively circle around the heir apparent and among these was Catherine's father, Thomas Parr. Like so many others, Parr waited impatiently for the death of the old king and the beginning of that golden age which the coming of the golden prince promised.

On 21 April 1509 Henry VII died, and Henry VIII became King of England. For nearly forty years and on through the reigns of his children, England was to ride the choppy seas into which Henry plowed his ship of state. Wives, children, ministers, religion, and political alliances were so many building blocks to the golden prince, to be piled up, tumbled down, used or discarded at will.

What came between Henry and his desires was ruthlessly eliminated. But the true nature of the king, fashioned as it was by genetics, inclination and the raw clay of circumstance, had yet to be revealed in 1509. With Henry's accession to the throne, the fortunes of the Parr family improved. As part of the new king's coronation festivities, Thomas Parr was created a Knight of Bath and granted the stewardship of all the royal lands in the old barony of Kendal.[7] Four months later, Henry cancelled debts to the crown amounting to 16,000 marks owed by Parr and his stepfather, Sir Nicholas Vaux, and by 1513, the king had cancelled entirely the remainder of Parr's huge feudal debt. In November 1509, he threw in a 50-mark annuity to Parr for good measure.[8] With Henry VIII's accession to the throne, life for the Parr family not only presented altogether more attractive prospects for advancement but for revelry as well. Between 1509 and 1515, during the early years of Catherine and William's childhood, their father and mother became active members of a court that sought to resurrect Camelot, that delighted in lavish amusements and display, in jousts, feasts and pageants, that saw Catherine's father and uncle dressed in Kendal green playing the part of Robin Hood's Merry Men and running 'for a gladness to the Queen's grace.'[9] The change in mood from the gloomy court of the late Henry VII could not have been more marked. The new king's marriage to his brother's Spanish widow, Catherine of Aragon, had provided the new Camelot with a queen worthy of the honour, and Catherine's mother, Maud, was soon appointed one of her ladies-in-waiting. A friendship was formed between the new queen and the young Lady Parr that lasted until Maud's death in 1531.[10]

By the time she was five years old, Catherine Parr had led an itinerant childhood, the lot of many children whose parents were in service at court. Her father seemed to be content to wander from residence to residence without ever actually establishing a family seat in the south. In 1509, three years before his elder daughter's birth, Thomas listed himself as 'of Kendal, Harrowden, Carlisle and Kirkoswald',[11] and by 1510, he had added 'of London' to the list.[12] In 1509 he joined his stepfather, Sir Nicholas Vaux, in an investment venture in the English Pale in France and spent some time during the next few summers across the Channel at the castles of Guisnes and Hammes.[13] How many years these summer holidays continued and whether the young Parrs ever travelled to France with their father is not recorded. Shortly before her birth, Catherine's parents had purchased or leased a house in the fashionable London area of Blackfriars. They were spending an increasing amount of time at court and wanted their own home in the city. Their family was growing as well. Their first son, with whom Maud had found herself pregnant shortly after her marriage, did not survive the vicissitudes of child mortality and the only remembrance of him was as a mourner on his parents' tomb in St. Anne's

Church in Blackfriars.[14] The Parrs' second child, Catherine, was born in 1512, probably in the month of August,[15] and was followed by their only surviving son, William, born on 14 August 1513.[16] Their second daughter, Anne, the future Countess of Pembroke, was born about 1515. When Catherine's father died in November 1517, her mother was pregnant again, but this child, like its eldest brother, did not survive infancy. The birthplaces of the Parr children, particularly of Catherine, have been hotly debated, with Kendal Castle edging out competitors in the mythology of Catherine's life. At the time of Catherine's birth, however, Kendal Castle was in less than sound repair and by 1572 it was derelict.[17] That Sir Thomas would carry his pregnant wife on a gruelling two-week journey north over execrable roads to give birth in a crumbling castle in which neither of them had ever lived seems improbable.[18]

On 25 November 1510, Sir Thomas Parr received a grant of the manor of 'Fenel's Grove or Whitingham's manor' in Great Kimble (near Aylesbury) in Buckinghamshire.[19] He held title to this manor until November 1512, when the Crown returned it to the family of its original owner, and in all likelihood if she did not give birth to her elder daughter in her Blackfriars house, Lady Parr did so here. With the loss of Great Kimble in the winter of 1512, and until the spring of 1516, the Parrs seem to have resided mainly in London. Then in March 1516 they were granted the manor of Lillingstone Lovell in Oxfordshire, together with the castle of Moor's End at Potterspury near the Buckinghamshire–Northamptonshire border. Maud Parr's father, Sir Thomas Green, had been constable of Moor's End castle and keeper of the park, so the area was no doubt familiar to her.[20] The Parrs' continued residence at Moor's End seems, however, to have been dependent on whether or not Sir Thomas held office in the area. In August 1517, Cardinal Wolsey notified the king that, 'Sir Thomas Parr will probably ask for [Sir Nicholas Vaux's] offices in Northamptonshire and if you grant it, he can resume the manor of Moor's End which [you] granted to him, his wife and son during their lives.'[21] In the event, the Parrs never did return to Moor's End. Sometime in the year or so before his death, Catherine's father secured the lease of Rye House in Hertfordshire.[22] It was at Rye House where Catherine, William and Anne spent the formative years of their childhood. For it was here after Sir Thomas' death in 1517 that Lady Parr and her children finally established a more or less permanent home, maintaining it until Maud Parr's own death in December 1531.

Sir Thomas' career at court acquired a new lustre in January 1512 when his first cousin, Lord Fitzhugh of Ravensworth, died, leaving Parr heir to a moiety of the vast Fitzhugh estates.[23] At a stroke, Sir Thomas became master of half the Fitzhugh lands in seven counties, which included twenty-three manors in the North Riding of Yorkshire and the palatinate of Durham alone.

Yet the baronies associated with Fitzhugh's lands – Marmion, St. Quintin and Fitzhugh of Ravensworth – eluded him, the titles going to the senior heir, Thomas Fiennes, Lord Dacre of the South.[24] Influence and income, if not title, both increased, Parr continued to look for ways to enhance his power at court. In the summer of 1516, he joined the nascent Tudor civil service when his cousin Sir Thomas Lovell,[25] made him an associate master of the wards, a hitherto unknown office. In 1513, Lovell followed Sir John Hussey as the second master of the Court of Wards and Liveries, founded in 1503 by Henry VII to regulate the income from these lucrative sources of feudal revenue. At the beginning of his tenure as master, Lovell was a busy royal servant, but by the summer of 1516, he had begun to withdraw from royal affairs. It may have been the onset of the unknown illness which killed him eight years later or an inability to accommodate himself to Thomas Wolsey's rising star that caused his partial retirement to his house at Elsing, near Enfield in Middlesex. He did not, however, give up the mastership of the wards entirely but continued to hold it until 1520.[26] Nevertheless, Lovell apparently desired to share the duties of the office with an associate master and his choice fell on Sir Thomas Parr. One document, a signet bill, bearing the joint signatures of Lovell and Parr, indicates the establishment of this new office,[27] and the inscription on Parr's tomb in St. Anne's, Blackfriars, read, 'Pray for the soul of Thomas Par, knight of the king's body, Henry the eighth, master of his wardes ... and ... sher[iff] ... who deceased the 11th day of November in the 9th year of the reign of our said sovereign lord at London, in the ...(Black)Fryers...'[28]

By the fall of 1517 Sir Thomas Parr was thirty-nine. He had been married for nearly a decade to a dynamic and intelligent woman half his age and was the father of three young children. He maintained homes in London and Hertfordshire. He was popular with the king, a master of his wards, and had served at court with such men as Sir Thomas More, but his career had not prospered as much as it might have done. Although rich in land, the title of baron had eluded him. At the beginning of November, Parr fell ill and quickly got worse. On 7 November he wrote his will leaving £400 apiece as marriage portions for his six-year-old daughter, Catherine, and his baby daughter, Anne. He provided for a younger son if the child with whom Maud Parr was pregnant should be a boy.[29] If Maud produced 'any more daughters', Sir Thomas states rather humourlessly, 'she shall marry them at her own cost.' The bulk of his considerable estate descended to his only son and heir, four-year-old William, with Maud, Cuthbert Tunstall, Bishop of London, Sir William Parr of Horton, and Dr. Melton as executors.[30]

Sir Thomas Parr died at his London house on 11 November and was buried in St. Anne's Church, Blackfriars, beneath an elaborate table tomb overlooked by images probably in stained glass depicting his wife, himself and their four children kneeling in prayer.[31] He died in a year that was to have overwhelming consequences not only for the history of Sir Thomas' children, but for the history of Western civilisation as well. For it was in 1517, less than two weeks before Parr's death, that Martin Luther pinned his 95 theses to the church door in Wittenberg and tore the first rent in the seamless garment of European Christendom. For the moment, however, it was Sir Thomas' death that was of primary importance to the Parr family.

Catherine Parr was barely five when her father died. That she felt his loss is certain for her widowed mother's lifestyle suddenly became far more circumspect. The carefree days of courtly gaiety while her father was alive were over. This early loss seems to have strengthened Catherine's feelings of responsibility for her brother and sister. For the rest of her life, as queen and after, she made certain that William and Anne had all that she could give them. With Sir Thomas Parr's death, the family's income was affected as well. Money had to be found to buy marriages for the children and without the royal favours which her husband had enjoyed, Maud Parr was forced to plan carefully. The head of the house of Parr was now a four-year-old child, Catherine's little brother, and the Parr estates were of necessity left in the hands of stewards, overseen by Maud and her brother-in-law, Sir William Parr of Horton. The obvious solution to the Parrs' altered situation was for Maud Parr to remarry as quickly and as advantageously as possible. Yet Maud Parr lived for fourteen more years and never seems to have contemplated remarriage. Fortunately for her, apparently, she had no near relatives apart from her elder sister, Anne,[32] to pressure her into remarrying. On the basis of the evidence, Maud appears to have discovered what her daughter, Catherine, was to discover some twenty-six years later, that widowhood for a woman could become a deliverance from the bondage of social and familial imperatives to the freedom of self-determined action.[33] Widowhood implied loss but it could also mean being set 'at liberty'.[34]

If the Parr children's father, Sir Thomas, fulfilled all of the conditions for society's definition of the perfect man, a 'courtier, resplendent with all the highest human powers and graces, to which only a court could give full scope,'[35] as a widow, their mother strove to find ways to circumvent society's requirements for the perfect woman: chaste, passive, submissive and silent. Although her chastity never became an issue, passivity, submission and silence were antithetical to Maud Parr's character. For a widow still of childbearing age, celibacy became the trade-off for conditional freedom of action and a voice in her own and in her children's lives. As Maud Parr's influence on the early perceptions of her children cannot be underestimated, it is of primary importance to take into account the patterns of behaviour which she set down for them, particularly for her daughters. A strong, intelligent and resourceful woman, Maud discovered that widowhood, with its freedom from both parental and spousal supervision, offered her the best arena for utilizing her strengths. By the time she was twenty-five, she had fulfilled society's prescriptions for a woman. She had borne five children and proven an admirable wife in her husband's house. She had also shown herself a capable lady-in-waiting and an ornamental accessory at the early Henrician court. Yet Maud Parr defied the misogynistic definition of the 'poor weak woman',[36] vessel of all human frailty, by her capable handling of the legacy left to her at Sir Thomas' death. Although she never openly challenged cultural prejudices and deep-seated fears against 'woman as master', the way in which she handled her various roles, particularly in her children's lives, reinforced their belief in a woman's capabilities. Maud was made chief executor for her husband's will and manager of his lands in the south. She was the chief architect of her children's education and of Catherine's and William's first marriages. She founded a school in her own home, where the customs of her class sanctioned merely a supervisory role in her children's religious education.[37] She also left money to found schools which was not customary for a woman. She made her own will without interference, leaving legacies to family, servants and friends, and when she died, she was buried beneath the monument which she herself had had erected for herself and her husband.[38]

Maud Parr was not a woman who actively sought to change the status of women. The money left in her will for 'the marrying of maidens' implies a belief in marriage as the God-given destiny of the female, as well as a more pragmatic realisation that apart from the convent, marriage was the sole career option open to a gently-born girl. However, Maud's actions as supreme authority in her own household during her widowhood partly ameliorated these socially condoned beliefs in the eyes of her children. Her daughters, particularly, received mixed messages about the role of women within the society. In the received cultural bias of the period, and prominently featured in the literature, the act of creation, biologically a female determinant, had been culturally encrypted as a male prerogative. Thus, God, generally perceived as a male demiurge, created a world order destroyed by the ambition of Eve. Arthur created Camelot; Guinevere caused its downfall. The Trojans achieved; Helen destroyed. Of interest is the fact that negative icons of female frailty, such as Guinevere and Helen, were portrayed as childless, denied in myth even their biologically creative aspects. Woman, giver of life, was culturally encrypted in a literature written and controlled by men, as the betrayer and destroyer of the very force she embodied. Catherine and Anne Parr could hardly have missed the message. Yet their mother's actions offered them an alternative to this gloomy interpretation of the nature of woman. Books used as traditional teaching tools, including the Bible, might stress woman's role as subordinate to man and insist upon the lesser mental capacity of the female. They might even set out the creed that all the evils of the world were due to the uncontrolled irrationality and rampant lasciviousness of women, necessarily controlled and repressed by the measured reason of man.[39] Maud Parr, however, was an ever-present example as both father and mother in the daily lives of three children, who had yet to deal with society's admonitions and prejudices at large, that such concepts had less to recommend them than those who wrote the books would have them believe.

An exposure to the subversive message of power as an achievement based not on gender but on fortune is given graphic illustration in the story told of Catherine Parr as a child. When ordered to her 'womanly' lessons in needlework, the young Catherine announced one day to her mother that a fortune-teller had proclaimed her 'hands were ordained for sceptres' and not for needles.[40] That a female child could so fantasise her adult role, assuming the story's veracity, is directly related to the role that she perceived her mother to play in the world. The mother–daughter bond was particularly strong between Maud and Catherine and probably, although not provably, between Maud and Anne. Their childhood observation of her apparent freedom of behaviour within a liberally interpreted definition of the role of widow executor in early sixteenth-century society helped to justify to themselves as adults the assertive lives they led. Catherine as queen and Anne, as the dominant member in her own marriage due to her relationship with the queen, entered as adults into that minority of women who have managed to make their voices heard in an age which gave little value to female voices.

William, too, must have been affected by the powerful role played by his mother in his childhood but at eleven, he was to enter the world of male power politics, a fact which undoubtedly eroded some of the impact of a mother-dominated childhood experience. Certainly his treatment of his first wife would imply a general acceptance of society's definition of the proper spheres and sanctioned behavioural differences between men and women. His mother, however, he seems to have considered unquestioningly as someone apart from normal female constraints,[41] a perception his sisters probably shared and one which would have considerable influence on their later interpretations of their own adult roles in society. Catherine and Anne, who did not leave home until their mid to late teens, were longer exposed to their mother's dominant position in the household. It was Maud Parr's pragmatic exercise of power as unchallenged queen within Catherine, William and Anne's childhood kingdom which set the pattern for Catherine's later exercise of power as queen within a national arena and her eager exploration of the possibilities of her position. It was Maud Parr, who laid the foundations of expectation and active achievement, of a participatory rather than a passive role in the shaping of one's own destiny which Catherine came to embody and so passed on to her stepdaughter, the future queen Elizabeth I.

2

'Ripe and Seasonable Knowledge'

A close friend and intimate of the queen, Catherine of Aragon, Maud Parr continued upon her husband's death as one of the queen's most devoted ladies-in-waiting.[1] Not all of her time, however, was spent at court. Ladies-in-waiting worked in shifts, with time spent at court and time spent about their own business. When regulations for the royal household were drawn up at Eltham in 1526, Lady Parr, Lady Willoughby and Jane, Lady Guildford, were assigned lodgings on 'the Queen's side' of the palace, 'when they repaired to [court].'[2] If an emergency arose and the queen required the presence of all her ladies, yeomen of the chamber were sent riding post haste with letters from the queen, 'warning the ladies to come to the court'.[3] Maud, then, had time to spend with her children at Rye House in between the requirements of her service to Catherine of Aragon.

With her husband's death, Maud realized that the responsibility of establishing her children in the world rested on her shoulders. From 1517 until the end of her life, all of her energies, and they were considerable, were focused on educating her children, in settling them in the best positions and making the most advantageous matches she could find for them. Like her royal mistress, Maud Parr appreciated the importance of education, and to further this, she gathered a small group of children in her household to share lessons with her own three. The Parr children's two cousins, the orphaned Elizabeth Cheyney (later Lady Vaux), and Sir William Parr of Horton's eldest daughter, Maud (later Lady Lane), appear to have been among them.[4] With her cousin, the younger Maud, Catherine Parr formed a close life-long friendship, but Elizabeth Cheyney's stubborn, outspoken nature seems to have been too like Catherine's own for their schoolroom days to translate into a close adult friendship.[5]

Educational opportunities for boys and girls were differentiated by the demands of the role that each sex was expected to play in society. While both were expected to learn the tenants of their religion, that religion was frequently used as a tool to reinforce a woman's sense of diminished self-worth, of subordination to a social order dominated by men.[6] The Bible, St. Paul, the Evangelists, and later religious writers such as St. Thomas Aquinas and St. John Chrysostome, all expounded the gospel of divinely authorized female submission to the established order, not only in the unshakable belief of lesser intellectual ability but also on the grounds of woman's fundamentally debased nature and its need for instruction, admonition and control. Catherine Parr was intimately acquainted with the writings of these men, as she must have been with both Christian and classical injunctions against the dangers of over-educating women.[7] To many, the image of the scholarly woman was anathema and against the social order ordained by God.[8] Yet Catherine seems to have responded to these attitudes as she later responded to those who feared that allowing the common folk to read the Bible in the vernacular would lead to heresy:

> ... it is a lamentable thing to hear how there be many in
> the world that do not well digest the reading of Scripture
> and do commend and praise ignorance, and say that much
> knowledge of God's word is the original of all
> dissension, schisms and contention and maketh men
> haughty, proud and presumptuous by reading of the same.
> This manner of saying is no less than a plain blasphemy
> against the Holy Ghost ... I pray God all men and women may
> have grace to become mete tillage for the fruits of the gospel,
> (for) ... It were all our parts and duties to procure and seek all
> the ways and means possible to have more knowledge of
> God's words.[9]

As there is no evidence that Maud Parr provided two sets of tutors – one for her son and one for her daughters – it is to be deduced that the quality of education provided in her household was, at least until William's departure in 1525, the same for both. Economics may have played a role in schooling William and his sisters together under the same tutors, but the quality of Anne's continuing education after William left home in 1525 to join the household of the Duke of Richmond demonstrates that the ideal of a humanist education for her son extended in Maud Parr's mind to her daughters. Marriage may have been the fate to which Catherine and Anne were necessarily destined, denying the girls any public forum for their scholarship, yet within the confines of that future destiny, and limited by the cultural constraints of domestic modesty and marital obedience, Catherine and Anne were to have whatever freedom and attainments a well-educated mind could give them.

As with so many aspects of Catherine Parr's life, the quality and extent of her education have been a matter of debate among modern scholars. The majority opinion allows her an adequate if not inspired grasp of the basics[10] – the quality of her Latin raising the most controversy – while a minority opinion allows her little above a rudimentary literacy.[11] The evidence available points to something more than either of these schools of thought. To understand the principals under which Catherine was educated, it is necessary to investigate the architects who designed her education – her parents and her father's cousin, Cuthbert Tunstall, Bishop of London (in 1522) and later Bishop of Durham.

Catherine's grandfather (actually step-grandfather), Sir Nicholas Vaux of Harrowden Hall, Northamptonshire, had been placed as a child in the household of Henry VII's mother, Margaret Beaufort, dowager Countess of Richmond.[12] Margaret Beaufort was a highly intelligent and unusually well-educated woman for her time. She was interested in scholarship and devoted time and money to raising the level of education among the male members of her own class. During her lifetime, her money also helped support scholars of the new humanism which was emerging on the intellectual scene and she was responsible for a variety of collegiate foundations at Cambridge, most importantly at St. John's College. It was from this college that so many of the religious reformers of the 1530s and 1540s – Roger Ascham, John Cheke, John Redman, George Day, William Grindal, Thomas Smith – were to come. Bishop Fisher in his *Morning Remembrance* recalled of Margaret that, 'She was also of singular easiness to be spoken unto, and full courteous answer she would make to all that came unto her. Of marvellous gentleness she was unto all folks, but specially unto her own, whom she trusted and loved right tenderly.'[13]

On 22 March 1487, Margaret Beaufort had been granted by her son, Henry VII, several manors in Hertfordshire and Northamptonshire, among them the manor of Colyweston. Margaret liked the area around her new manor and completed the half-finished house that its previous owner, Ralph, Lord Cromwell, had begun. It was 'a goodly, faire and stately house', and Margaret enjoyed visiting Colyweston and did so frequently between 1487 and her death in 1503.[14] At Colyweston, Margaret installed the scholar and teacher, Maurice Westbury of Oxford, and 'certain young gentlemen', including the son of the Earl of Northumberland, were placed in the household to be educated.[15] Not only education but important future political connections were forged among the schoolboys in such an establishment as Colyweston. The manor was just over twenty miles north of Sir Nicholas Vaux's own manor and as a Beaufort 'graduate', himself, it is more than likely that Vaux placed his young stepson, Thomas Parr, in the Beaufort household to study the art of being a gentleman under Maurice Westbury. Thomas Parr's late father, Sir William Parr of Kendal, had once been Margaret Beaufort's reversionary heir to her substantial lands in Westmoreland, known as the Richmond Fee.[16] Then, too, Margaret's third husband, Thomas Stanley, 1st Earl of Derby, had been married formerly to Eleanor Neville, the sister of Alice, Lady Fitzhugh of Ravensworth,

Thomas Parr's maternal grandmother. This complicated kinship and geographic interrelationship, combined with Vaux's long-time friendship with Margaret, would have provided sufficient credentials to admit young Thomas into the countess' household.

Parr has been described as, 'a scholar in Latin, Greek and modern languages',[17] and his associate mastership of the wards implies a degree of mental acuity in addition to an important family connection, but the only remnant of his scholarship is found in a book of hours, the *Horae ad Usum Sarum*, given to him by his aunt, Mabel, Lady Dacre, which contains a few carefully inscribed Latin tags in an adult hand and his name carefully printed in the manner of schoolboys.[18] Roger Ascham, in a letter concerning the joys of scholarship, written to Parr's daughter, Anne, about 1547, refers to 'the memory of your most famous father'.[19] Additionally, there are Parr's connections with Sir Thomas More to recommend him as a man with a keen interest in scholarship. More's first wife, Jane, the mother of his children, was Parr's niece,[20] and it was to More's household that Parr looked when seeking an educational plan for his own children.[21] With the notable scholar Cuthbert Tunstall as his cousin and executor of his will and Sir Thomas More as an in-law, Parr's interest in scholarship seems more than likely.

Catherine's mother, if not a scholar of the classics, was nevertheless a woman capable of running her own affairs and her husband's estates, of organizing the education and marriages of her children and of negotiating for marriage settlements on a one-to-one basis with Thomas, Lord Dacre, Lord Scrope of Bolton, and Henry Bourchier, Earl of Essex. In her will, Maud left 400 marks, a considerable sum, for the founding of schools and 'the marrying of maidens and in especial my poor kinswomen'.[22] She was fluent in French, may have read Latin, although this is not certain,[23] and like her royal mistress, Catherine of Aragon, was concerned that her children have the best education that she could give them. It was probably from her mother that Catherine learned much of that reputed knowledge of simples, herbals and medicines that was to become such a feature in two of her four marriages. One tribute to Maud Parr's interest in her children's education comes from her husband's cousin, Lord Dacre. In a letter of advice written in 1523 concerning his grandson, Henry Scrope, Dacre wrote: '... remembering the wisdom of my said lady [Parr]... I assure you he [Henry] might learn with her as well as in any place that I know, as well nurture, as French and other languages ...'[24] From this, it is apparent that the foundations of Catherine's education as well as her love of learning were laid in childhood by her able and versatile mother.

Lady Parr's careful management of her children's education was, according to her younger daughter, Anne, based on the programme of studies that Sir

Thomas More set out for his own children.[25] More did not credit the generally accepted view that a woman's mind was by nature 'bad and apter to bear fern than corn.' Given an equal educational advantage, 'both [men and women] bear[ing] the name of a reasonable creature equally,' were capable of a fruitful intellectual harvest.[26] More was 'one of a handful of Renaissance thinkers who either gave an equal education to daughters or advocated such...[thus] his was the most positive voice among male humanists during the sixteenth century in England.'[27] More and Sir Thomas Parr had been born in the same year, were related by marriage and served together at court. More's educational programme, which laid heavy emphasis on classical studies and languages for both girls and boys, was quite influential among the ambitious parents at Henry's court. This was true among those of the upper classes for whom education, particularly the new humanist version that included daughters as well as sons, soon became a popular fashion, although the goal of education for women was not to prepare them for any career other than marriage. To produce a daughter who could read Latin, argue philosophy or discuss mathematics was a novel sensation for aristocratic parents and this trend to educate daughters was encouraged by the fact that the heir to the throne of England was a girl, the Princess Mary.

Catherine and Anne Parr grew up during a time of increasing emphasis on female education, albeit within a restricted social circle and for private enjoyment alone. This emphasis was nourished by the appearance of a number of gifted teachers whose skills and enthusiasm were passed on to their gently-born pupils. Men like Juan Luis Vives, Thomas Linacre, Roger Ascham, Sir John Cheke, and John Palsgrave held well-earned reputations for their scholarship and the innovative quality of their teaching. It has been claimed that Catherine Parr was educated at court with the Princess Mary under the tutelage of Juan Luis Vives.[28] This is probably untrue for besides the fact that there is no evidence that Vives actually taught the princess personally – or ever left Spain for that matter – Catherine was four years older than Mary and in 1523, when Catherine of Aragon was hiring tutors for her daughter, Catherine, at eleven, was already well into her education.

Vives' 'Plan of Study For Girls' which advised an educational curriculum that prepared girls to become informed helpmates to their husbands, competent teachers to their children and servants, and capable students of religious lessons to be learned in Scripture, viewed a woman's education as necessarily more restricted than a man's as her socially and religiously dictated life-calling within the family was necessarily more restricted.[29] This was the prevailing view, even among the more enlightened of the new breed of teachers, yet given an apt and eager student with a precocious mind, particularly one who might some day rule a kingdom, the scholar might be tempted to overlook the sex of the student in the recognition of individual gifts worth encouraging. So theoretical dogmatic proscriptions on the advisable limits of female education were not always honoured in practice. Elizabeth I certainly enjoyed as good an education as her brother and John Aylmer's inability to endorse the concept of equality in education for the sexes did not preclude his covering the same material with Jane Grey that he would have covered had she been a boy. Catherine and Anne Parr, also, seemingly enjoyed equal educational opportunities with their brother, certainly until 1525 and probably beyond.

Who the tutors were that Maud Parr may have engaged to educate her children is not known but she had the advice of her husband's cousin, Cuthbert Tunstall, on which to depend. Her gratitude to him was so great that it is mentioned in her will, of which Tunstall was principal executor, where Maud leaves to 'my good Lorde Cuthberd Tunstall, Bisshop of London … a ring with a ruby'.[30] To Lord Dacre, Maud wrote in 1524, that she had a high regard for 'the advice of my lord of London'.[31] Tunstall was a clever and conservative man with a keen mind and a shrewd eye for opportunity. The illegitimate son of Thomas Tunstall of Thurland Castle and great-nephew of Sir Thomas Parr's paternal grandmother, Alice Tunstall, Cuthbert, named for a popular local saint, had studied civil law at Oxford, Cambridge and Padua. He found a patron in Cardinal Wolsey and worked for various periods as ambassador in Brussels and Cologne. Master of the Rolls in 1516, in 1522 he was made Bishop of London, in 1523 the keeper of the Privy Seal, and in 1529, Bishop of Durham. Familiar with Latin, Greek and Hebrew, Cardinal Pole considered him 'the best scholar in England'.[32] Tunstall had been one of the three executors of Sir Thomas Parr's will, would be principal executor of Maud's, and was a close family friend. A central figure in the English humanist circle, Tunstall was also one of Sir Thomas More's closest friends, an intimate of Erasmus, John Colet, Thomas Lupset, and William Grocyn, and the executor of the wills of Thomas Linacre and John Sistin. Tunstall and More were dubbed by Erasmus, 'the two most learned men in England – both very dear to me'.[33] The bishop was also a man known for his patronage of humanist scholars as well as his own scholarship, and was closely involved in the preparation of the second edition of Erasmus' Greek Testament. Of the three presentation copies of this great work which Erasmus had printed on vellum, one was presented to Tunstall. Tunstall also wrote the first treatise on arithmetic published in England, *De Arte Supputandi*. He confided to his friend, Sir Thomas More, his difficulties in turning his studies among the abstractions of arithmetic into elegant Latin.

During the time I was trying to do this and the business
was making little enough progress, overcome by weariness

I often threw down the books, hopeless of being able to
carry out what I had purposed – at times because the
subject-matter was hard to understand, at others because
many points often arose which seemed to offer no scope
either for Latin style or for eloquence ... So at last, determined
on my plan I put up with its tedium, and, forcing my way
through many obstacles, noted down these extracts of one
sort and another from among a great number. And I have
been for a long time past assiduously fashioning them at
home, thinking in the end to have licked them into shape at
my leisure, after the manner of a bear with her ugly cubs.

One of the many innovative things about *De Arte Supputandi* is that Tunstall,
who had an endearing fondness for children, recommends the study of
arithmetic for both boys and girls and invites parents to:

Pass the book on to your children for them to read – children whom you take care
to train in liberal studies. For to them it might be most specially beneficial ... since
by nothing are the abilities of young folk more invigorated than by the study of
mathematics.'

Mathematics, states Tunstall, is 'only to be understood by keen intelligence, good
memory and concentration', and offers an antidote to 'the eloquent but addle-
pated phrase-maker.' Here is an echo of Catherine's later acerbic statement that,
'speaking of the gospel maketh not men good Christians but good talkers.'[34]
Tunstall's varied and impressive abilities were summed up by Thomas More in
a letter to Erasmus in 1516, when he wrote, 'no one is better versed in all good
literature, no one is more strict in life and behaviour, yet no one whatever is a
more delightful companion ...'

Given the scholarly proclivities of those who had the organization of the Parr
children's education, the standard adhered to would seem to have been high.
One of the books used in their schoolroom has survived, their father's *Horae ad
Usum Sarum*, in Latin with a few prayers in English. That it was used in their
schoolroom is evidenced by the children's scrawls and ink blots and copied
words to be found in its pages. 'If you be not a robber,' one of the children has
written, 'there is none in all this county.'[35] 'Stella,' another child has carefully
copied out. The book is written in Latin and the children read it. Catherine
has chosen the page which describes '*Virgo Sancta Katherina grecie gemma urbe
alexandria costi regis erat filia*' to inscribe her name and a short dedication to her
uncle, William Parr of Horton:

Oncle wan you do on thys loke

I pray you remember wo wrete thys in your bo[ke]

Your louvynge nys Katheryn Parr.[36]

On the recto side of the page is a woodblock engraving of Catherine's patron saint, St. Katherine of Alexandria, an iconographic portrait of woman triumphant. She is shown holding a sword in one hand and a book in the other, her unbound hair streaming from beneath an elaborate crown, the severed head of her enemy overcome at her feet and the broken wheel of her martyrdom forgotten behind her. The glorious and victorious saint wears an ermine surcoat over royal robes, and, according to the text, mounted into heaven where she sits among the angels. For the young schoolgirl, Catherine, this must have been an image worthy of emulation, a point which she discloses by her choice of page in the book on which to write her name. As queen, Catherine was to chose a similar representation of her patron saint as her official emblem, issuing symbolically enough from a Tudor rose. The imaginings of all of the Parr children were formed by such images as the woodblock prints in this book of hours. A picture of the naked Bathsheba, bathing in a fountain beneath the lascivious eyes of King David, is printed under a picture of a younger David, 'being such a little one',[37] slaying the giant Goliath. Sex and violence served up in the unobjectionable trappings of religion played their part in the forming of childish minds. These imagines echo in Catherine's later writings, David being a special favourite, and their titillating quality no doubt had the result of encouraging the children in their study of Latin, a knowledge of the language being needed to satisfy their curiosity about the stories.

As queen, Catherine was the recipient of frequent correspondence in Latin by those who knew her, such as Thomas Smith and the Prince of Wales, and by those who served in her household, such as Francis Goldsmith. Roger Ascham corresponded familiarly in Latin with all three Parr siblings. It is unlikely that such people would have addressed correspondence, of great importance to them, to a recipient incapable of reading their words. 'You so possess that universal glory of learning,' Roger Ascham wrote in Latin to the queen in 1547. 'You learn more in the important business of your station, than many among us in the great leisure of our repose, and you do that also in the grandeur of your rank where other women are willing to despise learning, and also in that age when it is more usual to cast learning out of mind before it is received.'[38]

Catherine's Latin has been heavily criticized on the basis of the very few extant samples which have survived, primarily the drafts of two letters, one to Prince Edward[39] and one to the Princess Mary,[40] neither of which is in

Catherine's handwriting. Edward was five years old when Catherine married his father and not yet eleven when she died. A letter written in elegant, elegiac Latin would have been highly inappropriate for a five-year-old and Catherine would have formed her letter in a style comprehensible to her audience, a child. Yet given the fact that her letter to Edward is in someone else's hand, any conclusion made regarding the queen's own Latin must be dubious at best.

As for the letter written to Mary, it was actually written by the fourteen-year-old Princess Elizabeth, acting as her stepmother's amanuensis, in September 1547 while Elizabeth was living in Catherine's household.[41] Catherine may have dictated the letter, although this is unlikely as there is no other example of Catherine ever having written to Mary in Latin. What is more likely is that Elizabeth used an English letter of the queen's as an exercise in Latin translation, just as in 1545 she had used Catherine's *Prayers or Meditations* for such a purpose. The letter dealt with translating from Latin to English so Elizabeth neatly turned the original English communication into Latin, providing a sample of her abilities for both her stepmother, the sender, and her elder sister, the recipient. One extant tribute by Dr. Richard Cox to Catherine's fluency in Latin appears in a letter from Prince Edward to the queen.[42] In it, the young prince describes Cox's initial disbelief at Catherine's obvious ability in the language. The queen's progress in Latin and in *belles-lettres* commended by Edward in the same letter may, in fact, refer not to lessons such as the young prince delighted in but to the translation project from Latin into English which the queen had at that moment in hand.[43]

In her book, *Lamentation of a Sinner*, Catherine refers obliquely to her understanding of Latin, when she describes the surprise and disgust felt by those who 'very well understand the Latin tongue', upon hearing 'learned men persuade to the credit and belief of certain unwritten verities, as they call them, which be not in Scripture expressed, and yet taught as doctrine apostolic and necessary to be believed.' Her own disgust surfaces when she offers the opinion that those who understand Latin and hear such things, 'have been of this opinion, that the learned men have more Epistles written by the apostles of Christ than we have abroad in the canon of the old and new testament, or known of any but only to them of the clergy. Which belief I did not a little lament in my heart to hear that any creature should have such a blind ignorant opinion.'[44]

That Catherine studied Latin is evidenced by the *Horae ad Usum Sarum*. Her sister, Anne, had read and 'delighted' in Cicero,[45] and Juan Luis Vives suggested reading Quintilian, Plutarch and Cicero.[46] Bishop Tunstall recommended the reading of Quintilian, Linacre, Latin translations of Homer, Aristotle, Erasmus, and the French scholar, William Bude. A priest in Tunstall's household, Robert

Ridley, collaborated with Polydore Vergil in publishing the first edition of Gildas ever printed. The book, dedicated to Tunstall, appeared in 1525 when Catherine was thirteen, and this early source of the Arthurian cycle would have appealed hugely to the teenage girl. The romance of the Arthurian cycle, however, also reiterated the message of woman's destructive powers. Although Gildas never mentions Arthur by name, his diatribe against five princes of Britain reinforces the role of woman as destroyer. Of Gildas' five princes, Aurelius Conanus, Vortipore, the 'foolish tyrant of the Demetians', and Cuneglasse of Cambria are vilified as riddled by lust and culpable of adultery, charges to which they must answer not only to their people but to God on the Day of Judgement. Vortipore's 'shameless daughter', and Constantine's mother, 'the unclean lioness of Damnonia', have, in the mind of the sixth-century monk, defiled their family honour and defied the higher commands of Christian morality.[47] The cycle of Arthurian romance, appealing though it would have been in many ways to a teenage girl, restated in later French additions the role of woman, in this case Guinevere, as the catalyst for the end of Eden. The egalitarian round table and utopian Camelot are destroyed by the queen's lust for Lancelot and her unfaithfulness to her husband. The sorceress Morgan Le Fey is the archetypal Lillith, beyond the charmed circle of Christian salvation, plotting from the shadows the destruction of man's most noble and divinely inspired enterprises. In her later writings, Catherine's imagery, determined by her growing religious evangelicalism, became almost wholly biblical, but that she was exposed as a child to the world of classical humanism, of which her parents and cousin were so much a part, and to at least some aspects of the popular literature of the cult of courtly love, seems beyond doubt.[48]

In addition to Latin, the young Parrs studied French, the girls probably with the aid of John Palsgrave's French grammar published in 1525, William certainly so as he became Palsgrave's student shortly afterward. Catherine's fluency in French is attested to by the fact that several books in her personal library at Sudeley were printed in that language.[49] Also in this library is evidence of her fluency in Italian. Her copy of Petrarch, published in Venice and thus in Italian and not an English translation, later became the property of her stepson, Edward VI.[50] In addition to languages, there seems to be no reason to suppose that the Parrs did not also study the arithmetic textbook written by their cousin, Cuthbert Tunstall. It was first published in October 1522, when Catherine was ten but due to his enthusiastic endorsement of the study of arithmetic for children, Tunstall could very well have provided a study plan in that subject for the children prior to publication. Although none of Catherine's accounts from the years before her marriage to Henry VIII have survived, the earliest account that still exists from her years as queen is countersigned by her and implies that she was in the habit, as Mistress Borough and later as Lady Latimer, of checking the household accounting and signing off on merchants' bills, a prudent and not very surprising habit.[51]

A corollary to this habit of applied arithmetic was Catherine's fascination with numismatics and chess. No less than nine items relating to coins appear on the 1549 list of her belongings, several of them purses containing 'sundrye straunge coynes', or 'three frenche Crownes', or 'a Gilder of golde'.[52] This fascination may have been fostered by Cuthbert Tunstall, an avid coin collector and correspondent of William Bude, author of a 1514 treatise on classical coins and weights, *De Asse et Partibus*. Coin collecting was his hobby and ancient coins his passion. 'Tunstall,' wrote Erasmus from Antwerp in May 1517, 'is in the best of health, exultant in fact, because he has found such a number of old coins here.'[53] As for chess, Catherine's interest in the game may be inferred from the occasional chess images she uses in her writings, such as, 'St. Paul doth most diligently admonish us which arts are not convenient and mete to be made checkmate with Scripture.'[54] A new, faster form of the game which gave the queen unparalleled powers on the board had been introduced in Europe, probably from Spain, in the 1490s and had appeared in England by 1530. Henry Howard, Earl of Surrey, and a friend of Catherine's brother, used 'an elaborate chess conceit' related to this new form of the game in one of his poems.[55] Whether Catherine learned to play chess as a child or as an adult, the game required that 'good intelligence, keen memory and concentration' that Cuthbert Tunstall declared a study of mathematics inculcated in children.

Catherine's interest in medicine is well known. As queen, she not only concerned herself with the treatment of her husband's ills but even questioned the Spanish ambassador regarding the emperor's medical history.[56] In this regard it is of interest to consider that Thomas Linacre, physician and classical scholar, was at work on Latin translations of Galen during Catherine's childhood. Linacre was a close personal friend of Cuthbert Tunstall's, whom he named executor of his estate. Linacre died in the same year that Tunstall was advising Maud on the marriage of her elder daughter and some familiarity with his work would not be very surprising in a child in whose life and circumstances Tunstall had interested himself. The Parr children, moulded by their tutors, grew to enjoy scholastic pursuits and their schoolroom achievements may be measured by their intellectual accomplishments as adults.

At Catherine's death, that part of her personal library which travelled with her down to Sudeley Castle, contained twenty-two books printed or written in English, French and Italian, and possibly one in Latin as well.[57] Her chamber accounts record that she was studying the Spanish language but whether any of the books were in this language is not mentioned.[58] Only seven in the library are described specifically as religious works, among the rest being 'a little book covered with green velvet with stories and letters finely cut'.[59] Catherine's copy of Petrarch in Italian may have been among them as well. Catherine's younger sister, Anne Parr, has been called 'an accomplished scholar',[60] who employed in her household John Pindar, a fellow of St. John's, Cambridge, and was patron to another St. John's fellow, Reginald Middleton.[61] She sent her two sons to Peterhouse College, Cambridge, and corresponded in Latin on a familiar basis with Roger Ascham, who borrowed her copy of Cicero, quoted Ovid to her (an author felt unsuitable for study in the schoolroom), and praised 'the perfection of your Latin' and appreciated 'your affection for me.'[62] For New Year's, 1544, Anne's gift to the Princess Mary was 'a book covered with silver and gilt'.[63] In 1549, William Thomas, an Italian scholar and clerk of the council under Edward VI, dedicated to Anne, *The Vanitee of the World*, proclaiming that she excelled in virtue and bounty 'as the diamond among the jewels'.[64] The reference to her bounty no doubt implies some form of patronage relationship.

Catherine's brother, William, also had a reputation as a well-educated young man and had studied under John Palsgrave. It has been stated as well that William studied at Cambridge under the guidance of Cuthbert Tunstall.[65] Although no further information is given, this may account for the bestowal by the university of an MA degree on William on 18 March 1571. William's principal passion was music as his patronage of the brothers Bassano indicates, a tribute to his music tutor, William Saunders, but he had not wasted his time under Palsgrave either.[66] Sir Francis Bryant's 1548 English translation of Antonio Guevara's *A Dispraise of the Life of a Courtier* was, as Bryant states in the dedication, inspired by a French edition of the work which he had seen William reading. William's intellectual abilities manifested themselves not only in scholarship but in patronage. In the spring of 1546, William gave an exhibition or scholarship to a boy named Nicholas Steward and secured a passport for him and his uncle, 'repairing into parts beyond the seas to study.'[67] Roger Ascham presented his new work, *Toxophilus*, to William in 1545, commenting, 'Of all noble men you are the first and principal, very noble man, this book carries the imprint of your hands.'[68] Sir Thomas Hoby, who joined William's household in 1551, dedicated both his *Travels* and his English translation of *The Tragedy of Free Will* to Parr. Later in life, William acted as patron for Charles Bill, a probable relative of William Bill, master of St. John's College, Cambridge, under Edward VI, and of Dr. Thomas Bill, court physician to Henry VIII and Edward VI. Charles Bill, who was born about 1552, matriculated at King's College, Cambridge, in 1568 and was a fellow from 1571–1587. He was appointed to the post of secretary to William's brother-in-law, Lord Cobham, and wrote a series of poems in Greek, Latin and Italian celebrating William Parr's life and lamenting his death.[69]

In 1553 William founded a grammar school in Guildford, a royal manor of which he was keeper. His commitment to the University of Cambridge was acknowledged by Roger Ascham on numerous occasions. Regarding William's aid given on behalf of St. John's College, Ascham wrote about 1550:

> How much you alone sustain the present liveliness and future
> hope of our entire University, most noble Sir, almost everyone
> of us realizes with the highest benefit and acknowledges with
> the greatest thanks ... and in these last recent days you so
> mitigated with Thomas Lever as your agent, the poverty of
> many students and aroused the hope of all that this new ardour for
> study, bestowed through your efforts, will generate a new fruit
> of learning in these most difficult times to the immense benefit
> of religion and the republic.[70]

In 1546, Catherine Parr wrote in a draft of her celebrated letter to the University of Cambridge,

> 'you seem to have conceived, rather partially than truly, a favourable estimation
> both of my ~~learning~~, going forward and dedication to learning ... showing how
> agreeable it is to have, being in this worldly estate, not only for mine own part to
> be studious, but also a maintainer and cherisher of the learned state, by bearing
> me in hand that I am endowed and possessed of those qualities and respects which
> ought to be in a person of my vocation.'[71]

Her dedication to scholarship, in the tradition of that earlier patron and family mentor, Margaret Beaufort, founder of St. John's College, is indicated in this letter when Catherine announces to the Cambridge worthies that she has encouraged the king to 'advance [good learning] and erect new occasion' for its promotion. This 'new occasion' that she was urging Henry toward erecting was, in fact, the foundation of Trinity College.[72]

Some historians have pointed to Catherine's condemnation of 'dead, human, historical faith and knowledge, which they have learned in their scholastical books',[73] as evidence that Catherine condemned learning and as a corollary was herself unlearned. Yet this position cannot be maintained against the body of evidence to the contrary. Catherine was quite literally what the University of Cambridge declares her to be, 'a maintainer and cherisher of the learned state'. Her protests are focused on those who would put secular learning above the study of the Scriptures and substitute the wisdom of the classical academies for the wisdom apparent in 'the boke of the crucifix'. Learning, for Catherine, was a facet of good works, instituted and earned by man's efforts, fulfilling a human curiosity and a human need. Learning must, therefore, always take second place to God's grace, unearned by man, undeserved by man, yet offered freely by Divine Love as the only study inherently leading to spiritual salvation. Testimonies to the queen's own dedication to learning are numerous. Francis Goldsmith describes a mind 'formed ... for pious studies',[74] and John Bale praises her 'natural virtue, elegant writing, and generous benevolence ... truly in her can be seen the judgement of Socrates.'[75] Nicholas Udall extols the dedication of the queen, who 'with most earnest zeal, from the first hour of the day to the twelfth',[76] studied to improve her understanding of the Scriptures. Such habits are learned in childhood, and the apt pupil of a humanist schoolroom carried a love of study and a love of learning with her throughout her life even though the curriculum of her private moments altered as her religious ideas developed and the focus of her interests changed.

3

Civil War in the Household of the Duke of Richmond

In the summer of 1525, the educational and living arrangements for the Parr children were suddenly changed. While thirteen-year-old Catherine and ten-year-old Anne remained at home under their mother's tutelage and supervision, the eleven-year-old heir of the family was provided with a brilliant opportunity – a place in the household of the king's only (although illegitimate) son, the Duke of Richmond. This opportunity was secured through the offices of young William's uncle, Sir William Parr of Horton.

Although the Parr children grew up without a father in the household, in a sense this vacuum was filled by their uncle. It has not perhaps been fully appreciated how completely this uncle filled the role left empty by his brother's early demise. He was to the young Parrs, Catherine, William and Anne, an active and devoted surrogate father. All of them maintained close ties to him throughout his, and their, lifetimes, and Catherine's sense of loss at his death in the fall of 1547 is recorded in a letter written to Sir Edward North on behalf of one his servants. ' ... it hath pleased almighty god,' she wrote, 'to take unto his mercy my our entirely beloved uncle the late Lord Parr of Horton'[1] Her slip of the pen, writing 'my uncle', when for four years as queen all of her official correspondence had been couched in the impersonal royal 'we', shows more of her emotion than perhaps she knew. Her brother was also particularly close to Sir William, spending long periods at his home in Horton in the late 1520s and 1530s.

At heart, Sir William was very much the country squire, addicted to hunting, overseeing his cony runs and quarrelling with his neighbours. Knighted at Tournai during Henry VIII's less than brilliant foray into France in the summer of 1513, Sir William's early career was very much as the family lieutenant of his elder brother, Catherine, William and Anne's father. While Sir Thomas Parr was involved in overseeing his Cumbrian and Yorkshire estates, Sir William took care of family affairs in Northamptonshire,[2] but he was far from being a careful man of finance as his later career was to show. He had no head for accounts and little interest in balanced books. He lived in a constant state of debt and during the 1530s wrote numerous pleading letters to Thomas Cromwell, then

Lord Privy Seal, complaining frequently and volubly of his poverty. It appears from the evidence that Sir William was not so much poverty-stricken as disorganized, and while he could with great courage storm a Scottish castle 'right dangerfully' and could ride 'further and in more danger' than most, money, debts, bookkeeping and accounts left him frustrated and helpless.[3] It was to be Sir William's sad misfortune that his career came to depend far more heavily on his bookkeeping abilities than on his ability to storm besieged castles. He was a man whose overriding sense of family duty and family honour forced him into the very life that he would gladly have relinquished for the pleasures of the hunt and a quiet life at Horton.[4]

Sir William Parr was a client of Thomas Wolsey's and it was Wolsey who secured for him in 1525 the highly desirable position of chamberlain to the newly formed household of Henry Fitzroy, Duke of Richmond. Born in 1519, Henry Fitzroy was the illegitimate son of Henry VIII and Elizabeth Blount, a lady-in-waiting to Catherine of Aragon. At the time of Richmond's birth to Bessie Blount, Henry and his queen had been married for ten years and had no living son to show for it. Catherine's unfortunate history of miscarriages and stillbirths had left the king with but a single heir, his three-year-old daughter, Mary. Given the high rate of infant and child mortality at the time, Mary's chances of reaching adulthood could be reckoned no better than fifty-fifty. Henry's great joy at being presented with a living son, even an illegitimate one, was the direct result of his painful awareness of the fragility of his line. After ten years of marriage he must have had grave doubts of his wife's ever producing a living male heir. The future he intended for the royal bastard can be deduced from his actions during Richmond's first years of life. By the age of six, Henry Fitzroy had been created Duke of Richmond and Somerset and Earl of Nottingham, with precedence over all other dukes save the king's legitimate issue, of whom, other than Princess Mary, there were none. He had been made lieutenant and knight of the Order of the Garter and on 18 June 1525, he was appointed lieutenant-general of the north and keeper of the city and castle of Carlisle.

During the next four years, offices were heaped upon the child – lord high admiral of England, Wales and Ireland, a commission as warden-general of the marches toward Scotland, the lord-lieutenancy of Ireland. No one viewing the lands, offices and titles lavished on Richmond could doubt that the king had plans for the boy and every year that passed without the birth of a legitimate male heir increased the likelihood that these plans included the crown of England. After all, Henry had two such notable precedents to ponder as the rise of his grandmother's family, the Beauforts, the illegitimate (although later legitimised) descendants of John of Gaunt, not to mention his father's paternal line, the Tudors, who were the offspring of an alliance of questionable legality between Katherine of Valois, widow of Henry V, and her sometime clerk of the wardrobe, Owen Tudor. The possibility that Henry VIII might legitimise Richmond and name him his heir remained a very real one until the boy's premature death on 22 July 1536.[5]

The household of the Duke of Richmond, created by his godfather, Cardinal Wolsey, in 1525, was an interesting one. All of the families who were to become the core of the new religion party and who were to be the major architects of the policies of the turbulent years of the 1540s and early 1550s, had representatives in Richmond's household. Many of Catherine Parr's future friends and enemies were gathered together here. Arthur Plantagenet, Viscount Lisle, stepfather to John Dudley, future Duke of Northumberland, was named the young duke's lieutenant. Queen Jane Seymour's brother, Edward, the future Lord Protector of England, was Richmond's master of the horse. Catherine Parr's uncle was Richmond's chamberlain. Lady Jane Grey's father, Henry Grey, the future Marquis of Dorset, was Richmond's schoolfellow, as was Catherine Parr's brother, William, the future Marquis of Northampton. Sir Edward Baynton, brother-in-law of Queen Anne Boleyn, also seems to have placed his son, Andrew, in the care of Richmond's tutors, and other possible students included the future Earls of Cumberland and Rutland, and Lord Dacre and Greystoke.

Having achieved this desirable appointment as chamberlain,[6] Sir William Parr no doubt rubbed his hands in joy at the thought of the opportunities for enrichment and advancement that awaited him and his. As second in command of the duke's household with control over the household finances, he was in a position to enrich himself, provide for friends and relatives and offer rewards to personal retainers and clients. Both Wolsey and the king were far away in London and the titular head of the household was six years old. From Parr's later complaints, it appears, too, that Wolsey had told Parr at the time of his appointment that partial remuneration for the position would come in the form of offices granted from the duke's estates by the duke, himself, when they fell vacant. Certainly such an expectation would have been normal and understood as standard operating procedure by all parties. As events were to prove, however, service might have its rewards, but they are not always what – or as much as – one might hope. In Parr's case, service to the duke meant responsibility for the ordering and accounting of household expenses. It was not a duty for which he was well fitted by temperament or ability. In addition, Sir William, by virtue of his office, was expected to serve on the ducal council which it was hoped would offer some sort of promise of order in the ever turbulent north. Parr grew tired of both duties very quickly,[7] particularly when the rewards that he must have expected to fall into his lap proved extraordinarily elusive.

When on 26 July 1525, the child Duke of Richmond and his new household left London on their way to take up residence at Sheriff Hutton in Yorkshire, they spent the first night of their journey north with the Parrs at Rye House. Maud Parr welcomed the young duke to her home and it was reported back to London that, although he was not feeling in the best of health, the little boy 'was marvellously well intreated and had good cheer.'[8] Given Maud Parr's ambitions for her children, it is unlikely that she would have passed up the opportunity of presenting them all to the duke, and it was probably here that young William joined the duke's household as one of a group of gently-born boys destined to share Richmond's lessons and play in Yorkshire. Under his mother's coaching, William set himself to win the affections of the slight and apparently delicate duke and succeeded handsomely. By the time the party reached Yorkshire, young William and young Henry Fitzroy were best friends. If this child ever came to the throne, the Parrs were determined to see young William Parr standing on one side of him.

Nepotism in the Tudor era, as Professor Hurstfield has pointed out, was 'a moral duty rather than a vice.'[9] Publicly Parr deprecated the need for this. 'The common rule of favourites,' he is quoted as saying, 'is to bring in all their relatives about them, to adorn and support them. But a wall that hath a firm bottom needs no buttress, and that which wants it, is often rather tossed down than upheld by it.'[10] Privately, this selfless commitment to duty translated itself into aggressive action on behalf of the family interests. The opportunistic Parr of Horton soon found places in the duke's household not only for his nephew and namesake but for cousins and Parr family retainers as well. Sir James Leyburne, steward of the Parr estates in Kendal, joined the duke's entourage as did young Nicholas Throckmorton.[11] Throckmorton and his seventeen brothers and sisters were the abundant progeny of Catherine Vaux, half-sister of the late Sir Thomas Parr. Catherine Vaux had been married to Sir George Throckmorton of Coughton in Warwickshire, and together they produced a family far beyond the means of Sir George to provide for. Increasingly, they began to look to Catherine's brother, Parr of Horton, to do something for their brood.[12] He obliged them by taking young Nicholas into the Duke of Richmond's household to serve as a page. Though his mother was grateful for this patronage, Nicholas, himself, was less enthusiastic. He particularly resented Richmond's high-handed treatment of him.

> Soe with her (my mother's) Brother I was safely plac'd
> Of almes he kept me in extremitie,
> Who did misdoubt a worse calamitie ...

By parents' heast, I served as a page
To Richmond's Duke, and waited, still at hand,
For feare of blowes, which happen'd in his rage.[13]

Richmond apparently favoured his royal father in temperament and Throckmorton, seeing his cousin, young William Parr, placed as one of Richmond's companions, may have resented his own position as a mere page. Yet having ultimately been promoted to gentleman of the household, Throckmorton remained in Richmond's employ until the duke's death in 1536.

Further references to Parr of Horton's attempts to promote his own family began to surface almost as soon as the ducal household had established itself at Sheriff Hutton Castle. The size of the household had been set by Wolsey. In addition to the duke, his officers and councillors, Richmond's establishment contained some 34 gentlemen, 46 yeomen, 3 pages, 63 grooms and 79 gentlemen's servants. In October 1525, as the household was settling in, Parr secured permission to take on an extra yeoman. Three months later, Richmond's tutor complained to the king of members of the household who were 'entertaining friends and servants above their allowance and in finding (places for) Sir William Parr's house'.[14] Five days later, the complaint was reiterated and accusations made that much food and money were being wasted in entertaining Parr's friends and providing for Parr's own family. Sir William's actions in attempting to pack Richmond's household with as many of his family and clients as possible were in no way unusual. This was commonly done at all levels of society by those who had sufficient influence. Richmond's master of the horse, the young and exceedingly ambitious Sir Edward Seymour, had found a position among the gentlemen ushers for his own cousin, Christopher Wentworth.[15] It was not so much Parr's ambition that was at fault as the heavy-handed nature of his methods. No one apparently thought the worse of him for such flagrant nepotism apart from the Duke of Richmond's tutor, Richard Croke.

Richard Croke was a native of London, born about 1489 and educated at Eton and King's College, Cambridge, where he took his BA in 1510. Croke was a master of Greek who had had to struggle mightily for the funds with which to pursue his education. His scholarship was good enough to impress Erasmus and about 1513 Croke left England to study and teach on the Continent. He was a success as a lecturer in Greek at Leipzig. The major scholars of the day, such as Reuchlin and Hutien, corresponded with him. George, Duke of Saxony, became his patron. Everywhere he was honoured and respected. For a self-made man who had fought his way out of the abyss of anonymous poverty, the illustrious peaks of scholarship and respectability to which he had ascended on the Continent were heady and to some extent deceiving. Thanks to his Continental reputation as a scholar, Croke found employment back home in England as Greek tutor to the king. Croke was an ambitious ('I am insane enough to covet the doctor's laurel'), contentious, and suspicious man, who continually suspected others of plotting against him ('I could not forbear visiting the master of my college in order to understand the lies Smith has been telling ... '; 'I have been maligned to the bishop [of Lincoln]'). His favouritism in the classroom was chronic and resented ('require half a page of Lucian of each of the two boys ... Denton, who is my favourite, will be industrious. The other must be driven')[16] Croke's sense of self-importance had grown with his reputation and when in 1525 he was appointed tutor to the king's only son, he must have felt deep satisfaction at being entrusted with the education of the possible heir to the throne. This satisfaction did not last long.

From the first, Croke was at loggerheads with most of the duke's household, particularly Sir William Parr and his cronies, the clerk comptroller, Richard Cotton, and his brother, George Cotton.[17] Parr and his circle were bluff, gregarious, self-interested men to whom riding to the hunt was a far more important and noble activity than learning the verbs of a long-dead language. These men belonged for the most part to the gentry and knew it, and Parr at least had little patience and much contempt for men whom he felt came from the lower classes.[18] Croke, for his part, was a fussy and pedantic scholar, with a touchy pride about his origins and a high opinion of his achievements and his position. He felt that it was his responsibility to make the rules for the education of the duke. Parr and his circle, who in fact controlled the household, gave way to the attitude best calculated to enrage the tutor. They alternately laughed at him or ignored him altogether. What was worse, they taught the young Duke of Richmond to do the same.

Five months after the arrival of the duke's household at Sheriff Hutton, letters from Croke began to bombard the king and the cardinal. Croke wanted royal reinforcement of his position and his authority. He accused Parr and the Cotton brothers of using the duke's household funds for their own entertainment and amusements, of ignoring their duties and encouraging the duke to play truant from his lessons. Parr, accused Croke, failed to attend to either the household or the council and spent all of his time hawking and hunting. The disgruntled tutor even took to keeping a record of the number of days that Parr was absent altogether from Sheriff Hutton.[19] Dr. William Tate, another member of the council, supported Parr in the dispute, and Croke furiously reported this bias. The tutor was angry and indignant when Parr 'told the duke of Richmond in my presence and ordered him when Cotton was absent never to be alone with me or listen to me except when reading.' Parr had, continued Croke, 'appointed his young nephew to say matins and vespers with the Duke of Richmond and has thus got the duke to pay no attention to ... requests or threats ... His disposition will be spoiled by such masters who care only for their own pleasure and profit.'[20]

Yet it is hardly to be wondered at that a six-year-old boy would prefer to hunt and hawk with his older friend and hunt-loving chamberlain than to recite Greek verbs with an overly ingratiating and punctilious tutor. This household civil war soon spread to the group of boys surrounding Richmond. Among them were the heir of the second Marquis of Dorset, Henry Grey, and 'a boy named Scrope', who was probably John Scrope, son of Henry, Lord Scope of Bolton. Young John Scrope was Parr of Horton's cousin and took delight in taunting the tutor and his pets. Croke wrote to Wolsey on 25 May 1527, complaining that Scrope 'excites the [other] boys against me and calls me names and has ill-treated a boy of good disposition sent by the king, who lives with me.'[21] Croke retailed again in tedious detail how he had been prevented from forcing the boys to rise before daylight and from holding lessons at night. Yet he failed to fathom these boys' dislike of him. Although Richmond obviously preferred the company of the Parrs to that of his tutor, Croke was very careful never to accuse the royal bastard of ill will. Like most disaffected minorities, he saved his accusations and his vitriol for the 'evil councillors' around the seat of power.

What the king and Cardinal Wolsey thought of the complaints of this great Greek scholar who was proving incapable of controlling both his own temper and a group of rowdy schoolboys is not a matter of record, but no doubt it was close to impatience. After all, Croke was not Richmond's only tutor. William Saunders, who had once been a servant of Wolsey's, was at Sheriff Hutton teaching the duke and his companions singing and the virginals. John Palsgrave was there teaching French. No one apparently had a problem with them. Nor, although Croke was convinced of the contrary, were his supposed enemies dispatching messages to London attacking him. Not one letter from Parr complaining of Croke's querulousness survives and Parr was not a man to keep quiet in a quarrel.[22] It seems logical therefore to assume that Croke and his problems meant nothing at all to Sir William Parr. He had only contempt for the tutor and could not even be troubled to deny Croke's accusations of misconduct.

An important aspect of this feud, bearing on future religious attitudes among the boys around the duke, was its anticlericalism. 'Cotton,' Croke complained, 'allows buffoons to sing indecent songs and to abuse the clergy' in front of Richmond. 'The boys laugh ... and the grooms protect them from punishment.'[23] This anticlericalism in Richmond's household is apparent from the beginning. Even as the household was settling in at Sheriff Hutton, John Uvedale, the duke's secretary, reported to Wolsey that he believed Parr and others desired the duke to build a larger chapel and institute more elaborate religious celebrations. Parr, who had never been a particularly religious man, indignantly denied any such pious notion. Not for him, he proclaimed, 'a chapel like the Lords Darcy and Latimer', two of the pillars of piety in the north.[24] The anticlerical atmosphere in the household of the duke, originating with Parr, the Cottons and their cronies, produced in the succeeding generation the core of the English reformed party.

Then, during the summer of 1529, there was a changing of the guard in the household of the Duke of Richmond. Croke was relieved of his onerous duties as chief tutor to the duke and returned, with thanks and an appointment as Nottingham pursuivant at arms, to Cambridge.[25] In the departed Croke's place, John Palsgrave was appointed chief tutor. Palsgrave was a different man altogether from Richard Croke. He was a warm-natured, erudite teacher, who regarded learning as a pleasure in which to indulge rather than a duty to be performed. He was England's foremost scholar of French and had been tutor to the king's sister, Mary, Duchess of Suffolk, during her apprenticeship as Queen of France. She held him in very high esteem. At Palsgrave's appointment to Richmond's household, he had the courtesy to write to the duke's mother, now the wife of Sir Gilbert Tailboys, and describe the care that the king had for her son:

> '... the King's grace said unto me, in the presence of Master Parr and Master Page [Richard Page, member of Richmond's council], 'I deliver', quod he, 'unto you three, my worldly jewel; you twain to have the guiding of his body, and thou, Palsgrave, to bring him up in virtue and learning.'[26]

Such a flattering commission brought out the best in Richmond's new chief tutor:

> And to make the child love learning, I never put [him] in fear of any manner [of] correction, nor never suffer him to continue at any time till he should be wearied, [Palsgrave wrote to his friend, Sir Thomas More] but devise all the ways I can possible to make learning pleasant to him, insomuch that many times his officers wot not whether I learn him or play with him, and yet have I already brought him to have a right good understanding in the principles of the grammars both of Greek and Latin.[27]

Considering that one of the wise saws of the age was that 'a boy wears his ears on his back – the more he is beaten, the better will he learn,' a merry approach to study was a novel, even revolutionary idea. 'I understand by Sir William a Parre,' Palsgrave remarked to More, 'that the King's Grace demanded of you and Dr. Stevens (Stephen Gardiner, at this time royal secretary), whether you thought it convenient that the Duke of Richmond should learn Greek and Latin both at once ... And I remember that you showed me once how a little Latin should serve so the said Duke might have French.'[28] This was an interesting point of view from one of the two ablest scholars in England and partially accounts for young William Parr's fluency with that language.

Yet Palsgrave, too, faced the difficulty of weaning the duke from his passionate attachment to hunting, learned in the company of the Parrs.[29]

> ' ... on my faith I knew never a more singular wit, neither rich nor poor, than he hath, and albeit that he hath already and every day shall have more and more sundry callers upon him to bring his mind from learning, some to hear a cry at a hare, some to kill a buck with his bow, sometime with greyhounds and sometime with buckhounds ... to see a flight with a hawk, some to ride a horse, which yet he is not greatly combryed with because of his youth.'[30]

Palsgrave persisted in his attempts 'to make the child love learning', and succeeded in a far more constructive way than had Richard Croke.

If Croke's complaints about him raised little interest in London, Sir William Parr's own ineptitude as chamberlain began to catch up with him in October 1528. He was ordered to court by Wolsey to show what had been done 'in the executing of the king's high commandment ... for the reducing of my lord of Richmond's household to some better order and less charge than the same hath been at heretofore.'[31] In a way, this was rubbing salt in the wound, for in spite of Parr's attempts to enrich himself and his relatives at the duke's expense, he had not gained a great deal in the three years he had been in Richmond's employ. This unpalatable fact was apparently made quite clear to Richmond, himself, by his disaffected employees who had already complained to Wolsey of the appointment of 'divers persons not in the duke of Richmond's service to various offices in the duke's gift [which] has much discouraged his servants.'[32] Richmond was pressured by his council to write to his father about such discouragements and on 21 July 1528, he sent a letter protesting the granting of offices in his gift to other than his own household servants. Cardinal Wolsey had told him expressly, continued the boy duke, that, 'it is your wish that when any offices fall vacant, I should dispose of it considering the great number of my servants who have no other reward.' Parr and the council supported

Richmond's protests in their own letter, which described the animosity aroused by the practice of granting these appointments to other than those in the duke's household, to 'the great grudge and discomfort of all his servants; they be almost despaired to obtain or get any promotions by his service.'[33]

The king was not particularly interested or impressed by these pleas, and Parr was left fuming in Yorkshire over the offices and other perquisites that he had hoped to snap up and had in effect been led to expect and yet were being denied him. He was left with all the drudgery of his position while the rewards were granted out in London by the king and the cardinal. One case in point were the stewardships of two parcels of Richmond's lands held by Sir William Compton of Compton Wynyates. A close friend of Compton, Parr of Horton had been made a trustee for some of Compton's own lands in Northamptonshire and Yorkshire. When Compton died in 1528, Parr lobbied for the reversion of the stewardship of Richmond's lands, which Compton had held in Dorset. These included the manor of Canford, Corfe Castle, and a 100-shilling per annum stipend. Encouraged to be master of his own by the members of his household who stood to gain, the nine-year-old duke granted this stewardship to Parr. The grant was immediately overturned by the king and the stewardship given to Sir Edward Seymour. Richmond – and Parr – protested in vain.

4
In Search of a Title

As in education, family expectations for the marriages of the young Parrs differed. William was the heir to a large estate and for him, his mother's ambition was boundless. For her daughters, Maud's sights were set more conservatively. The girls had each been left £400 by their father as a marriage portion, a sum which guaranteed them some consideration among the more impecunious of the gentry families but little interest among those with the luxury to pick and chose. Unlike William's inheritance and his expectations as a member of the Duke of Richmond's circle, the legacies and expectations of Catherine and Anne were far more modest. Maud Parr, however, did not despair of a good match. Additionally, if she could secure an advantageous alliance for her elder daughter, the marriage prospects for her son might be enhanced. Although William was the family heir and only some twelve months younger than Catherine, Maud chose to begin match-making for her daughter first. No one knew better than the orphaned and widowed Lady Parr what insecurities could arise for a young girl upon being left an orphan in the world. Marriage was the only way, apart from the convent, for Maud Parr to ensure Catherine a secure future.[1] Without a father to defend her from the vicissitudes of sixteenth-century life, a husband was an immediate necessity. Catherine's uncle, Sir William Parr of Horton, had four daughters of his own for which to find marriages and was equally aware of the necessity of making arrangements for his nieces at the earliest opportunity. Although from a modern point of view it seems callously premature to attempt to marry off daughters barely out of childhood, it no doubt appeared to Maud Parr that marriage alone could provide the security and stability that she wanted for her daughters, especially as her own life was all that stood between her children and the arbitrariness of royal wardship.

Catherine was not yet eleven when her mother, with her child's best interests in mind, began negotiations for her marriage. Such negotiations were typical of the period and considered entirely appropriate and prudent. Child marriages were common and daughters of the upper classes were of political value as matrimonial pawns as soon as they reached puberty and the ability to bear children. They were the conduits through which estate inheritance was secured and blood alliances were formed to enhance family prestige. To submit to a marriage with an unknown boy who lived hundreds of miles away was a duty that Catherine owed to her family regardless of age. This was strongly impressed upon her and was to become a major theme in her life – marriage for the advantages it would bring to her family. It was not a move that was to bring her much personal happiness. Her own feelings on the matter at eleven years of age have not been recorded but as a mature woman, there is no missing the bitterness with which she wrote of forced alliances.

The object of Maud Parr's marriage plans for her daughter was young Henry Scrope, son and heir of Henry Scrope, Lord Scrope of Bolton, and his wife, Mabel, the daughter of Thomas, Lord Dacre. For over a century there had been a close and enduring connection between the Parr family and their cousins, the Lords Dacre of Gilsland. After Sir Thomas Parr's death in 1517, Thomas, Lord Dacre, who had a strong affection both for Parr and his young son,[2] became a sort of unofficial custodian for the Parr family's lands and interests in the north. Marrying Catherine to the future Lord Scrope of Bolton, Dacre's young grandson, would ensure for Parr interests in that area another generation of guardians linked by family ties, and both Lady Parr and Lord Dacre were quick to see the advantage to both families in such an alliance. Unfortunately for the proposed match, as they were soon to discover, Dacre's son-in-law, the surly Lord Scrope, did not agree with them.

Lady Parr began the negotiation process by approaching Lord Dacre with proposals for a marriage between her daughter and his grandson sometime before Dacre left for the Scottish border in April 1523. With Dacre's blessing, she wrote to his son-in-law, Lord Scrope of Bolton, who had little enthusiasm for the match. He put her off. In July, Maud wrote again to Dacre, reminding him of their original conversation and relaying to him a list of conditions for the marriage that had been sent to her by Lord Scrope. ' …The matter is not like to take effect except it be by your help,' Maud told Dacre.[3] She agreed to pay 1,100 marks as Catherine's marriage portion – 500 marks down and 100 marks a year for six years. In addition, Catherine was to have fifty marks a year until she turned twelve, when the marriage would be sexually consummated, and 100 marks thereafter. Maud confided to Dacre that this was as much as she could spare to buy the marriage for her daughter.[4] The subsequent response of the father of Catherine's proposed bridegroom, Lord Scrope, to Lady Parr's proposals was neither enthusiastic nor cordial. Lord Scrope informed Maud brusquely that in the unlikely event of their reaching an agreement, he would repay none of the dowry were anything to go amiss – such as Catherine's early death before the marriage or widowhood thereafter – nor did he intend to pay for bringing up the children during their nonage.

Maud was justifiably irritated by Scope's attitude and duly informed his father-in-law, Lord Dacre, of the fact. Dacre, for his part, responded in a letter to Maud a month later, on 30 July, assuring her that he would have a talk with his recalcitrant son-in-law. Lady Scrope, Dacre's daughter, had faithfully promised her father that she would arrange no marriage for her son without Dacre's own consent, 'which,' he reassured the indignant Maud, 'they shall not have for no person but unto you.' Lord Scrope was in dire need of money, Dacre confided, 'and his son's marriage is his only commodity. Do not be hasty. I will do all I can for you.'[5] It may perhaps be inferred that Lord Scrope's hostility to the match between Catherine and his son grew as much from his resentment of his father-in-law's interference in what was, after all, the marriage of Scrope's own heir than from any personal animosity toward the Parrs themselves.

Another month passed with no resolution and Lady Parr wrote again on 22 August to Lord Dacre, telling him that Lord Scrope had 'of late sent to a servant of mine that he would no longer give time in that matter with me but he would be at large and take his best advantage'.[6] There were others who would like to make a match with his son and who had made proposals to him. He named the Lord Treasurer as one.[7] 'I am always bold,' proclaimed Maud to Dacre, 'to put your lordship to pain and business which I pray to God I may some part desire (deserve).' Lord Scrope, although in no mood to be pushed around by his wife and father-in-law, had not totally written off the Parrs, and for form's sake if for nothing else, he wrote to Lord Dacre in December asking his opinion of the proposed marriage. This was an obvious stall as Lord Dacre's opinion had been quite clearly stated on a number of occasions. Dacre wrote back to Scrope from Morpeth, telling his uncooperative son-in-law that he thought well of both the match and lineage of the proposed child bride. He chided Scrope tactfully for trying to sell his son's marriage at too high a price and advised him to 'take the common course' or customary settlement that Maud Parr had offered.[8] Besides, he hinted slyly, only young Anne Parr stood between Catherine and an inheritance of £800, the sum left in their father's will to be divided between them, a fact that Dacre brought to Scrope's attention, 'because of the possibilities that fell unto myself by my marriage.'[9]

Scrope continued to stall, escalating his demands unreasonably, probably with an eye to forcing Maud to break off negotiations, which by the following spring she was prepared to do. She had taken a new advisor on the subject by this time, the ubiquitous Cuthbert Tunstall, then Bishop of London, and Tunstall and 'divers others of my husband's friends' had advised her against the Scrope marriage. In her last letter to Lord Dacre, written from Greenwich on 15 March 1524, one year after Maud had first broached the subject, she announced her decision to abandon the match. She thanked Dacre for his efforts and wrote rather plaintively that, '[I] never had any offer of marriage for my daughter that

I so wished to go forward as this.'[10] Dacre's response was unusually querulous and unusually prompt. On 25 March, he wrote again from Morpeth that he was sorry for her decision 'on account of the labour I have taken' with the business.[11] Lord Dacre's feelings were hurt. Maud had taken others' advice over his.

In the event, it was probably just as well for both Catherine and her family that the marriage plans fell through. Henry Scrope and his younger brother, Richard, both died the following year. If the marriage had gone forward with any expedition, Catherine would have been a widow before she even entered her teens. If the match had been renegotiated with the third Scrope son, John, as was customary and as Lord Dacre suggested, Catherine might not have found much contentment there either. John Scrope, ultimately Lord Scrope of Bolton, was an insufferable bully who outlived Catherine Parr by a year. If fate decreed that she must marry such a bully, surely a royal one was a better choice. Had Catherine married the unlovely Scrope, she would have lived an unremarkable life at Bolton Castle in Wensleydale with a quite unremarkable husband.[12]

Having been unsuccessful in her efforts to arrange an early marriage for her daughter, Maud's prospects now turned to her son. The failure of the proposed marriage between her daughter, Catherine, and the scion of the Scropes of Bolton had stung Maud Parr's pride. Instead of discouraging her and forcing her to set her sights lower, it seemed to spur her to new heights of ambition. Young William's placement in the Duke of Richmond's household encouraged in her ideas of achieving rank and title that had always been one of her husband's chief obsessions. In this quest, she was aided and abetted by two kinsmen, the ever-present, ever-useful Cuthbert Tunstall, and Sir William Fitzwilliam,[13] as well as by a loyal family friend, Sir Edward Montague.[14] When Maud Parr wrote to Lord Dacre in March 1524, telling him of her decision to break off the Scrope marriage negotiations, she had already cast her eye on a much more desirable marriage alliance, this time for her son. The bride whom William's ambitious mother had selected for him, with the encouragement of Tunstall, Fitzwilliam and Montague, was Lady Anne Bourchier (pronounced 'Bowser'),[15] the seven-year-old daughter and only legitimate child of Henry Bourchier, third Earl of Essex.

The Bourchiers were an old and eminently well-connected family. Directly descended from three of Edward III's sons, Essex was also the son of Anne Woodville, sister of Edward IV's queen. During his long life, the earl had been a soldier, sportsman, courtier, gambler and general rakehell. At the age of twenty-six, he had married the notable heiress, Mary Saye, daughter and ultimately sole heir of her father, Sir William Saye of Broxbourne in Hertfordshire. Rye House, where Maud Parr was living, was only two or three miles from the Saye home at Broxbourne and it may have been this proximity that first gave her the idea of Anne Bourchier as a bride for her son. Essex controlled vast tracks of land concentrated in the counties of Essex and Hertfordshire, with additional holdings in Buckinghamshire, Cambridgeshire, Suffolk and Kent.[17] Securing the marriage of the heiress of a peer of the realm for the son of a northern gentry family would be an expensive undertaking.

In 1526, at the age of fifty-four, Henry Bourchier was already an old man. Age and ill health compelled him to live more quietly than he liked. Fat, suffering from deafness and gout, with only one small daughter to mark the end of his line, the Earl of Essex was increasingly impatient with the exasperations and vicissitudes of life. He was a rich man on paper but his dissolute youth and lavish lifestyle had reduced him to living more or less permanently at his chief seat of Stansted Hall in Halstead, Essex. Here he spent his days trying to think up ways to outfox his creditors who more often than not were hounding him for payment. Occasionally he would haul himself into the saddle and ride west the thirty-some miles to his manor of Baas, near Broxbourne in Hertfordshire, for some hunting and a change of scene. If the king or Cromwell demanded it, he would serve on a county commission or ride up to London for an appearance at court, and his appearance, old and fat as he was, must have been impressive. In 1538, when the infant Edward, Prince of Wales, was still a baby, Essex was called to court to accustom the child to seeing stern faces and enormous beards before him. The baby prince seems to have had little trouble in getting used to this peculiar nursemaid but when the ambassadors from Saxe and Lansgrave visited and young Edward was trotted out to inspect them, no amount of coaxing by nurse or earl could persuade the baby to hold out his hand to the German representatives. Impulsively and in front of the affronted ambassadors, Essex informed the child that he did quite right in not trusting such men, a remark for which he was strongly rebuked, but a decade later, the incident still amused Stephen Gardiner, Bishop of Winchester.[18]

Having selected Essex's daughter and heir as her quarry, Maud Parr pursued the parents with a single-minded purpose. Tunstall, Fitzwilliam and Montague lent her advice and money. Essex, with his debts, was, as Lord Scrope had been with his heir, willing to marry his daughter only for the highest price he could get for her. Maud Parr borrowed widely on the strength of her son's inheritance and the proposed marriage to pay the earl's price.[19] At this period, the guilds supplied the place of a nascent banking establishment which occasionally lent out money. Maud borrowed money from the wardens of the mercers' guild to forward the great Essex merger.[20] Even the king was persuaded to a loan. On 22 July 1526, William Parr's marriage was sold by the King's Wards to Fitzwilliam and Thomas Englefield, sergeant-at-law, for £1,000 to the use of Maud Parr, the first step toward the realization of a two-centuries-old Parr dream of securing a title for the family.[21] Maud Parr undoubtedly hoped that at the death of the Earl of Essex, his son-in-law, for lack of a direct male heir, would be allowed by the king to assume the title. What service in war and peace had not achieved for the family, marriage ultimately would, or so the optimistic Lady Parr hoped. The king may even have given Maud some vague assurances of his goodwill toward his old friend's son and his own son's playmate. Essex, himself, seemed quite taken with young William Parr and this factor, together with Maud Parr's generous monetary inducements, persuaded the debt-ridden earl to agree to the match.

On 9 February 1527, a marriage license was issued by the Bishop of London for William Parr, esquire, and the Lady Anne Bourchier.[22] The wedding was celebrated in the chapel of Stansted Hall. The groom was thirteen and the bride barely ten. It was the beginning of a turbulent forty-four-year relationship that was to bring neither participant any joy. From the beginning they were an ill-suited pair.[23] Like his father before him, William grew up to be the perfect courtier – handsome, charming, well-educated, sports-loving, devoted to the reformed religion, an outstanding example of the Tudor (and later Elizabethan) gentleman. Anne was a country girl – solemn, stubborn, indifferently educated, devoted to the old religion,[24] uninterested in politics, court life or her husband's reputed charms. The boy bridegroom joined his father-in-law's household not long after the wedding but seems to have found it dull and took refuge in extended visits to his uncle at Horton[25] and to the household of the Duke of Richmond, which moved its headquarters south after Richmond's own marriage to Mary Howard, daughter of the 3rd Duke of Norfolk.[26]

Essex may have developed a real fondness for William but the boy failed singularly to charm his child-wife. Technically the marriage should have been consummated two years after the wedding, when William was fifteen and Anne twelve, but neither had any inclination for the task. Maud Parr, in her will written on 20 May 1529, offered a substantial collection of jewellery as a bribe 'to my lady Bourchier when she lyeth with my son'.[27] Neither baubles nor persuasion had much affect on Anne, and it was to be twelve years before she and William began to live together as husband and wife. Their sexual relations proved to be as great a disaster as their marriage.

Maud Parr could not have known that the brilliant match which held out the prospect of riches and title for her only son would end in emotional catastrophe. In 1527, conscious only of a job well done, Maud turned once again to the task of finding a husband for her elder daughter. Catherine was now nearly sixteen and from a contemporary viewpoint, it was high time she was married. There was no longer any question of a brilliant match for in the three years since the abortive Scrope negotiations, Maud had mortgaged all of her income to buy the marriage of the heiress of the Earl of Essex for her only son. Catherine's prospects had been sacrificed for William's, but as William was the son and heir neither he nor his sister would have expected anything else. Once again, as in the pursuit of the heir of Lord Scrope of Bolton, Maud Parr looked to the northern families for a husband for her daughter. The royal surveyor of the castle, manor and lands of Sheriff Hutton, where her son had lived in the household of the Duke of Richmond, was one Sir Thomas Borough of Gainsborough, who could claim distant kinship ties to the late Sir Thomas Parr.[28]

The Boroughs of Gainsborough in Lincolnshire were an old and well-established gentry family. During Edward IV's reign, Sir Thomas Borough, the first Baron Borough, had been an outstanding Yorkist in a neighbourhood of fanatical Lancastrians. He had proven himself a tough-minded, hard-handed individual and was given the Order of the Garter in 1496 by Henry VII, proving his ability to adapt himself to the winds of royal change. Lord Borough's son, Sir Edward Borough, who succeeded in 1496 to the barony, was not so fortunate. A few years after he inherited the title, Edward, Lord Borough, was pronounced 'a lunatic though with lucid intervals', and was kept under restraint in his own home, Gainsborough Old Hall. Insanity was not a novel occurrence among the Boroughs. Sir Edward's sister, Margaret, was the wife of Sir George Tailboys of Goltho, who was listed as a lunatic in 1531.[29] After Lord Borough's incarceration, his eldest son, Sir Thomas Borough, later the third Baron Borough, took over as head of the family. Both Sir Thomas and his first wife, Agnes Tyrwhit, were kinsmen of the Parrs and thus a marriage with the family if not brilliant was eminently suitable. Sir Thomas' eldest son, Edward, was in his early twenties and although almost nothing is known about his character, it appears that his health was not robust. Whether he was physically frail or had inherited the seeds of his grandfather's insanity is uncertain. There is also the unsubstantiated possibility that he was a homosexual. Whatever his difficulties, he was certainly competent enough for his father to allow him the duties and responsibilities of part of his inheritance, and he served both as a feoffee and as a justice of the peace.[30] For centuries, historians and antiquarians alike have confused the grandfather – Edward, Lord Borough – with the grandson – Edward Borough – throwing the Scrope-Parr marriage negotiations into the mix for good measure. These worthies have written in purple prose of the horrors suffered by the twelve-year-old Catherine packed off to Lincolnshire to marry an aged lunatic. This myth may now be laid to rest and although the truth is not quite so lurid, it has its moments of high drama.

It was probably in the late spring of 1529[31] that Catherine Parr, aged sixteen, set out for the wilds of Lincolnshire as the bride of Edward Borough, taking with her as a wedding gift from her mother two gold bracelets and a rosary of carved wooden beads. This was Catherine's first venture into the north, long considered a violent and uncivilised place by southerners, and given her closeness to her mother and her proven affection for the rest of her family, there can be little doubt that she was homesick. Life at Gainsborough Old Hall with an unfamiliar young husband, an overbearing father-in-law given to violent rages, and memories of a recently-deceased lunatic in the attic could not have been easy. Requiring absolute obedience from his children, Catherine's new father-in-law ruled his family with an iron hand. Nor did Borough scruple to interfere in his children's marriages. Some years after Catherine's own marriage, he had another daughter-in-law, Elizabeth Owen, the wife of his son Thomas, thrown out of the house and her children declared bastards. As queen, Catherine would later pay the impoverished Elizabeth a pension from her own chamber accounts.[32] If his brother Thomas is any example, Catherine's new husband lived in terror of his father.

Scholarship, Catherine's passion, eagerly encouraged at home, was for Sir Thomas an indefensible frivolity. He was also opinionated in matters of religion. When his ambitious reform-minded chaplain went up to London and found a new patron in Cromwell, Borough wrote asking that he be returned at once.[33] In May 1533, at the celebrations for the coronation of Anne Boleyn, Borough was severely rebuked for 'ripping Queen Catherine's (of Aragon) arms off of her barge and for seizing the barge'.[34] Having been appointed Anne Boleyn's chamberlain, he maintained a high profile at the subsequent festivities, rode with the new queen in her barge as she was received at the Tower and appeared in the coronation procession in a surcoat and mantle of white cloth of tissue and ermine.[35] This passion for the reformed religion that obtained in Sir Thomas Borough's household could hardly but have had some sort of effect on his new daughter-in-law. Like her godmother, Catherine of Aragon, Catherine may have taken refuge from the more unpleasant aspects of her surroundings by discussing religion with the Boroughs' chaplain. Religion was one of the few sanctioned areas of emotional release that women could claim in 1529.[36]

Yet Catherine's duty was not to debate religion but to bear sons, a duty she failed to perform although that failure may not have been entirely her fault. Having been raised in a liberal and enlightened home overseen by her mother, Edward Borough's new bride was unused to the paternal tyranny that dominated the household at Gainsborough Old Hall. If Sir Thomas attempted, as he no doubt did, to intimidate Catherine, he found her made of sterner stuff than his own sons, and if Catherine had only pity for Edward and little affection for his family, she could scarcely be blamed. What is more, Catherine's marriage portion had not yet been paid, for when Catherine's mother wrote her will in May 1529, she remarked, 'I am indebted to Sir Thomas Borough, knight, for the marriage of my daughter'.[37] The dilatory arrival of the marriage portion had put a strain on more than one marriage, but with Lady Parr's continuing indebtedness for her son's marriage, the delay could not be helped.

For a time Edward and Catherine lived with Edward's family at Gainsborough Old Hall. If Catherine was homesick and unhappy, she had reason to be and no doubt wrote to her mother for comfort and advice. Worried by her daughter's difficulties, Maud Parr travelled north into Lincolnshire to see Catherine, probably in the summer of 1530.[38] She stayed at her own manor of Maltby, some eighteen miles west of Gainsborough Old Hall, and it may have been at her urging that about two years after their wedding, Catherine and Edward moved out of the hall. Edward's father, Sir Thomas, held a patent for the office of steward of the manor of the soke of Kirton-in-Lindsey, a small village about ten miles northeast of Gainsborough.[39] In October 1530, he was persuaded to secure a joint patent in survivorship with his son. Edward and Catherine set up housekeeping at Kirton-in-Lindsey which lay in a valley beneath the crest of a limestone escarpment on the waters of the Idle. It was a modest enough residence but it had the virtue of being at least a little distant from Catherine's in-laws, and, as importantly for Catherine, it was a home of which she alone was mistress. In this move, the active, rebellious nature of Catherine's character can be discerned. Rather than play passive and patient Griselda[40] in a dysfunctional household, Catherine seems to have taken control of her own fortunes to the extent of moving them – or colluding in their movement – elsewhere. Yet joy at escaping Gainsborough was countered by grief at a loss in her own family. Catherine had been in her own home less than a year when the crushing news of her mother's death reached her.

Maud Parr was only thirty-nine when she died on 1 December 1531 and was buried next to Catherine's father in St. Anne's, Blackfriars. As a mother in an age when children and parents frequently had little more than a formal relationship, Maud had been unusually close to her children. She had been their companion and confidant, the guiding force in their upbringing, their education, and for Catherine and William, their marriages. Bereft of her mother and separated by marriage and distance from her sister and brother, Catherine must have felt herself alone in the world. In her will, Maud left Catherine a cross of diamonds with a pendant pearl, a cache of loose pearls, and ironically, or prophetically, a jewelled portrait of Catherine's future husband, Henry VIII. Maud also bequeathed 400 marks, a rather substantial sum, for the founding of schools and the marrying of maidens, particularly the more needy maidens of her own family. In learning, charity, and responsibility for the welfare of her family, Maud was the pattern from which Catherine constructed her own self-image and her loss was irreplaceable.

A year and a half after her mother's death, Catherine's marriage to the fragile Edward came to an end. In 1532, Catherine's husband was named to the various commissions of the peace that held session in the area, but by April of 1533, Edward Borough was dead. Unable to remain at Kirton-in-Lindsey, which belonged to her father-in-law, Catherine's options were limited. Her in-laws showed no desire to have her move back in with them and she, for her part, must have been more than happy that her relationship with the Boroughs was at an end. The cantankerous Sir Thomas Borough turned over to Catherine the income from two of his manors in Surrey and one in Kent as her dower and more or less washed his hands of her.[41] Barely out of her teens, young Mistress Borough was now a supernumerary, a relict, the superfluous widow of the undistinguished son of a country squire. She had a small income from her dower, but no child to give her any further claims on her father-in-law or his estate. Her mother's widowhood had been a period of liberation, but Maud Parr had been left with a large estate to manage and to support her and her three children, as well as the advice and interest of her husband's family. Catherine's first excursion into widowhood was far different. She had little money, no home and no support system among her late husband's kin. Isolated in the north, without sufficient funds to turn widowhood into freedom of action, Catherine was well and truly alone. Where to go and what to do with her life must have seemed difficult questions to answer.

There is a tradition in the family of the Stricklands of Sizergh Castle in Westmorland that Catherine spent the year of her widowhood – 1533 – with them, demonstrating her notable needlework on a piece of embroidery still at the castle. Although this tradition is unsubstantiated – apart from the needlework – it may well be true. In that year, Catherine Neville (born 1499), the daughter and coheir of Sir Ralph Neville of Thornton Briggs, was the widow of both Sir Walter Strickland of Sizergh, one of Catherine Parr's many cousins, and of Henry Borough. She was thus kinswoman to Catherine, Catherine's late husband, and Catherine's cousins, the Stricklands. Related by both blood and marriage, it is entirely possible that Catherine Neville, dowager Lady Strickland, invited the young widow to Sizergh.[42] But serving either as a comparatively poor relation in Lady Strickland's household or occupying a post as a superfluous houseguest were hardly attractive options for the energetic Catherine. As fortune would have it, Catherine Neville was also a kinswoman of Lord Latimer of Snape Castle in Yorkshire and by the following summer, Catherine had chosen him as her second husband.[43]

Twice Catherine's age and her father's second cousin, John Neville, Lord

Latimer, was 40 years old, the twice-widowed descendant of George Neville, Lord Latimer, Warwick, the 'Kingmaker's', 'idiot uncle'.[44] He had been knighted at the age of twenty on 14 October 1513 at Lille during Henry VIII's French adventure of that year. Latimer served on the usual Yorkshire commissions (Justice of the Peace for the North Riding in December 1530), and while still Sir John Neville, represented that shire in Parliament during the great 1529 session that debated the king's divorce from Catherine of Aragon. His first wife had been Dorothy Vere, the sister and coheir of John Vere, Earl of Oxford. Dorothy died in February 1527, leaving two small children, John (born 1520) and Margaret (1525). Latimer married as his second wife, Elizabeth, the daughter of Sir Edward Musgrave, who bore him no surviving children and died about 1530.

At the time of his marriage to Catherine, Latimer was experiencing financial difficulties. He owed the king large sums of money that at his death he had not yet been able to pay.[45] He wrote to Cromwell on 5 April 1534:

> As I have been at every prorogation of Parliament nearly these four years, which has been very painful and chargeable to me, as I have not yet paid the king all that is due for the livery of my lands, nor all the sums I am bound to pay by the wills of my father and mother-in-law, I beg you will get me leave to tarry at home and be absent from the next prorogation. I shall be in better readiness to do the king service against the Scots when we in these parts are called upon.[46]

Latimer added the rider usual in a letter of request to Cromwell, 'I send you a gelding by this bearer, the likeliest I could get.' Part of Latimer's financial difficulties stemmed from the £1,610 that he had paid in October 1534 for his nine-year-old daughter's marriage, as yet unconsummated, to the son and heir of Sir Francis Bigod,[47] who was having his own financial problems.[48] On 31 January 1535, Bigod wrote to Cromwell, begging his help in paying his debts. 'Lord Latimer is content to release me of so much land as would discharge them,' Bigod told Cromwell, 'yet my heart bleeds to part with any for my wife and children's sake.'[49] Bigod needed a loan of £2,200 to alleviate his debt and writing to Cromwell from Cambridge, confessed that 'I dare not come to London for fear of Mr. Gresham and Mr. Lodge.'[50] These economic troubles in the extended family into which Catherine married were to bear violent fruit by 1536.

Not only financial woes but family squabbles darkened the atmosphere at Snape Castle. Just after Christmas 1530, two of Latimer's younger brothers, George and Christopher, took legal action against him for property they claimed was owed them under the terms of their father's will.[51] The eldest male in the family was in line for the earldom of Warwick, a fact which exacerbated family sensibilities and sharpened the knives of family competition. Added to this, Lord Latimer's many brothers (there were fifteen children in the family) had a peculiar penchant for necromancy. Not for nothing was this clan of Nevilles descended from 'Kingmaker' Warwick's idiot uncle. Exactly two years after George and Christopher's lawsuit, on 30 December 1532, another brother, William Neville, a former servant of Wolsey's and seemingly in need of funds, was arrested for consulting a notorious necromancer named Richard Jones.[52] Jones prophesied to his eager client that William would shortly become the earl of Warwick. Not satisfied with this, Neville consulted 'one Nashe of Cirencester, who told Neville his wife would die and that he would marry an heiress of (Lord) Graystoke's kin and become Lord Latimer.' Seeking further supernatural reassurance that he would replace his brother at Snape, William next visited 'the wizard Johns of Oxford' and this time was promised a ring to be used by him and by brother Christopher, 'to obtain men's favour and to avoid northern wars'.

During this final session with the Oxford wizard, a number of seditious remarks were made, predicting Henry VIII's death and the succession to the English throne of James V of Scotland. William, still in hot pursuit of the earldom of Warwick, now believed that his eldest brother, John, 'shall be slain at one of the said battles, and then shall I have the ward of his son, and have both his lands and the earl of Warwick's.' William, rather unwisely, confided the results of his supernatural consultations to a gentleman named Thomas Wood, who in turn lost no time in reporting what he had been told to the authorities. George Neville was questioned, and Christopher Neville was compromised, for William stated that brother Christopher's distaste for 'the northern wars' was one of the reasons he had sought out supernatural aid in the first place. Two years after William's excursions into the occult, two more Neville brothers, Thomas and Marmaduke, were arrested for treason, although they eventually escaped the extreme penalty of the law. John Neville, Lord Latimer, with huge debts, a gaggle of garrulous, unstable brothers, a troubled son and numerous relatives depending on him for financial support was a man much in need of a wife to comfort him.

From the beginning, Catherine tried to be a good wife to her new lord and a good mother to John and Margaret. Her relationship with young John was undoubtedly a difficult one. Catherine's stepson grew from a troubled youth into a violent and emotionally unstable man, who was sent to the Fleet for violence done on a servant, Dorothy Wiseman, in the summer of 1553, arrested for attempted rape and assault in 1557,[53] and who killed a man with a rapier in 1563.[54] Lord Latimer declined to make his son and heir, although of age, the executor of his estate in his will, confining himself to entailing the property so that John could not meddle with his inheritance or interfere with his father's testated legacies.[55] That public violence, at least, occurred only after his stepmother's death may indicate that Catherine had some control over the wayward John. She later wrote of difficult teen-agers:

> And, contrary the younglings and unperfect are offended at small trifles, taking everything in evil part, grudging and murmuring against their neighbour ... when (these little ones) see one that is reputed and esteemed holy to commit sin. Forthwith they learn to do that, and worse, and wax cold in doing good, and confirm themselves in evil, and then they excuse their wicked life, publishing the same with the slander of their neighbour. If any man reprove them, they say such a man did thus and worse ... Their affections dispose their eyes to see through other men, and they see nothing in themselves .[56]

The frustrations of parenting young John Neville, a violent rebellious boy who grew into a violent unstable man, echo through Catherine's words.

Margaret, on the other hand, was a bright and articulate girl, secure in her father's affections and devoted to her stepmother, the only mother she ever really knew. Her childhood betrothal to Ralph Bigod was set aside after the Pilgrimage of Grace, and when, after Lord Latimer's death, Catherine married Henry VIII, she took Margaret with her to court and made her a maid-in-waiting in her household.[57] Margaret acted as liaison between her stepmother and her stepsister, the Princess Elizabeth, while the latter was out of favour between the summers of 1543 and 1544, visiting her at Ashridge during December 1543.[58] Because Catherine's stepdaughter, who died at Greenwich in 1546 at about the age of twenty-one, died at such an early age her importance both to the woman who raised her and to her young stepsister, Elizabeth, has never been adequately investigated. Both women loved her and certainly Catherine's close, affectionate, and supportive relationship with Margaret set the pattern for her future relationship with Elizabeth.

Catherine Parr became the third Lady Latimer probably during the summer of 1534, and during her nine-year marriage developed an affection for her husband deep enough to cherish a remembrance of him, his New Testament with his name inscribed inside the cover, which she kept with her until her death.[59] Socially Lord Latimer was definitely a step upward from Edward Borough and Catherine now had, despite Neville family problems, all that she could conceivably want – a home of her own at Snape Castle, a husband with position and influence in the north where her own family's lands lay, a ready-made family and a title. By a stroke of irony, Catherine was the first of Sir Thomas Parr's children to carry a title, and apart from her great-aunt, Mabel,

Lady Dacre, the only female Parr to marry into the peerage. Catherine had every reason to feel satisfied with this match, but whether or not she was ever completely happy in the north is a moot point. She had, after all, been raised in the cultured atmosphere of Hertfordshire, with close ties to the life at court. She was gently bred and well-educated, accustomed to southern society and southern manners. Northern society tended to be, as it had always been, rather rough and ready, and the thick Yorkshire dialect would have been unfamiliar to Catherine even after four and a half years in Lincolnshire.

Snape Castle was an isolated place surrounded by rough, wild country, unlike Gainsborough Old Hall which lay in flatter terrain and had a village adjacent to it. Nor was Catherine's character particularly suited to the sober privations that a life spent in the north could entail. Like the rest of her family, Catherine had a merry disposition. She was young, energetic and intelligent, with red hair, grey-blue eyes and a clear complexion. She loved fine clothes and, like her mother and her grandmother, had a passion for jewels, especially diamonds. She liked to ride and hunt with a crossbow, and like her father, was an excellent dancer, fond of music, revels and other courtly entertainments. Yorkshire must have seemed cold and dark and hopelessly provincial to the new Lady Latimer, as well as being painfully remote from family and friends in the south.

Twice her age, her new husband was Yorkshire born and bred, of a conservative nature, and as later events would prove, a man who would take foolish chances and crumble beneath the weight of the consequences. Yet there was kindness in him too, as the many bequests in his will to loyal servants and a variety of relatives, as well as his detailed instructions for the care of his widow and daughter attest. He forgave the necromantic machinations of his brother William to the extent that he provided for William's daughters in his will. Certainly of a more gentle and less authoritarian nature than her former father-in-law, Sir Thomas Borough, and not much of a soldier, Latimer combined kindness with fussiness, self-consequence with weakness, facts Catherine was to learn to her cost. Like many of his northern compatriots, Latimer was a fervent supporter of the old religion and was known for the elaborate private chapel he maintained. The establishment of the Church of England under the aegis of the king some three years after his marriage to Catherine was not to this northern lord's taste at all, and possibly, to Latimer's further discomfiture, although this is not certain, he found that his young wife was not completely in agreement with him. The new Lady Latimer moved to Yorkshire and for the next three years devoted herself to raising her two young stepchildren and trying to adapt herself to Yorkshire society. Conditions in the north, always volatile, were once again reaching a point of open revolt. When the explosion came, Catherine Parr was to find herself right in the middle of it.

5

The Parrs and the Pilgrimage of Grace

When Catherine Parr was born in 1512, she was named for Henry VIII's queen, Catherine Aragon, who in all probability acted as her godmother. The irony of Henry's first queen acting as godmother to his last is one that until now has been lost to history. Four years later, in February 1516, at the Greenwich christening of Catherine of Aragon's own baby daughter, Princess Mary, Catherine's parents played prominent roles.[1] Given Catherine Parr's close relationship with the Princess Mary in the early 1540s, it seems possible that Lady Parr may have encouraged her daughter as a child to make a friend of the princess, who might someday become queen of England. Yet even at their daughter's christening, the early, happier days of Henry VIII's marriage to his Spanish princess were coming to an end. By 1526, ten years after Mary's birth, no more revels were being run for 'a gladness to the Queen's grace'. Camelot had to all intents and purposes closed its doors and rolled up its round table for good. Queen Guinevere was stout and aging; King Arthur a middle-aged man on the make.

At forty-one, it was evident to Henry that his wife's childbearing days were behind her, without the burning necessity of a legitimate male heir having been satisfactorily achieved. Catherine had not conceived in nine years and the likelihood of her doing so again would require nothing short of a miracle. Nor could Catherine any longer command her husband's affections as she had been able to do in the early halcyon days of their marriage. Continual childbearing had left her stout, tired and humourless. Her health, too, was affected by the long succession of pregnancies that had ended in miscarriages and still births. She suffered from leucorrhea, a particularly unpleasant and odorous infection that sometimes follows on the heels of childbirth. Although she was by no means an invalid, Catherine's body no longer held any attractions for her husband. Sex had become a duty distasteful to both marriage partners and by 1525, it had ceased altogether between them.[2] Always pious, the queen now spent more time at her prayers, and her devotions were divided between her religion and her daughter. Mary's best interests were Catherine's chief concern. By 1525 Catherine of Aragon's concern for her disintegrating marriage included concern for her daughter's rights to Henry's throne.

As Catherine's sexual needs found a substitute for intercourse in the ecstasies of religion and a refuge from procreational failure in prayer, her husband's sexual appetite was at its peak. If his wife could no longer satisfy him, another woman's body must do. Restlessly he looked around for a new partner in desire. It was a quirk of Henry's emotional make-up that he found sex in marriage more attractive than sex on the side. The romantic aspects of his personality, complicated by his need for a legitimate male heir, led him to attempt love matches with five of his six wives. The results were to prove disappointing. As kings go, Henry was not a promiscuous man. Not for Henry a dozen mistresses to satisfy nothing more than some physical whim. He had been sincerely in love with Catherine of Aragon as a young man. The woman he chose to replace her would have to fill his heart as well as his bed.

Sometime around February 1526, Henry made a new romantic discovery and unleashed a sexual obsession in himself that was to last a decade and have incalculable consequences for his dynasty and his kingdom. Cool, ambitious, ruthless, gifted with a charismatic personality and a devastating ability for making enemies, Mistress Anne Boleyn was something novel in Henry's experience. Earlier interests such as Bessie Blount and Mary Boleyn, Anne's elder sister, had been content to become his sexual partner without demanding more. Anne was not. Unlike Catherine Parr, who some seventeen years later was reputed to have exclaimed, 'Better to be his mistress than his wife,' Anne Boleyn felt it infinitely preferable to become the latter rather than to settle for the former. Her impatient would-be lover began to ponder ways of shedding queen number one and replacing her with queen number two. This would not prove to be an easy thing to bring about.

By 1529, the year that Catherine Parr married Edward Borough, Henry VIII had tired of games and subterfuges and was determined to have his own way in the matter of his marriage as quickly as possible. He decided to take the bull by the horns and force the issue. The heretical and disreputable activities of many of the English clergy were exposed and denounced to the English populace in a public relations campaign run between 1529 and 1531 and stage managed by Anne Boleyn's supporters. With the fall of his former master, Cardinal Wolsey, Thomas Cromwell began to build a new career for himself predicated upon making the king head of the English Church and able to marry whomever he chose. By December 1532 Henry and Anne were having sexual relations. Anne Boleyn seems to have soon become pregnant and the following month, January 1533, in a secret and legally questionable marriage, the king made her his second wife and Queen of England.

During this volatile period, young William Parr, the son-in-law of the Earl of Essex, spent much of his time at court. There he made friends with the Duke of Richmond's brother-in-law, the Earl of Surrey, with Thomas Seymour, younger brother of the Duke of Richmond's former master of the horse, with Sir Thomas Wyatt,[3] ten years Parr's senior and the son of Sir Henry Wyatt, an old friend of William's father and uncle, and with Sir John Dudley, who had been raised in the family of Parr's great-aunt, Jane Guildford.[4] Poetry, music and literature, hawking, hunting, and martial posturing, combined with less elevated ambitions to form the common currency of these courtly gallants. With such important connections as these, William Parr found himself at the heart of an elite inner circle. His close relationships with a group of young court aristocrats led him to look with a less than kindly eye on the ambitions of Cardinal Wolsey's former secretary, Thomas Cromwell. Raised with the Duke of Richmond, friend of the arrogant young Surrey, Parr had no doubt been taught early on contempt for the man who was to become the king's chief minister and architect of the Great Divorce. Yet during the early days of Cromwell's ascendancy, Parr was caught in the not-uncommon position of trying to stay on the good side of the royal favourite while privately despising him. Parr's uncle, Sir William Parr of Horton, had exchanged his clientele position with the fallen Wolsey for one with Wolsey's successor and he was expected to pay a price for Cromwell's influence. Uncle and nephew both soon found that Cromwell regarded the Parr family's store of patronage as a larder to be raided at will. While his uncle was forced to put up with this, young William Parr appears to have resented it and to have considered Cromwell's demands as some form of upstart *lese-majeste* against the dignity of the upper classes. There was little he could do about it but protest, and this he did at length.

Early in 1533, Cromwell had a mind to the lease of the farm of Nasingbury in Essex which was part of the Parr holdings. Under his uncle's prodding hand, Nasingbury's owner, young William, was forced to write to Cromwell on 28 January 1533:

> I beseech your lordship that you hold me excused by answer I have so long delayed your lordship from your request in the fee farm of Nasingbury which was by reasons of my mother's will ... who did dispose the farm ... [but] considering your mind is so fervently set thereon ... I am content.[5]

Eighteen-year-old Anne Parr, William's strong-minded sister, however, was far from content. She had been left an interest in Nasingbury by her mother and had no intention of giving it up. By October, control of Nasingbury had still not been relinquished by the Parrs. William wrote to Cromwell once again, protesting that Nasingbury should be continued under Parr control for '[my mother] gave and bequeathed it to my sister Anne by her said will ... over and above her child's portion, the sum of 400 marks, toward her entertainment and marriage.'[6] More pressure was put on Sir William Parr of Horton to bring his stubborn nephew and recalcitrant niece into line, and on 24 October, Sir William wrote to Cromwell that his nephew was now reconciled to giving up Nasingbury.

This was just the beginning of Cromwell's depredations. Having obtained Nasingbury by the age-old method of intimidation, Cromwell now decided he wanted young William's steward, Thomas Pickering, as well. This was a tribute to Pickering's abilities and possibly to his ambitions, but it was a terrible blow to his twenty-year-old master, who relied on such trusted family servants to keep the wheels of estate management running smoothly. William, who had already learned one bitter lesson in the politics of power, gave way as gracefully as he could, but not without protest:

> It may like you to understand [he wrote to Cromwell in June 1534] that the good order and governance of such poor household as I shall have to keep at such time as I come to my living should not only have rested in his wisdom and experience but also [without his opinion] nothing can be done concerning of my poor affairs.[7]

Parr explained how his mother, Maud Parr, had had absolute faith in Pickering and how she had instructed young William to follow his advice implicitly. Such appeals to sentiment weighed very little with Cromwell, however, and young William was once again forced to concede to Cromwell's demands and write that 'considering it is your pleasure to have him, I am very well content that he shall be at your commandment.' It was a bitter pill to swallow and quite obvious that William was not in the least content. To add insult to injury, Cromwell appointed the appropriated Pickering steward for the appropriated Nasingbury. On 30 July 1535, Cromwell's servant, Thomas Thacker, reported rather smugly to his master: 'Thomas Pickering says he has inned you one hundred load of good hay and you shall yet have sixty load or more at Nasingbury.'[8]

If young William Parr resented the predatory habits of his uncle's patron,[9] he was not the only victim in the family.[10] In 1535, Cromwell decided he would like the lease of the manor of Pempole in Cornwall which happened to belong to Thomas, Lord Vaux,[11] and his wife, Elizabeth Cheyney, first cousins to Catherine, William and Anne Parr. Elizabeth Cheyney had been raised by her aunt, Maud Parr, and she was every bit as steel-willed as that formidable woman. When Cromwell demanded Pempole, Elizabeth proved adamant. Her husband, a talented poet but a weak-willed and moody man, would have given up without a struggle. Not Elizabeth. Cromwell began to put pressure on Parr of Horton to force his niece to accede to the inevitable. Parr wrote to Cromwell:

> Wherefore if it will please your mastership to send for her and by your great wisdom to take the pain to commune with her, I trust, or else she doth fair deceive me, she will apply herself therein according to the king's pleasure and yours. For more than I have done it neither lieth in my power nor wit to do.[12]

Lady Vaux, it seems, was stronger willed than her uncle, but even she could not hold out long against Cromwell's express desire.[13] All of these petty but irritating battles of the Parr family faded into insignificance, however, the following year when greater concerns overwhelmed the entire family.

With the accomplishment of the king's divorce and remarriage and the establishment of the English monarch as the head of the English Church, the question of church property became one of extreme importance. Thomas Cromwell had been created Vicar-General and king's Vice-Regent in all matters ecclesiastical in order to preside over the national dismemberment of church-owned property. In his capable hands the liquidation of church assets to the enrichment of the upper classes proceeded in a ruthlessly efficient manner. Yet for all of those who viewed the dissolution of English religious foundations as a grab bag of lands and money to get while the getting was good, there were those who viewed it as an affront to God and His Holy Church. Every revolution creates a group of disaffected whose mood is surly and whose instinct is violent. The destruction of one religious supremacy and the substitution of another produced its own group of religious refugees. This was particularly true in the north of England, traditionally a conservative area. Perhaps, many northerners thought, the true church did need reforming, but the king's arbitrary decision to cut the umbilical cord that tied London to Rome and endow himself with the power of God's temporal designate was more than many of the deeply conservative could stomach. As the liquidation of church property proceeded, the mutter of dissent in the north steadily grew in volume until it exploded in the violent confrontation of 1536 known to history as the Pilgrimage of Grace.

A number of factors were at work in northern society that led to the Pilgrimage of Grace. Northern society was suspicious of the south. Southern society was contemptuous of the north. The royal attitude toward the entire area was summed up by Henry VIII in his characterization of Lincolnshire as 'one of the most brute and beastly (shires) of the whole realm.'[14] Henry had no more patience with the stubborn conservatism of shires than he had with the stubborn conservatism of individuals. In Lincolnshire, itself, there was bitter outcry, not at the king but at his evil councillors, particularly Thomas Cromwell and those bishops who had supported the separation of the English Church from Rome. Men with personal grievances, men deeply in debt and desperate like Sir Francis Bigod, men seeking fresh opportunities, men who feared the new ecclesiastical order and the king's potential fiscal demands, men who hated their landlords and the new aggressive policies of enclosure, men of the commons, the yeomanry and the gentry classes formed the nucleus of a northern revolt that exploded on 1 October 1536 at Louth in Lincolnshire.[15] Three royal commissions that were then in the shire collecting subsidies, suppressing monasteries and imposing Cromwell's draconian regulations on the clergy provided the spark which quickly flamed into a conflagration. Within three days, the Louth riot had grown into a major uprising and on 4 October, the Earl of Shrewsbury wrote to the king that 3,000 rebels had gathered at Horne Castle and were threatening one of the few significant members of the gentry who had refused to join them, Sir Thomas Borough of Gainsborough Old Hall.

Married to Lord Latimer the year after Henry VIII's secret marriage to Anne Boleyn, Catherine Parr must have felt the growing emotional disturbances pulsing through the north. Her new husband bitterly opposed the king's divorce and remarriage and its religious ramifications. Catherine would have been privy to his outrage and to mutterings of anger and resentment at the government among the local people, feelings that her later actions imply she may not have shared. Sitting at home at Snape Castle, she must have received the news of the mob's threat to her former father-in-law and his household with mixed feelings but with some natural concern for her own family at Snape. Her old home, Kirton-in-Lindsey, had risen on the side of the insurgents. Worse news was to follow. Branded rebels by the government, the northern commons were infuriated. Many perceived themselves as fighting in the king's cause against those who would mislead him. To Henry, a mob in arms was a rebellion. Lord Latimer wrote somewhat naively that he did not think that the government would hinder people's desires 'as be reasonable'.[16] Unfortunately for Latimer, the government in the person of the king failed to see anything reasonable in the northern risings. This particular rebellion, begun in Lincolnshire, spread like a forest fire toward Catherine's home in Yorkshire.

Within two weeks of the riot at Louth, a mob appeared at night before Catherine's front door, threatening violence unless Lord Latimer joined them. Before Catherine's horrified eyes, her husband was carried off into the darkness by the rebels. Terror for his safety was soon compounded for Catherine by rumours of his treason. Now a prisoner of the rebels, conflicting stories concerning Latimer's conduct began to reach Cromwell and the king in London. On 17 October, Sir Brian Hastings commented in a letter to the Earl of Shrewsbury that both Lord Latimer and the new Lord Scrope of Bolton were 'sworn to the rebels, with the worshipful of their retinue.'[17] In another twist of fate, Catherine's husband and her almost-fiancé, John Scrope, were both living in the camp of the leader of the Yorkshire rising, Robert Aske. The signatures of Latimer and Scrope began to appear on documents detailing rebel demands and Latimer was reported to be on close terms with Aske. Quick to perceive and resent any behaviour that smelled of treason, both Cromwell and the king became convinced that Latimer served the rebels voluntarily because he secretly sympathized with their grievances. Stories of his having raised men for the cause under the banner and arms of St. Cuthbert and of having mustered them before the very doorstep of the Bishop of Durham added fuel to the flames of reputed treason licking at Latimer's heels.[18] Latimer, himself, later emphatically denied both stories and accusations, but to little avail.

John Neville, Lord Latimer, was forty-six in 1536, a middle-aged man of careful habits who worried about money, his health, and his own comfort. He was not a particularly well-informed or courageous man nor was he a particularly strong-minded one. The rebellion in Yorkshire had put him in a terrible dilemma. He did in fact sympathize with the cause of the rebels. He had no love for the king's friends or advisors and his religious beliefs were conservative. But neither had he any desire to suffer the extreme penalty for treason. The result was that Latimer tried hard to pacify all parties and ended up satisfying none. He became the spokesman for Robert Aske in order to appease the rebels who had appeared out of the night at his own front door clamouring for his support or his blood. This same violent ultimatum had been offered to the reform-minded Lord Borough and he had fought his way to freedom. Latimer tried appeasement, a position hardly calculated to endear him to the king. Henry was busy mounting an army to deal with the rebellion and he considered all who did not stand up and fight to be traitors. Latimer later protested that he stayed with Aske to try and end the uprising and stop the violence. As Latimer explained himself in a letter to his brother-in-law, Sir William Musgrave, in January 1537: 'Though I durst not much contrary [argue with] them [the commons], I did my best to reduce them to conformity to the king's pleasure. My being among them was a very painful and dangerous time to me; I pray God I may never see such again.'[19]

While her husband was off with the insurgents, Lady Latimer's uncle and brother were approaching with a royal army raised to crush the rebellion. Sir William Parr of Horton had been appointed, together with Sir John Russell (later first Earl of Bedford) and Sir Francis Bryan, to muster the levies of

Buckinghamshire, Bedfordshire and Northamptonshire. By 9 October, Parr reached Stamford with his troops and reported to the king that the city walls were weak, the town citizens reluctant to blow up the bridge that would strengthen the town's defences, and the commons were only prevented by the army's presence from joining the uprising themselves. Ordnance, money, horses, harness and artillery were all in short supply. The ever-martial Parr promised that despite these hindrances, he would 'put the offenders in despair and dread.'[20] The daring Russell disguised himself as a rebel and infiltrated their ranks in order to gather information. Sir William Fitzwilliam, future Earl of Southampton, was also on his way to Stamford, snorting fire, spoiling for a fight, and 'so earnest in the matter that ... [he swore] he would eat [the rebels] with salt.'[21] Men such as Parr, Russell and Fitzwilliam, besides liking a good fight, saw in the northern uprisings exactly the same opportunities for advancement that many of the rebels had seen. Careers could be made or broken on the battlefield according to the luck of the day, and Parr of Horton instinctively knew that this was his best arena. As civil servant, chamberlain or glorified bookkeeper, he was a singular failure. A blow well struck for the king against the tyranny of the mob might bring the rewards and recognition that he craved.

For young William Parr, the uprising was something to be put down as quickly as possible. William was a friend of Thomas Legh, who together with Richard Layton, both members of one of Cromwell's hated northern commissions, were the particular targets of the mob's fury.[22] But William's primary purpose in riding into the north with the Duke of Norfolk was not to save Legh. Parr hurried north because the uprisings had threatened his lands in Lincolnshire near Louth, as well as those in Yorkshire and Cumbria. He was concerned both about the possible destruction of his holdings and about growing rebel tendencies among his tenants. More pragmatically, he was also concerned about getting his rents on time which, if the north were up in arms and his tenants under arrest, would be unlikely to happen.[23] At twenty-three, William Parr had had little to do with his northern estates beyond receiving his stewards' reports and collecting his rents from their hands. Like the king, the younger Parr had no taste for the north, for its conservative customs or its clannish society. His tastes had been formed in the south among courtly society, and Parr felt himself to be of finer clay than his rude northern cousins. His commitment to the new religious establishment, rooted in his years lived in the Duke of Richmond's circle, left him out of sympathy with northern traditionalists and his position as landlord of northern estates precluded a tender concern for the complaints of oppressed tenants.

This basic indifference to his Cumbrian lands, apart from the income they generated, was tempered by a sensitive concern for his own feudal rights. When one of Parr's tenants, Richard Thornborough of Sleddall and Crosthwaite, died, he left as his heir a minor son, William.[24] Taking a page from Henry VII's book of feudal prerogative, Parr demanded the custody and wardship of the child as his feudal right. Richard Thornborough's widow, Margaret, refused to give up custody of her son. Parr tried to prosecute the case in court but could make no progress and finally in 1536, the year of the Pilgrimage of Grace and its violent demonstrations against oppressive landlords,[25] he resorted to that most ancient of northern customs – brute force – and ordered his cousin Walter Strickland, his acting steward in Kendal, to storm the Thornborough home and seize the child. Such arbitrary and violent actions on the part of demanding landlords must have served as a spur to alienated tenants to view the rebellion with sympathy. There is also some evidence that Parr was involved in land enclosure.[26] No wonder then that he was worried about his estates and the loyalty of his people and eager to ride north with the Duke of Norfolk to ensure the security and preservation of his lands and the obedience of his tenants.

For Catherine, Lady Latimer, the months between October 1536 and April 1537 were a time of violence and fear. Alone with two children, threatened by the mob and unsure from day to day what new calamity was about to fall on her head, Catherine struggled to survive. She could hardly have failed to understand that her husband's actions on behalf of the rebels could easily be interpreted by Cromwell and the king as treason. In such case, Lord Latimer would lose his head as well as forfeit his estates, leaving his widow and two children all but penniless. Nor is it likely, given Catherine's later devotion to the new religion, that she was much in sympathy with the rebellion. In fact her strong reaction against the northern violence probably strengthened her adherence to the reformed church. Her husband's ties to the uprising must have left her dismayed and afraid. Catherine's young stepdaughter, Margaret Neville, was betrothed to the son of Sir Francis Bigod, one of the rebel leaders and a close friend of Latimer's. Two of Latimer's brothers had been declared traitors.[27] Latimer's own bailiff, Walter Rawlinson, had been named one of the ringleaders of the uprising.[28] Another rebel and friend of Catherine's husband was Sir Christopher Danby, who later swore that he had been coerced into serving the rebellion. Sir Christopher's kinsman, Edward Danby, served in Latimer's home.[29] Two of Lord Latimer's household stewards, Robert and John Layton, may have been kinsmen of Robert Aske's.[30] Such friendships and associations with proven rebels could be enough to tip the balance of royal opinion against Latimer.

Throughout October and into November, Catherine stayed at Snape in what must have been an unbearable period of frightened expectation. The king's troops, concentrated at Stamford under Parr of Horton and Sir John

Russell, were joined there on 10 October by the retinues of the Duke of
Suffolk, Sir William Fitzwilliam and Sir Francis Bryan.[31] The coming of Parr
and Russell had quieted the countryside around Stamford and within ten days
the royal troops set out to recover Lincoln from the rebels. On 19 October, the
Lincolnshire insurrection collapsed and its leaders offered their submission to
the king's generals. Affairs in Yorkshire followed a similar pattern and when a
general amnesty was offered during the first week of December, Aske accepted
it. With difficulty, he persuaded his army of some 30,000 volunteers to disband.
Meanwhile, the king had written to the Duke of Norfolk to put pressure on
Latimer to induce him 'to condemn that villain Aske and submit (himself) to
our clemency.'[32] Latimer was more than happy to accede to the king's request.

Having returned home at the cessation of hostilities, Lord Latimer took
advantage of the amnesty to leave his once more unprotected wife and
children at Snape Castle shortly after a grim Christmas and hurry south to
plead the extenuating circumstances of his collaboration with Aske to the
king. The king's attitude was far from sympathetic toward gentlemen such as
Lord Latimer, who pleaded with him that fear for their lives and property, or
more altruistically a concern to bring an end to the violence, had led them
to cooperate with the rebellion. As Latimer's brother, Marmaduke Neville,
testified: '[I think] the mean gentlemen might have escaped, but the commons
suspected the nobles and gentlemen would deceive them. What might have
been done I know not for no man dared to try.'[33] Latimer might protest his
innocence all he wanted to, but the fact remained that he had neither tried to
escape nor to call up his tenants and face the rebels in arms. He had surrendered
without a fight and neither the king nor Cromwell was willing to forgive him
for it. Yet the evidence against him was counterbalanced by influential friends
at court. Fitzwilliam, the Lord Admiral, wrote a letter to the king on Latimer's
behalf. Nor was it likely that such kinsmen as Lady Latimer's brother and uncle
would fail to speak up for him. Parr of Horton now had some influence with
the Duke of Suffolk after so many weeks together in Lincoln. Latimer's survival
and exculpation were important to the Parrs' own position. His attainder and
execution could affect them all. Latimer, as it proved, was fortunate that he had
married a Parr. It was Catherine's connections and those of her family that were
instrumental in saving his life from charges of treason.[34]

While Lord Latimer was on his way to London trying to explain himself
to the king, word of his 'betrayal' of the rebel cause reached Yorkshire and
infuriated the mob. In the middle of January 1537, they stormed Snape Castle
and took Catherine and the children hostage. What particular violence or rape
Catherine suffered at their hands is not recorded, but the mob ransacked the
house and word was sent to Latimer that if he did not return immediately to

Yorkshire, Snape Castle would be burned to the ground and his family killed. Latimer was at Stamford when he received word of this new catastrophe. He was at his wit's end by this time. The king had ordered him north to meet the Duke of Norfolk at Doncaster. To ignore the king's direct order to care for his own affairs, even if it meant the lives of his wife and children, was dangerous in his present situation. Cromwell had made no bones about wanting him executed for treason and now the rebels wanted to hang him and murder his family for betraying their cause. Frantically, for Catherine and his children were now in the hands of the mob, Latimer wrote to Fitzwilliam begging him to ask the king what to do. 'I have no men and no strong house,' he wrote, and then added in despair, 'if it were the king's pleasure that I might live on such small lands as I have in the south, I would little care for my lands in the north.'[35] Latimer had been further compromised by his friend, Sir Francis Bigod's, new rebellion, and by the accusations of treason against his brothers, Marmaduke and Thomas Neville. But the family's tendency toward rebellion had apparently not impressed the men who still held his wife and children prisoner.

Latimer returned to Snape Castle and somehow managed to persuade the rabble to release his family and leave his house. His own life still hung by a thread and he wasted no time leaving the area, abandoning for a third time Catherine, Margaret and John to potential hazard. He rode to Pontefract to meet with the Duke of Norfolk, who on 3 February confided rather sarcastically to the Earl of Sussex: 'My lord Latimer should not have met me, unto [until] my coming to York, but he liked so ill his being at home, that he was content to meet me, or I came to Doncaster.'[36] The king's men under Norfolk had finally defeated Aske's army, formed once more during the abortive rebellion of Sir Francis Bigod, and the bloody business of arrest and execution began. The duke, who had Catherine's brother, William, in his train, was charged with gathering evidence against Lord Latimer. Cromwell minced no words when he wrote to inform Norfolk that, 'the King doesn't much favour Lord Latimer.'[37] Fortunately for Latimer, the duke did not much favour Cromwell, and Latimer's brother-in-law was at Norfolk's side and in Norfolk's favour and certainly would have encouraged the quality of mercy.[38] On 16 June, Norfolk wrote to Cromwell that he had contrived to 'make Latimer go to London as a suitor on his own affairs ... [but I] can't discover any evidence other than he was enforced and no man in more danger of his life.'[39] With the duke stubbornly refusing to supply the evidence that would indict Latimer for treason, there the matter rested. Latimer, however, was a marked man. He spent the last seven years of his life paying blackmail to Cromwell – small gifts of money, the sale of two of his southern manors, and even the lease of his London house – in order to preserve his lands and liberty.[40]

Having suffered the violence of the mob, Catherine, as Lady Latimer, now suffered the humiliation doled out to her husband. She had seen her family threatened and her house ransacked. She had been manhandled, held hostage and her life put in jeopardy both by the violence of the rebels and by the inability of her husband to protect her. As a result, Latimer's credibility with the king had been destroyed and his position in the north severely compromised. Catherine's actions after the executions which marked the bloody conclusion of the rebellion in the north indicate that the entire period had left deep emotional scars. She encouraged her husband to make good on his promise to leave the north and they moved south, first to Latimer's lands in Worcestershire, and then to Northamptonshire. Latimer owned a group of manors around Pershore, south of Worcester, notably Wick, Wadborough and Shilton, and it was at Wick that Catherine and her husband settled temporarily by the end of the year.[41] Latimer also pleased Cromwell and the king by this temporary removal to the south, for it had the virtue of taking him out of the area of his greatest influence, Yorkshire, and rendering him incapable of further rebellion should such a fancy enter his head.

For her part, Catherine must have been grateful for the quiet of Worcestershire after the frenzy of Yorkshire. She had been separated from her family since 1529 and after eight turbulent and traumatic years, Latimer was willing to indulge his wife's natural desire to be near them again. Catherine's uncle, Sir William Parr of Horton, who held a father's place in Catherine's affection, lived with his wife, Mary Salisbury, at Horton manor, a few miles southeast of Northampton. Within a ten-mile radius of this town clustered the manors of Catherine's cousins, aunts, uncles – the Greens, the Lanes, the Vauxs. For his wife's sake, Latimer may have bought Stowe manor in Northamptonshire. Stowe was only eleven miles from Catherine's aunt and uncle at Horton, and after the upheavals of the last eight years, it was at Stowe that Catherine would finally have found a measure of peace. When Latimer died in 1543, he left the manor to Catherine for her lifetime, probably at her own request, 'if she be so contented and do so accept the same', thus providing for her a safe haven in her mother's country that he had been unable to provide in his own.[42]

During the years 1538–42, the Latimers also spent time in and around York. In January 1538, they sold a manor in Bedfordshire, in which Catherine had an inherited interest, and used the money, together with some other land in Yorkshire, to exchange with the Crown for two former ecclesiastical properties just to the west of York, Nun Monkton and Kirk Hamerton. The increasing economic importance of York, combined with the amount of time Lord Latimer was required to spend there during these years on various commissions, made an estate in the area an attractive convenience. Another reason for the purchase was to provide Latimer's daughter, Margaret, with an income independent of the entailed estates which her brother would inherit. Kirk Hamerton with its Saxon church and Nun Monkton with its apple orchards, located at the confluence of the Ouse and the Nidd Rivers, were particularly attractive acquisitions, especially as the parsonages attached to them could provide the Latimers with a townhouse in York itself.

If, as it appears, Catherine spent much of her time in the south during the years 1537–42, her husband was forced by king and Cromwell to return to the north for long periods on what must have been distasteful duties.[43] With almost vindictive regularity, Latimer was named to commissions of assize, oyer and terminer and gaol delivery that continued the prosecution and execution of rebels and other malefactors. Between April 1538 and the summer of 1542, Latimer travelled regularly between York, London, and his southern manors. Having had his London townhouse in Charterhouse Yard seized during 1536, Latimer was forced to petition Cromwell for a place to stay when he went up to London at the start of Michaelmas term in the autumn of 1537. He bitterly regretted the loss of his London house, for 'it stands in good airs out of the press of the city ... and I do always lie there when I come to London.'[44] London residences, Latimer complained to Cromwell, were expensive, 'getting a lease costs 100 marks', and although Cromwell did not like Latimer and certainly was not likely to play house agent for him, nevertheless Catherine's husband had to spend time in the city while Parliament was in session if only to protect his own interests. As most of the townhouses of their Northamptonshire neighbours were located in Blackfriars, not known for its 'good airs' but with sentimental associations for Catherine, who had lived there as a child, it is likely that the Latimers leased a house in this district.[45] With Cromwell's fall and execution in 1540, the Latimers seem to have reclaimed their Charterhouse residence. Attending Parliament as a peer in January 1542, Lord Latimer spent that winter in London. For Catherine, these periodic visits to the city were to mark a turning point in her life.

6

'All Our Immoderate Affections'

London was a messy, sprawling, exciting, vibrant city during the last decade of Henry VIII's reign. Wracked by periodic plagues, pollution and poverty, it was nevertheless one of the world's great mercantile capitals. 'I did not see a house in London in which merchandise was not sold,' remarked one visitor in 1544.[1] The streets were crowded with citizens going about the daily press of business; the Thames was clogged with ships and swans. 'Never did I see a river so thickly covered with swans as this,' the foreign visitor marvelled. Boatmen, standing ankle-deep in water, ferried passengers, horses and cargo across the river with cries of 'Eastward ho!' and 'Westward ho!'. 'It is not possible in my opinion,' commented a nobleman from Spain, 'that a more beautiful river should exist in the world, for the city stands on each side of it, and innumerable boats, vessels, and other craft are seen moving on the stream.' Wrote another visitor:

> Ships arrive from every country, freighted with all kinds of merchandise; they import malmsey wine, for instance, from Crete; and they bring oil from Peloponnesus and Calabria, and a great quantity of provisions from Spain and France itself ... And a certain very large bridge is built, affording a passage to those in the city to the opposite inhabited bank, supported by stone cemented arches, and having also houses and turrets upon it. And one may see ferry boats and small barks, which are rowed with speed, plying great numbers on the banks, for the accommodation of the city.[2]

On the Southwark side of the river, taverns, stews and brothels, cockfighting and animal baiting drew the punters, the touts, and the pickpockets. The colourful pageantry of royal processions were gala events that the Tudor king had honed to a fine art. English architecture had begun to discover itself and leave its mark on the landscape. The glories of literature, painting, and music that would make the Tudor Age a golden one were beginning to flower. For a stranger to the city, some English customs were eccentric, even shocking:

> And one may see in the markets and streets of the city married women and damsels employed in arts, and barterings and affairs of trade, without disguise. But they display great simplicity and absence of jealousy in their usages towards females.

For not only do those who are of the same family and household kiss them on the mouth with salutations and embraces, but even those too who have never seen them. And to themselves this appears by no means indecent.

Loyalty to the house of Tudor by London's citizens was everywhere apparent:

... [the English] are martial, valorous, and generally tall; flesh-eaters, and insatiable of animal food; sottish and unrestrained in their appetites; full of suspicion. But towards their King they are wonderfully well affected ... so that the most binding oath which is taken by them is that by which 'the King's life' has been pledged.

For Catherine, the excitement of London was increased by her access to the glittering world of the English court, where she had a ready-made entree into courtly society and all saluted by a kiss on the mouth and an oath to the king. Her brother was the son-in-law of the Earl of Essex and a member of the fashionable circle of young aristocrats who had surrounded the king's son, the Duke of Richmond, until his death and now surrounded his brother-in-law, the Earl of Surrey. Catherine's sister, Anne, had entered court service about 1531 as a maid-in-waiting and had served in the households of Henry's successive queens. Between them, William and Anne knew all of the leading lights at court among the ambitious younger set. Catherine began to make the acquaintance of such up-and-coming courtier friends of her brother's as Sir John Dudley (the future Duke of Northumberland), the poet Sir Thomas Wyatt, and the handsome and dashing Sir Thomas Seymour, some four years her senior.

This atmosphere of intellectual discussion and courtly culture in London was very different from the rural and parochial pastimes that Catherine had found popular during the years she spent Lincolnshire and Yorkshire. London was the centre of all the latest trends, not only in serious matters such as religion but in the more frivolous matters of fashion and jewellery which Catherine loved. Her excitement at being back at the heart of courtly society after so many years in the north may be imagined. She alone of Sir Thomas Parr's children had attempted to establish an alliance with a northern family, first with the Boroughs and then with the Nevilles. It was what her mother, and probably her father as well, had wanted and Catherine had tried hard to make a success of it. But her inability to bear a living child to either husband left her, and her family, unconnected by blood in either alliance. Her husband, however, still had strong ties in the north and Catherine's excitement at being back in London must have been tempered by news of the continuing chaos on the northern borders and what it could mean to him.

In August 1542, continuing hostile relations with Scotland had led to troop mobilization and Lord Latimer was sent north with a thousand men to reinforce the king's troops on the Scottish border.[3] Like his brother, Christopher, Latimer dreaded fighting in the king's northern wars. At the beginning of October he was apparently assailed by intimations of mortality and fearing that he might be killed in some future battle decided to write his will.[4] He was particularly worried about providing for his daughter and left her to Catherine's guardianship. His wife was to act as steward for the manors of Nun Monkton and Kirk Hamerton, collecting 100 marks yearly for the five years until Margaret's majority, the money to be put aside as part of her dower. Catherine was to find 'sufficient sureties to my lord Archbishop of York or to the Bishop of Durham' to secure her stewardship for the payment of the bequest. The remainder of the income from these manors was to be used by Catherine for 'the finding and the bringing up of my said daughter, Margaret'. If Margaret did not marry within five years, Catherine was to take £30 per annum out of the income to support her stepdaughter. Any servant 'which shall fortune to be notably hurt or maimed with me now in the king's wars' was to be granted the compensation of a year's wages.

Latimer set aside money to hire a priest 'to sing for my soul' in the family chapel at Well Church in Yorkshire. Richard Harding, late of Gisborough, was to have the post during his lifetime. Dr. John Broughton, the Latimers' chaplain, was also remembered and Catherine's husband left money for a yearly 'obit' to be said in Well Church for himself and his ancestors. It may have been Catherine's influence that caused her husband to follow her mother's lead and endow a school at Well for the 'teaching of grammar there' and to fund a schoolmaster so that the tuition for students attending the school was free. The students were to come from 'the sons of the tenants and inhabitants of the lordship of Snape and Well', and it says much for the generosity of both Latimers that in establishing this school, they were providing for children, some at least of whom had fathers who had threatened them and theirs with violence and destruction. It may also have been in Lady Latimer's thoughts that by encouraging the literacy of the sons of her husband's tenants, they would in future be able to read the Scriptures for themselves and not need to rely on the questionable interpretations of others. In addition to founding the Well Grammar School, Latimer also left an endowment for six beds to be added to the hospital at Well and with all his worldly affairs in order, squared his shoulders to face the Scots. In the event, he did not die on the battlefield but shortly afterward returned to London to attend the session of Parliament scheduled to begin in January 1543. His health, however, had broken down and with his wife to nurse him, he spent the winter of 1542–43 in the city, his physical condition gradually getting worse.

Catherine faced the possibility in that winter, that after Lord Latimer's death, which the state of his health made predictable in the not too distant future, she would be forced into a country exile away from London and the court. This she refused to accept. Using her late mother's relationship with Henry's first queen and quite possibly the fact that she was Catherine of Aragon's goddaughter, Catherine took this opportunity to renew what may have been a childhood friendship with the Princess Mary. As relations with her father improved dramatically after her submission of 1536, Mary's household had become an increasingly attractive establishment in which to seek service. Mary, herself, must have had clear memories of Catherine's mother, who had been such a loyal servant in Catherine of Aragon's household. For this lonely and embittered princess, a genuine offer of friendship by a face from the past could only have been well received. Knowing that her husband was dying and determined not to return to rural exile, Catherine once again took her fate into her own hands and apparently sought and obtained a position in Mary's household as one of her ladies. Maud Parr had served Mary's mother and her daughter now sought the same security of employment in a royal household.

By 16 February 1543, Catherine had established herself with Mary and was close enough to the princess to order clothes for her, directing William Skutt, the tailor, to submit his bills to the king for payment.[5] Catherine's own fashionable tastes appear in the orders for French, Dutch, Italian and Venetian gowns that she placed for her royal friend, in the slope hoods, typets and kirtles that Skutt was commissioned to create. Catherine must have taken great delight in outfitting the princess, for the dowdy Mary loved clothes but lacked refinement in fashion and taste. Catherine's employment in Mary's household was to be of brief duration, for accidentally or deliberately it had the effect of calling her to the king's notice. By February, comment was being made that the king 'was calling at [the princess'] apartment two or three times a day.'[6] Relations with his elder daughter might have been good but it would not have been long before the court became aware of just whom the king actually had his eye on. Many women would have been flattered. Catherine was terrified. Her affections and ambitions were not centred on Henry. Coinciding with Catherine's entry into Mary's household in the winter of 1542, was the return of the king's brother-in-law, Sir Thomas Seymour, from his travels on the king's business to the Continent. When Lord Latimer died, Catherine would be free to take another husband, and it soon became apparent, to Catherine at least, just who this new husband was likely to be.

Sir Thomas Seymour, the brother of Henry's beloved and late lamented Queen Jane, was the antithesis of his sister. Where she was quiet, pale and plain, he was reckless, dark and handsome. She collected dolls;[7] he collected people. Ambitious, greedy, thoughtless, sexually aggressive, charismatic and wildly popular with women, he had begun his career serving his cousin, Sir Francis Bryan, while the latter was ambassador to France in 1531–32. By 1538 Thomas Seymour seemed about to make a highly advantageous match with Mary Howard, the dowager Duchess of Richmond.[8] 'Affection shall lead me to court,' the cynical Seymour is quoted as saying, 'but I'll take care that interest keeps me.'[9] Although Seymour had her father's consent, he was simply not a good enough match for Mary's proud brother, the Earl of Surrey, who additionally detested Seymour's elder brother, Edward. Jane Seymour, after all, was no longer queen and members of the Seymour clan were not the match they had been while she was alive. Although another of Sir Thomas' sisters, Elizabeth, was Cromwell's daughter-in-law, this family connection did little to help Seymour in his quest for the duchess. Whether Surrey was in fact the stumbling block in Sir Thomas' road to romance or whether there were other reasons for the failure of his suit, Seymour was still a carefree bachelor, known for his temper, his charm and his way with women when Catherine, Lady Latimer, began to spend increasing amounts of time in London.

Seymour had several added advantages which helped him cut a romantic figure at court. He had a magnificent speaking and singing voice, wrote poetry, dressed with flair and panache, and like his brother, Edward, could boast of actual exploits in battle. He loved the sea and captained his own ships, the 'Peter Pomegranite' and the 'Sweepstake', and besides all this, was one of the most widely travelled of Henry's courtiers. After his disappointed suit for the Duchess of Richmond in 1538, he had been sent to France on a diplomatic mission with Sir Anthony Browne. He returned at the end of the year and in the spring of 1541, just for the fun of it, left the English Pale in France disguised 'as a civilian' and travelled as far as Ardres, where he and his party were entertained unknowingly by the governor.[10] It was the sort of adventurous jest in which the king's brother-in-law delighted. And if more sober minds at court tended to condemn such actions as childish bravado, many of the ladies were not among them. In the summer of 1542, Seymour departed for Austria where he joined the emperor fighting the Turks in Hungary. Sir Thomas enjoyed himself greatly and on Henry VIII's orders, travelled in December to Nuremberg in the emperor's party.[11] The king had ordered Seymour to Nuremberg to investigate the possibility of hiring German mercenaries to fight English battles and to recruit not only soldiers but a party of Hungarian tambourine, drum and fife players as well.[12] While Catherine nursed her seriously ill husband in London, Sir Thomas enjoyed the Christmas festivities of 1542 in Nuremberg at the house of Joachim Gundelfinger, an English agent.[13] Seymour arrived back in England in January 1543 and it was probably at this time that his romance with Catherine became serious enough to warrant gossip. A miniature of him painted by Holbein, in the guise of the wooing lover with a pink in his cap, was probably painted for Catherine.[14]

Seymour was a supporter of the new religion, although his commitment to it was probably more that of a man seizing the new order as the road to advancement rather than any deep religious conviction. This commitment was one of the bonds that joined him to Catherine's brother, William, and brought him into direct contact with William's sister. Catherine had affection for the dying Lord Latimer, but she was not in love with him. This made her an easy mark for the amorous Seymour whose sexual prowess was well known at court. Both the Holbein miniature and Catherine's own words are explicit statements of a love affair, although given Catherine's position and her sense of the duties of a Christian wife, it is unlikely that the emotional affair was physically consummated at this time. Recalling her first romantic feelings some four years later, Catherine wrote in 1547: 'I would not have you think that this mine honest good will toward you to proceed of any sudden motion or passion for as truly as God is god, my mind was fully bent the other time I was at liberty to marry you before any man I know.'[15] For the prudent, practical and, to this point seemingly, sexually reserved Lady Latimer in the winter of 1542–43 to be ready to marry Seymour argues for an intimacy that Catherine believed could lead to marriage. Catherine Parr had fallen in love with the dashing Seymour and it was to prove a love that was to endure for the rest of her life.

For the first but not the last time in her relationship with Seymour, she put her heart before her common sense. Whether Seymour was worthy of the devotion she offered him is a matter of opinion. The king's brother-in-law was the closest thing the Tudor court had to an Errol Flynn-style matinee idol, and history, together with many of his contemporaries, has not been kind to Seymour. 'The Lord Seymour,' remarked Sir John Hayward, 'was fierce in courage, courtly in fashion, in personage stately, in voice magnificent, but somewhat empty of matter.'[16] Yet the poet Sir John Harrington, who was Catherine's cousin and served in Seymour's household, sincerely mourned him at his death, wrote an elegy for him and considered him a loyal friend and a leader worth following. Catherine's cousin, Nicholas Throckmorton, remembered him 'at all essays, my perfect friend'.[17] William Parr, too, had deep affection for him and remained loyal to Seymour's memory long after the latter's death. To Catherine, this charming and dangerous warrior against the Turks, this sophisticated and worldly wise sea captain, this would-be poet, magnificent singer, courtier, and lover of beautiful women, must have been irresistible. Handsome and dashing Seymour may have been, but he would also prove to be unreliable and emotionally unstable. He had an explosive temper, an enormous ego, and an elastic sense of ethics – attributes not particularly unusual at the court of Henry VIII. Catherine became very familiar with these failings, yet she continued over the years that followed to support him with unswerving love and loyalty. He was everything Catherine's first two husbands had not been – energetic, aggressive, virile and romantic.

Seymour, for his part, appeared to be in love with Catherine. Although credited with the statement that, 'Love is but a frailty of the mind when 'tis not to ambition joined,' he seems to have been thinking of things other than ambition as he courted Catherine. Despite the inventions of Grigorio Leti,[18] there is no evidence that from the time he met Catherine until her death, he ever proposed marriage with anyone else. Yet marriage to the soon-to-be-widowed Lady Latimer would hardly have advanced his personal ambitions greatly. Catherine was not a rich widow; her jointures were not extraordinary and the manors she held were for her lifetime only. Childless, twice-married and approaching her thirtieth birthday, Catherine was no great catch for the brother-in-law of the king. Reasons for Seymour's courtship must be looked for elsewhere and the notion must certainly be considered that he may have been more interested in becoming Catherine's lover than her husband. Yet his pursuit of her was so widely known at court that when the romance was thwarted, Seymour contrived to spend as much time as possible on extended government assignments to the Continent and away from England.

Between 1537 and 1543, Catherine was not the only member of her family to cherish dreams of love. Her brother, William, and her sister, Anne, both made during those years – or in William's case, contemplated making when circumstances would allow it – that most eccentric of sixteenth-century unions, a love match. The consequences of her siblings' affairs were to have a significant impact on Catherine's life as well as on the power politics of the next twenty years. Maud Parr arranged no marriage for her second daughter, Anne, which given the efforts she had made on Catherine's behalf when her elder daughter was no more than ten years old, is odd. Anne had been left £400 toward her marriage by her father's will but the amount of money needed to secure William's marriage had necessitated the postponement of payment of Catherine's jointure on her marriage to Edward Borough and may have precluded the payment of one for Anne altogether. Then, too, with both William and Catherine gone, Maud may have been loath to see Anne married before it was absolutely necessary. Whatever the factors involved, Anne was unmarried and unbetrothed when she was orphaned at sixteen. Either under her mother's auspices shortly before Maud's death or on her own behalf following her mother's example shortly after, Anne Parr chose service at court as a career.

Four generations of women, beginning with her great-grandmother, the redoubtable Alice Neville, Lady Fitzhugh, and continuing through her grandmother, Elizabeth Fitzhugh, Lady Parr, and her own mother, Maud Parr, had served England's queens since 1483. This tradition of court employment by the women in Anne's family was carried on in this the fourth generation by Anne herself, and by her sister, Catherine, in the household of the Princess Mary. Anne Parr had neither husband nor father to speak for her and so, most unusually for the period, achieved a career on her own application and merit. Vivacious, fun-loving, and well-educated, Anne served in the households of Henry VIII's successive queens, first as maid-in-waiting, and after her marriage, probably early in 1538, as a gentlewoman of the privy chamber. For Jane Seymour's state funeral in November 1537, Anne travelled to Windsor among the maids – Mary Zouche and the Misses Holland, Ashley and Norris.[19] Anne Parr was successful enough in her career that when the unfortunate Katherine Howard became Henry's fifth queen in July 1541, Anne was made official keeper of the new queen's jewels.[20] She relinquished the post to fellow gentlewoman of the chamber Elizabeth Tyrwhit briefly between September and December of that year when she retired from court to give birth to her elder son, Henry, but returned to court and Katherine's household at Hampton Court in December.[21] Anne apparently managed to achieve the tricky balancing act of gaining and keeping the trust of both king and assorted queens. She had Katherine Howard's confidence but was never implicated in her extracurricular amours. Anne served the queen during her brief marriage, and afterward, during her arrest and incarceration, first at Syon House and then in the Tower.[22] She was witness to the traumatic spectacle of that giddy, hapless girl's gruesome end on the block in February 1542. In addition to the traumas at court, the ebullient younger Parr sister met and fell in love with a tall, 'strong set but bony',[23] red-haired Welsh soldier known for his temper and his ambition.

William Herbert (born c.506) was some ten years Anne's senior. His father, Richard Herbert of Ewyas in Herefordshire, was the illegitimate son of the first Earl of Pembroke. The hot-tempered Richard had been forced to flee the Welsh border country during the reign of Henry VII after having killed a man. He took service with the King of France and his son, William Herbert, was born a French subject.[24] The Herberts returned to England while young William was still a child, and like his father, William, too, was a violent man. In 1533 he was involved in brawling and the murder of 'one honest man', in Newport, South Wales,[25] and the following year, 1534, his servant, Richard Lewis, was convicted of murdering yet another Welshman.[26] Despite his reputation for violence, William took service at the English court while still in his teens. By 1526, when little more than twenty years old, he was appointed one of the Spears, the king's corps of bodyguards. By 1535 he had been made esquire for the body, as well as joint Attorney General for Glamorgan, where his stepfather, John Malefaunte, had influence.[27] At heart, William Herbert was and remained a soldier. Although he inclined toward the new religion, he was capable, without much moral strain, of changing his religious colours, first under Mary Tudor, then under her sister, Elizabeth, and later, in 1569, in the cause of the Duke of Norfolk's marriage to the Queen of Scots. With him, ambition was a far stronger creed than any other. Anne Parr's marriage to William Herbert probably took place at the beginning of 1538, when Anne was twenty-two and Herbert about thirty-one.[28] Herbert quickly became an intimate of Anne's brother, William Parr, and owed the rapid progress of his career to Anne's sister, Catherine, after she became queen. Parr interests and Herbert interests found much common ground for well over thirty years.

Anne and Catherine were not the only Parrs who had fallen in love. Their brother, William, now Lord Parr, had formed a romantic connection at court, necessarily kept secret because he was already married. William Parr and his wife, Lady Anne Bourchier, daughter and heir of the Earl of Essex, had been an incompatible couple since the early days of their childhood marriage, when he was thirteen and she was ten.[29] While Lady Anne much preferred life in the country, Parr loved the life of a courtier and spent much of his time either at court or visiting the various residences of his childhood playmate, the Duke of Richmond. Consorting from childhood with the sons of the upper aristocracy such as Richmond and the Earl of Surrey had given Parr an elevated idea of his own importance, and as the husband of the heiress of the Earl of Essex, he came to fancy himself a prince without a title. With Richmond's death in 1536, it was impressed upon Parr that the days of his boyhood were behind him. He was, after all, twenty-three years old. High time to settle down with his wife and begin work producing a family heir. No doubt Parr's uncle, Sir William Parr of Horton, and his father-in-law, the Earl of Essex, both gave the young man stern lectures on family duty. The Earl and Countess of Essex as a gesture of encouragement even moved from their principal seat of Stansted Hall in Essex and took up residence at their manor of Baas near Hoddesdon in Hertfordshire, leaving Lord and Lady Parr together to play at being lord and lady, husband and wife. This experiment in marriage was not a success.

Although Lady Anne grudgingly followed her husband to court, she was not happy there. Her first recorded official appearance did not take place until 22 November 1539 at a banquet for Anne of Cleves, fourteen years after her marriage. A staunch supporter of the old religion, Anne Bourchier was not interested in religious reform, intellectual pursuits or the garnering of patronage, all of which were of profound concern to her husband. Nor was her pride untouched by the fact that her husband was in the process of achieving quite a reputation as a ladies' man, involving himself in two successive affairs with ladies of the court. It must have been painfully obvious to Parr's friends that while many ladies at court found him fascinating, his wife was not among his conquests. It must have been equally obvious to Anne that her marriage was a trap out of which it would be difficult if not impossible to escape. Yet Parr was determined to maintain control of Anne as the heir to lands and titles he intended should be his and Anne had little recourse but to comply.

Knighted in 1538, William Parr was made a baron the following March,[30] presumably to prepare him for inheriting the earldom of Essex when his father-in-law died.[31] Exactly one year later, the expected happened. On 3 March 1540, the old, deaf, unwieldy earl fell from his horse and was killed. One month after Essex's death, on 18 April 1540, not Parr but royal favourite Thomas Cromwell was created the new Earl of Essex. Parr's feelings about this creation may well be imagined, but having his anticipated title stolen from him was not the worst that was to happen. In 1541, Parr received yet another terrible blow when his wife, Lady Anne, created a major public scandal by leaving him for good and eloping with a penniless cleric, 'one Hunt or Huntley'.[32] This was probably John Lyngfield, 'alias Huntley', the prior of St. James, Tandridge, Surrey, whom Catherine Parr had presented to the parish church of her dower manor, Oxsted, in May 1534.[33]

The head-strong, impulsive Lady Anne soon found herself pregnant by her lover[34] and informed her estranged husband that, 'she would take her pleasure and live as she listed [liked]'. She also informed him 'that she never loved him, nor never would.'[35] Parr was publicly humiliated and privately enraged. First the Essex titles and now the Essex heir and her estates seemed to be slipping through his fingers. If the stubborn and independent Lady Anne were to secure an annulment of her marriage, her entire inheritance would be lost to him. To forestall such a catastrophe, Parr secured a legal separation from Anne in the following year on the grounds of his wife's open adultery, and on 13 March 1543, using the growing influence of his sister Catherine at court, he managed to have a bill passed in Parliament condemning Anne's adulterous actions and barring any child of hers born out of wedlock from succeeding to her inheritance. Parr declared in the bill that he had 'admonished' his wife for her flagrant adultery, but 'she being very obstinate ... [did] refuse his said good counsel and godly exhortations.' Lady Anne, in fact, defied both Parr and Parliament, an act at once courageous and foolish. She was to spend much of her life in exile at the remote manor of Little Wakering in Essex.[36]

However angry William Parr was at his wife's behaviour, he soon found comfort not only in legal vengeance but in the arms of another woman. He entered into a brief but passionate affair with Dorothy Bray, one of Anne of Cleves' maids-in-waiting. The Bray–Parr affair became so notorious that it was mentioned in testimony given at Katherine Howard's trial for adultery in 1542.[37] By Christmas of 1543, Catherine Parr's first Christmas as queen, Dorothy Bray was a thing of the past, for William had fallen deeply in love with one of his sister's most charming ladies, Elisabeth Brooke,[38] the daughter of Lord Cobham of Kent, and the niece of the poet, Sir Thomas Wyatt. Elisabeth Brooke was everything that Lady Anne Bourchier was not, beautiful, lively, witty, musically accomplished, totally in sympathy with the new religion. There had been rumours in 1542 that the king himself had his eye on her. Although Elisabeth's education had been neglected and she never pretended to be an intellectual, nevertheless her beauty, warmth and charm won her, over the next two decades, the appreciative praises of such continental sophisticates as Francois, Duc de Vendome of Chartres, and the imperial ambassador, Guzman de Silva. More importantly, Elisabeth also won the friendship and affection of the young Princess Elizabeth, Catherine Parr's stepdaughter.

By the end of 1544, the Parr–Brooke affair had become an open secret at court and by 1545, Elisabeth's father, frightened of possible repercussions, was having his daughter watched and her activities reported to him.[39] Yet despite Lord Cobham's fears, William Parr and Elisabeth Brooke continued their affair with every attempt at discretion. With Parr's sister on the throne, a scandal was to be avoided at all costs. Henry VIII's position on adultery was well known. And although the King of England could marry and divorce with impunity, or so it seemed to many, there was little likelihood under the legal system of the period that William and Elisabeth would ever be allowed to marry so long as Lady Anne Bourchier lived.

While Anne Parr married for love and William Parr languished without its legal consummation, Catherine Parr dreamed of marriage with Thomas Seymour and continued to fulfil her duties to her husband, nursing the sickly Latimer to the end. Catherine achieved something of a reputation for her devotion and her nursing skills, with an interest in medicines and their curative powers. But all the cures known to the Tudor pharmacopoeia proved powerless in the case of her husband. John Neville, Lord Latimer, finally obliged his enemies by dying in February 1543.[40] He was just fifty. On 2 March, Catherine had her second husband buried in all solemnity at St. Paul's Cathedral and for the second time in ten years put on the habit of mourning.[41] But Latimer's death did not leave his widow free to choose her third husband. That selection had already been made for her by the king and the new candidate for her heart and hand was Henry, himself.

Life for Catherine, William and Anne Parr, as the winter of 1542–43 wore to a close, was about to take a drastic turn which would soon affect every aspect of their lives. Twice widowed and now economically provided for by the late Lord Latimer, Catherine deliberately declined to take the path her mother had taken, that of conditional freedom within the socially recognized parameters of widowhood. Her service in Princess Mary's household offered her the choice of continued residence in the south where, through the changes of fortune and her own efforts, she had now returned. Yet Catherine apparently felt that such a life choice would be unfulfilling for her and her desire for Thomas Seymour predisposed her to accept the cultural and religious bonds of matrimony once again with him. Her sister, Anne, had risen at court by her own wits and ability in service to Henry's successive queens to become one of the unfortunate Katherine Howard's most trusted gentlewomen. Her career at court, however, depended very much on patronage and connections. Secure in the middle ranks of the nascent Tudor civil service as the younger daughter of a landed gentry family without claims to aristocratic consideration, Anne could not command the patronage necessary to advance above the place she had already earned for herself. Wherever Anne's ambitions lay, a higher rank such as lady-in-waiting in the queen's household, should there be a new queen, was denied her so long as her husband was plain Master Herbert.

Paradoxically, given the advantages that had been offered him, William Parr had done the least with his opportunities. Maud Parr had called upon every family friendship, borrowed money and encumbered the family estates in order to provide William with a titled heiress as a bride. Sir William Parr of Horton had provided a place for his nephew in the household of the king's son, the Duke of Richmond, ensuring him the finest education available in England. Yet in the nine years since his coming of age, William had made little use of these advantages. Much of William's time and energy had been given to his dysfunctional marriage with a woman undeterred by threats and legal pronouncements and willing to flout all the most cherished precepts of English society by living openly with a lover from the lower classes. Forced to the expedient and expense of securing a legal bar to inheritance against his wife's illegitimate child, Parr's troubles became common coinage for court gossip, a factor that did his pride little good. William's education, too, may have placed another kind of bar in his political path, for by raising him as a companion to the most nobly born boys of the aristocracy, he came to see himself as above those who sought to secure bureaucratic offices which might have led to political roles in the government and subsequent career advancement. Offices such as the Mastership of the Wards, co-occupied briefly by William's father, were not something that would have tempted William. Content to play the gentleman with his cronies, absentee landlord with his tenants and stewards, and wait, probably somewhat impatiently, for his father-in-law's death to bestow on him the earldom of Essex, William lacked both political acumen and practical ambition. His passion to establish an image of himself as a Renaissance prince conveniently precluded the more distressing aspects of that image, such as leadership in war and active interest in government. Catherine's evolving position at court, however, would soon require William to make an effort in both fields of endeavour.

During the winter of 1542–43, Henry VIII's mind was not only on love and marriage among kings and widows, but also on the marriage of nations, especially that of England and Scotland in the persons of the young Prince of Wales and the infant Mary, Queen of Scots. With the death of James V of Scotland after the defeat of his army at Solway Moss in the winter of 1542, Scotland was left vulnerable. A determined Henry pushed to follow up his advantage by trying to gain physical custody of the new Scottish baby queen. He hoped to unite the peoples of Scotland with England under his personal regency. The Scots, in spite of a pro-English element at the Scottish court, were less than pleased with the whole idea. The infant queen's mother, Mary of Guise, was a woman devoted both to the House of Guise and to the 'Auld Alliance' between France and Scotland. She was determined to allow the English no advantage which she could prevent.

Among the lords of Scotland and the ruling council under James Hamilton, Earl of Arran, most viewed union with England as nothing short of catastrophe. Through the winter and spring and into the summer of 1543, Henry tried by negotiation to bring the Scots to terms. He dealt first with Arran, who outfoxed him, and then with the Earl of Angus, who betrayed him, and finally with the Earl of Lennox, who proved too weak to bring the Scots to their knees at Henry's feet. On 1 July 1543, England signed a peace treaty with Scotland at Greenwich which left Henry boasting of his conquest but which in fact promised him exactly nothing. As part of the king's matter in the north, William, Lord Parr, received money to supply 100 foot soldiers under a captain and his second in command for combat. Parr's banner saw action but Parr, himself, did not. Sir Thomas Wharton wrote to Edward Seymour, now Earl of Hertford, on 26 November 1542, before the Battle of Solway Moss, that, 'he was with the English standard which went further into Scotland than Lochmaben Castle (where James V was staying) on the day prior and with him both days were the standards of Lord Parr in the rule of Walter Strickland.'[42] Wharton went on to say that Parr's men, together with other northern levies, 'all served the King better than I can write.' Parr's men continued to acquit themselves well under Strickland's leadership, including the two hundred Kendal archers that fought at the Battle of Solway Moss. Parr, himself, seemed disinterested in participating personally on the field of battle. His experiences in the north of England during the Pilgrimage of Grace some six years before had apparently given him a distaste for soldiering and his residence as a child at Sheriff Hutton in Yorkshire had done little to endear the area to him. Although he spent time with the Duke of Suffolk in the north between January and March 1543, it was not until April of that year, when the king appointed him Lord Warden and Keeper of the Western Marches towards Scotland, that Parr became seriously involved in Anglo-Scottish affairs.[43]

Parr's appointment as Lord Warden owed more to his friend, John Dudley, Lord Lisle's, active lobbying for him and a conspicuous lack of other aspirants to the office than to any outstanding personal qualifications for the job. Lisle had served as Lord Warden prior to Parr's own appointment in April and it was he who lured Parr into the north and encouraged him to involve himself in the affairs of this particular sphere of Parr family influence. The Earl of Hertford, Lisle's own predecessor in the office, had suggested Parr's appointment to the wardenship to the Privy Council as early as the winter of 1542. Both Hertford and Lisle had discovered that the pathway to opportunity did not at this particular political juncture lead through the office of Lord Warden. Lisle wanted out and Parr wanted the earldom of Essex that Cromwell had so infuriatingly deprived him of in 1540. Cromwell was now dead and the earldom unclaimed. Parr's appointment as Lisle's replacement in the northern office might provide an opportunity for Parr to prove himself to the king and so secure the earldom.

This opportunity, however, might not have been granted to William – the king, after all, had shown little interest in him prior to this – if it had not been for Henry's rapidly developing interest in William's widowed sister, Catherine. By March 1543 when Lord Latimer died, Catherine must almost certainly have been aware of Henry's interest in her. Toward the end of April, an outpouring of grace and favour upon her brother pointed the direction that the winds of the king's intentions were blowing. During the week of 23–29 April, William, Lord Parr, was created chief steward and receiver of Writtle, near Chelmsford in Essex, and granted the office of chief steward of the Honour of Beaulieu in Hampshire. More importantly, he received the office that Lisle had encouraged him to seek, that of Lord Warden and Keeper of the Western Marches towards Scotland. Even the practical considerations of appointing to this once important northern office a man whose family estates were largely in the north could not camouflage Parr's sudden promotion to royal regard. This was particularly true when Parr was elected to that most exclusive of English men's clubs, the Order of the Garter. Nor was he the only family member to receive tokens of royal friendship at this time. Catherine's sister, Anne, was remembered through her husband, William Herbert, who in May 1543 was granted the governorship of the castles of Aberystwyth and Carmarthen.[44] His sisters, Catherine and Anne, had more active characters and more determination than their brother, but none of them could have imagined that it would not be William's career that brought glory to the Parrs but Catherine's. Nor could any of the Parrs have imagined that one sudden turn of fortune's wheel would make Catherine Parr Queen of England and architect of her siblings' future lives and fortunes.

William Parr's career had up to this time been a brilliant example of mediocrity. If Catherine and Anne had inherited the so-called masculine characteristic of active self-assertion and Catherine, especially, courageous endurance, William had inherited the so-called female characteristics of passive pleasure and self-indulgent idleness. Intelligent and charming but lacking any personal ambition, William, like his father before him, had been content to drift at court, his elevated position defined by his titled friends and brilliant but spectacularly unsuccessful marriage. It is unlikely that he had any real desire to take up a post in the north. Nor did the past experience of John Dudley, Lord Lisle, argue for the office's advantages as a proving ground for ambitious courtiers. In 1543, the most desirable venue for pleasure and politics was the court. Yet Parr was caught in a cleft stick. His sister's rising star had generated an interest in his own fortunes by the Crown. Though interest in Catherine led the king to look more favourably on William, Henry apparently did not mean to hand over the earldom of Essex to Parr unless that lord bestirred himself and proved his worth. Dreams of establishing his reputation as a power to be reckoned with in the north, fed by Lisle's encouragement, as well as finally securing the earldom of Essex went to William's head. Ambition for glory, markedly latent until now, seems to have stirred in Parr's breast. Perhaps there was an element of sibling rivalry as well. If his sister attained a crown, her brother could do no less than distinguish himself in those fields of endeavour proper to men. Lisle's motive for promoting his friend to the wardenship was probably not altogether disinterested. Lisle was a shrewd enough observer to read which way the wind of the king's affections was blowing. If Henry married Catherine Parr, then the more influence that William Parr could achieve from such an alliance, the better for Lisle. For William depended and would continue to depend on his best friend's political judgement. Lisle could and would use Parr for his own purposes. In the event, the king, with his eye on Parr's sister, was more than happy to send William into the north to see what he could do.

Appointed the last week of April 1543, Parr was given wages for a personal retinue of one hundred soldiers and the aid and council of a man with considerable experience of border conditions, Sir Robert Bowes. The Duke of Suffolk was already in the north as Lord Lieutenant and Parr was to serve under him as Lord Warden. Upon his arrival in Newcastle-upon-Tyne, Lord Parr proved that he intended to take up his new office, in spite of his lack of experience, with both enthusiasm and attention to duty. The new Lord Warden chose Warkworth Castle, seven miles from Alnwick, as his chief residence. It 'being something decayed and out of reparation',[45] he ordered it to be repaired and refurbished under the direction of Robert Horsley, seneschal of the castle. Work was done between 17 May and 11 August on the great hall, kitchens and living quarters. The brew houses, towers and out-buildings were also returned to a useable state by a large corps of carpenters, masons, smiths, plasterers and painters. Parr chose to reside in a group of buildings connected with the great hall, which after the rebuilding were probably quite comfortable although Parr's enjoyment of them was brief. He was a man who valued luxury and seemed to be planning on a lengthy tenure in the north. He soon began to change his mind.

His duties as outlined by the Privy Council were to take musters, to carry out reprisal raids, to secure redress for Scottish raids during periods of truce, and to keep the king and council informed of border activities within his jurisdiction. Parr's principal difficulty lay in a chronic tendency to overreach that jurisdiction. With the knowledge that his sister had captured the fancy of the capricious king, Parr, now thirty-one years old, decided that the time had come to distinguish himself. Unfortunately he had left it rather late. Arriving after the fighting which climaxed at Solway Moss, Parr remained mostly with the Duke of Suffolk at Darlington in Durham, the seat of his long-time mentor, Cuthbert Tunstall, while the Earl of Hertford made a daring raid that saw Edinburgh partially sacked and burnt by the English and the town of Leith all but destroyed. This policy of attacking a neighbour he was trying simultaneously to woo with diplomacy only helped to defeat Henry VIII's goals in the long run but at the time he was lavish in his praise of Hertford's efforts.

Parr became the middle man between Sir Ralph Sadler, the king's secretary in Scotland, and the Duke of Suffolk, his superior in the north of England, passing letters, news and gossip back and forth. Untried before in any position of real responsibility, Parr soon became both overzealous in his duties and overconfident of his powers. This was increasingly true as it became apparent to him and to everyone else that he would shortly become the brother-in-law of the king. Parr's reports to the Privy Council got longer, his advice more freely given, as his self-importance swelled. Yet in the tone of his letters there was a boyish ingenuousness that was disarming. Parr's cousin and friend, Cuthbert Tunstall, Bishop of Durham, tried to protect and reprove him. When Parr wrote angrily to Tunstall that some of his letters to the Privy Council had not arrived in London, the bishop reassured him that all his letters had been forwarded except one which 'my lord of Suffolk only stayed ... out of love lest the Council should think you were too curious ... and were meddling.' Tunstall also admonished Parr that it was the duke and not he who was responsible for reporting to the Privy Council, as Suffolk 'has chief charge both within and without your wardenry and must account to the King for the whole country.'[46] William responded like a mutinous schoolboy. He assumed judicial powers in a local civil case and Tunstall and Suffolk were forced once more to remind him of the limits of his office, patiently explaining that he was not empowered 'to judge murder as warden among the King's subjects unless they also commit some March treason.'[47]

Due to the Duke of Suffolk's dominant position as Lord Lieutenant in the north and to the characters of the two men, Parr never managed to throw off the aura of tutelage under the duke that persisted as long as his tenure as Lord Warden lasted.[48] The Privy Council itself rebuked Parr's excessive zeal, writing irritably that he 'should meddle with none of his Grace's servants.' But like the eager puppy he was, Parr ignored Tunstall's sage advice, the Duke of Suffolk's warnings and the Privy Council's rebukes, bombarding both Suffolk and the council with ideas, stratagems, plots, plans and intrigues. When Sir Ralph Sadler wrote to Parr advising him that ' ... it is more than necessary that your Lordship have good espials, and the more the better, for, though they tell some lies, yet they may now and then stumble on the truth.' Parr enthusiastically began spy recruitment.[49] His star recruit, one Sandy Pringle, served well at first, but was later discredited by Sadler himself. Yet Parr kept trying. 'As to the secret affairs of the realm of Scotland, devised by the Council of the same,' he wrote in a report of 24 May, 'it will be very hard and almost impossible for me, as far as I can yet perceive, to have notice thereof ... [yet] in success of time by experience I trust to come ever more and more near to the perfection of His Majesty's service therein, like as my heart most earnestly desireth.'[50]

Although William protested that 'mine intent was, at my first entry into this office, to gather and acquire knowledge, and to be perfectly instructed of the present state thereof, or ever I would take upon me to advertise things scarcely known or perceived,'[51] yet he continued more to talk than to listen, more to advise than to receive and follow the advice of others. He was both overassertive and unsure of himself, eager to impress, particularly the king, and to get as much political advantage out of his appointment as possible. It was apparent to Suffolk and Tunstall, if not to Parr, himself, that he was floundering out of his depth. Despite his heritage, an atavistic hostility to the Scots, and his family's position in the north, apart from his schooldays, he himself had had almost no contact with the land of his fathers. He had visited briefly during the Pilgrimage of Grace, an area that to him, raised as he had been as a royal courtier, must have seemed cold, dirty, uncouth and barbaric. The northern hardihood of five quarrelling generations of Parrs had been bred down to a courtly gentility in this, the last of their line.

Parr not only stepped on toes with his meddling, he soon began to make misjudgements as well. His recruitment of Sandy Pringle and his family as spies was not a resounding success. When William granted immunity to a group of renegade Scots who assured him they were friends of England, he was subsequently informed that in a battle near Norham, 'the heaviest enemies [of England] were Douglas' servants and friends and those to whom you granted immunity as England's friends.'[52] By September 1543, Parr no doubt agreed with Sir Ralph Sadler that 'never so noble a Prince's servant was so evil entreated as I am among these rude unreasonable people, and never had man to do with so inconsistent and beastly a nation.' Darkly, Parr proclaimed: 'I can perceive nor learn none other but that the Scots hath intended deceits and fraud towards the king's majesty's proceedings, which now beginneth to appear.'[53] He went on to denounce, 'the continual crafty and malicious working of the Scots against his highness and his realm.' His disgust with the Scots was compounded by his boredom with the minutiae of routine required by the office he held. He was certainly clever enough to see that kept in leading strings as he was by the higher powers, he had no hope of becoming himself a power to reckon with north of the Trent.

Not only Parr but many of the English leaders living in the marches south of the border were equally sick of the place, the people, and especially of the weather: '... leave the enemy to the mercies of the weather,' wrote Suffolk, Parr, Tunstall and Sir Anthony Browne on 30 September, 'which will cause as much damage as invading armies.'[54] Reproved by Tunstall, corrected by Suffolk, sick of the Scots and their wars and betrayals, unhappy and uncomfortable, Parr was also receiving letters from his friends at court, such as Lord Lisle, which only served to increase his restlessness. On 20 June 1543, Lisle wrote to him that, 'I have made your commendations [to your sisters at court] as directed; and also to other friends, of whom there be numbers [here] that desire your short return.'[55] By this time, the very word 'court' must have had magic in it for the beleaguered Lord Warden. Things were happening in the south. A war with France was predicted. The king had left for Harwich. The Duke of Norfolk was conveying troops to Guisnes, and Catherine Parr had become Queen of England. William, Lord Parr, was beginning to feel left out of things, his northern opportunity turned into a northern exile. As autumn wore on he decided that he had had enough. On 26 October 1543, Parr's cousin, Nicholas Throckmorton, wrote to the Duke of Norfolk that he had arrived in Darlington from Berwick only to find that my Lord Warden had 'gone to Court'.[56] Two days before Christmas, courtesy of the new queen's influence, Parr received what he had been hoping for all along – the earldom of Essex. He never again returned to the north.

Part Two: 'Kateryn, The Quene'

7

'The Quene's Grace'

On Thursday, 12 July 1543, Henry VIII took his sixth and last bride before a small audience of family and intimates in the private oratory of the Queen's Closet at Hampton Court. Squeezed into the small room[1] on that warm summer's day were John, Lord Russell, the Lord Privy Seal: Sir Anthony Browne, captain of the King's Pensioners; Sir Thomas Heneage; Edward Seymour, Earl of Hertford; Sir Henry Knyvet; Sir Richard Long; Sir Thomas Darcy; Sir Edward Baynton; Sir Thomas Speke; Anthony Denny and William Herbert.[2] As supporters of the bride stood her sister, Mistress Anne Herbert; Jane Guildford, Lady Lisle; Anne Stanhope, Countess of Hertford; Katherine Willoughby, Duchess of Suffolk; the king's daughters, the Ladies Mary and Elizabeth; and his niece, Lady Margaret Douglas. The license for the marriage had been issued two days before by Thomas Cranmer, Archbishop of Canterbury, but the marriage service was performed by Stephen Gardiner, Bishop of Winchester.[3]

When asked if he took this woman to be his wife, the tall, corpulent king replied with a glad cry of 'Yea!' His slim, red-haired bride, speaking in a more subdued voice told the bishop that the marriage was also her wish.[4] The ironies of this moment in the Queen's Closet at Hampton Court were many. A number of the guests like Sir Edward Baynton, Sir Thomas Heneage, and the Earl of Hertford owed their careers to one or the other of Henry's former queens. Thomas Cranmer, the man who had issued the marriage license, was to prove a staunch friend to Henry's new bride, while Stephen Gardiner, who performed the ceremony, was to become her most bitter enemy. It cannot have been far from the thoughts of the reluctant bride as she glanced at the faces of the surviving relatives of Anne Boleyn, Jane Seymour and Katherine Howard that no more than a few hundred feet from where the wedding party stood was the infamous long gallery down which the frantic Katherine Howard, her predecessor at Henry's side, had been dragged screaming just over a year before on her first step to the block. Nor could the bride help but notice as she stood next to her bridegroom on that July day in 1543, that Henry VIII was a distorted echo of the golden prince who had ascended the throne of England with such bright hopes and noble ambitions twenty-six years before. The bride must almost certainly have remembered this golden prince from her childhood but the aging, gout-ridden, overweight, red-faced man next to her bore little resemblance to her memories. He suffered from excruciating headaches, chronic indigestion, depressions, erupting leg ulcers, excessive corpulence and high blood pressure.[5] He had a dozen different complaints and an unpredictable temper to go with them. He had married five wives and buried four of them, two of whom were executed by his own orders. Catherine Parr, Lady Latimer, bride number six, knew only too well that marriage to Henry Tudor was a very chancy affair.

Catherine Parr was thirty years old when she married the king. Twice widowed, she was considered a mature and stable woman in the minds of those who knew her. Henry's intentions toward Catherine in the months prior to their marriage must have been fairly obvious, for the king, it seems, took little trouble to hide his partiality. By December 1542, Henry had been a widower for less than a year, having sent the hapless Katherine Howard to the block on 13 February of that year. The king was restless without a wife, but he was not about to repeat his mistake with Katherine Howard and marry a young and flighty girl who could for a third time put public cuckold's horns on his head. As so often in Henry's career, he examined the ladies about the court and his eye fell on a member of the household of the Princess Mary, a lady who was the daughter of a friend from the past, had a soothing way with elderly, ailing men, and who although still married, had a husband whose health was failing fast. As early as December 1542, Chapuys was writing to Mary of Hungary that the king, 'who since he learnt the conduct of his last wife, has continually shown himself sad ... but now all is changed and order is already taken that the princess [Mary] shall go to court this feast, accompanied with a great number of ladies; and they work night and day at Hampton Court to finish her lodging.'[6] The mention of Mary's ladies is significant. Among them was the Lady Latimer, a woman who had a spotless reputation, was well thought of for her prudence and wisdom, was religiously sound and was known to be a skilled nurse, a definite plus for Henry in his deteriorating physical condition. Henry, however, was not a man to endure a wife he did not find desirable. He also appears to have been a man who needed a great deal of psychological stimulus to allow him to perform sexually.[7] Catherine, the object of sexual attraction for Thomas Seymour, must have had similar attractions for the king.

One drawback to the union, of course, was Lady Latimer's inability to bear children. The king was still obsessed with producing more male heirs, for apart from two daughters, who had both been declared bastards by their father, only one son, the child Edward, stood between Henry and the end of his line. Although Catherine had no children living at the time of her royal marriage, it is possible that she had been pregnant during one or the other of her two previous marriages.[8] Such a condition would have given the king hope for future issue. In any event, Henry seems to have taken an optimistic view. Catherine, too, may have been expressing her own hopes when she wrote some months later, that, 'if it pleased [God]', He could bless a marriage, 'with such a like jewel, if gladly and quietly [we] submit and refer all to his pleasure.'[9]

By late spring, and possibly as early as the end of March, Lady Latimer had become a fixture at court. John Dudley, Lord Lisle, wrote to Lord Parr on 20 June that both Catherine and Anne were 'in the court with the Ladies Mary and Elizabeth.'[10] By custom, Catherine should have retired for a period of mourning after her husband's death. But no deference to custom or respect for the dead, no concern for general opinion prevented Catherine's public appearance at court. Given the reluctance with which she greeted the king's proposals, it is to be assumed rather that Henry required her to be there than that her presence at court was due to any initiative of her own. Certainly if she wished to marry Thomas Seymour, then keeping out of Henry's way would have been a wise thing to do. It appears that she was not offered the choice. To any keen observer, it must have been fairly obvious that the king had developed a sudden interest in the Parr family, the reason for which would not be hard to find.

If Henry was 'joyful' at his choice of a bride, the rumour ran that Catherine was not. 'Better to be his mistress than his wife,' she is alleged to have cried out when the royal will was made known to her. Unfortunately for Catherine, too much was at stake for such personal feelings and fears to dictate her response. She was passionately in love with Sir Thomas Seymour, only waiting until she could be free of the ailing Latimer to marry him. The king's desire, however, changed the equation – for Catherine, for her family, and for the circle that supported the reformed religion. The queen's gambit had been proposed and set out on the political chess board of the court. There was nothing for Catherine to do but to play the game. For the Parrs, Catherine's marriage to the king was a stroke of luck they had never hoped for in their wildest dreams. Her elevation as Queen of England would mean titles and offices, lands and annuities, as the windfalls of April had proven. During the months of her courtship by the king, Catherine's brother was in the north exploring the possibilities of his new office as Lord Warden. He, too, urged the marriage in spite of the fact that he must have known his sister to be deeply in love with his friend, Thomas Seymour. 'You are', Catherine wrote him somewhat bitterly at the time of her wedding, 'the person who has most cause to rejoice.'[11]

This argument of family benefits might not have been enough to persuade Catherine to accept Henry as her husband, but she could not long hold out when the reformer group, friends of her brother's and her erstwhile lover's, made the argument that her marriage to the king should be interpreted as

God's will. That the reformers would support the king's match with the niece of the outspokenly pro-reformist Sir William Parr and sister of the equally sympathetic William, Lord Parr, is hardly surprising. In Tudor society, whatever her personal views, Catherine would be expected to urge those that her family supported. The conservatives, on the other hand, may have counted on Catherine's long association with the conservative Lord Latimer in the equally conservative north to produce a queen with similar tendencies, tendencies strong enough to override family religious pressures. Just how avid a reformer Catherine, herself, was at this juncture is debatable, but her family's connections with the reformers were well established and such an opportunity for advancing both family position and religious righteousness was not to be missed.

The enemies of the English religious revolution, led by Stephen Gardiner, Bishop of Winchester, and Thomas Howard, Duke of Norfolk, had supported the king's ill-fated marriage to Katherine Howard, Norfolk's niece. Her use to them as an influence with the king had been brief. With Katherine Howard's fall, they themselves fell, temporarily at least, out of favour. Now – Catherine Parr was almost surely told by her reformer friends and relations – now is the time to strike a blow for the new thinking, for the true, reformed religion. The king had grown increasingly conservative with the onset of age and illness; a new wife in sympathy with the reformed religion could control this alarming royal trend.[12] Cranmer, who himself had narrowly survived a recent conservative attempt to topple him,[13] and Catherine's other friends, all ardent supporters of the new order, must certainly have presented the proposed royal marriage as God's will, as a stroke of divine intervention on their behalf, as a marriage literally made in Heaven.

Writing later about this difficult decision, Catherine said that, 'God withstood my will most vehemently for a time, and through his grace and goodness made that possible which seemeth to me most impossible; that was, made me renounce utterly mine own will.'[14] Catherine's God voicing His imperatives in the voice of the new religion forced her to subordinate her personal desires to His. The force applied to accept God's will in the matter of her marriage was not only a metaphysical imperative but a human one, urged by the reformers. Catherine quickly came to perceive her marriage in terms of a divinely authorised mission, a mission not only to the king and his family, but to the nation as a whole. It was an easier notion to embrace than trying to switch the love that she felt for Seymour to the unknown and terrible Henry. Catherine's sympathies for the reformed school of thought were known at court but for the first year of her marriage, finding herself in a new and potentially dangerous position, she turned a prudently self-effacing front to the world while conducting a private, reformist-inspired examination of spiritual

Truth in her own conscience. Her connections with the late Lord Latimer and the conservative north may have given religious conservatives at court the idea, one that was later to occur to the imperial ambassadors, that under the right influence, the new queen's religious views could be brought back to the Roman Church. If this were the case, the conservatives must have realized their mistake before too many months had passed.

As to the question of her marriage with the king, Catherine had already learned self-denial in a hard school; she believed that she must continue to practice it for a higher good, for that was the duty of the true Christian woman.[15] She tried hard to follow the admonition expressed some months later to Lady Wriothesley, 'not so to utter your natural affection by inordinate sorrow that God have cause to take you as a murmurer against his appointments and ordinances.'[16] It would have been impossible for Catherine to hold out against such a combination of pressures brought to bear on her and she submitted with grace but not with joy. ' ... Let me sometime hear of your health as friendly as ye would have done if God and his majesty had not called me to this honour,' she wrote rather wistfully to her brother.[17] So Catherine renounced her love for Seymour and for the love of God agreed to marry the king. Thus on a summer's day, crowded into the Queen's Closet at Hampton Court with nearly two dozen other people who all had private ambitions they were hoping to further, Catherine Parr, Lady Latimer, became Henry Tudor's wife and Queen of England.

Congratulations on the marriage poured in. Edmond Harvel, the English ambassador to Venice, wrote to the king praising the new queen's 'goodness, prudence and virtue.'[18] Everyone in Venice, according to Harvel, felt that the English king had made a splendid choice. The imperial ambassador to the English court, Eustace Chapuys, was charmed both by Catherine's graciousness and particularly by her kindness to the Princess Mary. Francis Goldsmith, who joined the queen's household, remarked that, 'God has so formed her mind for pious studies, that she considers everything of small value compared to Christ.'[19] Goldsmith begged the queen to grant him but a coin from her treasury of grace. Sir Ralph Sadler, the long-suffering English ambassador to Scotland, voiced the reformers' joy when he wrote to Catherine's brother, 'This revived my troubled spirits and turned all my cares to rejoicing. And, my lord, I do not only rejoice for your lordship's sake ... but also for the real and inestimable benefit and comfort which thereby shall ensure to the whole realm, which now with the grace of God shall be stored with many precious jewels.'[20] At first even the conservatives spoke glowingly of the new queen. Sir Thomas Wriothesley, later Catherine's implacable enemy, wrote to the Duke of Suffolk that the new queen was 'a woman in my judgement, for virtue, wisdom and gentleness, most mete for his highness; and sure I am his majesty had never a wife more agreeable to his heart than she is.'[21] He was soon to change his mind. Yet in the early days of the marriage, the court seems to have felt a sort of euphoric relief at the king's marriage to a virtuous widow with no pretensions to premarital virginity, a woman who it appeared could satisfy the king but would cause no one trouble.

Catherine Parr's marriage to Henry began on a somber note with an outbreak of the plague in London. Whether it was fear of the plague or some of the more unsavory aspects of her husband's various ailments, the new queen's first order of business the day after the wedding night, was perfuming the nuptial bedchamber.[22] On 13 July, Catherine issued an order to her apothecary for 'fine perfumes' for her bedchamber at Hampton Court.[23] Four weeks later, she placed another order for three pounds of sweet pouches 'to make sweet the queen's bed'.[24] Odors, some of which emanated from the kitchens located beneath the royal bedchamber, were camouflaged by sackloads of sachets and perfumes as Catherine tried her best to fulfil her marriage vows and be 'blithe and buxom in bed'. Fearing contagion from the plague, the court remained in the relative safety of the countryside where Catherine formed her new household, appointed ladies-in-waiting, household officers and lesser servants and gradually grew accustomed to her exalted position.

The queen's apartments at Hampton Court were built on the east side of the inner court where the private lodgings of the royal family were located.[25] As they stood, these were apartments which had been built for Jane Seymour on a grander scale over the bones of Anne Boleyn's more modest range of lodgings. Anne Boleyn had not lived to see the completion of her rooms and Jane moved into the greatly altered and expanded apartments just in time to give birth to Edward VI. On the ground floor, these apartments consisted of the queen's privy kitchen and wardrobe.[26] Both king and queen had privy kitchens which catered exclusively for them and were set up directly under their privy chambers. A small spiral stairway linked the chambers on the two floors, allowing the yeoman of the wardrobe to deliver clothes or the waiters to bring up food from below without actually entering the queen's private apartments.[27] A practical advantage of this arrangement was that the heat from the kitchens below helped to warm the queen's privy chambers above. Unfortunately, together with the heat, cooking odors, old and new, were also wafted to the upper rooms and may in part account for Catherine's standing orders for sweet smelling herbs.[28] On the first floor, above the privy kitchen and wardrobe lay the queen's presence chamber, the queen's closet, her privy chamber and bedchamber. This wing of rooms connected at right angles with the queen's gallery, built for Jane Seymour, which ran some 175 feet along the eastern front, facing the park, until it made a right angle at the top of the square, joining a council chamber and beyond that, the apartments of the Prince of Wales. To the southwest of the queen's presence chamber lay her watching chamber which connected with the king's gallery.

These official privy chambers had by 1543 become more used for public functions than for the private residence and occupations of the queen.[29] Expansion of the apparatus and personnel of the privy chamber in the second two decades of Henry's reign had put enormous pressure on that most precious of royal commodities, privacy. By the year of Catherine's marriage, functions once accustomed to being confined to the presence chamber had so lapped over into the private royal apartments that like an ever-more intricate series of Chinese boxes, king and queen required the use of a growing number of retiring rooms, withdrawing chambers, 'utter prevy chambres' and finally secret lodgings, where they could achieve some measure of personal privacy. Like Henry, Catherine, too, used her official privy chamber as a place of public audience, distributing Maundy money there in April 1544.[30] This royal lack of privacy must have been difficult for Catherine to adjust to, accustomed as she had been to living in households far smaller and more compact than that which obtained at the Tudor court. The apartments in which she actually lived at first were located on the south end of the east front of the inner court. In a line of five adjoining rooms lay Catherine's bedchamber followed by a withdrawing chamber which enclosed a tower on three sides where her guarde-robe was no doubt situated. To the south of this was a privy chamber, another withdrawing chamber, probably used by the king, and lastly one of the king's several private bedchambers with windows opening on the park and the privy garden. Here Henry usually slept when he desired to have sexual relations with his wife, although this event could also take place in the queen's own bedchamber.[31] The king's bedroom connected on the west to another of his privy chambers and to private stairs leading outside.

These rooms with their echoes of Henry's former wives – Jane Seymour died and was embalmed in the bedchamber – were abandoned by Catherine shortly after her marriage. Within six months, a lavish new set of apartments had been created out of rooms around the southeast corner of the outer or base court, including some of Wolsey's 1526 south range. The ceilings of the rooms were raised and coved ceilings inserted. Even the wall supporting Henry's magnificent astronomical clock was built up so that the room behind it could have a higher ceiling. New partitions and wainscoting were installed; stair turrets were built to connect the new apartments to the courtyard. The queen's new apartments faced south, looking out onto the pond gardens with their sunken fishponds surrounded by striped wooden poles supporting brightly painted heraldic beasts set among low-walled flower beds.[32] The creation of a grander, more spacious, more impressive set of rooms for the royal consort in what had, over the previous fourteen years, become the 'public' area of the palace reflects the increasing importance of Catherine's influence at court and her determination to impress her own identity on the office of England's queen.

The royal household ran on a precisely detailed schedule. The pages of the chamber rose at 7.00 a.m., made up the fires and wakened the esquires of the body and their counterparts in the queen's household, the gentlewomen of the chamber, so that they could dress and be in the king or queen's chamber 'by 8.00. at the latest'.[33] Dinner was served at 10.00 a.m. and supper at 4.00 p.m. in the hall for as many as 540 people.[34] Often the numbers of people eating required that they eat in shifts. Those above the degree of baron, numbering about sixty people, could claim the privilege of eating in the king's dining room or great chamber and the queen's vice-chamberlain, council, chaplains, waiters, sewers and ushers dined in her watching chamber. On holidays, meals were served after the king and queen had gone to chapel. Tudor cuisine relied heavily on cooked meats, roasted, boiled or stewed, fish, game and poultry. Fine or coarse bread, sweets, ale and wine, generally completed the menu. Those entitled to lodge in the royal palace at the royal expense and dine at the royal table were the most important or the most cherished of the lords and ladies that served at court. The elaborate rituals which controlled life in the royal household could be daunting to an outsider unfamiliar with the intricacies of prerogative, pedigree and ceremony. Yet Catherine was determined to fulfil all expectations of her and proved to be an exceptionally adept queen. Her chosen motto, 'To Be Useful In What I Do', she took as a rule of life, and her life during the next three and a half years was a peripatetic one. She rarely spent more than a few weeks at any one residence and sometimes no longer than a few days. During the first five months of 1544 for example, she stayed in no less than fifteen royal residences. Harbingers or royal messengers were sent ahead on a three-day search of the countryside around for any signs of contagious illness. Then other servants followed to prepare the privy chambers and set up the beds for each successive move.[35]

Two reasons for this gypsy life were the limited fresh food supplies available for a large household in any given area, and the period's sanitation arrangements or lack thereof. Few residences, with only the most primitive methods of refuse disposal available, remained pleasant places to stay for very long when burdened with several hundred occupants, their horses, dogs, hawks, and other assorted livestock. A frequent purchase for the queen's privy chamber were 'flowers for the closet', 'herbs and boughs', or 'perfumes for the chambers'. Catherine also purchased or had mended numerous clocks for her privy chamber to keep hours and moves running smoothly. So dependent was she on these that in September 1544, while on a progress through Surrey and Kent, she sent one of her chamber grooms on a three-day ride back to London to have a clock mended. Such frequent shifts of residence required both efficiency and organization and the new queen soon became an expert at both.

The reports and letters of Catherine Parr's contemporaries paint a picture of a lively and attractive woman with a kind and affectionate nature. She could be vain, imperious and outspoken, and beneath her pleasant demeanour she had a fiery temper of which she occasionally lost control. She was a staunch and loyal friend, a loving wife and sister, but she could be a bitter enemy as well. She was certainly no plaster saint and her patience had limits. Catherine had a quick wit and was fond of intellectual arguments, but she also took pleasure in music and dancing and in the excitements of the hunt. Like her brother and sister, Catherine was at heart a sensualist, but this aspect of her personality was only allowed full expression after Henry VIII's death.

The new queen's growing understanding of the potential of her own position can be charted in the charges of still extant household account books. These indicate a woman gradually awakening to the possibilities of her new state. Early orders for clothing show Catherine ordering conservatively, usually subdued gowns of black and purple, almost as if she were afraid of calling too much attention to herself. Bills for jewels and luxuries are conspicuously absent.[36] An apothecary's bill, dated December 1543, carries the queen's signature as well as Sir Edward Baynton's, Catherine's first lord of the bedchamber.[37] Unlike all of her predecessors as Henry's wife, Catherine had neither been raised a princess nor spent any significant time as an adult at court. She was expected to assume the mantle of queenship without any of the background or training for the position generally enjoyed by those women newly elevated to the throne. Queens, unlike Yorkshire housewives, did not countersign their apothecary bills. But Catherine learned quickly. The *faux pas* was not repeated.

By 1544, the new queen had acquired more confidence. Her chamber accounts show orders for 'sumptuous clothes'.[38] As she became further accustomed to her newly exalted position, Catherine became an increasingly enthusiastic supporter of the pomp and circumstance that was the prerogative of England's queen. Her clothes and jewels consciously began to reflect the florid, nearly mythical image of a Tudor monarch built up by Henry VIII. This image flaunted magnificence and opulence as a way of impressing citizens at home and visitors from abroad. God's word might enjoin simplicity but the king's word commanded magnificence. Catherine's personal tastes seem to have fit right in with this Tudor appetite for luxurious wearing apparel. Not since the thousand days of Anne Boleyn, which saw the accelerated acceptance of French fashions by the nobility and new and more flattering dress and cap styles for ladies, had the court had a queen more conscious of fashion trends and continental styles and more determined to set her mark on the dress at court than was the case with Queen Catherine Parr.

Crimson was Catherine's colour of choice. It appears in her own clothing, her household liveries, and the hangings she later chose for her infant daughter, Mary Seymour's, nursery. Crimson velvet covered the back of Catherine's looking glass, bound up her books and upholstered the seat of her commode. The ladies of her chamber, such as Anne Herbert, Maud Lane and Elizabeth Tyrwhit, were given a kind of uniform dress of black double jean velvet with the queen's badge on their cap displaying the head of St. Katherine adapted from the woodblock print in the old *Horae ad Usum Sarum* Catherine had dreamed over as a child. The royal consort's own metamorphosis from black dresses to 'fine cloth of silver', and 'sumptuous clothes' of russet and yellow velvet, red cloth of gold, blue, green, white and red silk, trimmed and lined with fur and heavily embroidered with gold thread was well under way by Christmas 1543.

Catherine was very conscious of fashion and the contemporary Continental influences on dress. She patronized Italian drapers and hat makers. Her embroiderer, Guillaume Brellant, was French. Her jeweller, Peter Richardson, was Dutch.[39] These knowledgeable foreigners kept the queen abreast of the latest Continental fashions. When she ordered clothes for the Princess Mary in February 1543 from John and William Skutt, who became her own tailors as queen, the gowns were a veritable pot pourri of continental styles – Venetian, French, Italian and Dutch. The Dutch gown may have been the cone-shaped farthingale skirt brought into fashion by the ladies of the Hapsburg family which ruled the Netherlands at this time, a style worn by Catherine Parr, herself, in her full length portrait (NPG no. 4451).[40] The loose gown of patterned red silk which the queen is wearing in the half length portrait (NPG no. 4618) also owes its origin to continental modes, another example of which can be seen in the costume of Christina, Duchess of Milan, by Holbein.[41] Her dress, very *à la mode*, contrasts in this painting sharply with most other aristocratic women's portraits of the period and presents the queen as the arbiter of fashion at the Tudor court.

Catherine's nightwear seems to have been designed to please a king who favoured black silk nightgowns. Anne Boleyn's black nightgown has gained notoriety but Catherine had two of them. Among the first articles that she ordered upon her marriage to Henry VIII in 1543 were 'eleven yards of black damask for a nightgown' and 'for the making of a nightgown of black satin with two burgundian garde[s] [or sleeve trim], embroidered and edged with velvet'.[42] This may well be the first record of a peignoir set in existence.

The queen's accessories were as advanced as her dress styles. It has been claimed that Catherine de' Medici introduced the feather fan into France from Italy upon her marriage to Henri II in 1533. If so, the fashion quickly spread across the Channel. At her death, Catherine owned 'a fan or screen for to hold in the hand of black ostrich feathers set in gold, garnished with six counterfeit stones and some pearls.'[43] Another interesting item in her wardrobe was 'a muffler of black velvet garnished with twenty rubies coarse, and fully furnished with pearl, with a small chain hanging at it of gold and pearl.'[44]

Catherine's jewels were as opulent as her dresses, kept carefully wrapped in or sewn to yellow cotton bunting and locked in wooden jewel coffers that were stacked with nests of fitted trays. She had a particular passion for diamonds which as queen, she could indulge. Anne Herbert had been in charge of Katherine Howard's jewels from the time of that queen's marriage and could thus have described to the new queen her predecessor's possessions. Some of these pieces, like a *tau* cross of diamonds, had belonged to Jane Seymour and may even have belonged to Anne Boleyn. Like clothing, jewellery, too, had its fads and fashions, and the settings and styles worn by Catherine of Aragon and her ladies in the early part of Henry's reign looked dated and old-fashioned next to the heavier, more ornate designs of Henry's later queens. Many of these new designs may have originated with Peter Richardson, a Dutch goldsmith from Haarlem, who came to England about 1536 to work for Henry's third queen, Jane Seymour. Richardson subsequently became Catherine Parr's official jeweler upon her marriage to the king in 1543.[45] By January 1547, Richardson was in partnership with Hans (John/Jan) of Antwerp, an executor of Holbein's will, an indication, perhaps, of just how much in demand at court Richardson's talents were.

The designs for two covered gold cups by Holbein with finials of St. Katherine holding a lettered scroll and a heart, crafted after Holbein's death in 1545, attest to the queen's interest in goldsmith's work. A drawing of one piece of jewellery which may also have been designed for Catherine by Hans Holbein still exists and shows an ouche or brooch of a half-figure maiden's head, holding a rectangular plaque of gold on which is inscribed the legend, 'Well Loyvdi Well', and garnished with hanging pearls.[46] The maiden's head was the queen's personal emblem. It has been suggested that the richer, heavier court jewellery, seen in such paintings as Holbein's portrait of Jane Seymour, his miniatures of Lady Audeley and Lady Margaret Douglas, in the family portrait of William Brooke, 10th Lord Cobham, at Longleat, and in the half-length painting of Princess Mary and Catherine Parr's two portraits in the National Portrait Gallery, were originally crafted from Holbein's designs. The extant sketches attributable to Holbein, however, do not bear this out. They show an extensive use of pearls and gemstones in combination inside the gold bezels for brooches and pendants. Yet none of the above portraits include pearls used in this way, reserving them for trims, links or hanging pendants. It is probably Peter Richardson, therefore, who was primarily responsible for much of the elegant jewellery on display at the English court between 1536 and 1553 (when Richardson was employed to fashion jewellery for Catherine's brother, the Marquis of Northampton and his wife), although the possibility of a mutual influence on style and design between Richardson, Holbein and the more obscure Hans of Antwerp should not be ignored.

The queen's crown, possibly made for Anne Boleyn, was not so elegant. It is described in 1550 as being of gold bordered with six sapphires and smaller sapphires, six balas (red spinals), 'not fine stones', a small balas 'of little value', twenty-four big pearls, 'not fine', and eight small pearls. Around the rim were six crosses of gold, each set with a sapphire and a balas and four pearls, 'not great', and six fleur-de-luces of gold, each set with a sapphire and balas and five small pearls, the 'sapphire and balas not fine'.[48] This red, white and blue hodgepodge of inferior stones was topped with a diamond and a cross of gold, 'not garnished', and lined with a cap of purple velvet. Whether Catherine Parr actually wore this crown is unknown.

Clocks and watches both fascinated the queen. Some she inherited from her predecessors as Henry's wife and others she had made for herself. These included everything from large chamber clocks run by weights to small pieces of delicate jewellery which could be worn hanging from a chain or girdle or pinned to a bodice. Among the more interesting specimens in Catherine's collection was one which was found among her effects at her death and consisted of 'two sables skins with a head of gold, being a clock, in each eye a rock ruby and about the collar three small table rubies and three small table diamonds with (the sable having) four feet of gold.'[49] She also owned 'a tablet of gold being a clock fashioned like a hart garnished with three rubies and one fair diamond lozenged' and 'a tablet being therein a clock, on the one side the king's word wrought of diamonds furnished, and on the other side a cross of diamonds furnished with twenty-four diamonds with a button hanging thereat having two diamonds and two rubies'.[50]

In a time when few people paid much attention to personal hygiene, Catherine indulged in milk baths taken in a leaden bathtub. Orders were sent out for expensive oils, almond, olive and clove, for perfumes and unguents, rose water and breath lozenges. Her privy was canopied with crimson velvet and cushioned with straw pillows covered in cloth of gold. The seat was of crimson velvet and the removable pan beneath it covered with red silk and ribbons held in place by gilt nails.[51] Catherine was as meticulous in her personal habits as she was increasingly extravagant in her dress.[52] She had a personal launderer for her private linen; she owned silver tweezers to pluck her arched eyebrows,[53] and, like the small snuff boxes of the late eighteenth century, she carried with her small jewelled boxes of lozenges flavoured with liquorice or clove or cinnamon for sweet breath.[54]

The new queen appeared determined to enjoy her new position. She added a company of players to her household as well as a company of Venetian minstrels, the Bassano brothers. Music was particularly important to her, as it was to her brother, and a number of servants in the queen's household doubled as musicians. Men with household offices, such as Walter Erle and Robert Cooch, were also proficient in the art of music. Cooch, for example, was, according to Bishop Parkhurst, 'a very accomplished man, and well skilled in music (and when) I was preacher in Queen Catherine's household, he was steward of the wine cellar.'[55] In a letter to Princess Mary,[56] the queen remarks on their mutual delight and pleasure in music, and one of the surviving comedies that Nicholas Udall wrote for Catherine, *Ralph Roister Doister*, is remarkable for the number of songs and musical interludes that are included in the text.

Besides music and plays, the queen also employed two fools, Jane and Thomas Browne, for entertainment and apparently had a pet spaniel named 'Rig', who wore a dog collar of crimson velvet embroidered with gold.[57] She kept parrots which she fed on hempseed, a number of expensive horses, a grey, a white and a 'sumpter gelding', in the care of Robert Tyrwhit, her master of the horse. Hunting livestock included a kennel of greyhounds fed on milk, and a mews of horsemeat-eating falcons for hunting. She was determined to improve her skill with the crossbow and had archery butts set up in the garden of the manor at Slough for private target practice away from critical or mocking eyes at court.[58] About her abilities on the dance floor, however, Catherine had no need to be embarrassed, and she enjoyed performing in public, dancing for guests of the court like Ambassador Chapuys. Her obvious love of dancing and the pleasure she took in learning new dance steps was such that her prim stepson, the Prince of Wales, wrote to her in May 1546, begging her and Princess Mary, 'to attend no longer to foreign dances and merriments which do not become a most Christian princess.'[59]

An account of a visit in February 1544 of Don Manriquez de Lara, Duke of Najera, from Spain demonstrates that in just seven months, the widow from Yorkshire had metamorphosized into an English queen of elegance and splendor.[60] On Sunday, 17 February, William Parr, Earl of Essex, and his friend, Thomas Howard, Earl of Surrey, dined with Najera and brought him to Whitehall. After an audience with the king, Najera was conducted to the queen's chambers, who had been entrusted with the task of entertaining the foreign dignitary. Accompanied by the Princess Mary, Lady Margaret Douglas and 'other ladies [who] were dressed in different silks, with splendid headdresses', the queen welcomed Najera. 'The Duke kissed the Queen's hand, by whom he was received in an animated manner. From thence they conducted the Duke to another apartment, where stood another canopy of brocade, with a chair of the same.' The secretary of the Spanish duke, Pedro da Gante, was very impressed with the queen:

> The Queen has a lively and pleasing appearance, and is praised as a virtuous woman. She was dressed in a robe of cloth of gold, and a petticoat of brocade with sleeves lined with crimson satin, and trimmed with three-piled crimson velvet: her train was more than two yards long. Suspended from her neck were two crosses, and a jewel of very rich diamonds, and in her head-dress were many and beautiful ones. Her girdle was of gold, with very large pendants.

Catherine had arranged an evening of music and dancing for the duke which his secretary, at least, enjoyed very much:

> The Queen entered with the Princesses and ladies, and having seated herself, she commanded the Duke to sit down, and musicians with violins were introduced. The Queen danced first with her brother, very gracefully; then the Princess Mary and the Princess of Scotland danced with other gentlemen, and many other ladies did the same. Among these gentlemen danced a Venetian of the King's household some *gallardas* so lightly, that he appeared to have wings in his feet. Never did I witness such agility in any man. After the dancing was finished (which lasted several hours) the Queen entered again into her chamber, having previously called one of the noblemen who spoke Spanish, to offer in her name some presents to the Duke, who again kissed her hand; and on his requesting the same favour of the Princess Mary, she would by no means permit it, but offered him her lips, and the Duke saluted her, and did the same to all the other ladies.

With the help and advice of experienced court servants such as her sister, Anne Herbert, and Mary Wotton, Lady Carew, Catherine Parr had managed in only seven months as queen to find her political and social feet at court.[61] The liveliness and animation which the Spanish visitors discerned in her behaviour and the grace and elegance of her carriage and dress, demonstrate a woman who had managed outwardly at least to shed the trappings of a chaotic life in the north, a double widowhood and a non-aristocratic background. They also demonstrate a queen who enjoyed the full confidence of her royal husband, a husband who had left in her hands the reception and entertainment of important foreign guests. Energetic by character and eager to excel in this, the most important role of her life, by the beginning of 1544 Catherine had appeared to have succeeded in her ambition to be more than simply the sixth in succession of Henry Tudor's many wives.

'Most Honourable and Entirely Beloved Mother'

Catherine Parr's talent for captivating useful allies such as the Archbishop of Canterbury and imperial ambassador Chapuys and impressing haughty Spanish noblemen was employed soon after her marriage in the important task of winning the confidence and friendship of Henry's children. The dysfunctional royal family presented a challenge to which the new queen was quick to turn her talents as diplomat. Her approach varied with each child and it is the measure of her real affection for them and her understanding of their characters that with each child she had considerable success. Towards the lonely Mary whose life had been so twisted and difficult, Catherine acted the elder sister. Within a month of her marriage, the queen had made her stepdaughter an almost permanent companion.

'The King continues to treat the Princess kindly,' Chapuys reported to the emperor, 'and has made her stay with his new Queen, who behaves affectionately towards her.'[1] Catherine set herself to amuse Mary, discussing clothes and jewels with the princess, who like her stepmother had a passion for such things. Catherine also delighted in presenting her stepdaughter with gifts, such as a pair of gold bracelets set with rubies, emeralds and diamonds that she gave Mary shortly after her marriage to Henry.[2] Mary's chamber accounts show that Catherine also gave her stepdaughter sums of money. Their friendship became so close that a courtesy letter written in June 1544 to the Countess of Hertford was written by both of them on the same sheet of paper.[3]

Chapuys, one of whose duties it was to keep an eagle eye out for the interests of the princess, rarely mentions Mary without also mentioning the queen's manifold kindnesses to her. The two women seem to have been almost always together and when Chapuys thanked the queen in the name of his master for such attentions, Catherine replied, 'very graciously that she did not deserve so much courtesy from your Majesty; and what she did for Lady Mary was less than she would like to do, and was only her duty in every respect.'[4] Catherine liked Mary, who suffered from a variety of physical ailments including bad eyesight and bouts of profound melancholia, and made herself the princess' champion, a gesture that was to have important consequences for the royal succession.

Mary had been removed from the line of succession by her father, who had declared her a bastard. Catherine set out to reconcile father and daughter and to restore Mary as a potential heir to her father's crown. In the imperial ambassador's report, dated 18 February 1544, Chapuys related that, '[the] Queen favours the Princess all she can; and since the treaty with the Emperor was made, she has constantly urged the Princess' cause, insomuch as in this sitting of Parliament she has been declared capable of succeeding in default of the Prince.'[5] Both Chapuys and through him, Mary's cousin, the emperor, realized the importance of Catherine's influence in the matter of the English succession. ' ...You are doing the right thing in keeping on good terms with the Queen,' the emperor advised Chapuys on 5 March, 'do not fail whenever the opportunity offers, to address her.'[6] On 3 January 1545, Chapuys assured the emperor that he had, 'thanked [the queen] for the favour she showed the Lady Mary.'[7]

This correspondence between the emperor and his ambassador, observant and sensitive to anything affecting Mary's interests, indicates that Catherine was intent on ensuring Mary's place in the line of succession, that she urged Mary's cause at every opportunity and succeeded in her purpose when Mary was named heir to the throne after her brother. The queen was equally bent on maintaining cordial relations between England and the Empire. For Catherine, the two goals were interconnected and she appears to have given her servants standing orders that when the imperial ambassadors appeared at court, she was to be immediately informed. In January of 1545, the ambassadors of Charles V wrote to him that, 'we were conducted without the slightest hint of a desire on our part, to the oratory of the Queen, who shortly afterwards herself entered ... [and] with regard to the maintenance of friendship [between England and the Empire], she said, she had done, and would do, nothing to prevent its growing still firmer and she hoped that God would avert even the slightest dissension as the friendship was so necessary and both sovereigns were so good.'[8]

A lengthy dispatch written on 9 May from Chapuys to Charles V, paints a vivid picture of the queen in action and it is worth quoting the text of it as it relates to her efforts at international diplomacy:

When I had entered the back door of the King's apartments, [Chapuys relates], having traversed the garden facing the Queen's lodging, and arrived nearly at the other end close to the [main] entrance of the King's apartments, my own people informed me that the Queen and Princess were following us quickly. I hardly had time to rise from the chair in which I was being carried before she approached quite near, and seemed from the small suite she had with her, and the haste with which she came, as if her purpose in coming was specially to speak to me. She was only accompanied by four or five women of the chamber; and opened the conversation by saying that the King had told her the previous evening that I was coming that morning to take my leave of him. Whilst on the one hand she was very sorry for my departure, as she had been told that I had always acted well in my offices, and the King had confidence in me, on the other hand she doubted not that my health would be better on the other side of the water. I could, however, she said, do as much on the other side as here, for the preservation of the amity between your Majesty and the King, of which I had been one of the chief promoters. For this reason she was glad that I should go; and although she had no doubt that so wise and good a monarch as your Majesty, would realise the importance and necessity of maintaining this friendship, of which the King, on his part, had given so many proofs in the past; yet it seemed to her that your Majesty had not been so thoroughly informed hitherto, either by my letters or otherwise, of the King's sincere affection and goodwill, as I should be able to report by word of mouth. She therefore begged me affectionately, after I had presented to your Majesty her humble service, to express explicitly to you all I had learned here of the good wishes of the King towards you; and likewise to use my best influence in favour of the maintenance and increase of the existing friendship. She asked me very minutely and most graciously, after your Majesty's health and expressed great joy to learn of your Majesty's amelioration ... I then asked to be allowed to salute the Princess, which was at once accorded, she, the Queen, being anxious, as it seemed to me, that I should not suffer from having to stand too long.[9]

As Chapuys spoke with Princess Mary, the queen 'drew seven or eight paces, so as not to overhear my conversation with the Princess. The latter, however, appeared unwilling to prolong the interview, in order not to detain the Queen, who stood apart regarding us ... ' – Catherine was waiting for another chance to lobby the ambassador:

When the Queen saw that I had finished my talk with the Princess, she returned immediately to me, and asked if, perchance some of the gentlemen who accompanied me had come from your Majesty. She then made many enquiries as to the health, etc. of the Queen-Dowager of Hungary, to whom she desired to be most affectionately remembered. She said that the King was under great obligation to her Majesty for having on all occasions shown so much good will towards him; and she continued with a thousand compliments on the Queen-Dowager's virtue, prudence and diligence. After some other conversation, the Queen returned to her lodgings without allowing me to stir from where I was.

Several aspects of the queen's position at court and her intimacy with the king are revealed by this letter. Her urging of Mary's cause, her understanding of England's precarious position in the international community at the time, following the unfortunate diplomatic repercussions of the 1544 invasion of France, her realization of the necessity for rapprochement with the empire are apparent. Also revealed are her political conversations with the king, who had told her about the importance of Chapuys' role in bilateral negotiations and his concerns that Charles V had not been sufficiently reassured about England's intentions. Catherine even took it upon herself to express the king's sense of obligation to the emperor's sister, Mary, Regent of the Netherlands, and bestow upon her the encomium that she herself desired, a reputation for virtue, prudence and diligence. That Catherine spoke for the king is made apparent later in the dispatch when Chapuys relates in his conversations with the Privy Council, that the councillors 'expressed regret at my departure, for reasons similar to those stated by the Queen; but entertained the same hope with regard to it as that expressed by her.'[10] This dispatch establishes Catherine's important contribution to Anglo-Imperial diplomacy with its ramifications for Mary's place in the English succession.

Van der Delft, Chapuys's successor at the English court in 1545, found the same political dynamic when he chatted with the queen while watching a hunt at her brother's house at Guildford that August, and like his predecessor was moved by Catherine's 'kindness and graciousness' toward himself and toward Mary.[11] The queen, doing all she could to favour the princess, felt that Mary's inclusion in the succession was a necessary link in the chain of friendship between England and the Empire. Her lobbying toward this end, combined with the king's warmer relations with his daughter, brought about Mary's return to the recognized order of succession.

Having been a member of the princess' household, Catherine knew that Mary's real allegiance was to Rome and to the old religion, just as hers was to the new, but it speaks for her humanity, her optimism, and her intimacy with the princess that she felt Mary's beliefs were alterable and should not therefore be a stumbling block to her rights of inheritance. Catherine's actions underscore her sense of mission to her husband's children. Then, too, the princess had been the acknowledged heir to the kingdom throughout Catherine's childhood and adolescence. There must have seemed to the queen a sense of moral rightness, of welcoming back the prodigal child, of restoring the lost lamb to the proper order of things, in the return of Mary to her father's good graces and a recognized place in the succession. As for her religion, Mary had publicly acknowledged the Henrician Settlement and the Royal Supremacy, all that remained was to encourage moderation toward reform. Soliciting Mary's participation in the great Reformation translation project of Erasmus' *Paraphrases*, transferring her personal chaplain Francis Mallet to Mary's service,[12] and including the princess in social activities dominated by the inner circle of reformers, such as the November 1545 party to the Duchess of Suffolk's for the christening of Lady Lisle's child, tended to this end.[13]

Catherine appeared to be confident that gentle pressure would ultimately wean Mary away from any false ideas she might have entertained toward the infallibility of the papacy and the old religion, open her eyes to the truth as the queen defined truth, and attach the princess' whole-hearted loyalty to England's new religious establishment. Three years later, adherents of the Roman Catholic Church, unaware of the tenacity of the queen's own religious convictions, discussed a similar program to bring Catherine back to their church by less gentle forms of persuasion.[14] The notion that a woman's mind was less firm, less committed than a man's and could therefore be swayed by appropriate persuasion was current in Tudor society at all levels. No amount of evidence to the contrary, and there were numerous examples of evidence to the contrary in women such as Elizabeth Barton and Anne Askew, could crack society's implicit belief in this received wisdom of moral frailty, intellectual imperfection and sexual differentiation into stronger and weaker orders. Catherine believed that Mary could be wooed down the road to reform and she herself undertook to guide her first steps. The re-establishment of the princess in the line of succession to Henry's kingdom and Henry's church would make a strong beginning.

Based on comments in the ambassadorial reports, it was Catherine who was the chief instrument of Henry VIII's decision to name all of his children in his will as heirs to the throne. The inclusion of Mary, and subsequently of Elizabeth, whom Catherine reclaimed from rural exile in the summer of 1544, were the result of the queen's three and a half year campaign to make the princesses, after their brother, the acknowledged heirs of their father's crown. The terms of Henry's will later legitimised both Mary's seizure of the crown from Lady Jane Grey and Elizabeth's succession after Mary's death. The princesses may have been the daughters of a king, but it was their stepmother who helped to insure their legitimacy as queens. The argument that Catherine Parr was a negligible political influence falls before the weight of such evidence.

Almost from the beginning of his reign, the king had depended on the abilities of one keen-witted favourite after another. With Cromwell's death, Henry found himself for the first time since the rise of Wolsey, so many years before, without the sort of advisor that his political short-sightedness and short-fused temperament seemed to demand. Now handicapped as well by diminishing physical abilities, Henry needed a person whom he considered to be a trustworthy councillor. Catherine satisfied this need by evening discussions and debates with her husband on politics and religion. Her marital obligations were satisfied through a combination of sexual submission, an attitude of affectionate encouragement and a game plan of calculated coaxing that flattered Henry's ego and satisfied his emotional and physical desires.

In a sense, the queen had little competition for the position of councillor so long as she was subtle in her suggestions, liberal with her body, and clever in her handling of the king. The result achieved was an influence with her husband, at least during the first two and a half years of her marriage, that was second to none. Without the challenge of a Wolsey or a Cromwell to check it, the strength of the queen's position with the king was apparent both to those at court ('I have so urgently requested you to use your influence and kindness in the Queen's presence,' Roger Ascham wrote to Sir Anthony Denny in 1545;[15] '[I] signify these things that they may suggest something to the queen for a suit to the king,' Matthew Parker wrote in 1546),[16] and to those abroad ('Do not fail whenever the opportunity offers to address [the queen],' Charles V commanded his ambassador).[17] It was her influence, recognized by the emperor and his ambassadors seeking rapprochement with England after the king's divorce, that not only brought Mary back into the line of succession but also did much to heal the breach between England and the Empire.

With her younger stepdaughter, Princess Elizabeth, the queen was on loving and intimate terms as well. It is significant that of the five surviving letters which Elizabeth wrote before the age of sixteen, four were written to Catherine and one was written to Catherine's fourth husband, Sir Thomas Seymour, about the queen's health. The precocious daughter of Anne Boleyn was nine years old when her father married his sixth wife. She had never had a real mother apart from her beloved nurse, Katherine Ashley (or Astley), and she and Catherine took to each other at once.[18] There is a wistful, almost pleading tone in Elizabeth's correspondence with her stepmother, a desire to return in full the affection that Catherine offered her. 'I know that I have your love and that you have not forgotten me,' Elizabeth wrote at one point, 'for if your grace had not a good opinion of me you would not have offered friendship to me that way, that all men judge the contrary.'[19] And at another, 'And in this my exile, I well know that the clemency of your Highness has had as much care and solicitude for my health as the King's Majesty himself.'[20]

Elizabeth sought to please the queen with gifts that she knew would particularly appeal to her. As a New Year's gift in December 1544, Elizabeth sent Catherine a copy of one of the queen's favourite works, 'The Mirror of the Sinful Soul' by Marguerite of Navarre, which the young princess had translated from the original French into English prose.[21] Elizabeth had made the translation, written out the text in her own hand and then bound the pages together in a cover that she had embroidered herself. Elizabeth begged Catherine's indulgence for any faults in the gift. 'I hope that ... there shall be nothing in it worthy of reprehension, and that in the meanwhile no other [but your Highness only] shall read it or see it, lest my faults be known of many. Then shall they be better excused [as my confidence is in your Grace's accustomed benevolence] than if I should bestow a whole year in writing or inventing ways for to excuse them.'[22] The following year, 1545, Elizabeth fashioned two New Year's gifts for her parents. For her father, the young princess translated her stepmother's own work, *Prayers or Meditations*, into French, Italian and Latin. For Catherine, Elizabeth translated the first chapter of John Calvin's *L'Institution de la vie chrestienne* as 'How we ought to knowe God' and bound both offerings in elaborately worked covers that she herself had embroidered. [23] Such efforts were not mere courtesy gifts. Elizabeth, too, like her sister Mary, in and out of favour with the increasingly hard-to-please king, had found a champion in her new mother.

With Prince Edward, Catherine tried another tactic. She praised his schoolwork and appealed to his sympathies as a fellow student and scholar. '... with what great diligence you have cultivated the Muses,' she wrote to him, 'the letters you recently sent me can already be very ample witnesses – epistles which seem to me to shine both with the elegance of Latin discourse and more polished structure far surpassing all the others you sent me.' If she did not hear from him daily, she would understand and attribute it to 'your admirable studies rather than to any negligence, since I affectionately and thoughtfully consider with what great love you attend both me, your mother, and scholarship at the same time, so that love toward your mother on the one hand and desire of learning on the other entirely free you from any suspicion of negligence even without a hearing.'[24] This was a recurring theme in Catherine's relationships with her stepchildren – involvement in their education and interest in their progress.

Because Catherine had had an unusually advanced education as a child, she delighted in study and intellectual endeavours. As the wife first of Edward Borough, and then of the conservative Lord Latimer, with households to run and the daily press of family affairs, such pleasures as scholarly studies would no doubt have been regarded as frivolous, particularly for a woman, and an inexcusable waste of time. As queen these impediments did not exist. Catherine could work with the finest minds available in her favourite fields of interest – humanist learning and religious reform. It is typical of her inquiring mind that, not satisfied with French, Italian, English and Latin, the queen undertook the study of Spanish during the summer of 1546.[25] Her active and continuing interest in educating others is demonstrated by her involvement in the administration and curriculum at the college of canons at Stoke in Suffolk, part of her marriage jointure, whose supervision she continued in the capable hands of scholar and reformer Matthew Parker.

In the spring of 1546, Parker wrote to the queen and her council that, 'The Queen's tenants round about [the college] are refreshed with alms and daily hospitality and instructed in God's word, while their children are taught grammar, singing and playing, with other suitable exercises by sundry teachers.'[26] Both scholars and children were profiting, Parker asserted, from the queen's care and patronage. This active commitment to scholarship combined with Catherine's growing friendships among, and correspondence with, the humanist community would have certainly recommended her to her new stepson, Edward, a cold and somewhat priggish child, but her fellowship with the prince as an earnest student endeared her to him as well. 'Wherefore since you love my father,' Edward wrote to his stepmother shortly after his father's death, 'I cannot but much commend you; since you love me, I cannot but love you again: and since you love God's word I will love and admire you from my heart.'[27]

One of the most debated issues of Catherine's influence on the royal children, and later on Lady Jane Grey, is her impact on their education. The underlying significance of this is, of course, that Edward and Elizabeth's tutors – Richard Cox, John Cheke, Roger Ascham, Anthony Cooke and William Grindal – were part of that enthusiastic group of religious reformers whose impact on the minds of their two royal students helped to confirm the commitment of two future rulers of England to the Protestant Reformation. Henry VIII, in spite of the increasing conservatism which coloured his personal religious views at the end of his life, allowed his children to be taught by those whose religious attitudes coincided with the reform group centred around the queen. The very selection of these men as royal tutors, protégés as they were of the 'queen's party', suggests that Catherine Parr may have had more impact on the appointment of her stepchildren's teachers than some present critics would allow her.[28] In order to form an idea of what her role was, it is necessary to analyze her influence with the king, ultimate arbiter of royal education, her personal relations with the group of tutors who oversaw the children's studies and her basic interest in and commitment to Edward, Elizabeth, and even Mary's scholastic efforts.

In July 1544, on the verge of his departure for France and at the same time that he was drawing up the documents that would make Catherine Parr the Regent-General of England, the king was also setting up the new household of Prince Edward. The prince was six years old and would soon be released from his nursery establishment of women to begin schooling with a group of carefully selected tutors. Catherine's involvement in the selection of these tutors – Dr. Richard Cox and John Cheke – has been called into question, and they may not have been her personal candidates, yet her approval or veto at this time in her marriage carried weight and it may be inferred that if she did not nominate them, she approved of their selection.

John Cheke had been the pupil and was the protégé of George Day, Bishop of Chichester, who was also Catherine's almoner.[29] Day became Catherine's friend as well and if any man acted as the queen's religious and literary mentor after her marriage to Henry, it was George Day. It was for him that she ordered presentation copies of her works, beginning with the 1544 translation of *Psalms or Prayers*, a work he may well have encouraged her to undertake in order to improve her rusty Latin.[30] In June 1547, she sent the bishop presentation copies of two books bound in white satin which appear to have been the *Enchiridion* by Erasmus, a man whose thought was a strong bond between Day and the queen, and another Erasmean work, *The Preparation to Death*.[31] On the evidence, the queen seems to have been sincerely attached to Day and it is certainly within the realm of possibility that Day prevailed upon his royal mistress to use her influence with the king on Cheke's behalf. By the end of her reign if not earlier, Cheke and the queen were on particularly close terms. She sent him gifts of game from the hunt[32] and, according to Roger Ascham, writing to Cheke in 1548, 'I do not believe [the queen] will do anything without consulting you.'[33] Richard Cox, too, was part of the same Cambridge group of reformers that included Cheke, Roger Ascham, William Grindal, Matthew Parker and Hugh Latimer. Whether or not Catherine actually suggested Cox and Cheke, it is naive at least to quibble that the king would have been unwilling to take the queen's advice in the matter of his son's tutors when he was not only willing to take her advice on the royal succession by reinstating Mary but to publicly acknowledge his faith in Catherine's abilities by making her Regent-General of England.

The queen's influence with the king is apparent in the appointment of her regency council. In the Privy Council minutes which named the council, a separate minute was added to include Catherine's uncle, Lord Parr of Horton, among the councillors.[34] This was almost certainly at Catherine's own request. The queen's ascendancy with the king was also testified to by her cousin, Sir Nicholas Throckmorton, whose father, Sir George Throckmorton, had been imprisoned for religious transgressions. Lady Throckmorton pleaded for Catherine's help and the queen gave it. According to Sir Nicholas:

And, when the King was in the pleasing moode,
She humbly then her suit began to crave.
With wooing times denyalls disagree,
She spake, and sped: my Father was sett free.[35]

Throckmorton's conclusion is clear. Sexuality was a tool that Catherine used with great dexterity and such a tool, when used with subtlety by a clever woman, rarely fails to achieve the desired end. When in 1544 Catherine turned author, the king allowed her to publish two of her works using his licensed printer, publicly voicing her religious concerns in literary additions to the English vernacular press. This was something unheard of before in a queen of England. In 1545, when Sir Anthony Denny required an influential spokesman 'on behalf of literature' and good learning, he turned to the queen.[36] In February 1546, when the University of Cambridge needed the most powerful ambassador to the king that they could recruit, they, too, turned to the queen. These instances together with Lord Parr's appointment and Sir George Throckmorton's liberty attest to the queen's influence with her husband.

Catherine Parr's relations with the tutors of the royal children were invariably cordial ones. Roger Ascham's friendship with the Parrs is well documented.[37] The son of John Ascham, house steward to that irascible Lord Scrope of Bolton, who had nearly become Catherine's father-in-law, Ascham may have met Catherine during the years that she was living in the north. Certainly he knew her at court and even though Catherine attempted to instate her attorney, Francis Goldsmith, as Elizabeth's tutor after William Grindal died, she was persuaded without too much effort by her stepdaughter's arguments to accept Ascham in Grindal's place.[38] With Richard Cox, the queen appears to have been on friendly if not intimate terms. 'I perceive,' Prince Edward wrote to his stepmother on 10 June 1546, 'that you have given your attention to the Roman characters, so that my preceptor [Cox] could not be persuaded but that your secretary wrote them, till he observed your name written equally well.'[39] Cox, it would seem, did not know Catherine's scholastic abilities well. The case was just the opposite with royal tutor, Anthony Cooke,[40] who although tutor to Edward after Catherine's death, yet had her goodwill while at court during her lifetime. Cooke had married Catherine's cousin, Anne Fitzwilliam. Cooke's mother-in-law was Catherine's first cousin, close friend and lady-in-waiting. Catherine's recommendation of Cooke at court would have been entirely in keeping with her proven proclivities for promoting members of her own family.

On the evidence, Catherine took an active and very personal interest in her stepchildren's education. As Maud Parr's daughter, a woman who had set up a school in her own household and bequeathed money in her will for education, it is hardly surprising that Catherine's taste for learning was formed young and continued throughout her life. The free school set up at Well in Yorkshire by her second husband's will almost certainly owes more to her inspiration than to his. 'I am never able to render to her grace sufficient thanks for the goodly education and tender love and bountiful goodness which I have evermore found in her highness,' wrote Margaret Neville, Catherine's stepdaughter, in the spring of 1545.[41] Prince Edward echoed these sentiments in the following year:

> 'I have me most humbly recommended unto your grace with like thanks, both for that your grace did accept so gently my simple and rude letters, and also that it pleased your grace so gently to vouchsafe to direct unto me your loving and tender letters which do give me much comfort and encouragement to go forward in such things wherein your grace beareth me on hand that I am already entered. I pray God I may be able in part to satisfy [your] good expectation.'[42]

As for Elizabeth, Ascham noted that 'Our most illustrious queen and my most noble mistress Elizabeth are superior by all praise, because they have devoted themselves to this study of the graces of women of older days ... who flourished in that praise of literature.'[43] To Catherine, he wrote, 'you so possess that universal glory of learning that you willingly acknowledge it taken away from all the others but shared with great sweetness of mutual association with Lady Elizabeth only.'[44] Filling the role of loving mother, devoted friend and studiously inclined companion from the princess' ninth year until she was two days short of her fifteenth birthday, Catherine's influence on Elizabeth's life and education was seminal. Not only were her stepchildren grateful for her interest in their studies so were their teachers. The royal tutors were eager to maintain their pupils' interest in their books and so encouraged them to correspond frequently with their sympathetic stepmother describing their progress. Numerous letters survive written between Catherine and the children in English, Latin, French and Italian, discussing their intellectual efforts.

As far as the education of Lady Jane Grey is concerned, Catherine's fourth husband, Sir Thomas Seymour, held Jane's wardship during 1547 and 1548, including the last nineteen months of Catherine's life. Jane Grey's tutor, John Aylmer, was indisputably chosen by her parents yet he was also a close friend of Catherine's own chaplain, John Parkhurst, and her almoner, Miles Coverdale. Given the queen's leaning toward learning and her affection for Jane, it is probable that Catherine had some effect on the direction of Jane's education during those two years. This would have been particularly true during the summer of 1548, when Jane lived with Catherine in her household at Sudeley

Castle. Jane's own affectionate attachment to Catherine, a woman so markedly different in warmth and interest from her own abusive parents, was demonstrated in 1553, five years after Catherine's death, when Jane, then in the throes of a nervous breakdown, chose the queen's own beloved manor of Chelsea, still resonant with Catherine's memory, as a refuge in which to recuperate.

In the art of endearing herself to the royal children, Catherine employed an additional tactic, that of doing special favours for valued members of her stepchildren's households. She wrote a letter in favour of George Tresham, one of Edward's gentlemen of the privy chamber, and befriended Sir William Sidney, his chamberlain.[45] She pressed a suit for Mary's chaplain, Richard Baldwin, to have a prebendary in Newark College in Leicester.[46] She liberally rewarded certain servants in Elizabeth's household and set herself to be especially friendly to Elizabeth's beloved nurse, 'Kat' Ashley. ' ... my Mistress (Ashley) wisheth ... your Highness most humble thanks for her commendations,' Elizabeth wrote to her stepmother.[47] Catherine helped arrange a marriage for Edward's servant, Philip Gerrard,[48] and she allowed her own chaplain, Francis Mallet,[49] to transfer service to Lady Mary's household while she found space for one of Mary's maids in hers.[50]

With tact and kindness, Catherine managed to gain the love and trust of the royal children. During her three and a half years as queen, all of Henry's children had their portraits painted *en large*, Mary and Elizabeth probably for the first time. Catherine was fascinated with portrait painting and had her own done many times. She understood intuitively how court portraiture could be used as a tool of effective propaganda for the royal family, particularly for herself and her stepchildren. Royal portraits were the concrete iconography of divinely authorised rule. They reiterated the consequence of their subjects' birth and position, of their spiritual and terrestrial inheritance, of the supreme imperative of their right to the Crown and to the loyalty of their subjects. As visual reminders of their royal descent, these portraits were an effective device in the queen's campaign to establish Mary and Elizabeth as legitimate heirs to the English throne. When Catherine Parr married Henry VIII, only Edward, the royal heir, enjoyed his father's full attention and approval. Mary's relationship with her father had been twisted and soured by the years of punishment that Henry had inflicted on his elder daughter in an effort to force her to deny the validity of her mother's marriage and to acknowledge her own illegitimacy. Although Mary's relations with Henry had vastly improved in the last seven years, who knew when the king 'might turn again and rend her'? Elizabeth's relations with Henry, too, were coloured by the bitter residue of his memories of Anne Boleyn. All three of Henry's children lived apart from him and from each other. It was Catherine Parr in her mission as family peacemaker who brought them together under the same roof for extended periods of time. This she accomplished within a few months of her marriage.

On 16 December 1543, Richard Layton, Dean of York and the English ambassador to Flanders, wrote in his report to the king, that the Emperor's sister, the regent of the Netherlands, had demanded of him 'how the Queen's Grace, my Lord Prince, my Lady Mary, and my Lady Elizabeth did; and whether Your Grace and they continued still in one household.'[51] Such a sudden and drastic change in Henry's domestic arrangements had become the gossip of Europe. In August of the following year, 1544, Lord Russell wrote to Sir William Paget, cheered to hear that 'the queen and all the royal children are together at Hampton Court.'[52] Henry was in France at this time, leaving Catherine as Regent-General of England for three months. While the king was away, she kept the children with her, reporting on their health in almost all of her letters to her husband.[53] Catherine and the children hunted together at Woking in September,[54] sending prizes of the hunt by assorted yeomen of the chamber to various of their friends and went on a progress through Surrey and Kent until the first week of October. Each of Henry's children had their own household establishments and certainly they did not live with the queen on a permanent basis, but for the first time in any of their lives, they had found a parent who concerned herself with bringing them and their father together as a functioning family and in securing their legal rights of inheritance in his kingdom.

9

Patronage and the Queen's Household

Catherine Parr's income as queen was derived from a dower package of lands and manors which had been passed down from her predecessor, Katherine Howard. These were located principally in Essex, London, Suffolk, Herefordshire, Wiltshire, Dorset, Northamptonshire, Worcestershire and Gloucestershire, with a scattering of lands in various other counties. Like the thrifty housewife she had become, Catherine took a keen interest in her estates and instituted a full survey of them upon her marriage to the king. Their extent, income and condition were matters in which she interested herself personally. 'We [are] not willing such unlawful demeanour be used in any [of] our said forest nor parks,' she wrote in the remains of a stern letter concerning wastage to one of her servants, 'and specially not within our said forest and park of Gillingham.' Reform your ways, she commanded, repair the damage and stop the decay and ruination of the forest, '[as we] desire you and also straitly demand you,' or suffer the consequences.[1] Catherine's conservation-conscious attitude had practical aspects for ruined forests made for ruined hunting, one of the ruling preoccupations of the Parrs and their contemporaries. Another ruling passion was gardens, particularly those at Greenwich and at her dower manors of Chelsea and Hanworth. At Chelsea, the queen planned a 'little garden' or privy garden for her own pleasure. For John Colman, head gardener at Chelsea, she authorized his hire of two women undergardeners and gave him sufficient funding for all things 'to be bought needful to be sown and bestowed in and upon the same garden.'[2] At Baynard's Castle, which became the London residence of Anne Parr and William Herbert, Catherine authorized payment to Morgan Lloyd, the gardener, 'for weeding and dressing of the garden there and other charges by him sustained about the same.'[3] Catherine also paid money from her own pocket for 'necessaries' for the gardens at Greenwich and Hanworth. Given the queen's interest in medicine, it is possible that these necessaries included plants such as borage which Catherine used in solution to relieve melancholy,[4] and other plants and herbs commonly used to treat various ailments. Apart from parks and forests and gardens, the queen's major concern in the first days of her marriage was the organization of her household.

The new queen's household was typical of most royal households of the sixteenth century in structure and composition.[5] It was an amalgam of four interrelated groups – the members of her family and close affinity who formed Catherine's innermost circle, the professional civil servants who had served in the establishments of Henry's former queens, the appointees who had been given places as favours to friends and relatives, and the servants from the queen's own former households. Professional civil servants Sir Thomas Arundell, Sir Philip Hoby and Sir Edmund Walsingham were appointed the queen's chancellor and auditor, her receiver for foreign receipts, and her vice-chamberlain. Wymond Carew,[6] and later John Coke, was made the queen's treasurer and receiver-general, and Sir Robert Tyrwhit, originally the queen's master of the horse, later became her comptroller. Apart from her uncle and newly appointed chamberlain, Lord Parr of Horton, these men were the chief officers of her household, professionals in court service, seeking and getting political appointments in the new royal establishment. Together with her secretary, Walter Bucler, her legal councillors, Francis Goldsmith and 'Mr. Neville', possibly a relative of the late Lord Latimer's, and her almoner, Dr. Day, Bishop of Chichester, they formed her household council.[7]

Under these men were others such as Sir Edward Baynton, first lord of the queen's bedchamber, who had been vice-chamberlain to his sister-in-law, Anne Boleyn, and who had also served in Katherine Howard's household. By his very presence, he must have raised unpleasant reminders of the past for the new queen. Sir Robert Tyrwhit, on the other hand, the new master of the queen's horse and later her comptroller, was a distant cousin and he and his wife, Elizabeth, became Catherine's close friends. Richard Dauncey transferred service from the king's household to the queen's. John Thynne and William Sharington, both to have well-known careers, secured appointments as men of Catherine's household.[8] John Bassett, the queen's new surveyor-general, and his sister, Anne Bassett, one of her maids-in-waiting, were court professionals and close friends of Anne Herbert's, having served with her in the household of Katherine Howard. From her ill-fated predecessor, Catherine inherited jewels, servants, lands, furniture and the constant reminder of her delicate position. One exotic in the queen's new household with strong ties to Dublin was Elizabeth Garrett, born Elizabeth Fitzgerald, a kinswoman of the Irish Fitzgeralds, particularly of Lady Elizabeth Fitzgerald, the teen-aged bride of Sir Anthony Browne and granddaughter of Thomas Grey, Marquis of Dorset.[9] Elizabeth Garrett became the particular friend of Catherine's stepdaughter, Margaret Neville.[10]

At the bottom of the household structure, down among the butchers and the bakers and the candlestick makers, the launderers, scullery workers and grooms of the stables, there was a continuity of employment from queen's household to queen's household. To this more or less entrenched *domus providencie* or working commissariat, supervised by professional court servants and capped by political appointees, the new queen added her own substructure of well-wishers. Her uncle, soon to become Lord Parr of Horton, was appointed her chamberlain although he was really too old and infirm to ever be more than an honourary one.[11] A place was found for the late Lord Latimer's brother, Marmaduke Neville, for Catherine's ubiquitous and chronically impoverished Throckmorton cousins – Nicholas, Clement, George and Kenelm – as well as for David Seymour, son-in-law of Catherine's first cousin, Elizabeth Parr of Horton. Other cousins, Armyll Green and Adam Lane, became, respectively, a yeoman of the chamber and sumpterman. Catherine's brother-in-law, William Herbert, probably nominated George Herbert, Henry Jones and John Lygon to their positions as gentlemen waiters, and Henry Seymour, the brother of Catherine's former lover, Sir Thomas Seymour, was appointed her carver.[12]

A variety of place-seekers with old ties to the new queen sought and found employment. Of Catherine's gentlewomen, Elizabeth Bellingham, wife of Cuthbert Hutton, belonged to a family closely associated with the Parrs for centuries in Kendal, and Elisabeth Brooke was the niece of Sir Thomas Wyatt and quickly became William Parr's paramour. Anne Blechingham (also written 'Blechington') was another of the queen's conspicuous well-wishers and gentlewomen, as was Mistress Syllyard, a kinswoman of William Parr's friend, Sir John Syllyard. Among Catherine's chamberers were the daughter of Lord Parr of Horton's bailiff of Rothwell, Edward Osborne, and Mary Woodhull (spelled 'Odell' in contemporary records), the daughter of Elizabeth Parr, the queen's first cousin. Among her maids was a relative of Dr. Huicke's, the stepsister of John Dudley, Lord Lisle, Sir Anthony Browne's daughter, a Guildford, a Carew, and a Windsor. Mistress Stoner of that ancient Yorkshire clan, a relative of Lady Hoby's, became mistress of the maids.[13]

Sir Anthony Cope, long-time friend of the Parr family, was made master of the queen's hawks and rose to become her vice-chamberlain. William Kynyatt, third husband of Catherine's cousin, the dowager Lady Strickland of Sizergh, was appointed the queen's vice-auditor. Radcliffes, Lees, and Aglionbys of Cumberland,[14] all kinsmen of the new queen, managed to find place or patronage while such household members as Catherine's stepdaughter, Margaret Neville, Dorothy Fountain, Margaret's maid,[15] Nicholas Pygot,[16] John Broughton and William Parkington came with the former Lady Latimer from her Yorkshire household at Snape.[17] Another addition from Yorkshire was Dr. Thomas Layton, employed as one of the queen's chaplains.[18] The obvious advantage of this core affinity within the household was that the queen maintained servants who were reliably loyal because they depended solely on her for employment and preferment. They would also be useful as eyes and ears among the household at large which undoubtedly contained those who might not be as loyal or as reliable. If there was any friction between the Yorkshiremen and the civil servants in the queen's employment, no record of it has survived.

In ever expanding circles, other would-be place-seekers brought pressure for admittance to the new royal establishment. Friends of Catherine's brother, William, pressed him to place relatives looking for preferment in his sister's service. Sir Richard Manners, who became keeper of the queen's manor of Fotheringhay, was kinsman to William's friend, the Earl of Rutland, while William Savage, who became a groom of the chamber, was probably a kinsman of Anne Savage, the wife of Parr's close friend, Thomas, Lord Berkeley. One of Catherine's chaplains, a Mr. Reynolds, may have been the same Thomas Reynolds who served Parr in the north earlier in the year.[19]

Besides the affinities of relatives and distant Cumbrian kin, the new queen's household found places for poor relations from Northamptonshire as well. Mary Woodhull, who had served Maud Parr and was one of a family of poor cousins descended from Catherine's uncle Parr of Horton, maintained the tradition of service to the Parrs by becoming one of Catherine's most trusted chamberers.[20] It was Mary Woodhull whom Catherine sometimes chose to share her bed when she was lonely or in need of company and it was Mary Woodhull who felt Catherine's unborn baby move for the first time when she became pregnant by Thomas Seymour late in 1547. Margaret Paye, another chamber servant like Mary Woodhull, must surely have been related to Maud Parr's servant, Clemence Paye. The Payes belonged to the tradition of gentry feudalism,[21] a tradition which tied together over time those families who had served the Parrs or the Fitzhughs or Catherine's mother's family, the Greens, for generations. It was the continuity of this inner community of family servants and retainers that Catherine brought with her that made the myriad of houses she was to live in over the next five years seem more welcoming and protective.[22]

In addition to her inner affinity, Catherine also trusted and depended on her secretary, Walter Bucler; her personal physician, Dr. Robert Huicke;[23] and the clerk of her closet, William Harper, who in fact handled most of her daily secretarial work.[24] Harper came from Axbridge in Somerset and was a fellow of New College, Oxford. Since 1526, he had been vicar of Writtle in Essex, where William, Lord Parr, was chief steward and receiver, which is probably how Harper came to Catherine's notice. Harper functioned as the queen's jack of all trades. He was her acting secretary, oversaw the washing of the closet linen, ordered books for her, organized luggage carts for the removal of the royal boxes from residence to residence, ordered flowers for her closet, and saw to the mending of the clerical vestments. Harper consequently was on particularly close terms with his mistress. He was also religiously conservative yet Catherine kept him as a functionary of one of the most intimate aspects of her chamber. This liberality of employment which occasionally included those whose religious views differed markedly from hers continued to the end of Catherine's life.

There were many ways that the members of the queen's household could enrich themselves and some did very well indeed. In the counting house sector of Catherine's establishment was a coterie of clerks, receivers and stewards who collected the queen's rents on her 139 manors and the lands she held in 23 shires, saw to the care of her properties and kept tabs on her tenants. They participated in periodic audits, such as the one for household expenses held on 28 March 1545, 'in Kellates' house at Westminster'.[25] Kellate's wife baked the queen's bread. Members of the household might also on occasion be called upon to perform other duties than those habitually assigned to them. Robert Warner, receiver for the queen's estates in Northamptonshire and Huntingtonshire, was seconded in 1544 to the role of messenger between the king in France and the queen and her regency council in England.[26] Walter Bucler, her secretary, became a discrete ambassador to the Protestant princes of Germany during the winter of 1544–45.[27] These men submitted their accounts to the queen's auditor, technically Sir Thomas Arundell. In fact, however, the accounting was done under the supervision of an assistant, first William Kynyatt and, after December 1544, Anthony Bourchier.

Anthony Bourchier, the son of Maurice Bourchier of Berkeley in Gloucestershire, probably owed his appointment to a family connection with William, Lord Parr's close friend, Lord Berkeley. The new vice-auditor soon found himself besieged by petitions for preferment and offers of substantial rewards if he would use the influence of his office to grant them.[28] John Walsh of Somerset begged preferment for his under-employed son, George, 'to give him occasion to avoid idleness.' William Boys asked Bourchier to take his son, Thomas, into his service, offering rewards for this favour – 'I will conclude with you for the premises if you be reasonable.' A widow, Joan Beak, petitioned Bourchier to find her son a place in his service as a clerk. John Capelyn, auditor for Lostwithiel, desired help with a delinquent fee. Giles Forster wanted a discharge of debt. Walter Compton wanted preference for the paling of New Park in the lordship of Berkeley. William Sheldon of London wanted to buy the reversion of Shraveley manor in Worcestershire. Even Bourchier's own family badgered him with unending requests. His father wanted preferment for friends and relatives. His brother, John, wanted a special grant of land, a wardship, trees from the royal forest, venison for the celebration of his wedding supper.

Inundated with such pleas and petitions, Bourchier was blunt about the sale of offices and influence. To Giles Forester, he wrote that he would have the debt discharged for the price of a fine gelding. No doubt he was equally frank with the rest of his petitioners, and the system worked. Forster sent Bourchier not only the best gelding he had but the venison off half a buck as well.[29] Notes scribbled by Bourchier in the spring of 1545 itemize the numerous *doucements* which merchants, solicitors, tradesmen and even various members of the queen's own household, such as Wymond Carew and Clement Throckmorton, had paid him for a variety of favours.[30]

A household official did not need to work in the counting house, however, to find himself with influence to peddle and opportunities for patronage that he could turn into saleable commodities. Clement Throckmorton, whose only source of income seems to have come from his office as cupbearer for the queen which he received in 1543, was doing so well by July 1545, just two years later, that he could afford to pay £654 for a grant of lands in Warwickshire and Worcestershire.[31] This was a large sum for a man in Throckmorton's position and simply reinforces the impression that contemporary records give, that the queen took care of her own.

Catherine Parr's generosity with the members of her household seems to have reached down to the lowest levels – to Walter Erle of the squillery and woodyard, to Thomas Beck, page, to Amyas Hill and William Parkinson, yeomen of the queen's chamber, to Giles Bateson, footman, to Henry Webbe and Laurence Lee, gentlemen ushers of the queen's chamber. Catherine even undertook to write to the king while he was in France on behalf of one of her maid's pages who had committed theft and for another poor petitioner, one 'Archer's wife'.[32] These household employees in turn used the queen's patronage to provide themselves with a consequence that they could market to a lower level of society, their own clients and petitioners.

The descent of grace and favour filtering down the ranks is apparent in the career of Anthony Bourchier, whose family connections secured him his office in the first place. Bourchier family influence was then responsible for finding a position for Henry Webbe as yeoman usher of the queen's chamber, even though Webbe actually preceded Bourchier, himself, into the queen's household.[33] Webbe, too, prospered at Catherine's hands and in April 1546 secured the position of yeoman waiter in the Tower for his client, William Slack. Slack, no doubt, had clients of his own. Each man bought and sold places within his control right on down to the bottom of the grace and favour ladder. Like all royal households, Catherine Parr's establishment was a marketplace, avid for grant and reward, preferment and favour, sensitive to shifts of popularity and dangerous alliances and liaisons, knowledgeable about which cliques and which individuals were worth cultivating or best left alone.

Within the queen's household, in addition to the officers of the counting house and the *domus providencie*, was the reginal equivalent of the regnal *domus magnificencie*, the aristocratic heart of Catherine's retinue. The queen's closest female confidant and constant companion was her younger sister, Anne Herbert.[34] Margaret Neville, Catherine's stepdaughter, and Lucy Somerset, the wife of Catherine's stepson, John Neville, 4th Lord Latimer, were also close companions. Others in Catherine's innermost circle of ladies-in-waiting were the widowed Maud, Lady Lane, Catherine's first cousin and childhood playmate; Elizabeth Oxenbridge, Lady Tyrwhit, the wife of Sir Robert Tyrwhit whose great-aunt Agnes Tyrwhit had been Catherine's first mother-in-law; and Mary Wotton, Lady Carew, a veteran at court and an old acquaintance of Catherine's own mother, Maud. Lady Carew (b.1500), was the widow of Sir Henry Guildford and the aunt of Jane Guildford, Lady Lisle. Her second husband, Sir Gawain Carew, a captain in the navy, was a member of the populous Carew clan of Devon which managed to place in the new queen's household several of their number, including Wymond Carew, Catherine's treasurer. It was Lady Carew, together with Anne Herbert, whom Catherine chose to assist her in donning linen aprons for her first Maundy Thursday ritual before Easter 1544,[35] where she was expected to show Christian humility by washing the feet of a group of poor women. This ritual was an example of both religious and social imperatives that demanded the performance of public charitable acts by women in general and queens in particular.[36] These four then – Ladies Herbert, Lane, Tyrwhit and Carew – were Catherine's closest friends. There was gossip at court that the king was annoyed by the lack of physical attractions among Catherine's ladies. In plain words, he thought them a pack of crows, a reference not only to their looks but to the black double jean velvet that was the daily uniform of her gentlewomen.[37] But Catherine, besides having a lifetime's commitment to the women closest to her, was shrewd enough to know that any queen of Henry's who cultivated lovely ladies in her household ran a grave risk of cultivating her own successor.

Another woman who soon became an intimate of the new queen's was Katherine Willoughby, Duchess of Suffolk. The duchess was six years younger than the queen but they had much in common. The daughter of Maria de Salinas, who like Catherine's mother had been a lady-in-waiting to Catherine of Aragon, the Duchess of Suffolk's father had been a considerable landowner in the north and had left his only child and heir an extensive patrimony based on the Willoughby de Eresby lands in Lincolnshire. Katherine Willoughby's wardship had been bought by Charles Brandon, Duke of Suffolk, for his son and heir, but usurping the expectations of the sickly boy who died a year later, the elderly, thrice-married duke wed the fourteen-year-old girl himself. Katherine Willoughby had the same hard-headed yet passionate temperament as the queen and when her considerably older husband died in 1545, she fell deeply in love with Richard Bertie, her master of the horse, and married him some years later. Their romantic natures, however, were not the only things that bound these two women together. They both had a lively sense of humour and a strong streak of no nonsense practicality, but their strongest tie was their mutual commitment to the new religion.

This commitment was shared by the extended circle of the queen's court-within-a-court, whose members included Jane Guildford, wife of John Dudley, Lord Lisle; Joan Champernowne, wife of Sir Anthony Denny, known for her looks and her learning; Anne Sapcote, wife of Sir William Fitzwilliam and granddaughter of Sir Nicholas Vaux; Lady Anne Grey, wife of Sir Edmund Walsingham; Mary Arundell, wife of Henry Fitzalan, Earl of Arundel; Elizabeth Stoner, wife of Sir Philip Hoby; Anne Calthorp,[38] wife of Henry Radcliffe, Earl of Sussex; and Anne Stanhope, wife of Edward Seymour, Earl of Hertford. Yet it was not only religion but a commitment to education, too, which cemented the bonds between these women. The fashion for educating the daughters as well as the sons in upper-class households, begun when Catherine was a child, continued throughout her lifetime. The precedent-setting educations of the royal Tudor princesses encouraged a century-long trend. Within the queen's circle were such intellectuals as Lady Denny and Mary, Countess of Arundel, who had translated the writings of Emperor Severus.

To the Tudor mind, education and religion were inextricably linked. Christian humanism early in the century, within the parameters of the Roman Catholic church, had allowed a place for education in the lives of upper-class women inside the private world of their own households. With the king's break from Rome and the beginning of England's Protestant Reformation, this allowed place for female education became a necessity. In order to fulfil the spiritual requirements laid down for communicants of the new religious order, a constant reading of the Scriptures was essential. Religious literature, heretofore beyond the access of most women as it was published in languages in which they were untrained, began appearing in the vernacular and offered a religious 'library' of reading material incumbent upon them as communicants in the new English Church to study. Literacy became essential for proper religious devotion and as such, an aim of the new religion evangelicals at court. During her reign, Catherine Parr was the active centre of these efforts. Piety and literacy became conjoined, interactive elements of a new vision of faith with unforeseen consequences for the future social order. Women, however, were still expected to practice both inside their own households and were actively discouraged from becoming practitioners within a public sphere.[39] Yet having been given an ell, some like the queen, herself, were now preparing to take a mile.

By supporting this trend toward education among her ladies, Catherine's influence on the intellectual accomplishments of a number of leading lights of the next generation was assured. Jane Guildford's daughters by her husband, John Dudley, Lord Lisle (later the Duke of Northumberland), received a thorough education. Their daughter, Mary Dudley, became particularly well known, both for her own intellectual achievements and as the mother of the poets, Sir Philip and Lady Mary Sidney. Anne Stanhope's six daughters by Edward Seymour, Earl of Hertford, were equally well educated, the three eldest – Anne, Margaret and Jane – eventually publishing their own verses on the death of Marguerite of Navarre. The five daughters of Sir Anthony Cooke of Gidea Hall, Essex, Catherine's cousins, became paradigms of female intellectual achievement. In 1548, the same year the queen's great project, the translation of Erasmus' *Paraphrases*, was published, her cousin Anne Cooke at twenty published an English translation of five sermons by the Italian Calvinist Bernardino Occhino, a particular Parr favourite.[40] Catherine Parr's own daughter-in-law, Lucy, Lady Latimer, left a bequest in her will 'of all my books'.[41] Susan Bertie, the future Countess of Kent and daughter of the Duchess of Suffolk by her second husband, was set to learning early and became a patron and scholar during the reign of Elizabeth I. It was a corollary both of the new religion and of the new attitudes of the age that a woman need not forfeit her true place in God's universal pattern by receiving an education. Indeed, she might profit from it, using it to clarify the tenets of her faith in her own thoughts and so help pass orthodoxy on to her children. The glue that bound this inner circle around the queen together was a combination of blood ties, self-advancement, an interest in scholarly pursuits and a missionary zeal to define and disseminate the tenets of the new religion. Patronage of those involved in such pursuits, as well as those who formed the artistic matrix of the rapidly maturing English Renaissance, became an important aspect of the queen's life and an active factor in her household as well.

All three of the children of Sir Thomas Parr were conspicuous patrons of the arts during their time at court. In music, William Parr was the most outstanding patron. As a child, he studied singing and the virginals under William Saunders with his schoolfellow, the Duke of Richmond, during his years in Richmond's household at Sheriff Hutton. This love of music continued into his adult life. In 1553, as Marquis of Northampton, Parr paid £10 10s to Mr. Bytton 'for a pair of royalls with virgenalles with a reward to his men for setting them up'.[42] In a small, extant fragment of the Northamptons' household bookkeeping, the importance of music is very apparent. During the first few months of 1553, entries appear for:

10 March: to my lord Westmorland's singing men: 20s
03 May: to my lord Admiral's musicians: 20s

In December 1541, Northampton, then Lord Parr, had become enough of a fixture at court to take under his patronage a group of foreign musicians who served at the English court, primarily the five brothers Bassano from Venice.[43] On 19 December, a warrant for the Christmas wearing apparel of six minstrels was passed on by Sir Brian Tuke, treasurer of the chamber, to Lord Parr. There followed numerous bills and warrants during the succeeding year which were diverted by Tuke to Parr, all dealing with the court musicians:

2 February 1542, a licence for the brethren minstrels (the five Bassano brothers: Alvise, Anthony, Jasper, John, John Baptist) to bring in 300 tuns of wine.
16 April 1542, a lease of the manor of Fiddington in the county of Gloucester for Mark Anthony (the king's musician).
21 September 1542, a passport for Jasper Bassano, musician, his horse and £20 in ready money.
18 October 1542, a warrant to deliver to Mark Anthony, Anthony Simon Nicholas Andrew, Piligryne Simon, Anthony Mary, William de Troches, William du Vaiet, Peter John (or Petit John), Nicholas Puvall, John Pettrey, Hans Garrett and Bonntannce (John Bontempe), the king's minstrels, £40 by way of reward.
18 October 1542, a warrant to pay monthly to Alexander Penax Demislader (the king's drummer), 12d by the day from the last day of August last past.
12 November 1542, a warrant to deliver to Alvise, Jasper, Anthony, John, and John Baptista Bassano, musicians to the king, the sum of £20 by way of reward.[44]

Whether Parr actually held some official sinecure connected with the court musicians or undertook an unofficial patronage is unclear. His care and concern for them was interrupted during the spring of 1543 when he took up his duties in the north as Lord Warden of the Marches, but upon his sister's marriage to the king, he passed the patronage of the brothers Bassano on to her.[45] The new queen took them into her household and so the link between the Parrs and the Venetian court musicians continued.

A court musician could and did provide more services than just playing a musical instrument. Foreign musicians such as the Bassanos, who lived in England but still held property in Venice, naturally spoke several languages and had occasion to travel to the Continent. During the reign of Queen Elizabeth, the Crown made frequent use of them as spies[46] and it is not too great a stretch to suppose that the same held true in the 1540s.

Jasper Bassano, traveling on business to Venice in September 1542, was in a very good position to gather news along the way. So in 1546 was Mark Anthony Petala, 'one of your Majesty's sackbuts, repairing into Italy to visit his friends', for whom William Parr secured a letter of commendation.

It was not just the foreign musicians who could be used as tools in court politics. Catherine Parr's servant, Walter Erle, is a case in point. Erle began his career as a page of the chamber to Anne of Cleves and progressed to an office in the squillery and wood yard of the king's household. He subsequently found favour in the household of Catherine Parr. The key to this favour may lie not only in his apparent discretion in matters relating to the queen's private affairs but also in his great skill on the virginals. Erle progressed rapidly from the king's squillery. Within four months of Catherine's marriage to Henry VIII, he had received from the queen the office of bailiff and hayward of the manor of Collaton in Devon and the keeping of Colcomb park with attendant fees. On 1 July 1545, the grant was turned into a forty-year lease of the manor and park, and on 1 July 1546, the lease was re-granted to Erle rent free. This adept royal servant appears frequently in chamber records receiving gifts, some 'at the queen's suit', and Catherine even helped to arrange Erle's marriage with his cousin. Erle functioned as both groom of the queen's privy chamber and as her musician on the virginals. After Henry VIII's death, he carried letters between Catherine and Sir Thomas Seymour and was a party to their romantic conspiracy. Seymour refers in one letter to 'my old friend, Walter Erle', as the chief messenger between himself and the queen. After Catherine's marriage to the lord of Sudeley became public, Erle went briefly into Seymour's household, and he knew some uneasy moments during Seymour's attainder and trial for treason. He soon found his feet again after Seymour's execution, and entered the household of Edward VI as a groom of the privy chamber. Erle continued to add to his holdings in Devon, was promoted to gentleman of the privy chamber under Queen Mary, and died in the early years of Elizabeth I's reign as the venerable 'Master Walter Erle', the queen's official player on the virginals. His place at court was filled only 'after a prolonged gap' by Orlando Gibbons, which gives some indication of the level of musical ability that Erle had achieved.

If William Parr's passion was for music, Catherine Parr's artistic obsession was with painting. At her death in 1548, Catherine left behind a legacy of numerous portraits, both paintings *en large* and miniatures.[47] Her chamber accounts show payments made for portraits to John Bettes, Margaret Horenboult, and Giles Gering,[49] who carved the queen's portrait as a cameo from a portrait miniature by Bettes. Unlikely though it seems given the quality of the likeness, William Scrots has traditionally been considered the best candidate to have painted the half-length portrait of the queen, and one 'Master John' is credited with the full-length portrait, both now in the National Portrait Gallery. Among the last work that Holbein designed before his death in 1543 were two covered cups for the queen and a brooch with a maiden's head dressed in the latest Tudor fashion which may have been intended as a small royal portrait in gold. Catherine's sister, Anne, Countess of Pembroke, was the patron of miniaturist Levina Teerlinc and thus it seems very likely that the queen would have been painted by Teerlinc as well. William Parr, captain of the gentleman pensioners, even found a place for Levina's husband, George Teerlinc, in that exclusive band.[50] The queen's passion for portraits is well documented as is her fashion for giving portrait miniatures as gifts to close friends. The Duchess of Suffolk, the Duke of Somerset, Edward VI, Sir Thomas Seymour, the Earl and Countess of Pembroke[51] and almost certainly Catherine's brother, the Marquis of Northampton, were all in possession of portraits of her. 'A picture of Queen Katherine, that last died, in a box' is recorded at Westminster Palace in 1553, stored, together with two other portraits, one of the Duchess of Suffolk and one of Italian hero Andrea Doria, 'within a coffer of murrey [dark red] velvet, plated with copper'.[52] Sometime after Henry's death, the full-length panel portrait of her (NPG 4451) was given to her cousin and lady-in-waiting, Maud, Lady Lane.

One reason, apart from this passion for art, which may have impelled Catherine to order so many portraits of herself as queen was the no doubt profoundly irritating custom of the king to have new portraits of the royal family include not his present wife but his former one. The great mural at Whitehall, begun by Holbein in 1537 but copied a number of times in later years by different artists, depicts Henry VII, Henry VIII, Elizabeth of York and Jane Seymour as the founding parents of the Tudor dynasty. Two other portraits painted while Catherine was queen and undoubtedly representative of a whole genre of portrait painting show Henry, Jane and the young Prince of Wales as the secular (and politically correct) embodiment of the Holy Family, with the princesses Mary and Elizabeth outside the inner sanctum, flanking the central trio like petitioning virgin saints.[53] This insistence throughout the final years of Henry life on the late, great Jane Seymour as mother of his heir and thus his true queen must have been deeply annoying to his current one. A multitude of portraits insisting on her rightful royal place at Henry's side was one way in which the living queen could tactfully and wordlessly combat the pervasive cult of Janeolotry outside the framework of Henry's own beliefs. Giving Henry a second, living son would have been the only way for Catherine to supplant Jane within that framework.

Besides Catherine Parr's passion for painting and William Parr's passion for music, the Parrs shared an interest in the advancement of printing and bookbinding that flowered in the sixteenth century. This, of course, was a corollary of their desire to spread the Word of God, but the results for the nascent English book industry were great. As queen, Catherine helped to advance the careers of publishers of reformed religious literature, such as Richard Grafton and Edward

Whitchurch. She took an aesthetic as well as a spiritual interest in their products. She ordered books bound in stamped and gilded leather, in a variety of coloured velvets, garnished with silver, with gilt, with enameling, and with precious stones. Her copy of the works of Petrarch had her arms and quarterings 'richly worked on its sides, highly embossed upon velvet.'[54] Catherine patronised the printer, Thomas Berthelet, by giving him her own works to print, ordering lavishly bound presentation copies for family and friends. As queen, she was also interested in the 'lymmyng and ingrossing' of her patents. The limning or the drawing of small images of the monarch on formal patents represented the early stages of English miniature painting. In one instance the responsibility for limning one of Catherine's patents was given to George Haydon, clerk to the council for the duchy of Lancaster. The order to him for the work appears in Catherine's chamber accounts and this combined with her interest in bookbinding and portraiture leads Erna Auerbach to conclude that 'Henry VIII's last Queen thus seems to earn the right to be included in the list of royal patrons: and we may surmise that the high artistic standard in document portraiture and related arts reached in the last period of Henry VIII is due not only to his but also to her patronage.'[55]

Catherine Parr and her brother, William, were the subjects of numerous book dedications. John Leland included an encomium to the queen's virtue in the dedication of his *Itinerary* in 1546, and Sir Anthony Cope and Nicholas Udall both dedicated works to her. Sir Thomas Hoby dedicated his English translation of the *Tragedie of Free Will* to William Parr in 1550. Catherine's sister, Anne Herbert, was also a well-educated woman, the patron of miniature painter Levina Teerlinc, and of Cambridge scholars John Pindar and Reginald Middleton. She may also have been the subject of one of Holbein's most expressive drawings, executed during the period that Anne served as a gentlewoman of the queen's privy chamber.[56] She commissioned several portraits of herself, one of which hung in Baynard's Castle in 1561.[57] Anne was, too, a friend and correspondent of Roger Ascham, and she had a book, entitled *The Vanitee of the World*, dedicated to her. Written by William Thomas, a scholar of Italian and clerk of the council, it was published by Thomas Berthelet in 1549. Anne Herbert excelled, wrote William Thomas, 'in vertue and bountee ... as the daimond amongst the jewells.'[58]

From 1541 to 1571, the Parr family acted as patrons for nearly every aspect of the artistic Renaissance in England. Catherine, as queen, and William, first as the Earl of Essex and then as Marquis of Northampton, both maintained companies of players, and Nicholas Udall wrote plays for the queen's players to perform.[59] In the graphic arts, besides paintings and miniatures, Northampton commissioned Stephen van Herwijck to cast two silver medallions of himself and his second wife, Elisabeth Brooke, in 1562. In architecture, the marquess may never have been impelled to put up a stately home, but he built additions to homes he held at Stansted Hall and Nymph's Green in Essex. Anne and William Herbert's contributions to architecture during Catherine's lifetime consisted of the upkeep of Baynard's Castle, property of the queen, who turned it over to her sister and brother-in-law to use as a London residence. With the fall of the Duke of Somerset and Herbert's elevation to the peerage, as partial payment for his support of the Duke of Northumberland's coup, Anne and William had at last an income that they could use to indulge their architectural ambitions. These resulted in the creation of the glories of Wilton House (completed after Anne's death) and in a £600 facelift for Baynard's Castle.[60]

Catherine Parr's own interest in architecture and the property that supported it may be deduced not only from the grandeur of the new apartments she commissioned for herself at Hampton Court but also from the fact that during the years of her reign, the royal acquisition of lands and manors nearly doubled from its 1535 level.[61] A design for the interior of a room, calculated as at least fifteen feet high and thus probably a public reception room, has survived. It features the queen's maiden's head badge superimposed on a Tudor rose in a complex and highly sophisticated pattern of animals, grotesques and mythological antiques. Simon Thurley has noted that: 'Its affinities with the Galerie Francois Ier at Fontainebleau suggests that the drawing could be connected with decorative work undertaken by French craftsmen at Whitehall in the 1540s.'[62] A second group of architectural fragments connected with Catherine Parr are six painted panels, now at Loseley Park near Guildford in Surrey, which carry designs incorporating the royal motto, 'Dieu et mon droit', the Prince of Wales' feathers and Catherine Parr's initials. The curious thing about the delineation of these initials is that they have been painted precisely as Catherine, herself, signed them on all extant documents. This would tend to the conclusion that she personally oversaw the decoration of the panels herself.[63] As a number of architectural elements including an elaborate mantel and overmantel from Nonesuch ended up at Loseley after the destruction of the royal palace in the seventeenth century, it might be conjectured that this was the original location of the panels.

The list of artists and artisans patronized by one or the other of the Parrs between 1541 and 1571 reads more or less like a catalogue of seminal names in the early English Renaissance – Holbein, Horenboult, Terlinc, Scrots, Gering, Udall, Berthelet, Richardson, Hans of Antwerp, Stephen van Herwijck, Leland, Ascham, not to mention the significant group of scholars, teachers and divines which Catherine befriended and helped to preferment during her time as queen. This legacy of artistic and scholastic patronage by the Parrs, first inculcated in her children in their schoolroom at Rye House by that extraordinary woman, Maud, Lady Parr, was carried forward into the seventeenth century by the children, grandchildren, and great-grandchildren of Anne Parr – the earls of Pembroke.

Regent-General of England

Of the three turbulent titans who ruled most of Europe during the first half of the sixteenth century, Henry VIII, Francois I and Charles V, the latter two had in 1539 taken advantage of the English king's schism with the papacy to set aside their normal attitudes of mutual hostility and consider a joint military strike against England. Such a move was effectively countered by Cromwell's policy of rapprochement with the German Protestants of the Schmalkaldic League which culminated in Henry's marriage to Anne of Cleves in 1540. Masterminded by Cromwell and instrument of his downfall, this royal marriage was meant to be the cornerstone of an alliance made to balance the combined forces of France and the Empire. The possible political and religious ramifications of Henry's 'Protestant' policy had led to an uneasy and purely temporary truce between the French king and the Hapsburg emperor, but with the dissolution of Henry's marriage, they returned to their normal attitudes of mutual aggression. Henry had actively been seeking closer ties with the emperor since late 1541, and had wanted to join the continental brangle on the side of Charles in 1542. By 1542 also, Francois was seven years behind in payment to Henry of the French pension stipulated by earlier war indemnities, a point the English king was unlikely to overlook. Marital difficulties and affairs in Scotland had forced Henry to postpone his efforts on the continent but he signed a secret treaty with the emperor on 11 February 1543. Charles' scruples about allying himself with the schismatic English king were offset by the scandal of Francois I's alliance with the Turks. While Henry was making plans to join Charles in a continental campaign against France in the summer of 1543, trouble with France's traditional ally, Scotland, took centre stage.

For some time, Henry had been determined to subjugate his nephew, James V of Scotland, force reform upon him and bring both king and country under English control. Henry had adopted a highhanded attitude toward the Scottish king, and after a series of abortive efforts to bring James to the bargaining table, had demanded that his nephew meet with English commissioners at York in December 1542 to negotiate a treaty of mutual friendship – or else. Henry's demands were anything but friendly and the probability of military action against Scotland became a certainty when, not surprisingly, James refused to cross the border. Henry ordered the Duke of Norfolk on a six-day devastation raid into Scotland, hoping by such shock treatment to bring James to Henry's definition of reason. What it brought was the Battle of Solway Moss on 23 November 1542, in which England defeated the Scottish army and produced the death (reputedly of grief) of the Scottish king. On 1 July 1543, just eleven days before his marriage to Catherine Parr, Henry VIII signed a peace treaty with Scotland at Greenwich which, despite the king's boasts, did not end the friction between the two nations nor lead to the deliverance into his hands of James' infant daughter and heir, Mary, Queen of Scots.

The following year, just prior to his departure for France, the king turned his attention to James' half-sister, Lady Margaret Douglas, using her not-unwilling hand in marriage as a bargaining counter to secure what he hoped would be a powerful ally in his quest for dominance over Scotland. Henry's twenty-nine-year-old niece, now aunt to the Scottish queen, was a high-spirited and romantic girl who had led a high-spirited and romantic life. Seized as a child from her mother, Henry VIII's sister and the dowager Queen of Scotland, Lady Margaret was taken by her father, the Earl of Angus, into exile in France when she was no more than six years old. At the age of thirteen, having returned to Scotland with her father's changing fortunes, she was sent by Angus again into exile for safety, this time into England. Once at the English court, Lady Margaret followed a headstrong and dangerous course. Twice secretly and imprudently engaged to members of the Howard clan, one Anne Boleyn's uncle and the other Katherine Howard's brother, both engagements had ended in disaster when Henry found out about them. One fiancé, Lord Thomas Howard, had languished in the Tower until his demise and Margaret, herself, had spent several years in and out of favour and in and out of house arrest. In October 1538, while Margaret was temporarily between fiancés, Henry had tried to use her as a marriage pawn in one of his complicated European diplomatic strategies. Nothing had come of it, however, and by the time that the king married Catherine Parr, Margaret was still a rather unhappy, very unmarried maiden.

Catherine befriended Margaret, who was an intimate of the Princess Mary's, and made her a familiar in her household. When Margaret was in residence at her manor of Stepney, the queen was a frequent guest.[1] By the spring of 1544, Margaret's marriage had become a factor in the campaign that Henry was waging to secure Margaret's niece, Mary, Queen of Scots, in marriage for his son. He decided to use her as the carrot to entice some powerful Scottish lord to the English cause. The Scottish regent, the Earl of Arran, seemed to be in Henry's pocket after arresting the hitherto most powerful Anglophobe in Scotland, Cardinal Beaton, and signing the Greenwich treaty of July. Yet another Scottish ally would not come amiss, particularly in Henry's pet project of joining the baby queen with the child Prince of Wales in marriage. Where

Scotland's queen went, in Henry's opinion, her kingdom could be made to follow. In the event, the Scottish lord selected for promotion by marriage to Lady Margaret Douglas was Matthew Stewart, Earl of Lennox.

The Earl of Lennox, who had spent much of his youth in France, was, according to Chapuys, 'young and handsome'. He was also described as 'liker a woman than a man, for he was very lusty, beardless, and lady-faced'.[2] Tall, striking, with a quick temper and a small understanding, he appealed greatly to the romantic Margaret Douglas, who in this case at least, did not mind acting as her uncle's pawn. The descriptions of Lennox by his contemporaries are so nearly identical to ones made of Sir Thomas Seymour that it may be imagined without too much license that the queen found him attractive as well. Given her situation with regards to Seymour, Catherine could hardly help but sympathize with Margaret's several frustrated romances. On 29 June 1544, 'this morning at Mass, the King and Queen attending.'[3], Lady Margaret Douglas was married to the 'lusty, beardless' Earl of Lennox. Whatever the queen's role may have been in bringing about the marriage of Henry's frequently unmarried niece to the handsome Lennox, Catherine attended their wedding at St. James and grew ever closer to the earl's new countess.[4]

Cheered by the fall of Beaton and the acquisition of Lennox and having achieved what he was publicly promoting as a great victory over a traditional enemy by the treaty of Greenwich, Henry now turned to the other partner of the 'Auld Alliance' and his long-anticipated invasion of France. Vanity and a desire to reassert his self-perceived greatness in the European theatre of action spurred him on, as no doubt did the would-be gallants at court, untested in battle and eager to chase 'the bubble reputation even in the cannon's mouth.' But Henry had not been born a general. Despite commanding the largest expedition that England had organized since the glory days of Henry V,[5] the king launched a campaign in the summer of 1544 that 'was a muddle even by the generous standards of the times.'[6] It is easy to see that Henry felt a resurgence of youthful vigor as he planned his French invasion. Newly married, in the full flush of enthusiasm for his bride, feeling in better health than he had for a long time, the king was determined to clap on armour, hoist his considerable bulk onto horseback and ride victorious into France at the head of a conquering English army. Charles V had a more pragmatic and less optimistic view of Henry as a battlefield commander, especially after Henry's health suffered a sudden setback. The emperor did everything in his power to persuade the English king to send his troops by all means but to stay at home himself. Henry was not to be dissuaded. His bull-in-a-china-shop approach to the Scottish situation was followed by a stubborn determination to lead his troops into Paris.[7]

In the summer of 1513, during another campaign in France, Henry had left his wife, Catherine of Aragon, as regent of the realm. Now, thirty years later, Henry repeated this gesture of trust with his bride of barely a year and appointed her Regent-General of England during his absence. Although some at court may have felt that Catherine's function would be essentially to preside as a decorative figurehead over a regency council which made all actual decisions, she took the position and the appointment as a royal reiteration of her importance not only to the king but to the country as well. That she intended not merely to preside but to rule was made quite clear from the outset. The appointed regency council consisted of Archbishop Cranmer, Sir Thomas Wriothesley, Edward Seymour, Earl of Hertford, Thomas Thirlby, Bishop of Westminster, and Sir William Petre as clerk of council.[8] In a secondary memorandum, at the queen's request, her uncle Lord Parr of Horton was added to the council roster.[9] Two days after Catherine's commission as regent was signed, another commission was drawn up granting Catherine and any two of her councillors the right to disburse money from the royal treasury. With her uncle's vote assured and Cranmer and Hertford sympathetic, Catherine obtained functioning control of the council.

Where in 1513, Catherine of Aragon wrote letters concerned with Henry's health and lack of clean underwear, Catherine Parr tended to concentrate on money, transport, musters and supplies, with the occasional fulsome praise to God for Henry's success. Her approach to the regency put into practice those humanist dictums she had learned as a child – that man is meant to be an active not a contemplative creature and that power and wealth need not be evil if those possessing them use them to do good. What was new in the queen's application of these dictums was that she appeared to interpret 'man' generically and not as a definition of one specific gender. With her appointment as regent-general, Catherine had at last fulfilled the vision of herself she had cherished from childhood embodied in the image of St. Catherine of Alexandria in her father's *Horae ad Usum Sarum*. With a sword in one hand and a book in the other, a crown set on the flowing hair of maiden head, the head of her enemy at her feet and the broken wheel of her suffering behind her, she now embodied that old prophecy that her hands were ordained for sceptres. Her two contemporaries whom she most admired, Marguerite of Navarre and Mary of Hungary, had set the pattern for enlightened but dynamic female rule which Catherine now strove to emulate. The active way in which the queen undertook her duties was to have repercussions two years later, when religious conservatives anticipating another regency after the king's death, feared the queen's aggressive attitude toward the new religion and her tendency to give orders rather than to take them.

The general cultural opinion toward women as rulers, as expressed in the literature of the period, was that power placed in the hands of woman was power abused.[10] John Knox in his 1558 diatribe, *The first blast of the trumpet against the monstrous regiment of women*, was only a later extreme instance of a generally held belief. What made Catherine Parr's tenure as regent palatable to the more conservative at court was that it had been instituted by a king not given to abrogating crucial powers to females, that it was to be exercised under the guidance of an all-male regency council, and that it was intended to be an expediency of short duration. Yet even a regency of short duration such as Catherine's, let alone a rule of over four decades such as Elizabeth I's, could cause unease. The general condemnation of women rulers took its stance on a body of belief in women's basic inferiority, a belief bolstered by countless cautionary tales – biblical, folk and classical. Yet what was latent in these tales of such mythic figures as Eve was the unacknowledged subtext of power. God had created the world, hub of a cosmic order centred on Eden. Eve, formed from a human rib, possessing only those qualities with which God had endowed her, made a conscious choice to destroy that order, evincing a power, although denounced unequivocally as evil, far greater than her male counterpart's. The actions of a single woman, be she Eve, Guinevere, Delilah or Cleopatra, had in these tales the power to destroy the plans of kings and upset the stratagems of councils. The vain, beautiful and frivolous Helen brought to naught all the time-honoured might of Troy. Implicit in all these cautionary stories of destructive and damned women was a clear subtext of power and a fear of its being recognized and unleashed. 'Better to reign in Hell than serve in Heaven,' was a battle cry that the predominantly male architects of the sixteenth-century social order feared to hear from a woman's mouth.

During her tenure as regent Catherine signed five royal proclamations, mostly concerned with war-related matters such as French citizens resident in England, the pricing of armor, and the arrest and trial of military deserters, as well as a proclamation prohibiting persons exposed to the plague from appearing at court.[11] The variety of issues with which she had to deal during this time demonstrate a quick and decisive mind. When in July the Earl of Shrewsbury, Lord Lieutenant of the northern marches, complained that the Earl of Cumberland was hunting illegally and throwing down hedges, the queen responded sharply that, '[Shrewsbury] was to remind [Cumberland] how unmeet a time this is for such things, the King being out of the realm.'[12] Shrewsbury was commanded in no uncertain terms to bring his fellow earl to heel. Two months later, in September, the queen was dealing with a band of gypsies in Huntingdon, two of whom had offered to pay £300 for a pardon for a robbery conviction. She felt that since 'it would be hard to attain this money otherwise', the pardons should be granted. A few days later, she informed the king that, 'divers aged and impotent French nationals' resident in England and threatened with deportation were requesting toleration, as discrimination against them was so strong that they 'are like to perish in the street'. 'We are,' Catherine wrote shortly, 'wearied of their continual clamour.'[13] Henry answered that the gypsies should be allowed to purchase their pardon and the French nationals placated.[14] The result of Catherine's intercession was the royal proclamation of 30 September permitting French nationals to remain unmolested in England.[15]

On 28 September, the English fishing industry took centre stage when the queen reported of the 'annoyance' done to fishermen in 'the time of the taking of herrings' by certain Scottish and French ships of war.[16] This attack on an important source of food in the English diet was a matter of immediate concern. Dealing daily with such a wide variety of problems and issues on a competent basis, as the queen so demonstrably managed to do, required a keen wit and a quickness of perception and understanding. Yet amid such devotion to duty, amid hard-bargaining gypsies with surprisingly well-lined purses, clamouring French nationals, aggrieved herring fishermen, the ever-changing situation on the border, the delicate political balance at the Scottish court, and the organization and transportation of much-needed ordnance to the English army in France, the queen found time to report to Henry about his children and to press personal suits for such needy individuals as 'Archer's wife'.[17] In the same message that details the plight of the herring fishermen, Catherine entered a plea with the king for a pardon for a young servant of one of her maids. The boy had 'picked certain pieces of goldsmith's work from his mistress', and been caught. Catherine informed Henry that the boy was very penitent and because of his youth and that the crime 'is but hardly construed felony', she asked the king for a pardon, remarking in a characteristically pragmatic manner that the boy's present terror of punishment would be a salutary example to others.

In addition to appointing Catherine regent before he sailed for France, Henry also made out his will. There is every reason to infer from her actions immediately following the king's death two and a half years later that in this instrument, too, provisions had been made for Catherine to be appointed regent for her young stepson if anything happened to the king while away with the army. There is also every reason to infer that Catherine knew of these provisions and that this gave her a measure of confidence during the summer of 1544 that may not have been to the taste of all of her councillors. She certainly demonstrated a marked desire to prove herself worthy of the king's trust in her on this trial run of a Parrian regency, and her aggressive handling of the office, if it earned her censure in some quarters, earned her praise in others.

While practical preparations for the invasion of France continued in the hands of Henry's more experienced councillors such as Wriothesley and Gardiner, the court gallants rattled their swords and prepared for plunder and glory. Catherine's volatile stepson, John Neville, Lord Latimer, prepared to join the English army. William Parr, now Earl of Essex, who had replaced Sir Anthony Browne as captain of the exclusive band of gentlemen pensioners, also planned to lead them across the channel as part of the royal army.[18] The fifty gentlemen pensioners, mostly promising young men of good birth, were a quasi-military group whose function was basically an honour bodyguard to the king. Their actual military duties were minimal; parades and ceremonials were their *forte*. Only once between Parr's inception as captain in 1543 and the king's death in 1547 were they actually engaged in combat on foreign soil and that was during the summer campaign of 1544. In spite of what the new Earl of Essex or his sister might have wished for the good of both their reputations, Essex did little to distinguish himself on the field of battle, but then, there was little enough opportunity.[19]

With the anxious prayers and best wishes of his queen and a mighty army before him, Henry set forth in the second week of July 1544 to do battle with the French. Shortly after the king's departure, Catherine wrote to him from Greenwich that:

> The time, therefore, seemeth to me very long with a great desire to know how your highness hath done since your departing hence ... whereas I know your majesty's absence is never without great respects of things most convenient and necessary, yet love and affection compelleth me to desire your presence. God, the knower of secrets, can judge these words not to be only written with ink, but most truly impressed in the heart.[20]

While Henry set sail to challenge the lilies of France in their own field, Catherine used her new powers as regent to bring her stepdaughter, the Princess Elizabeth, back to court.

Elizabeth had been at court during her father's pursuit of her stepmother and was one of the witnesses to their marriage in the Queen's Closet at Hampton Court on 12 July 1543.[21] Shortly afterward, she left court and did not return for nearly a year. For most, if not all, of that time she lived at Ashridge near the Hertfordshire–Buckinghamshire border, three miles north of Berkhamsted where the queen held the lordship of the manor. The buildings of Ashridge had once housed the religious College of Bonshommes and little had been done to convert it to a comfortable habitation for a ten-year-old girl. The aisled church and cloister still stood and the living quarters of the dissolved college included a great hall, great chamber, presence and privy chamber. Elizabeth's bedroom was directly beneath the old infirmary and were she of a nervous frame of mind, the empty religious college must have on a grey winter's day seemed ghost-haunted enough. So little fondness did Elizabeth have for the house that after she became queen, she allowed it to fall apart and finally sold it altogether.[22] The length of time that Elizabeth was away from court and the distance she was sent may imply some sort of banishment although the reasons behind her exile remain obscure. That she felt it to be a banishment, she confided to her stepmother by letter, referring to her residence at Ashridge as 'this my exile'.[23]

That this exile originated with the king and not the queen is indicated by the efforts Catherine made to stay in contact with the princess. She sent Elizabeth gifts of elegant clothing, a kirtle of cloth of silver, a pair of sleeves of purple velvet and a gown of purple cloth of gold.[24] In July 1544, just before being reunited with her stepmother, Elizabeth wrote to Catherine that 'I understand [you have] not forgotten me every time you have written to the King's Majesty.'[25] There is a possibility, too, that Catherine sent Hans Holbein to Ashridge 'in late summer or early autumn' of 1543 to paint Elizabeth, reinforcing a belief in Catherine's determination to remind the court of her stepdaughter's existence as well as her position as a daughter of the king, despite her exile to the wilds of northern Hertfordshire.[26] With the possible addition of the royal portrait painter, Catherine's main liaison with her stepdaughter during this time was through another stepdaughter, Margaret Neville, whom Catherine had raised from childhood, educated, and trusted implicitly. To all intents and purposes, their relationship was that of mother and daughter.

Margaret Neville was ideal for carrying messages between her royal stepsister, Elizabeth, and the queen. Margaret was trustworthy, young, and lively enough to provide compatible companionship for Elizabeth. She travelled up to Ashridge in December 1543, sent by the queen to spend much of the month with her stepsister.[27] On Henry's departure for France, Catherine ended Elizabeth's exile. Although the details are not fully known, it seems likely that before he left for France, Catherine managed to secure the king's agreement for Elizabeth's return to court. The king set sail for France on 9 July and shortly afterward, the queen arranged for the princess to travel up to London and join her at St. James' Palace. After Henry's departure, Catherine had moved from Greenwich to Westminster, where she was in residence through the third week of July.[28] During that time, she spent a night or two at St. James, apparently expecting Elizabeth's arrival, but when the princess was delayed, Catherine had her coffers sent from Westminster to Hampton Court, arriving there herself on 22 July in her royal barge decorated with a brightly painted wooden panther.[29] Elizabeth arrived at St. James' nine days later and was distressed to find that Catherine had already left. On 31 July, she wrote her stepmother a letter condemning 'inimical fortune', which having deprived her 'for a whole year of your most illustrious presence, and, not thus content, has yet again robbed me of the same good; which thing would be intolerable to me, did I not hope to enjoy it very soon.'[30] Elizabeth's immediate disappointment at having to wait a little longer to be reunited with Catherine was appeased somewhat by the knowledge that her stepmother had 'had as much care and solicitude for my health as the King's Majesty himself.' Elizabeth went on to confide that she 'had not dared' to write to her father and begged Catherine to intercede for her with the king and secure 'his sweet benediction'.

Within a day or two, Elizabeth travelled down to Hampton Court and was finally reunited with her stepmother and her assorted siblings.[31] It was a happy reunion as Elizabeth had longed not only to see Catherine but to see her brother, 'Signore Iddio', as well. Having actively supported the re-establishment of Mary in the line of succession, Catherine had now been instrumental in returning Elizabeth to her father's favour, in securing 'his sweet benediction' for her, and in assuring the young princess her own place in Henry's disposition of his kingdom. Her success was demonstrated by a letter from Henry dated 8 September, the day after Elizabeth's eleventh birthday, requesting Catherine 'to give in our name our hearty blessings to all our children,' a request that both the queen and the princess could read as Elizabeth's official release from exile.[32]

If the queen and her stepchildren were playing happy families at Hampton Court at the beginning of August, the king was less than comfortable across the Channel in his great French adventure. The Dukes of Norfolk and Suffolk had preceded Henry to Calais in June but their orders had been so vague that the army was uncertain what it was meant to do. The English commissary at Antwerp complained vehemently to Suffolk about the lack of supplies, and Norfolk was reduced to sending acerbic letters to the council asking that someone tell him what his military objectives were. It was not an auspicious way in which to begin a campaign of conquest, especially as the council could do little but pass on the commissary's complaints and commend the exasperated duke to do as he thought best. Since his arrival in France on 14 July, the king had lost much of his original zest for campaigning. He was reluctant to move too far from his own supply lines in the Pale, and he was having trouble with his unpredictable ally, Charles V. While Catherine acted as regent at home, Henry decided on a change of plan. Rather than march on Paris, distant and demanding of much effort, he would instead besiege the closer, less demanding town of Boulogne for the glory of England and St. George. The king 'enjoyed the siege hugely, supervising every move and appearing to be in better spirits and health than had been seen for years.'[33] This was Henry's kind of war – small, manageable, not too messy, not too expensive, and quickly concluded. A pious Thomas Wriothesley had written to the queen and her council, that, 'God is hable to strength his own against the Devil, and therefore let not the Queen's Majesty in any wise trouble herself, for God shall turn all to the best.'[34] What Henry wrote, less in piety than in exasperation, was 'that we be so occupied, and have so much to do in foreseeing and caring for everything ourself, as we have almost no manner [of] rest or leisure to do any other thing.'[35] The siege continued and despite his complaints, the king enjoyed taking charge of all the details.

Catherine's own capacity for work and her active interest in the various demands of her position as regent were apparent back in England. On 7 September, the queen sent her chancellor, Sir Thomas Arundell, to London to 'take order for sending of powder in the Tower and also a like order for ships and bulwarks'.[36] Some days later she was called upon to investigate the Bishop of Bath and his finances. In early August she secured a pardon for murder for three labourers and a gentleman in the jurisdiction of her cousin, the Bishop of Durham.[37] For a woman who had been at court barely a year and a half, the queen's competency at managing the myriad details of a royal regency was impressive. Her full command of the regency council is demonstrated by her use of her own household servants, such as Sir Thomas Arundell, Sir Robert Tyrwhit, Walter Bucler and Robert Warner, as agents to carry out the council's instructions in the countryside and to the king's council in France. She even dared to question the king's own commands when she found them inappropriate. When Henry ordered quantities of lead for the war effort shipped to France at the beginning of August, Catherine wrote back that the naval convoy could not at present be assured of adequate protection during a Channel crossing and so 'it is better the said lead should remain here then be with danger sent forth.'[38]

Catherine was also at some pains to assure her husband of her ability to handle any emergency that might arise. When rumours of a French landing on the English coast reached the court at the beginning of August, Catherine dashed off a letter to the king that, 'We dispatched in post immediately to the Justices of [the] Peace of the counties adjoining [the rumoured landing] ... to have further knowledge of the truth therein, and shortly after received other letters that the thing was begun upon no ground.' 'Vain rumours', the queen assured Henry, were now under control. 'And because we know that vain rumours fly fast, we thought good to advertise you of the same, lest any other vain report passing over might have caused the king's majesty to have conceived other opinion of the state of things here, then, thanks be unto God (they are) ... all things here are in very good quiet and order.'[39] The purpose of Catherine's letter was not only to reassure the king of the baselessness of idle gossip but to fill out her own report card, something she did repeatedly while Henry was in France. All things in the realm were quiet and in good order, Catherine wrote over and over to her husband and, although she was too modest to say it, 'lest I should seem to go about to praise myself or crave a thank', her letters implied that the king had no need to look any further than his own wife for the cause of this laudable state of affairs.

Yet beneath Catherine's calm assurances to Henry, by September she may have been feeling the strain of her responsibilities for she took the uncharacteristic step of consulting a noted astrologer, presumably about state affairs. Nicholas Kratzer, or Crazer, was a German who held the position of king's astronomer at a time when astronomy and astrology were inextricably linked. In September while Henry was besieging Boulogne, Catherine's secretary, Walter Bucler, was sent from Woking to London to 'speak with Nicholas Cratesere and others about [the queen's] affairs'.[40] It is unlikely, much as she trusted Bucler, that Catherine would have charged him to discuss with Kratzer any matter that was of too personal a nature and thus state affairs rather than something more intimate seem indicated although this was dangerous enough. The queen's flirtation with fortune-telling dated to her childhood, according to an anonymous marginalist who annotated a copy of John Bale's *Centuries* with what may have been a true or an apocryphal tale. When adjured as a child by her mother to spend more time practicing her embroidery, so the story ran, Catherine announced that a fortune-teller had predicted that crowns not needles were in her future and that her 'hands were ordained for sceptres'.[41] Maud Parr's brisk response to such nonsense may be imagined, if, in fact, the tale is true. Yet if it is, Catherine's weakness for some form of predicting the future may date from the fulfillment of this childhood prophesy.

A fascinating light is thrown on these summer months by a comedy written by Nicholas Udall to amuse the queen and probably acted by her small company of household players. Entitled *Ralph Roister Doister*, it appears to have been performed during the period that the king was in France. Although various dates have been attached to the play, the internal evidence supports the 1544 dating. It was revised by Thomas Wilson in January 1553 and must therefore have been written before that date. Scheurweghs points to 1545 as the most likely date for the play yet acknowledges frequent references to a queen – 'But when Roister Doister is put to his proof/To keep the Queen's peace is more for his behoove'[42] – and to her 'most worthy counsellers', which ' [does] not at all suit the reign of Queen Mary', as the queen is also referred to as 'the protector of the Gospel', which to Mary 'would sound like an insult'.[43] Scheurweghs also notes the references to shooting off handguns in the street

in Act 4, Scene 7, which he believes connects the material to a statute of 2 &
3 Edward VI against such activities. Yet a royal proclamation of 6 July 1546[44]
against the wanton discharging of handguns in public places shows that the
problem was current then, and this would have been particularly true in the
summer of 1544 when large groups of armed citizens were coming and going
to the wars in France. A reference to the war exists in Act 3, Scene 4, where
Roister swears 'by the arms of Calais'. A third piece of evidence Scheurweghs
interprets as a reference to the Usury Act of 1545 but again this may actually
refer to the period of abuse immediately preceding and therefore initiating the
act. The successful debasement of the English coinage in 1542 led to a much
larger scale of debasement which coincided with the French invasion of 1544,
as the need for money to pay for the war manifested itself. A monetary system
being steadily and deliberately debased would lend itself handily to an increase
in illegal profits on loans.

Finally, there is the similarity of language between Udall's references to the
queen in his dedications for the English translation of Erasmus' *Paraphrases* and
his encomium to the 'queen' of *Ralph Roister Doister*. In the *Paraphrases*, Udall
refers to Catherine's 'hire (of) other workmen to labour in the same vineyard of
Christ's gospel', a tacit reference to her role as 'protector of the Gospel':

> Where your excellent highness, most gracious Queen Katherine, since the time
> of your first calling to the estate and dignity of espousal and marriage ... hath
> never ceased by all possible means that in you might lie, to mind, to advance and
> to increase the public commodity and benefit of this commonweal of England ...
> (Preface to St. Matthew)

> Therefore most virtuous Lady although your demerits are so set above all prais-
> es of man, that how far soever I would in magnifying your virtuous disposition,
> your devout study and endeavour to do good things, I shall be sure not to incur
> any suspicion of flattery. Yet do I at this present, omitting all other things, only
> in England's behalf make one among the rest in rendering public thanks to your
> highness, as well for your other godly travail in furthering the knowledge of God's
> word, as also most specially in setting men in work to translate the Paraphrase of
> Erasmus . (Preface to St. John)

A comparison with the last song in *Ralph Roister Doister* exhibits such similar
thought and phrasing that it seems like a continuation of the dedications:

> The Lord preserve our most noble Queen of renown,
> And her virtues reward with the heavenly crown.

The Lord strengthen her most excellent Majesty,
Long to reign over us in all prosperity.
That her godly proceedings the faith to defend,
He may establish and maintain through to the end.
God grant her as she doth, the Gospel to protect,
Learning and virtue to advance, and vice to correct.
God grant her loving subjects both the mind and grace,
Her most godly proceedings worthily to embrace.
Her highness' most worthy counsellors God prosper,
With honour and love of all men to minister.
God grant the nobility her to serve and love,
With all the whole commonality as doth them behoove.
(Act 5, Scene 6)

Nicholas Udall, who had been dismissed in 1541 as headmaster of Eton for possible complicity in robbing his own school (unproven) and for engaging in sexual activities with his students (confessed), had found a refuge with the queen. It is possible that she had met him previously when she lived in the north during her first two marriages as Udall spent the years 1529–33 teaching in that region. As queen, Catherine funded both the impoverished scholar and his great project for translating Erasmus' *Paraphrases* into English. Udall was deeply grateful for her patronage. He wrote, translated and organized plays for her amusement, one of which was an English version of Italian Calvinist Bernardino Occhino's *Tragoedia de Papatu*.[45] Another may have been *Thersytes*, a classical comedy that he originally wrote for the celebrations surrounding the birth the Prince of Wales in 1536, and the earliest known English comedy.[46] *Ralph Roister Doister*, another court comedy, was written especially for Catherine. Udall made her his heroine, the virtuous widow 'Christian [Kitte] Custance', a recognizable play on Catherine's former condition and nicknames, 'Kate' and 'Constance'. Her voice, too, can be heard in speeches whose phrasing sounds very like her letters as regent. In a reproach and not too thinly veiled threat to her idle and giddy maid, Kitte commands:

Will not so many forewarnings make you afraid? ...
Good wenches should not so romp abroad idly,
but keep within doors, and ply their work earnestly;
if one would speak with me that is a man likely,
ye shall have right good thank to bring me words quickly.
But otherwise with messages to come in post, from
henceforth I promise you, shall be to your cost.[47]

'[I look] as far beyond the people, as one may see out of the top of Paul's steeple,' Kitte tells another character.[48] Thus Udall proclaims the elevated condition of his heroine.

In the play, the absent king becomes 'Gawain Goodlucke', the heroine's betrothed, absent on important matters overseas. In a curiously proto-Shakespearean way (some of the wooing scenes are strikingly reminiscent of the emotional dynamic between 'Petruchio' and 'Katharina' in the later *Taming of the Shrew* for which this play served as a source),[49] Udall proceeds to tell the tale of a boisterous, handsome courtier (a proto-Petruchio) who brags of his military prowess and of his affairs with women. This courtier, the 'Ralph Roister Doister (RRD)' of the title, is almost forty, still unmarried, has a good singing voice, is conscious of dressing well and intends to have the fair and wealthy Kitte (CC), whether she is willing or not. 'Yes, in faith, Kitte,' Roister announces, 'I shall thee and thine so charm, that all women incarnate by thee may beware':[50]

CC: Speak not of winning me: for it shall never be so.
RRD: Yes dame, I will have you whether ye will or no.
I command you to love me, wherefore should ye not?
Is not my love to you chafing and burning hot?

'I will not be served with a fool in no wise,' Kitte retorts. 'When I choose a husband, I hope to take a man.'[51] Roister's servant tells Kitte, ' ... though ye were a queen, (Roister will) 'break marriage between you twain.'[52]

During the proceedings, Udall satirizes various members of the queen's household in a far from gentle manner. Only the absent Goodlucke and Kitte, herself, are exempt from Udall's barbs yet he does not hesitate to poke sly fun at her. 'Her talk is as fine as [if] she had learned in schools,' Roister remarks in exasperation,[53] while another character explains how he tried to tell Kitte of Roister's love for her, but she would not stop talking long enough for him to get a word in edgeways. 'I could not stop her mouth,' he exclaims.[54] Yet Udall gives Kitte an undeniable sense of wit and humour, that same 'pregnant wittiness joined with right wonderful grace of eloquence' which he attributes to Catherine in his dedication to *St. Luke*. When Roister is praised to her as a jewel among men, Kitte dryly remarks, 'Yea, no force, a jewel much better lost than found.'[55]

How the queen felt about the comedy, if Udall intended, as seems probable, the cruel caricature of the hero to be a portrait of Sir Thomas Seymour, is problematic. Lady Constance she might outwardly appear to her royal husband

and the court, but inwardly, as later events were to show, she continued to be deeply in love with Seymour. 'I know she loveth me,' Roister confides to his servant, 'but she dare not speak.'[56] Traces of a suppressed but underlying passion colour the scenes between the overly protesting Kitte and the amorous, roistering Ralph, and although the queen may have laughed during the performance, in fact there was little else she could do, these ever so delicate allusions could only have made Catherine uneasy. As for Seymour, a quick man with a sword when provoked, he was fighting by the king's side in France and would shortly be promoted to Admiral of the Navy. His appearances at court had become so infrequent that Udall probably had little concern about repercussions from this quarter. Seymour's brother was away from court after the first week in August on the Scottish border and his sister-in-law detested the soon-to-be admiral. No one therefore was likely to lodge a protest of character assassination with the playwright. The king, as 'Gavin Goodluck', is shown as a just man of probity and good sense, a characterization that Henry would hardly have considered an insult.

Another interesting plot device Udall employs is Goodlucke's suspicion that Kitte has played him false, when upon his return from overseas the officious meddler Sym Suresby (Thomas Wriothesley?), Goodlucke's servant, reports Roister's pursuit of Kitte but not her rejection of him. Here the icon of female chastity appears as the ultimate determinant of a woman's character.[57] Udall's protestations of innocence in Kitte's mouth were eerily prophetic of events still to come. He has the beleaguered Kitte turn to Heaven for help as she exclaims:

> Oh Lord, how necessary it is now of days,
> That each body live uprightly [in] all manner [of] ways,
> For let never so little a gap be open,
> And be sure of this, the worst shall be spoken.
> How innocent stand I in this for deed or thought?
> And yet see what mistrust towards me it hath wrought
> But thou Lord knowest all folks' thoughts and eke intents
> And thou are the deliverer of all innocents.[58]

This closely paraphrases a verse from Catherine's *Prayers or Meditations*, published the following year. 'Truly it is no good spirit that moveth men to find fault at everything, and when things may be well taken, to pervert them into an evil sense and meaning.'[59] Fortunately for the queen, 'God, the knower of secrets' would stand by both her and her literary *doppelganger*, Kitte. Udall closes his play with the newly returned 'Goodlucke', now fully aware of Roister's plottings against Kitte, nevertheless offering to shake the hand of the man who has pursued her so remorselessly. Kitte is left seething inwardly, forced to entertain with gracious civility the man who has tried symbolically to rape her while 'Goodlucke' was away by mounting a mock attack upon her house and person. This attack scene is a curious choice on Udall's part, too, even though he has adapted it from a classical model. The all too real attacks on Catherine's house and person in 1536, during the Pilgrimage of Grace, could only be grim memories for the queen and hardly suitable for satiric comedy. Udall, of course, may have been ignorant of those events.

While there is no evidence to support any accusations of infidelity or impropriety on Catherine's part during Henry's excursion into France, nor it is likely that Udall would have turned such an accusation into a comedy expressly for the queen if there had been, yet the very material that Udall selected for his farce was in its own way a warning. Catherine felt herself secure on the heights where Henry had raised her but that was because, since the early days of her marriage, she had never been forced to consider just how far it was possible for her to fall. Her elevation as regent had given her an increased sense of security in her husband's trust and affections. Were Henry to die in France – and given the precarious nature of his health, that prospect was not an unthinkable one – Catherine stood, already appointed at the head of a regency council, ready, willing, and able to take up the reins of government. Apparently unperceived by her, this delight in the exercise of power was beginning to make her enemies.

By the beginning of September, the king was still managing things at the siege before the defenses of Boulogne. Despite his personal attention to every detail, the city had not yet fallen. On 8 September, however, it looked as if the end of the siege were near and in great excitement, Henry dashed off a personal message to his wife at the bottom of an official letter:

> At the closing up of these our letters, the castle aforenamed, with the dyke, is at our commandment, and not like to be recovered by the Frenchmen again, as we trust, not doubting with God's grace, but that the castle and town shall shortly follow the same trade, for as this day, which is the eighth day of September, we begin three batteries, and have three mines going, besides one which hath done his execution in shaking and tearing off one of their greatest bulwarks. No more to you at this time, sweetheart, both for lack of time and great occupation of business ... Written with the hand of your loving husband.[60]

Finally five days later, on 13 September, Boulogne surrendered. The queen's brother-in-law, Sir William Herbert, mounted a fast horse and headed for the coast and England with the news while the impressive Tudor propaganda factory rolled into action. Five days after the surrender, Henry, in his role of *le monarch magnifique*, rode into the city in triumph:

> The 18 day, the king's highness having the sword borne naked before him by the Lord Marquis of Dorset, like a noble and valiant conqueror, rode into Boulogne and the trumpeters standing on the walls of the town sounded their trumpets at the time of his entering to the great comfort of all the king's true subjects, the same beholding. And in the entering there met him the Duke of Suffolk, and delivered unto him the keys of the town, and so he rode toward his lodging, which was prepared for him on the south side of town.[61]

King David, himself, taking the capital of the Ammonites could not have announced his victory to the captive populace with greater pomp. In a gesture guaranteed to alienate that said populace, Henry ordered the town's Lady Chapel to be torn down and the stone used to raise a monument to his victory. With Henry, pomp and pettiness went hand in hand. Wriothesley's assurances to the queen that, 'God is hable to strength his own against the Devil,' had been vindicated. The king and his chancellor congratulated themselves on the fact that God was an Englishman, and Henry celebrated his triumph in the conquered town until the end of the month.

His queen was equally delighted by the victory and sent messages out to the surrounding countryside similar to the one the Earl of Shrewsbury received:

> The Queen having this night advertisement by Sir William Herbert of the Privy Chamber, that Boulogne is in the King's hands without effusion of blood, [Shrewsbury] shall cause thanks to be given to God, by devout and general processions in all the towns and villages of the North, and also signify to the Wardens of the Marches this great benefit which God has heaped on us.[62]

The king's victory celebration, however, was not unalloyed. His ally, Charles V, had cut his losses and much to Henry's fury signed a separate peace with France on the very day that Boulogne capitulated to the English.

Meanwhile, the Duke of Norfolk, with half the army, was starving in a miserably disorganized siege at Montreuil. Informed of the fact by the imperial ambassador, Catherine sent an unusually tart reply back that shows the queen in full command of the logistics of military supply.

> Thus, if the English campaign happens to be in want of provisions, it will certainly not be the fault of the Queen, who has not failed to give all possible attention to the matter, making the usual requisitions, and issuing proclamations for people to

go to the English camp with provisions for sale. In fact, the Queen has hitherto acted in this affair in such a manner that the English ought to be perfectly satisfied. Nor has it been the Queen's or her ministers' fault if the vanguard or rearguard of the English army have stayed so long on the road ... Indeed, the Queen would be very sorry if any one should attempt to inculpate her, or her ministers, on that score, of deficiencies and faults, which are not theirs, and she cannot do less than declare on this present occasion that unless better provisions be made for the future, it is to be feared the English may feel still greater wants than those they now complain of, which would be very distressing for her to hear.[63]

Catherine Parr minced no words in her communications with all except the king.

With the fall of Boulogne and the expectation of an end to the hostilities in the not too distant future, Catherine decided to take the children and go on a progress into Surrey and Kent. Together with most of her council – the Earl of Hertford left for the north at the beginning of August – the queen had spent the last half of July and all of August at Hampton Court, with only a few days off before the earl's departure to travel to Syon House in a closed barge for the christening of the Hertfords' latest child and a night at Richmond Palace.[64] The queen was ready for a change and an outbreak of the plague in London which prevented a return to the capital, plus the victory at Boulogne, provided the opportunity for some royal rest and recreation.[65] Sir Thomas Wharton, deputy warden of the western marches, had sent Catherine a gift of falcons and a tercel.[66] She took these, her crossbow, her horses, her dogs, her children and her council and proceeded at a leisurely pace to Edward IV's palace of Woking, where she left the council in residence.[67] With periodic returns to Woking to check on the council's work, Catherine and the children travelled to Mortlake,[68] Byflete, Catherine's brother's house at Guildford, Chobham, Beddington Place and Eltham. She visited friends at Merewood, Sir Robert Southwell's home, and at Allington Castle, home of the Wyatts.[69] The weather turned cold – Catherine sent for some furred gowns from London – but the hunting was excellent.[70] Gifts of the hunt went out to friends and a present of venison was even dispatched to Henry at Boulogne.[71]

While Catherine and the royal children were on progress, the army still with the Duke of Norfolk was exhausted by the freezing weather and a chronic lack of supplies before a stubbornly resistant Montreuil. The duke finally managed to retreat with his men from the futile siege and join Henry at Boulogne, but the army and its generals were very near mutiny. Fortunately for everyone concerned, the king decided that he had had enough of war and made plans to return to England at the beginning of October, full of his exploits and conquest.

A rumour that the French intended to waylay him en route concerned the queen enough to send Wriothesley up to London to discover what he could. On 25 September, he wrote to her that 'the King's person is out of danger and so, doubtless, are the rest, for it shall not yet enter into my creed that the Frenchmen will cope with us, what brag soever they set upon it.'[72] Three ships, continued Wriothesley, the *Sweepstake*, the *Primrose*, and the *Jennet*, were to set forth immediately with all possible speed with money and letters for the king. Catherine must have read this news with mixed emotions as the former captain of the *Sweepstake* had been Sir Thomas Seymour.

Henry returned to England while Catherine was at Eltham, about to depart for Otford, but she sent word that she intended 'to remain here without going to Otford until the king's further pleasure be known.' Henry agreed to meet her at Otford. Despite his benedictions on all of his children, Catherine dispatched Elizabeth back to Beddington Place[73] and although the princess returned to Ashridge before Christmas, her brother Edward, his tutors and household, and her father's blessings went with her.[74] The queen sent her cast of falcons on to Westminster[75] and travelled to Otford alone for her reunion with England's conquering hero. From Otford, the royal progress continued to Leeds Castle, probably to inspect the gun emplacements, and thence back to Otford and finally on to London. In November, Catherine contrived to go on progress to Buckinghamshire and Bedfordshire and spent two days during the last week of the month with Elizabeth and Edward at Ashridge.[76] Her interest and care for them was one of the few constants in the constant unpredictability of their lives.

Catherine's approach to rule during her regency of 1544 is particularly important for a number of reasons. Not only was it a trial run for a minority regency, should fortune so decree, but success in handling the demands of the office gave Catherine a vastly increased self-confidence in her role as queen. During her lifetime Catherine was compared both to the biblical Esther, the commoner whose attractions in the royal marriage bed raised her people to greatness at the court of King Ahasuerus, and to Sheba's queen, who travelled from a far off place to pay homage to the great Solomon and perhaps seduce him. The events of Catherine's regency led to another comparison, this with the classical Penelope, the clever and faithful spouse who fended off importunate suitors and governed her husband's estates during his long absence at the Trojan War. Wrote John Parkhurst of the queen:

> If the Greek and Roman poets had known of you, would they have heaped so much praise on Penelope? Surely they wouldn't have. For you surpass in virtues not only Penelope but all Argolis.[77]

Yet it was Diana that a successful ruling queen was forced by the requirements of the position to emulate. Diana, who in ancient Greek mythology cut off the right breast of her womanhood in order to use her masculine weapon, a bow, with greater swiftness and accuracy, is the paradigm of the Renaissance queen. Womanly in body, the female ruler was forced to adopt a metaphorically male shape, to appropriate male gendered attributes, to assume 'the stomach of a king' in order to reinforce the legitimacy of her rule.

Although Catherine was a queen-consort and not a queen regnant, she laid down during her 1544 regency an androgynous approach to rule closely observed by her ten-year-old stepdaughter, Elizabeth, who was with her for most of that time. From the age of nine until two days before her fifteenth birthday, Elizabeth's acting mother and mentor was Catherine Parr. The queen's androgynous approach to the regency, observed at first hand by her young stepdaughter, was to form the basis for Elizabeth's later approach to rule as a woman.[78] The pattern of queenship that Elizabeth learned was the pattern of queenship that Catherine Parr provided. This perception of a woman's need to emulate male characteristics in the prosecution of power is apparent in Catherine's letters written at that time and it was crystallized a year and a half later in *Lamentation of a Sinner* and in the ideas expressed in the queen's letter of February 1546 to the University of Cambridge. To read Catherine's letters to Henry, juxtaposed with her orders to those over whom she had command, is to read clear evidence of this bi-gendered mind set. While Catherine played the devoted and self-abasing wife in her letters to the king, writing that 'the same zeal and love forceth me also to be best content with that which is your will and pleasure',[79] she gave short shrift to those under her command who wearied her with 'their continual clamour'[80] and responded sharply and unapologetically that she had 'hitherto acted in this affair in such a manner that the English ought to be perfectly satisfied.'[81]

The qualities required for the ideal Christian woman of chaste piety and self-effacing obedience seem – and were – mutually exclusive with the self-assertive command and active disciplined leadership required of an ideal king. Catherine to a lesser extent and Elizabeth later, to a far greater one, were forced by circumstance to try and find a way to impersonate both sets of qualities. Catherine's period as regent, brief though it was, introduced her to the same liberating possibilities for the exercise of self-determination that her mother had apparently found in her fourteen years of widowhood. Having been introduced to the male preserve of power politics, the queen had developed an appetite for the kind of decision-making control that was not usually the sphere of women. With the return of the king, her regency was at an end.

Yet another possibility for power, the exercise of which would have given her greater freedom of action than she had ever known, was an ever-present reality given the fluctuations of the king's health and the parliamentary statute which, in the case of Henry's death, provided for a regency council under the king's mother, a title that Edward had willingly bestowed on his stepmother and the king's will of 1544 almost certainly endorsed.

Whatever her private expectation, publicly Catherine displayed a quiet satisfaction with her own performance as regent during the crisis. Yet if the queen had achieved a reputation for a wisdom greater than Penelope during her time as regent and had managed to re-establish the Princess Elizabeth back in her father's favour, the actual adventure in France availed the king, himself, little positive gain. The effort, in fact, seemed greater than the achievement. Boulogne now needed to be refortified and garrisoned and the garrison needed to be paid. Thanks to his French adventure, Henry faced enemies not only in Scotland and France but, due to his inability to deal diplomatically with Charles V, he had also caused another serious rift between England and the Empire. By the summer of 1545, a year after the capture of Boulogne, England stood in greater peril than it had since the early days of Henry VII. Due to Henry VIII's severe defects as a solo statesman and military strategist, all the ruling hands of Europe, from Scotland in the north to the Pope in Rome, seemed turned against him.

The idea of an alliance among the Protestant princes of Europe in the winter of 1544–45, after Henry's return from France, may or may not have originated with the queen. Certainly it was an idea that she would have supported with enthusiasm and, as she had with the settlement of the English succession, one whose merits she began to press on her husband. The alienation of England and its ruler from the rest of Europe after Henry's unproductive invasion of France appears to have led Catherine to emulate the policies of the late Thomas Cromwell by pushing the king once again toward soliciting a secret alliance with the Protestant princes of the Schmalkaldic League. Between 1531 and 1540 various approaches for the foundation of such a league were made by the German Lutheran princes to the English king and by the English king to the Duke of Saxony. But after Cromwell's death in 1540, the idea had lain dormant until resurrected in 1545.

The formation and dispatch of a mission to the continent was kept a secret between the king and queen and their agents. In February 1545, the queen's trusted secretary Walter Bucler, and Dr. Christopher Mont, former ambassador to the court of Saxony, were given instructions to proceed to the continent, via Antwerp, and propose a league between the English king, the King of Denmark, the Duke of Holstein and the Landgrave of Hesse, as well as any other German prince willing to join such a league.[82] Henry offered to seal the alliance by arranging a marriage between the Duke of Holstein with either of his daughters, the twenty-nine-year-old Princess Mary or the twelve-year-old Princess Elizabeth. A Protestant League sponsored by the English king, whose health and temperament did little to recommend him, was at best a forlorn hope. Daughters who had been declared bastards, one too old and the other still a child, were hardly realistic temptations in the royal marriage market. Catherine, full of zeal for defining a common religious ground among right-thinking princes and for establishing a working political union that would help increase England's role in Europe, could not have known this. Full of the flattery of foreign ambassadors, the indulgence of a royal husband, and the taste for power that the regency had given her, she was too new to the game of international politics to judge the chances for success of such a league correctly. But she did know how to keep a secret. Dispatches written in cipher and sent back to London by Mont and Bucler also helped maintain secrecy although Bucler, at least, complained volubly about the need for such labourious precautions.

It was not until the third week in June 1545, three months after Bucler and Mont had received their instructions, that Charles V's ambassador, Van der Delft, wrote, 'the Queen's secretary, Richard Butler (*sic*), has been sent to Germany to solicit secretly the German princes to form a league with this king.'[83] In July, Charles V replied to Van der Delft's dispatch that his own attempts had failed to discover anything about Bucler's mission. Although the mission seemed to be making little headway with the Protestant princes, Catherine did not give up her plan easily. By October, although Dr. Mont appears to have been recalled, the queen's secretary was still on the continent and it was not until December, after nearly a year's absence, that Bucler, himself, returned to London.[84]

'The Boke of the Crucifix'

It is a truism to say that Catherine Parr grew up in a time of religious ferment. She was five years old when Martin Luther nailed his ninety-five theses to the door of All Saints Church in Wittenburg on 31 October 1517, nine when Philipp Melanchthon published *Passion of Christ and Antichrist* and Luther defied the emperor and the religious establishment at the Diet of Worms, and twelve when Erasmus published *De libero arbitrio* ('Concerning Free Will'), attacking Luther's doctrine of predestination. In 1529, the same year Catherine travelled north into Lincolnshire to marry Edward Borough, the second Diet of Speyer coined the term 'Protestant', and the following year witnessed Melanchthon's Augsburg Confession, which, together with his Apology of 1531, eloquently voiced the Lutheran position and gave it a definitive statement of faith that moved Lutheranism into realms unacceptable to Roman Catholic dogma.

From her birth in 1512 to her first marriage in 1529, arguably formative years, Catherine grew up in the south. She was the child of a courtier father and of a mother who served the queen, both of whom were friends to the king's great minister, Cardinal Wolsey.[1] Just how aware Catherine, herself, was of the momentous changes happening on the Continent and how, if at all, they affected her own religious thought is a question that may never be answered satisfactorily. Books defining the ideas which galvanized the Lutheran religious revolution began to appear in England in English editions in the early 1530's, shortly after Catherine had moved to the north. Yet this hardly rules out the importing of those ideas, well in advance of their official publication, by the great multi-national mercantile community of London or of their reaching in Latin editions the consciences and privy chambers of the upper echelons at court.

During the last years of Henry's reign, five to eight per cent of the total population of London was alien, many of them refugees from religious persecution who practised the specialized luxury trades such as clockmaking, weaving, and goldsmithing that brought them into direct contact with the court.[2] Hanse merchants were effective conduits for the flow of Protestant literature into the city and from the late 1520s, energetic efforts were being made by the government to control the flood of heretical literature. Given her apparently lifelong fascination with religious doctrine, her quick mind and her mother's connections at court, it is difficult to believe that Catherine left for the deeply conservative north in 1529 without the least exposure to the ferment that Luther had initiated in 1517.

That Catherine was born into a Roman Catholic family and trained in that faith is unarguable. The wills of her parents are testaments to a proper Catholic piety and Catherine's Latin training among the woodblock prints of her father's *Horae ad Usum Sarum* spells out the prayers central to Catholic orthodoxy that she would have been required to learn. Dr. Melton, Sir Thomas Parr's chaplain, would have been the first perhaps to instruct the child Catherine in her catechism. Yet Maud Parr, despite having chosen a dramatic picture of the Passion beneath which to inscribe her name in the *Horae*,[3] demonstrates in her letters and particularly in her bequests for the founding of schools, a stronger streak of secular pragmatism than of religious fervency in her nature. It would not be too wide of the mark to characterise her as a woman more interested in secular than in religious matters. This holds true for most of Catherine's immediate family. Her father does not appear to have been a profoundly devout man and his brother was a bluntly secular one. Catherine's brother and sister, while conforming to all the devotional requirements of the English Church and doing everything in their power to ensure its firm and lasting establishment, give every indication of having chosen such a course because it led to worldly advancement as surely as it led to spiritual salvation. Catherine's so-called conversion, therefore, must be seen not in terms of switching allegiances from a passionate attachment to the Roman Church to a passionate attachment to the English one, but more in terms of finding for the first time the seed of religious passion latent in herself. That this emotional discovery seems to have occurred between the violent months of the Pilgrimage of Grace and her sudden capitulation into love with Sir Thomas Seymour sheds some light on the psychological foundations of her conversion.

Humanism, with its desire to reform religious institutions by a direct study of the original language of the Bible, by its emphasis on languages in general and its openness to classical learning were part of Catherine's early religious as well as scholastic training. 'I professed Christ in my baptism when I began to live,' she later wrote, 'but I swerved from him after baptism, in continuance of my living, even as the heathen which never had begun.'[4] Regarding her religious education, she remarked, 'I had a certain vain blind knowledge, both cold and dead.'[5] Religion was propounded to her, as Catherine relates, 'by book, admonition, [and] learning',[6] but she admits to little emotional attachment to the doctrines that she learned. The emotional distance between her feelings and the religion in which she was raised is later characterized in her writings as 'cold and dead'. Whatever doubts, if any, she may have had about the state of the church in England or the infallibility of its doctrine, she took them with her into the turbulent north in 1529.

Catherine spent nearly a decade in the conservative bastions of orthodoxy north of the Trent, but even there, heterodoxy had already raised its head. Her first father-in-law, Sir Thomas Borough, was Anne Boleyn's chamberlain and a violent and outspoken proponent of the Protestant Reformation. In July 1530, he was one of a group of peers who wrote to Pope Clement urging him to grant Henry a divorce from Catherine of Aragon. Given the sort of patriarchal control that Borough exercised over his household, there is little doubt that his chaplains promoted the same viewpoint as their master. Dr. Thomas Rose, who held the office of chaplain to Borough's family in 1537–38 and who 'instructed all of his household', may have been chaplain at Gainsborough Old Hall during Catherine's marriage to Edward Borough.[7] He left Lincolnshire in 1538 and obtained a licence to preach at St. Margaret's, Lothbury, in London, but Borough wanted him back and petitioned Rose's new patron, Cromwell, for his return. On 29 June 1543, an inquisition post mortem on one Thomas Rose shows that he held lands in the north worth £20 per annum, half of them he held as tenant of the king and the other half as tenant of Catherine's brother, William Parr.[8] Whatever relationship if any that Catherine had with Thomas Rose, Gainsborough Old Hall offered her a heady and disturbing jolt of the Reformation in action.

Things were considerably different in the rigorously orthodox household in which Catherine found herself at Snape Castle with her second husband, John Neville, Lord Latimer. Latimer was known throughout the countryside for the conservative character of his beliefs and for the large chapel and ostentatious observances of the mass that obtained in his household. As Latimer's wife, Catherine was an integral part of these observances and her habit of hearing mass several times a day probably dates not from childhood but from Snape. During this time, as Catherine later explains:

> I had a blind guide called Ignorance, who dimmed so mine eyes, that I could never perfectly get any sight of the fair, godly, straight and right ways of [Christ's] doctrine, but continually travelled uncomfortably in foul, wicked, crooked and perverse ways. Yea and because they were so much haunted of many, I could not think but I walked in the perfect and right way, having more regard to the number of walkers, than to the order of walking, believing also most assuredly with company to have walked to heaven ...[9]

That Catherine describes herself as traveling 'uncomfortably' along the road of orthodoxy raises the possibility that even at this time she may have been having doubts about the infallibility of her received beliefs. The controversy over indulgences and the moral erosion visible in many church offices and officials was a state of affairs familiar to most Englishmen. Catherine later condemned the pope as, 'a setter forth of all superstition and counterfeit holiness, bringing many souls to hell with his alchemy, and counterfeit money, deceiving the poor souls under the pretence of holiness.'[10] Intimations of these later convictions would indeed have caused her to ask questions in her own conscience about the validity of established religious practices. She comforted herself with the notion that other minds, infinitely more knowledgeable than hers, seemed certain, in spite of ecclesiastical corruption, of the core righteousness of those beliefs and practices, and that if the majority of what men called 'the godly' walked along the same road, it must be the right road after all.

These doubts may have reached a crisis point during the terrifying months of the Pilgrimage of Grace in 1536, when Catherine very nearly lost husband, home and even her own life. 'The passions of the flesh,' she later commented, 'are medicines of the soul.'[11] She was perhaps remembering this time of anarchy and the bloody conflict of warring religious factions when she wrote ten years later:

> Truly the Devil hath been the sower of the seed of sedition and shall be the main-
> tainer of it, even till God's will be fulfilled. There is no war so cruel and evil as
> this, for the war with sword killeth but the bodies and this slayeth many souls for
> the poor unlearned persons remain confused, and almost everyone believeth and
> worketh after his own way ... I am able to justify the ignorance of the people to be
> great, not in this matter alone, but in many other ... Because I have had just proof
> of the same, it maketh me thus much to say with no little sorrow and grief in my
> heart for such a miserable ignorance and blindness amongst the people. I doubt
> not but we can say all, 'Lord, Lord'. But I fear God may say unto us, 'This people
> honoureth me with their lips, but their hearts be far from me.[12]

Hard upon the heels of the conservative religious uprisings and their bloody aftermath, Catherine moved with her husband to his southern manors in Worcestershire and then to Northamptonshire. Here the influences on her beliefs changed completely. Latimer was a spent force, his devotion to orthodoxy had nearly caused his – and his wife's – ruin. Catherine's uncle, Sir William Parr of Horton, was now her near neighbour and an ardent supporter of the reformed religion. His relationship with Catherine was that of surrogate father and throughout his life, Lord Parr was to be as devoted to her as she was to him, serving her as queen in the office of chamberlain of her household, and as her councillor and loyal friend. When Henry VIII sailed for France during the summer campaign of 1544, it was Lord Parr of Horton whom Catherine requested be added to her regency council. When the terrors of 1546 were to nearly lead to her arrest, it was to her uncle that she would send for help. Old and sick as he was, he left his much beloved manor at Horton to return to court, pick up the threads of his office as chamberlain and remain by his niece's side throughout the crisis.[13] His influence on her should not therefore be minimized, nor should the influence exercised by Catherine's brother, the younger William Parr, whom Catherine loved, encouraged and protected throughout her life. Both of these men were committed to the religious change that was then occurring in England. Parr of Horton was, as one of the commissioners delegated to dismantle the monasteries in Northamptonshire, a servant and well-wisher of Cromwell and the Reformation. He threatened to hang any who interfered with his work, had laughed at the priests in the household of the Duke of Richmond, and in September 1537, he 'caused a person's ear to be nailed to the pillory for seditious speech' in Northampton.[14] The younger William had little love for Cromwell, but an abiding love for the new – and fashionable – religion, as did his friends, Sir Thomas Seymour and John Dudley, Lord Lisle. The doubting Catherine, traumatized by the excesses of orthodoxy, may have been only too willing to listen to their views.

There is a persistent tradition, unverified and presumably unverifiable, that when the Latimers moved more or less permanently to London in the early 1540s, Catherine entertained such notable divines as Miles Coverdale, Hugh Latimer and John Parkhurst in her home.[15] If this is true, she can hardly have done so with her husband's blessing, which is not to say that, given his frequent absences in the north, she did not do it anyway. The point has been hotly debated by scholars as an indication of the future queen's religious beliefs.[16] Yet it should be pointed out that listening to an opinion or belief is not the same thing as agreeing with it. '[God] called me diversely,' Catherine remembered, 'but, through frowardness, I would not answer.'[17] She thus testifies to some sort of exposure to the reformed beliefs that she ultimately embraced, not only at Gainsborough Old Hall but also perhaps during these years. Given her family ties and their connections with the circle of religious reformers in London, it would be amazing if Catherine were not exposed to the most exciting and controversial topics of conversation of the day – apart from rumours of war and the king's marriages. It might perhaps be said of Catherine that the period from 1537 to the early 1540s, was one in which 'she pondered all of these things in her heart'.

If the factor of religion entered into her choice of the household of the Princess Mary in which to seek employment, it was a religion in transition, as Catherine testified to herself. More practical matters, such as her mother's ties to

Catherine of Aragon and thus the greater likelihood of employment, probably played a larger role than religious compatibility. Mary's faith, like Catherine's, had been well and truly tested, but the crucible in which the princess' beliefs were hardened had only made Catherine's beliefs more malleable.

Where then stood the new Queen of England in the matter of religion on Thursday, 12 July 1543, as she exchanged vows in the Queen's Closet at Hampton Court? On this point, a letter written to her in Latin at this time by Francis Goldsmith, one of Catherine's solicitors and a gentleman of her privy chamber, is illuminating.[18] Thanking her for taking him into her household, he asks Catherine for 'the smallest coin out of her rich treasure of grace' to enable him to serve her properly. The new queen, Goldsmith affirms, 'has made every day like Sunday, a thing hitherto unheard of, especially in a royal palace.' This particular piety, however, is not rooted in the old religion but in the new. 'God has so formed her mind for pious studies,' states Goldsmith, 'that she considers everything of small value compared to Christ ... Her piety cherishes the religion long since introduced not without great labour to the palace.' Goldsmith finds it difficult to express adequate gratitude for the queen's acceptance of his services as one in her household where Christ is celebrated daily, '*in tam sanctum tuum famulitin, ubi quotidie chrs' celebrat'*, *admittere dignanta sit* [in such a virtuous household as yours, where Christ is celebrated daily, I have the honour to be admitted].'

It is difficult to know what to make of this letter unless it is accepted as a statement of the new queen's commitment to the reformed faith. That Catherine cherished the religion introduced, 'not without great labour to the palace', can really only have one interpretation. From Goldsmith's letter, it becomes clear that 'learning of the crucifix, the book of our redemption, the very absolute library of God's mercy and wisdom'[19] had already become the focus of the queen's study. 'I am of this opinion, that if God would suffer me to live here a thousand year and should study continually in the same divine book, I should not be filled with the contemplation thereof,' Catherine wrote in 1546. 'Neither hold I myself contented, but always have a great desire to learn and study more therein.'[20] By the time she had become Henry's queen, Catherine was in the habit of interpreting that 'boke of the crucifix' from the reformed side of a chasm growing steadily wider, dividing what had gone before from what was to come after. Goldsmith's letter supports the impression given by Catherine, herself, in her later writings that she was reading omnivorously, weighing deeply the questions raised by the religious revolution and searching in her private conscience for new answers to old questions.

The queen's first personal statement of faith appears to have been written only months after her marriage to the king. It is found in the draft of a letter to Jane

Cheyney, the wife of Sir Thomas Wriothesley and niece of Stephen Gardiner, consoling her on the death of her baby son, Anthony.[21] It is a letter notable for its lack of sentimentality and one reason for this may lie in Lady Wriothesley's own character. In the letter, Catherine warns the bereaved mother against 'inordinate sorrow', 'excess sorrow', and 'immoderate and unjust heaviness', as well as remarking on the 'godly consolations given unto you, as will be by my lord your husband as other your wise friends'. Lady Wriothesley appears to have been both an emotional woman and a particularly possessive mother. The loss of this child, her second son to die as a baby, seems to have completely undone her. When her third and only surviving son, Henry (born 1545), was ordered to court in 1564 at age nineteen, Lady Wriothesley refused to permit him to leave her. A special order had to be initiated by the Privy Council to force her to allow Henry to appear, 'without further delay or protract of time, [and] notwithstanding her former excuses',[22] and when the boy wanted to make a perfectly respectable marriage a year later with his cousin, the daughter of Sir Anthony Browne, he had to make it in secret and 'without the consent of my Lady, his mother'.[23] This overabundance of dramatic and emotional motherlove may perhaps be blamed for the queen's rather brusque tone in her letter of consolation.

'Understanding it hath pleased God of late,' Catherine writes, 'to disinherit your son of this world, of intent he should become partner and chosen heir of the everlasting inheritance, which calling and happy vocation ye may rejoice.' This felicitous thought is followed by an acknowledgment that as 'you are a mother by flesh and nature, [doubting that] you can give place quietly to the same, in as much as Christ's mother endowed with all godly virtues did utter sorrowful natural passion of her son's death whereby we have all obtained everlastingly to life.' Despite the precedence for motherly sorrow set by the Virgin Mary, the queen points out sternly, to give utterance to excessive grief is to risk being taken by God, 'as a murmurer against his appointments and ordinances':

> For what is excessive sorrow but a plain evidence against you that your inward mind doth repine against God's sayings, and a declaration that you are not contented that God hath put your son by nature, but his by adoption, in possession of the heavenly kingdom?

To the queen's way of thinking, Lady Wriothesley by immoderate sorrow has put herself in danger of appearing a rebel against God's holy will:

Such as have doubted of the everlasting life to come, doth sorrow and bewail the departure hence, but those which be persuaded that to die here is life again, do rather long for death, and count it a solace than to bewail it as an utter destruction. How much, Madam, are you to be counted godly wise that will and can prevent through your godly wisdom, knowledge and humble submission that thing that time would at length finish.

What baby Anthony might have become as a man is, to Catherine, immaterial. 'And as of his towardness, you could but only hope, his years were so young ... It seemeth that he was now a mete and pleasant sacrifice for Christ.' The queen concludes on a note of admonishment, 'If you lament your son's death, you do him great wrong and show yourself to sorrow for the happiest thing there ever came to him ... being in the hands of his best Father. If you be sorry for your own commodity, you show yourself to live to yourself.' A quiet submission to God's will, adjures the queen, is the only acceptable path for a Christian woman to take, and she closes with the observation that God, 'can at His pleasure repay your loss with such a like jewel, if gladly and quietly ye submit and refer all to His pleasure.'

How this rigorously unsentimental document was received by the hysterical mother may well be imagined. How it was meant to be received as a statement of faith gives a glimpse into the mind of Henry's new queen. The concept that it was better to die young, the sooner to join God in his heavenly bliss, was a concept current in medieval Catholicism. It was an attitude effectively voiced in *The Mirror of the Sinful Soul* by Marguerite of Navarre, a work with which Catherine was much taken. The thought and tone of the letter give little indication of a mind 'infected' with heretical doctrine. The longing for death which Catherine defines as the corollary to a belief in a life everlasting was not a new idea. But it is possible that the very harshness of her manner in this letter stems not only from a personal dislike of the lady to whom it is addressed (apparently at Sir Thomas Wriothesley's urging) but once again reflects that same sense of 'discomfort' with the received doctrine that had been given her as a child to deal with life's emotional crises. Catherine was still suffering under her own secret sense of loss, having been persuaded against her will to give up her love for Sir Thomas Seymour in order to marry the king (' ... shall my sorrow ever endure: shall my wound be uncurable and never healed ... I beseech thee (O lord god) take away from me this pain and sorrow: or at least wise mitigate and assuage it, either by comfort or by council, or by what means soever it shall be seen good to thee.').[24] These feelings were doubtless all the more intense, because, unlike Lady Wriothesley, she could not give them public voice. This, to her irrevocable, sacrifice for Christ may have made the queen less than sympathetic to a woman who could with time look for a replacement for the baby whose unknown character made a mother's sorrow generic rather than unique and therefore ultimately consolable. One demonstrable aspect that does emerge from this early writing is the fluency and power of Catherine's use of the English vernacular. There is no hesitation or vagueness of thought. The queen possessed a vigorous style, a broad vocabulary, a clarity of meaning and a sureness of expression that gives lie to the notion that she arrived at the Tudor court, a country bumpkin without education or intellectual accomplishments.[25]

Catherine's spiritual journey from orthodox Catholic dogma through Henrician Anglicanism to evangelical Lutheranism and the radical fringes of Calvinism seems to have happened not as a sudden light on the road to Damascus but, in her own words, as a gradual awakening from the spiritual sleep of ignorance. If on the day she accepted the king as her husband, she had already accepted his established church in her heart, the spiritual battle within her was far from over. Initially, Catherine attempted to fulfil the strictures laid down by St. Paul for Christian wives, 'to be obedient to their husbands and to keep silence in the congregation and to learn of their husbands at home.' Christian wives, even queens, should:

> Wear such apparel as becommeth holiness and comely usage, with soberness. Not being accusers or detractors, not given to much eating of delicate meats and drinking of wine, but [as] they teach honest things, to make the young women sober-minded, to love their husbands, to love their children, to be discrete, chaste, housewifely, good, obedient unto their husbands, that the work of God be not evil spoken of.[26]

This was undoubtedly the philosophy with which she had been raised, never mind that there was no husband in the household to apply it to, and initially Catherine tried to practice as she preached. But she quickly discovered that she was a housewife no longer, and was, in fact, married to a king who understood better than most the propaganda aspects of ostentatious display, of opulent and splendid attire, of jewelled magnificence and the dazzling panoply of courtly pomp and circumstance. The austerity of God sat uneasily on the shoulders of any Tudor queen, and as Catherine strove to master the pitfalls and prerogatives of her new position, worldly splendors fought in her conscience with spiritual imperatives.

> I regarded little God's word [she wrote], but gave myself to vanities and shadows of the world. I forsook him, in whom is all truth, and followed the vain, foolish

imaginations of my heart. I would have covered my sins with the pretence of holiness. I called superstition godly meaning, and true holiness error. The Lord did speak many pleasant and sweet words unto me, and I would not hear.[27]

This theme of truth offered but ignored is dwelt upon at length in Catherine's writings and may recall her years in Lincolnshire when she lived in the household of a man committed to the English Reformation who had a reputation for violence and household tyranny. If Truth knocked on Catherine's door in Lincolnshire, the man often got in the way of the message. 'For only speaking of the gospel maketh not men good Christians,' she remarked dryly, 'but good talkers.'[28] Nicholas Udall mentioned Catherine's spiritual awakening in 1545 when he wrote that the revealed Truth in the gospel of St. Luke, 'is the same treasure hidden under the cloddy hard ground in the field of the letter which your grace, after ye had found, did for joy sell all that ye had to buy that same field withal.'[29] Whether the metaphor, taken from St. Matthew, was chosen by Udall or one that he had heard his royal mistress use, again the message is unmistakable – Catherine was reading widely in order to understand that one book of supreme value to the reformers, 'the boke of the crucifix'. William Cecil, in his preface to the queen's *Lamentation of a Sinner*, also refers to her spiritual conversion as an inner labour aimed at 'Removing superstition, wherewith she was smothered, to embrace true religion, wherewith she may revive.'[30]

The process, described by Catherine, herself, was one in which God in his mercy opened her eyes to Christ. 'I never knew mine own miseries and wretchedness so well by book, admonition, or learning, as I have done by looking into the spiritual book of the crucifix ... Thus, I feel myself to come, as it were, in a new garment before God ... ':[31]

When God, of his mere goodness, had thus opened mine eyes, and made me see and behold Christ, the wisdom of God, the light of the world, with a supernatural sight of faith. All pleasures, vanities, honour, riches, wealth and aids of the world began to wax bitter unto me. Then I knew, it was no illusion of the devil nor false nor human doctrine I had received. When such success came thereof, that I had in detestation and horror, that which I erst so much loved and esteemed, being of God forbidden that we should love the world or the vain pleasures and shadows in the same. Then began I to perceive that Christ was my only saviour and redeemer, and the same doctrine to be all divine, holy and heavenly, infused by grace, into the hearts of the faithful, which never can be attained by human doctrine, wit nor reason, although they should travail and labour for the same to the end of the world.[32]

Her principal spiritual mentor, particularly during the first year of her marriage, was George Day, Bishop of Chichester, who became Catherine's almoner. Day was a moderate reformer whom the accelerating pace of religious reform, throughout the reign of Edward VI, was to leave behind in the dust of reactionarism. But for the moment he stood just far enough down the road to reform to suit the queen's own beliefs. It was undoubtedly Day who inspired Catherine to study the works of Erasmus, a study which became a lifelong preoccupation and may have had early roots in the schoolroom at Rye House. It was almost certainly Day, too, who suggested to the queen that she undertake an English translation of a book of psalms, *Psalms or Prayers taken out of Holy Scripture*, originally published in Cologne in Latin about 1525 and attributed to John Fisher, Bishop of Rochester, whom the king had executed in 1535. Catherine's ambivalence toward Latin is demonstrated both in her study of the language and in her denunciation of it. In 1546, she protests her ignorance of Latin in a letter to the University of Cambridge, yet in answer to that letter, Roger Ascham responded in Latin, 'Spurn not this name of learning, most prudent Lady, for the glory of your application and ability is greater than all the distinction of your station.'[54]

This public ambivalence toward classical languages by the queen sprang not from an ignorance of them but from a fervent commitment to the emphasis put on the vernacular by the evangelicals and their condemnation of Latin as a language too frequently used to exclude all but an inner elite from a study of the gospels. There was also a secular side to this religious fervency. A celebration of vernaculars only just beginning to discover the literary potential latent in their music was symptomatic in an age of discovery. Even such a classicist as Sir Thomas More realized this. As John Palsgrave reminded him in 1529, 'I remember that you showed me once how a little Latin should serve so the [Duke of Richmond] might have French ... '[35] The queen's public modesty regarding her abilities was a literary pose common to the time as well. When Sir Anthony Cope presented the queen with his book, *A Godly Meditation Upon XX select and chosen Psalmes of the Prophet David*, as a New Year's gift in 1547, he protested that he had accomplished the work despite 'having very small learning, but only to gratify your mind and to avoid idleness ... ' Humility in public voices was a becoming attribute in the last years of Henry's reign and particularly so in a Christian woman. Yet Catherine's ability contradicts her literary modesty. That she turned to vernacular translation as early as she did was not only an example of the intellectual exercise she craved but yet another indication of the direction in which her religious thinking was tending.

George Day had been the chaplain to the late Bishop of Rochester, and the appeal of Fisher's book, with its mildly humanist origins and psalm-like format, was, despite its executed author, an unexceptional work to recommend to a queen who had a special fondness for the Psalms of David. The thematic material of *Psalms or Prayers* includes prayers for the remission of sins, for the obtaining of godly wisdom, for protection from enemies, and assurances of confidence and trust in God. The Fourth Psalm, 'A complaint of a penitent sinner which is sore troubled and overcome by sin', anticipates the queen's *A Lamentation or Complaint of a Sinner*, written two years later. As in Catherine's *Prayers or Meditations*, published the following year, the queen has taken an essentially Catholic text and given it a subtle Protestant colouration and emphasis. This interpretive translation of an early humanist work was the queen's first effort to render holy works that she admired relevant to an emerging reformed consciousness.

The queen's translation speaks out in the first person, acknowledging a belief in the unique bond between the individual soul and an all-merciful God. 'Thou art father of mercies, and God of all grace, peace and comfort, which wilt not the death of a sinner, nor delightest in the damnation of souls.'[36] The voice of the speaker in the queen's translation is no longer identifiable as a privileged member of the ecclesiastical elite but a simple human soul, undifferentiated from its fellows, seeking union with the grace and forgiveness of God not only in the heaven to come but in the immediate realities of this world. Although the psalms are set out as the plaints of a 'Christian man', on several occasions the voice is distinctly female. 'I never unto this day turned truly unto thee with all my heart: but as a woman that breaketh her fidelity and promise unto her husband, even so (o lord god) I have broken my promise unto thee.'[37] Yet overall, apart from the headings, the speaker is given an ungendered voice, a soul which speaks out to God in the name and service of all men and women wandering in the wilderness of the world. Catherine's voice can be heard rising in powerful counterpoint above Bishop Fisher's older harmonies. Word usage, phrasing and commonality of ideas all mark it as a product of the queen's able mind.

Psalms or Prayers	Letter to Lady Wriothesley
... behold thy son, which is given to us, whom thou hast not spared, but given to death for us all, to be a sweet offering and a sacrifice to thee.	... it hath pleased God of late to disinherit your son of this world, ... it seemeth that he was now a mete and pleasant sacrifice for Christ.

Psalms or Prayers	*Lamentation of a Sinner*
Thou hast spoken to me, but I would not hear.	The Lord did speak many pleasant and sweet words unto me, and I would not hear.

Psalms or Prayers	*Lamentation of a Sinner*
My pride and arrogancy have beguiled me and the foolish boldness of my heart hath brought me into desolate ways.	My pride and blindness have deceived me, and the hardness of my heart withstood the growing of truth within it.

Psalms or Prayers	*Lamentation of a Sinner*
(Thou) has saved us by the fountain of regeneration and new birth and the renewing of the Holy Ghost.	There is no man can avow that Christ is the only saviour of the world but by the Holy Ghost.

Psalms or Prayers	*Prayers or Meditations*
Hear the prayers of thy servant: and cast not away the humble fruits of thy poor creature.	But what am I, Lord, that I dare speak to thee? I am thy poor creature.

Psalms or Prayers	*Lamentation of a Sinner*
Turn me to thee, and I shall be turned: for thou art my maker: and I am the clay and work of thy hands.	Then I began to see perfectly ... that I was in the Lord's hand, even as the clay is in the potter's hand.

Psalms or Prayers	*Lamentation of a Sinner*
The fountains of thy goodness be ever full and flow over. Thy grace never decayeth.[38]	Even he is the water of life, whereof whosoever shall drink ... it shall be in him a well of water springing up into everlasting life.[39]

One of the strongest themes developed in this book, in the 8th, 9th, 10th, and 13th psalms and in part of the 11th and 12th, is a desire to smite one's enemies. 'Let thy zeal suddenly come upon them: the fiery thunderbolts and the spirit of the whirlwind be portion of their part ... let the wrath of the fury vex and trouble them. Let them be confounded forever: yea let them tremble and perish together.'[40] This is a side of the queen's character that surfaces only rarely, her temper and desire to be revenged on her enemies. It shows up in unguarded moments in her later letters to Thomas Seymour and is reflected in some of the scalding dialogue given by Nicholas Udall to her alter-ego, 'Kitte Custance', in *Ralph Roister-Doister.*

Catherine's reasons for an inner anger at the Byzantine court of Henry VIII are not hard to imagine. She had become queen over the heads of many who had spent a lifetime in royal service, who were connected by marriage, mutual interest, and common background and who came from the highest ranks in the kingdom. Lady Latimer of Yorkshire, irrespective of her new husband's capricious nature, would have found her sudden elevation as queen difficult to handle with tact and patience. Many no doubt considered the king's choice a strange misalliance, dangerous as it might be to voice such a view. Backbiters would have been plentiful not to mention those who disagreed with Catherine's attitudes on religion, orders of succession or women who 'meddled' in politics. 'They gather themselves together in corners,' laments the 10th Psalm, 'they watch my steps, how they may take my soul in a trap ... They do beset my way, that I should not escape: they look and stare upon me ... I am so vexed that I am utterly weary.' This lament speaks to the heart of the queen's situation.[41]

One of the major emotional steps taken by Catherine in the next two years is a change in emphasis in her writings from the wrathful anger expressed during the first year of her marriage to the compassionate charity expressed in her last, an indication of the spiritual journey she has undertaken:

> Charity suffereth long and is gentle, envieth not, upbraideth no man, casteth frowardly no faults in men's teeth, but referreth all things to God ... the men regenerate by Christ ... have a desire to do good to all men, and to hurt no man, no, though they have occasion given.[42]

In this change may be traced the growing confidence she had in herself, her marriage and the security of her position.

Psalms or Prayers taken out of the Holy Scripture was published first in Latin on 18 April 1544 by the king's printer, Thomas Berthelet. It was published without any reference to Fisher and although his name remained connected with the book on the continent, it was conveniently forgotten in England. The Latin publication of *Psalms or Prayers* was almost certainly the queen's first patronage project, her connection to it evidenced by the appendage of her 'Prayer for the King' at the end. The prayer, however, was in English and with its publication, Catherine takes her place as a published author in the vernacular within the first year of her marriage. Catherine's early championing of the vernacular can be seen as both the fulfillment of an Erasmean ideal learned in the schoolroom and a defined goal compatible with the tenets adopted by the Henrician church. But it was also the language of radicalism.

The English translation of *Psalms or Prayers* again printed by Berthelet, was published a week after the Latin edition, on 25 April, and ran through eighteen editions by 1608, so great was its popularity. The English translation was published anonymously and Catherine has never received credit as translator.

1 Dressed in clothes inscribed with heraldic devices, Maud and Thomas Parr, together with their children, kneel on their tomb in St Anne's, Blackfriars.

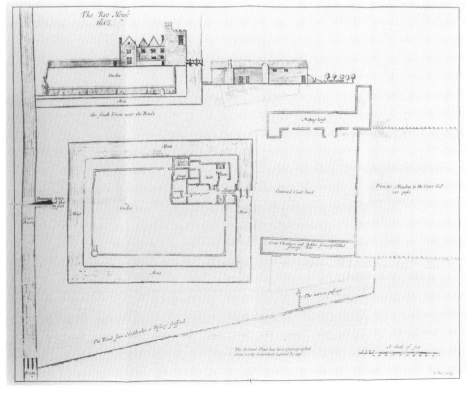

2 Childhood home of the Parrs, an early plan of Rye House in Leicestershire shows the hall, kitchen, great and small parlors, courtyard and gatehouse.

C hic incipiut comendacioes animau

3 The interior of a late fifteenth-century house from Sir Thomas Parr's
prayerbook illustrates the affluent lifestyle in which the young Parrs were raised.

loke / I pray yow remember yowre lovynge niviw, William Parr.' The figue of St Katherine at the top of the page became the royal badge of William's sister on her marriage to Henry VIII.

5 'Oncle wan you do on thys loke / I pray you reme[m]ber wo wrete this in your bo[ok] / your louvynge niece Katheryn Parr.' The bottom three lines of the page begin the account of St Katherine of Alexandria. The idiosyncratic spelling was typical of the entire age.

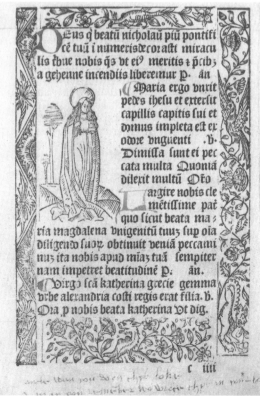

Left: 6 Cousin of Sir Thomas Parr and exector of his will, Cuthburt Tunstall, Bishop of London and Durham, was both churchman and scholar and together with their mother, the architect of the young Parrs' education.

Right: 7 'Brother et es another sayeng / That owt of siyt owt of mind / But I troste in yow / I shallnot fynd et treu. Mawd Parre'
Jesus carries the cross from the walls of Jerusalem at right and is offered vinegar on a sponge by a caricatured Jew at left in this graphically rendered Crucifixion scene.

Left: 8 Cousin of the Parrs, Elizabeth Cheyney, later Lady Vaux, was raised in the household of Maud Parr, together with her own two daughters.

9 Scenes of sex and violence decorate the young Parrs' prayerbook. David in the act of killing Goliath and secretly observing Bathsheba in her bath.

Left: 10 The earliest known portrait of Catherine Parr, probably painted about the time of her marriage to John Neville, Lord Latimer, and demonstrating her early interest in portraiture.

Below: 11 Gainsborough Old Hall in Lincolnshire where Catherine Parr came as bride in 1529.

is dressed as the Renaissance nobleman he believed himself to be. This drawing was probably executed about the time Parr was appointed loyal warden of the marches toward Scotland in April 1543.

Below: 13 Snape Castle in northern Yorkshire where Catherine Parr lived as the wife of Lord Latimer during the traumatic Pilgrimage of Grace in 1536.

Left: 14 This late drawing by Holbein of a gentlewoman of the privy chamber may represent Anne Herbert during the period she served in the household of Katherine Howard. The resemblance to portraits of Catherine Parr is striking.

Below left: 15 Sir Thomas Seymour wears a lover's pink cap in this Holbein miniature, possibly painted for Catherine Parr, Lady Latimer, in early 1543.

Below right 16 The queen has left her autograph and some carefully inscribed injunctions in this book which once belonged to her and which contains a sermon by John Chrisostome.

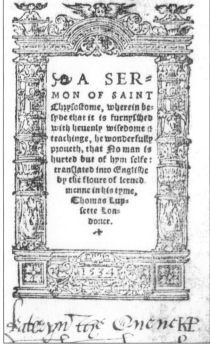

Above left: 17 Edward Seymour, Earl of Hertford(?). Although traditionally thought to be a portrait of Henry Howard, Earl of Surrey, new evidence suggests that this may be a drawing of the ambitious elder Seymour brother.

Above right: 18 This Holbein drawing, executed at the same time as the drawing of William Parr, may represent his closest friend, John Dudley, Lord Lisle, about 1542.

Right: 19 William Paget, one of the Tudor court's most outstanding self-made men, began his career as Gardiner's protégé but switched sides in the last months of Henry VIII's life.

Rich Lo: Chancelor

was one of the chief
conspirators in the 1546
plots against the queen's life.

CATHARINA REGINA VXOR HENRICI VIII

Left: 21 A recently
discovered portrait of
Catherine Parr shows her
about 1546, the year of the
plots against her life.

Right: 22 Sir William Petre served as secretary to the queen's council in 1544 and later supported her brother and the Earl of Warwick in their overthrow of the lord protector.

Right: 23 Sir William Parr of Horton acted as a surrogate father to the young Parrs and as adviser to Catherine as queen until his death in 1547.

KATHARINE PARRE

Left: 24 This late portrait of the queen shows her dressed in crimson, her favourite colour, and wearing a pendant which may have belonged to Katherine Howard.

Left: 25 Katherine Willoughby, Duchess of Suffolk.

Right: 26 Mary Salisbury, Lady Parr of Horton. Catherine's aunt.

Below left: 27 A poem by Thomas Seymour written in Catherine's prayerbook

Below right: 28 Catherine's writing.

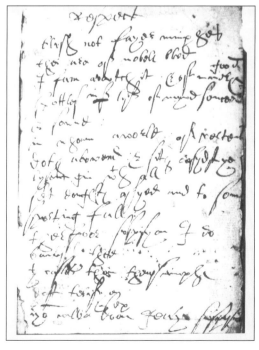

Above: 29 Hanworth Palace.

Below: 30 *Design for a Presence Chamber*, attributed to Nicolò da Modena. Present whereabouts unknown.

31 Portrait medals (1562) of William Parr, Marquess of Northampton, and his second wife, Elisabeth Brooke, by Stephen van Herwijck.

Left: 32 Catherine Parr's royal great seal.

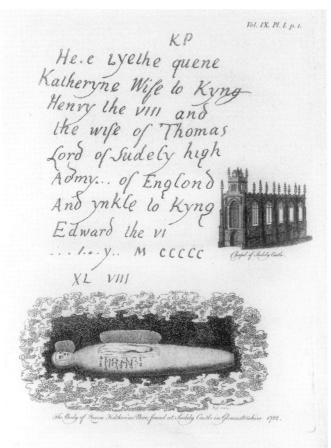

Left: 33 A 1789 sketch of the opening of Catherine Parr's lead coffin after its accidental discovery at Sudley Castle.

The reasons for her choice to publish anonymously are undoubtedly the same as those expressed by a later author on religious themes: 'Perhaps [the author] is not altogether insensible to praise or blame; and this might have been one reason why he preferred being anonymous, that at a safer distance, and through a wary loop-hole, he might so behold the fate of his little work, that whatever it might be, he who intended no harm, might receive none.'[43] Also no doubt initially intimidating to the queen was the culturally pervasive belief that the translation of accepted works, although just permissible for ladies of high birth, violated the divinely authorized sanction enjoining womanly silence.[44] 'How far more convenient,' Giovanni Bruto wrote about women in his 1579 conduct book, *The Mirror of Modesty*, 'the Distaff, and Spindle, Needle and Thimble were for them with a good and honest reputation, then the skill of well using a pen or writing a lofty verse.'[45] If Christian piety was 'the bedrock of subordination for women,'[46] the promotion of piety in others could hardly act as an excuse for a women, even a queen, to boast of scholarly achievement by publishing under her own name. Or as another contemporary writer has put it: 'When even ordinary women of the time saw the publication of a book by a woman as a symptom of mental instability, it is no wonder that women used pseudonyms.'[47] If Catherine published anonymously, what evidence is there, besides the internal parallels discussed above, to indicate that it was indeed the queen who translated Fisher's psalms?[48]

A majority of the subsequent editions of the work, particularly the 2 July 1545 edition, are bound together with Catherine's next religious production, *Prayers or Meditations*, and entitled *The King's Psalms and the Queen's Prayers*, without any other source of authorship being given. The inclusion by Berthelet of the *Psalms or Prayers* in the 6 November 1545 inaugural edition of Catherine's new publication, *Prayers or Meditations*, would not have been undertaken without the queen's permission. The persistent publication of the *Psalms or Prayers* jointly with Catherine's acknowledged *Prayers or Meditations* in editions dating from the later book's first printing, indicates that in Thomas Berthelet's mind, as well as in the queen's, an integral relationship existed between the two works. Nicholas Udall, in his dedication to the English translation of Erasmus' *Paraphrase of the Book of Acts*, refers to the queen as having composed and set forth 'many goodly Psalms and diverse other contemplative meditations'. In the *Preface*, he compliments the queen, telling her, '[You] deserveth no less than to be esteemed and called the chief patroness: not only for diverse most godly Psalms and meditations of your own penning and setting forth.'[49] His repeated use of the word 'psalms' rather than 'prayers' is significant, as are two bills for books to be found in Catherine's chamber accounts.

The first bill, dated January 1547,[50] records an order of books from Berthelet in special bindings delivered to the queen, among which are some thirty of her own *Prayers or Meditations* bound variously in white satin and leather, embossed with gilt. One item on the bill refers to 'a book of psalm prayers covered in white and gilt on leather'. These presentation copies indicate that the queen was in the habit of giving such copies to her friends and well-wishers. In light of that must be interpreted another bill, dated 1 May 1544,[51] and written in Thomas Berthelet's hand, recording charges for some eight of the 'books of the psalm prayers, gorgeously bound and gilt on leather', six of which had been ordered as presentation gifts for Catherine's almoner, George Day. Three days later, on 4 May,[52] another bill from Berthelet records six more copies 'likewise bound and gilt on leather' delivered to George Day. Fourteen presentation copies 'of the psalm prayers' ordered by the queen from the king's printer, half of them sent to her almoner, who was presumably the inspiration for the project, less than a week after the publication of the English translation of *Psalms or Prayers*, and including prayers known at court to have been written by the queen, is a fairly strong indication of the royal source of the translation. So, too, are recurrent charges in the queen's chamber accounts for the delivery of 'a book', almost certainly presentation copies of *Psalms or Prayers*, that occur throughout the summer of its publication. Copies were sent to the Duchess of Norfolk, Lady Kingston and Archbishop Cranmer, as well as those that went to the Bishop of Chichester.[53] As the queen's accounts are fragmentary, more than these may have been sent out or personally presented at court.[54] In his list of Catherine's works, John Bale lists 'Meditations Psalms',[55] a confusion of the titles of the two works, *Psalms or Prayers* and *Prayers or Meditations*. On 13 June 1546, the queen ordered another four copies of *Psalms or Prayers* bound in crimson velvet, one of which she kept with her until her death.[56] Among Catherine's belongings sent up to London from Sudeley in 1549 after the queen's death, was Catherine's personal library of books, some twenty in number. Among the items catalogued was, 'a book of Psalmes covered with crimson velvet and garnished with gold.'[57]

By the summer of 1544, the year that produced the *Psalms or Prayers*, the queen's religious beliefs were moving toward the more radical ideas current in the Reformation. Nicholas Udall's English translation for Catherine of Italian Calvinist Bernardino Occhino's attack on the papacy, *Tragoedia de Papatu*,[58] which like his play *Ralph Roister Doister* probably dates from this year, indicates that the queen's religious beliefs had gone well beyond the mild Erasmeanism of her childhood. In October 1544, Catherine personally intervened in a case before the Court of Aldermen in London in which a schoolmaster had been charged with voicing heretical opinions and printing radical religious books. Stephen Cobbe, a tutor employed in the household of the king's financial agent in Antwerp, Stephen Vaughan, was called before the Court of Alderman in London to answer these charges. The queen's silkwoman, who had died the month before, happened to have been Vaughan's wife and the mother of the children whom Cobbe was educating. In the process of acquiring a reputation at court as a reader of radical books, Catherine involved herself in the case by sending a member of her household, Edward Warner, to plead for Cobbe. Warner managed to have Cobbe released, and the queen's tendency toward religious radicalism was made public knowledge.

Her interest in Calvinism is implied both by Princess Elizabeth's 1545 New Year's gift of an English translation of the first chapter of John Calvin's *L'Institution de la vie chrestienne*, originally published in Geneva in 1541, and also by John Strype, in his *Ecclesiastical Memorials*, where he credits Catherine with an English translation about this time of Savonarola's *A goodly exposition, after the manner of a contemplation upon the li Psalm called Miserere mei deus*, first published in Paris in 1538 in Latin and English.[59] The only external evidence for this is John Bale's comment, '*Et alia*', at the end of his list of Catherine's known works.[60] Although definitive evidence for this attribution is lacking, internal evidence lends credence to the claim.

Psalms or Prayers	*51st Psalm*
Behold I was begotten in iniquity, and my mother brought me into the world defiled in sin.	Behold I was shapen in iniquity; and in sin did my mother conceive me.
Cleanse me (o holy father) with the blood of the new testament of thy well-beloved son.	Wash me thoroughly from mine iniquity, and cleanse me from my sin.
Hear the prayers of thy servant: and cast not away the humble fruits of thy poor creature and handiwork.	Cast me not way from thy presence; and take not thy holy spirit from me.
O most mighty god of angels and of men: whose judgements be unsearchable: and whose wisdom is profound and deep.[61]	Behold, thou desirest truth in the inward parts: and in the hidden part thou shalt make me to know wisdom.[62]

In the 6 November 1545 edition of *Psalms and Prayers* which was bound in with Cranmer's new *Litany* and Catherine's second work, *Prayers or Meditations*, a new prayer was added to the end of Catherine's translation of Fisher, entitled 'A prayer for forgiveness of sins'.[63] This prayer, undoubtedly by the queen as it was published in a book she had translated and under her auspices, echoes the phrasing and sentiments of the Fifty-first Psalm, Savonarola's sermon, and Fisher's psalmic commentaries:

> I have strayed abroad as a lost sheep: seek for thy servant (o lord) for I have not forgotten thy commandments. Remember not (lord) the offences and ignorances of my youth. Mind me according to thy mercy, Lord, for thy goodness sake, keep my soul, deliver me, for I have hoped in thee. Turn my wailing into joy. Cut my sack of sorrow in pieces and clothe me with gladness, and I will sing thy glory.

Catherine's apparent fascination with the Italian school of Calvinism, represented by Bernardino Occhino and Savonarola, sprang from her hostility toward the papacy and the 'worshipping of images and idols' she believed that institution encouraged:

> I forsook the spiritual honouring of the true living God, and worshipped visible idols, and images made of men's hands, believing by them to have gotten heaven … I sought for such riffraff as the bishop of Rome hath planted in his tyranny and kingdom, trusting with great confidence by the virtue and holiness of them to have full remission of my sins … For [the bishop of Rome] is a persecutor of the gospel, and grace, a setter forth of all superstition, and counterfeit holiness … [64]

While the mainstream of her religious thought came from Luther, as evidenced in her last work, *Lamentation of a Sinner*, written in 1546,[65] there were aspects of the more extreme Calvinist thought that appealed to her as well. Udall's translation of Occhino for the queen points to a religious radicalism that by 1544 had already moved well beyond the contents of the Henrician Settlement.

Radical ideas touching on social as well as religious matters were evolving in the mind of the queen too.[66] These found expression in Catherine's prayers included in *Psalms or Prayers*. The one she wrote, 'for men to say entering into battle', almost certainly written shortly before her husband's departure to campaign in France in July 1544, was intended as a public statement of religious affirmation rather than a private confession of faith. Although it must have called to mind personal and painful memories of the ravages of war witnessed by the queen in 1536–37, it is men engaging in a just war whom the queen addresses and not protesting peasants. Catherine's clever use of language is again apparent in the vivid image of David, 'being but a little one, unarmed and unexpert in feats of war', but, armed with courage and strength by God, going forth 'with his sling to set upon and overthrow the great huge Goliath.' The woodblock prints of David in her father's *Horae ad Usum Sarum* come vividly to mind as Catherine describes the drama in the pictures she knew so well from childhood.

In this same prayer, Catherine brushes briefly against a favourite symbol of John Calvin, who saw in war a metaphor for the struggles of a reformed Christian Church with the Goliath of Catholic Rome. 'Our cause now being just, and being enforced to enter into war and battle,' Catherine writes, quickly dispensing with the notion that England has any choice in the matter, 'we most humbly beseech thee, O Lord God of hosts, so to turn the hearts of our enemies to the desire of peace, that no Christian blood be spilt', and, as this seems unlikely in a military campaign where both sides are Christian, she adds, 'or else grant, O Lord, that with small effusion of blood, and to the little hurt and domage of innocents, we may to thy glory, obtain victory.'

The radical aspects of this prayer are not so much in the imagery and word usage but in its very creation and publication. These demonstrate a startling and unprecedented public display on the part of the queen. Without apology or any apparent gender-based self-consciousness, the queen asserts her public voice in a published work. To find a woman, particularly a woman from a non-royal, non-monastic background, taking it upon herself to speak directly to God, not in the voice of a humble female suppliant but in the voice of a soldier about to enter into battle, is in 1544 an incredible presumption.[67] The prayer is written 'for men to say', not by another man but by a woman, a daring and novel concept that forces an assessment of Catherine as a strong-willed, surprisingly unorthodox woman of conviction and courage. If it is true that the Reformation, 'with its emphasis on individual salvation and the reading of scripture, was ... the single most important influence on women writers', it is also true that evangelical religious belief led women to speak out who had before cultivated a submissive silence.[68] The evangelical need to bear witness forced the private conscience to assume a public voice. It also gave women something to say.

Catherine's facility with language and her pre-eminent position, combined with a newly awakened religiosity, had given her a voice, a desire and ability to use that voice, and a national forum, all but unique in England in this century. Women like Margaret Beaufort and Margaret More and later the Cooke sisters translated pious works for publication but not even they dared to put their original writings before the English reading public and sign their name to them.[69] 'To keep silence in the congregation' had proven to be too hard a commandment for Henry's energetic queen. In a letter that appears to be the first written by Catherine, then at Greenwich, to Henry on his way to France in the second week of July 1544, the queen closes with the comments, 'I finish this my scribbled letter, committing you into the governance of the Lord, with long life and prosperous felicity here, and after this life to enjoy the kingdom of his elect.'[70] The concept of divine election to spiritual salvation was a central tenant of Luther's teaching, and Catherine's use of the phrase in a letter to the king at this early date demonstrates not only how far her beliefs had evolved but also how free she felt in voicing those − not always compatible − beliefs to her husband.[71] The queen, entrusted in July 1544 with the care of the nation, and having seen one of her works popularized in print, had every reason to believe that God no less than Henry had chosen her for election to His kingdom.

The demands of her months spent as Regent-General of England encouraged the queen in a continued quest among competing and often conflicting religious ideas for those which represented for her a paradigm of God's Will. Catherine owned a copy of Thomas Lupset's English translation of *A sermon of Saint (John) Chrysostome, wherein beside that it is furnished with heavenly wisdom and teaching, he wonderfully proveth, that no man is hurted but of himself.*[72] This translation had been published in 1542 but as Catherine has written her royal cognomen, 'Kateryn the Quene KP', in the front, she probably did not acquire the book until after her marriage. Its message was one that the queen took deeply to heart. '...Though all be lined up against you, they can do you no ill but you yourself ... '[73] A particular virtue available to the mind of man (or in Catherine's religious vocabulary, offered through the grace of God), renders man immutable to human animosity. '...What is this virtue of man's mind? It is to think right of God, and to do right amongst men. For all the aforesaid vanities may be taken from man against his will: but this said virtue, he that hath it, cannot lose it by no man's violence nor yet by the devil's, except he himself destroy it.'[74] In her copy of the sermon, in the queen's hand, are written eight biblical-style verses which appear at once to be self-help memoranda and a list of spiritual guidelines that Catherine followed as regent while Henry was in France:

> Delight not thou in the multitude of ungodly men and
>   have no pleasure in them, for they fear not God.
> Trust not in wicked wretches, for they shall not help
>   in the day of punishment and wrath.
> Be not carried away with every wind and walk not in every
>   path, for so doth the sinner that hath a double tongue.
> Be gentle to hear the word of God, that thou mayst understand
>   it, and make a true answer with wisdom.
> Be swift to hear and slow in giving answer.
> Be not a privy accuser as long as thou livest, and use no

slander with thy tongue.
  See that thou justify small and great alike.
  Refuse not the prayer of one that is in trouble, and turn not
    away thy face from the needy.

The sentiments expressed are not novel but they indicate that the book was with her often enough to be used as a convenient journal and that John Chrysostome's sermon on the words of Jesus – 'Thou shalt love the lord thy God with all thy heart and with all thy soul and with all thy might, and thy brother as thyself. There is no greater commandment than these' – were words 'most truly impressed in the heart' of Henry's queen.[75]

It is important to understand that the ferment of religious ideas on the continent, preached in pulpits, argued in university lectures, propounded in diets, published in biblical commentaries and in attack and counterattack tracts and books had not yet calcified along hard dogmatic lines of antiecumenicalism. The field of the Word was still being plowed and harvested and the varieties of grain to be found there had not yet been meticulously separated. The same multiplicity of ideas existed in England where around the structure of the Henrician Settlement, dependent on the oscillating beliefs of England's mercurial monarch and supreme head of the English church, radicals such as Hugh Latimer, Nicholas Ridley and Edward Crome fought a daily religious battle of the word with both moderates such as the Bishop of Chichester and with conservatives such as Stephen Gardiner, Bishop of Winchester, and Thomas Thirlby, Bishop of Westminster. 'It is much to be lamented,' wrote the queen in 1546, 'the schisms, varieties, contentions and disputations, that have been and are in the world about Christian religion, and no agreement nor concord of the same among the learned men.'[76] The Eucharist and sacrificial character of the mass, clerical celibacy, a belief or disbelief in the efficacy of religious processions, icons and images, the definition of divinely authorized Sacraments, and the existence of Purgatory were all hotly debated issues with sensitive political implications. Exposed to the noise and confusion of this religious maelstrom, yet married to the unpredictable creature that was its centre in England, Catherine in her own religious thinking realized the necessity of tempering a fearless declaration of religious conscience with a public voice of political expediency. So 'anonymous' became the identity of the translator of *Psalms or Prayers*, and Thomas a Kempis and 'other holy works' the culpable parties if *Prayers or Meditations* hit amiss.

While the queen's beliefs continued to maintain a foundation sympathetic to Erasmean humanism and secular learning, as evidenced by her support of Cambridge University and its scholars, she incorporated in the superstructure rising above that foundation most of the major ideas of Luther, plus some of the more radical ideas of the Calvinists. Even when she attacked Erasmus' ideas, as she began to do in 1546, she continued to read his books.[77] By the time her religious beliefs had matured, inevitably, an undercoat of humanism could still be glimpsed beneath the high gloss of Lutheran evangelicalism. And if by 1546 she had become one of those who secretly patronized the Zwinglian sacramentary views of Anne Askew, as her enemies believed, she had by that year without doubt become the heretic that Gardiner believed her to be.

At times, Catherine's writings seem to include ideas from mutually contradictory sources and to avoid taking public positions on particularly sensitive points of doctrine, begging off with the disclaimer that, 'I have certainly no curious learning to defend this matter withal, but a simple zeal and earnest love to the truth.'[78] This disclaimer should probably be attributed not so much to a lack of defined personal position on these points as to a realization that publishing any but moderate religious views in her husband's lifetime could be a very dangerous thing. The Reformation was an on-going process – Luther died only two years before the queen – and if Catherine had not yet resolved to a purist's satisfaction all of the particular points of dogma in dispute in her own mind by her death, she had at least isolated those that were of overriding importance to her.

On 23 March 1545, Catherine's stepdaughter, Margaret Neville, whom she had raised since a child and taken with her to court, wrote her will.[79] That Margaret, an unmarried maiden, had the self-confidence to compose her own will and believed in her legal and moral right to do so is almost certainly due to her stepmother's encouragement and example. The first part of Margaret's will is a passionate statement of Protestant belief:

> I bequeath, yield up and commit to the hands of my most merciful father my soul, (yea) all my whole substance as well spiritual as corporeal, most steadfastly trusting unto his mercy that he through the mercies of my saviour and only mediator Jesus Christ will now perform his promise unto me, that death may have no power over me but that through his grace I may boldly say 'o death where is thy victory. O hell where is thy sting,' being above all other things most certain that all that trust in him shall not be confounded. I know that thou wilt retain me under the wings of thy mercy, not for my worthiness but for the worthiness of Christ my saviour in as much as thou hast promised to glorify all his members for whom he prayed here that they might be glorified.

This is followed by an equally passionate declaration of love and loyalty by Margaret to her stepmother. 'I am never able to render to her grace,' she avows, 'sufficient thanks for the godly education and tender love and bountiful goodness which I have ever more found in her highness.' This document connects the goodly/godly education provided Margaret by Catherine with the emergent Protestantism proclaimed in the will, a document witnessed by Catherine's brother, William, then Earl of Essex, her cousin, Nicholas Throckmorton, and her solicitor, Francis Goldsmith, all ardent supporters of the reformed religion. This declaration of the Protestant faith in Catherine's stepdaughter, whom she raised and educated and continued to keep in her household, admits to a private bond of shared religion between them. Even Margaret's choice of biblical imagery, taken from St. Paul, 'O death, where is thy victory, o hell where is thy sting', seems learned from the queen and is echoed in Catherine's last and primarily Lutheran work, *Lamentation of a Sinner*, written in the following year, 'Then shall the children of God rejoice on him, saying, 'O death, where is thy victory and sting?'[80]

In the same year that Margaret wrote her will, Catherine was organizing the English translation of Erasmus' *Paraphrases* and also working on a paraphrased edition of portions of Thomas a Kempis' highly popular early fourteenth-century religious work, *The Imitation of Christ*. Although arguably more than a paraphrase as original additions by Catherine were interpolated into the text, *Prayers or Meditations* was published as a 'collection' of excerpts from 'holy works' and written in two parts. The first part, or meditations, is a paraphrase of portions of Chapter 3 of Thomas a Kempis' work, filtered through an English translation by Richard Whitford, published in 1530.[81] The meditations are arranged in 288 short verses of no more than one or two sentences each. The second section of Catherine's book contains five prayers, the most frequently published and therefore best known being, 'A prayer for the king' and 'A prayer for men to say entering into battle'. It should be noted that in the title of the book, the publisher has given Catherine's prayers precedence over the paraphrased meditations. The first part of this work, which begins with a quote from St. Paul, Colossians 3:1-2, has been studied by modern scholars who have arrived at diametrically opposing viewpoints. On the one hand, it has been judged, 'a piece of schoolboy plagiarism ... which could hardly have a Protestant tone',[82] to, 'a sensitive and discerning contribution to a Cranmerian literary program on popularizing Protestant lines.'[83] The second part, the five prayers, are either closely considered statements of public piety along reformist lines or works, 'which are perhaps not original', and evince a theology 'distinctly Catholic'.[84] How should this work then be interpreted?

Initially the book must be seen in the context of the queen's on-going program of vernacular translations of primarily humanist-inspired religious works for popular consumption. The choice of publishing it in octavo form, undoubtedly the queen's, made it inexpensive to buy and thus ensured the book a wide popular audience. Like Thomas Cranmer, Catherine seems to have been concerned with building up a library, available to the general reading public, of religious works in the vernacular, as quickly, as reasonably priced, and as expeditiously as possible. This library would provide both validation and explanation of the Word by the word, and help a literate laity in understanding the changes taking place in the English religious establishment. Various volumes, such as the 12 October 1544 publication of the *Litany* with *Psalms or Prayers*, were intended to be used in the new vernacular forms of worship that were replacing Latin services. The audience thus envisioned for these works was a broad-based one, the non-specific gendering of the text rendering it suitable for the use of both sexes. Modern claims that Catherine's work was intended 'for women only' are not supported by the manner in which the works were written or the way in which they were published and distributed.[85] The queen's work at translation and paraphrase was her contribution to digging 'under the cloddy hard ground in the field of the letter' for the jewel of the Gospels that Udall refers to in his preface to the translation of 'St. Luke'. *Prayers or Meditations* must also be seen in the light of Catherine's sincere desire to bring the writings of holy men to the attention of those unable to study them in Latin. She admired the work of Thomas a Kempis just as she admired the work of John Chrysostome and of Erasmus. A very real dislike of throwing out the baby with the bathwater compelled her to reclaim and rephrase the core wisdom to be found in these holy writings for the new and reformed church. Thomas a Kempis' work had grown out of an exclusive world of privileged masculine monasticism. Now in a new age, in a time of great change and spiritual soul-searching, the queen was attempting to make the thought of a Kempis relevant to an inclusive and secular group of literate men and women, instead of allowing it to be relegated to the dust heap of abandoned ideas. But revisions were obviously necessary to make the work relevant to its target audience. Thus through the aegis of Whitford's translation, a Kempis' ecstatic dialogue with Christ was reworked by Catherine into a vernacular monologue of urgency and immediacy, suitable for the oratory of a queen with Protestant convictions or a parish church whose parishioners were seeking guidance and fresh inspiration.

Prayers or Meditations deals with frequently discussed Christian concepts, such as the individual's unworthiness, the vanity of worldly things, God's power and his mercy and the grace of God through Jesus Christ. The queen offers them up, however, in a new, less delicately erudite and more vigorous, accessible and universal manner. Passages expressing the author's burden of troublesome affliction and beseeching God's aid are juxtaposed with confessions of personal sin and unworthiness. Catherine, as narrator, chastises herself for delighting 'in men's praisings' and acknowledges that, 'mine old man, that is my carnal affections, live still in me, and are not crucified, nor perfectly dead.'[86] She utilizes Marguerite of Navarre's image of Jesus as 'most loving spouse' and makes use of the always viable themes of vanity ('... nothing under the sun may long abide, but all is vanity and affliction of spirit'),[87] and the impotence of men (' ... it is a vain thing, to trust in man: For the true trust and health of man, is only in thee.')[88] Yet there are subtle alterations in the material's presentation that mark it as a product of the early English Reformation. No longer is the text a dialogue between Christ and monk. As has been rightly pointed out,[89] Catherine demasculinizes the text, making it a generic one suitable for use by man or woman, and by stripping away the dialogue-dependent structure of the original, by condensing and subtly refocusing the viewpoint, she has intensified the power of the message.

In a medieval work, the clarion call of the Reformation can now be heard. 'When shalt thou be to me all in all; and when shall I be with thee in thy kingdom, that thou hast ordained for thine elect people from the beginning?'[90] Catherine as narrator asks of God. Not content with this, the queen has interpolated lines of her own that do not appear in the original but which magnify the soul's need to study the 'boke of the crucifix' to achieve salvation. 'O what thanks ought I to give unto thee, which hast suffered the grievous death of the Cross, to deliver me from my sins, and to obtain everlasting life for me?'[91] The theme of grace is a constant one. 'Lord, give me grace gladly to suffer, whatsoever thou wilt shall fall upon me, and patiently to take at thy hand good and bad.'[92] That this was a passionately-felt personal statement is reflected in a letter written two years later by Sir Thomas Seymour, then Catherine's husband:

> As I was perplexed heretofore with unkindness, that I should not have justice of those that I thought would in all my causes [have] been partial, which did not a little trouble me; even so, the receiving of your letter revived my spirits; partly, for that I do perceive you be armed with patience howsoever the matter will weigh ...[93]

A patient attendance on the will of God as revealed by the 'boke of the crucifix' was primary both to the Reformation and to the queen's religious beliefs.

The five prayers written by Catherine, which comprise the second part of *Prayers or Meditations* and are given priority of place in its title, were particularly popular. In 'A devout prayer to be daily said', Catherine prays the Lord to grant, 'that the kingdom of thy grace and mercy may reign continually in our hearts,' and that 'all other nations, beholding our goodness and virtuous deeds, that thou workest in us, may be stirred to hallow and glorify thee.' This is an idea frequently found among the writers of the English Reformation, that God in his mercy has blessed the present age by awakening it from the sleep of papistical evil and ignorance to a new dawn of resurrected truth. Henry the king in this schema becomes Moses, David, Josias, and Isaiah, a divinely ordained latter-day prophet designated by God to lead the footsteps of his wandering people into an apostolic Promised Land. England, then, should be acknowledged as God's Paradigm, the spiritual model against which Europe must measure itself. Catherine, as Henry's queen, assumes the guises of Miriam and Zipporah, of Deborah, Esther, the Queen of Sheba and even Mary Magdalene.[94] Whether or not Catherine saw herself in precisely this way, that she did see herself as a missionary to the nation is manifest in her writings.

The theory that *Prayers or Meditations* should be considered a work of conservative Catholic piety rather than part of the new vernacular reform canon does not hold up against a scrutiny of its text or the evidence of its publication record. It was reissued at least seventeen times by the end of the century – twice between December 1545 and December 1546, four times during the reign of Edward VI, and nine times during the reign of Elizabeth I. Only one edition, published by Henry Wykes and now in the British Library, can be dated to the reign of Mary I. Besides the printed editions of the book, there is one in manuscript allegedly in the queen's handwriting belonging to the city of Kendal.[95] It has been further condensed from the published edition with 'a very intensive resequencing of the printed text',[96] which may perhaps indicate that it is an earlier version of the final published work. The enthusiasm with which Catherine's book was received at court is evidenced both by the fact that it saw three editions in its first year and by the Princess Elizabeth's choice of a New Year's gift for her father. For New Year's 1546, Elizabeth translated her stepmother's work into French, Italian and Latin as a gift for the king, an exercise she would hardly have undertaken if she had not been certain of his approval of the project.

In defining the queen's religion, an examination of the men and women with whom she surrounded herself is a useful indicator of Catherine's convictions. Those for whom she acted as patron, who served in her household and who were among her inner circle of friends, all these formed her religious affinity. Catherine supported Nicholas Udall, employed Miles Coverdale, John Parkhurst, Matthew Parker, and Francis Goldsmith. She acted as patron to John Cheke,[97] befriended Nicholas Ridley,[98] and answered Dr. Thomas Smith and Roger Ascham's call for aid for the University of Cambridge.[99] Philip Gerrard, yeoman of the chamber for the Prince of Wales, who wrote *A Godly Invective in the defence of the Gospel*, was one of the lesser lights of the English Reformation whom the queen patronized – in March 1546, she arranged for him to marry the widowed Elizabeth Cotton[100] – as was Sir Robert Tyrwhit, Catherine's master of the horse, whose wife, Elizabeth, wrote a devotional work similar to *Prayers or Meditations*.[101] In 1547, Sir Anthony Cope, the queen's master of the hawks, published as a New Year's gift for the queen, a book entitled *A Godly Meditation upon XX select and chosen Psalmes*. In addition to these, the queen employed Dr. Robert Huicke, whose kinsman Dr. William Huicke,[102] was prosecuted for heresy, and Dr. Edward Layton, brother of Cromwell's aggressive ecclesiastical commissioner, Dr. Richard Layton.[103]

Apart from the Princess Mary and Lady Margaret Douglas, adherents of the old religion, the queen's friends were overwhelmingly adherents of the new. Catherine Willoughby, dowager Duchess of Suffolk, Anne Stanhope, Countess of Hertford, Jane Guildford, Lady Lisle, Jane Champernowne, Lady Denny, Anne Parr, wife of Sir William Herbert, Mary Howard, dowager Countess of Richmond, Elizabeth Stafford, Duchess of Norfolk, Anne Calthrop, Countess of Sussex, Frances, Mary, Lady Kingston, Anne Grey, the wife of Sir Edmund Walsingham, Margaret, Lady Long, the wife of Sir Richard Long, Katherine Skipwith, who married Sir Thomas Heneage, the elder, all of these were sworn to the reformed religion. Two of these closest to Catherine, the dowager Duchess of Suffolk, patron of Hugh Latimer, and the Countess of Hertford, flirted with sacramentarianism during 1546 and sympathized as did their royal mistress with views that would earn them the label of Calvinist after Henry's death.

'All the Words of Angels'

Between the spring of 1544 and the spring of 1546, the queen involved herself in a number of projects related to humanist scholarship and to the reformed religion that ultimately earned her the ire of the conservatives. Her involvement in these projects should also have earned her the interest of posterity but as she chose to keep much of her activity out of the public limelight, the bits and pieces of extant evidence connecting her with such major publications as Cranmer's *Litany*, the Grafton-Whitchurch primer, and the English translation of Erasmus' *Paraphrases* vary in strength and number. Her connection to the founding of the Trinity College, Cambridge, is also a matter of reading between the lines. 'She was a right noble lady, and had done an abundance of good things,' Strype informs us, 'but yet cared not that they should be known or spoken of.'[1] This may have been a laudable display of matronly modesty, according to the canon of behaviour laid down for Renaissance women, but such reticence is frustrating for historians. The one project of which she was indisputably sole author was her final book, *Lamentation of a Sinner*, written in all probability in the winter of 1545–46 and later revised for publication in November 1547.

Catherine's life during her years as queen was full of contradictions. A zealous advocate of the reformed religion, she flirted with Calvinism but also supported rapprochement with Spain. She vilified the papacy but read Italian authors. She spoke fluent French and studied the literary efforts of French writers but unsurprisingly had little sympathy with French political aspirations. An aspect of Catherine's psychology which should be emphasized is the fact that she grew up in a household presided over not by a man but by a woman. As her later actions imply, it was impressed upon Catherine, as the eldest surviving child, that she owed a responsibility to her younger siblings, but it was also part of the wisdom she received as a child that a woman alone was capable of managing a great estate, of handling the business involved in such management, and of establishing an individual identity apart from her father or her husband. Maud Parr had neither father nor husband alive to interfere with her running of her own affairs. Catherine's surrogate father, her uncle William Parr of Horton, lived in another shire and maintained a respectful relationship with his sister-in-law. This early sense of perceived individual identity for women may have been the reason that throughout her life, Catherine signed documents not with her married name but as 'Kateryn Parr, KP'.

In a sense, growing up in an effectively functioning, female-dominated household provided a false prototype for the young Catherine, offering her a skewed idea of how the adult world of sixteenth-century England operated. Marriage, in the forms which presented themselves to her between the years 1529–1547, must have come as a salutary awakening. When she described her brief period of widowhood in early 1542 in a letter, she referred to that time 'when I was last at liberty'. Yet whatever unfortunate surprises and hard life lessons these later experiences may have had for her, they never quite eradicated the hopefulness with which a woman, raised to believe that women can accomplish much, faced the prejudices and challenges of her world. This in part accounts for the energetic eagerness with which Catherine took on a number of important projects between the spring of 1544 and the spring of 1546.

Although religion may have been the most obvious focus of Catherine's attention during this time, a copy of the works of Petrarch, with exposition by Alessandro Vellutello, published in Venice with her name in it, shows a continued interest in the evolving world of humanist *belles-lettres*, as her stepson, Edward, noted in 1546.[2] Petrarch's sonnets had had a seminal impact on the courtier-poet circle to which the queen's brother belonged. Sir Thomas Wyatt combined rhyme schemes popularized by other Italian poets with the subject matter of love and loss dealt with by Petrarch, such as that in *Sonnetto in Vita* 91, which became Wyatt's 'The Long Love That in My Thought Doth Harbour' as well as the Earl of Surrey's 'Love, That Doth Reign and Live Within My Thought'. Wyatt thus introduced the sonnet form into English poetry and his friend, the Earl of Surrey, adding a more fluid standardized rhyme scheme, transformed it into the English sonnet form. Surrey also added unrhymed iambic pentameter or blank verse to the English vocabulary of poetic forms. That the queen owned and read Petrarch shows that she, too, was aware of the momentous things happening on the secular side of the English vernacular blanket. Whether she, herself, attempted to write poetry or was content to read her brother's and his friends in the various manuscripts that circulated at court has yet to be established. But what is certain is that Catherine did not spend all of her waking hours reading Scripture alone.

As far as their wide-ranging effects on the practice of religious devotions in England, among the most important of the projects of 1544–46 with which the queen involved herself were the publications of Archbishop Cranmer's 1544 *Litany*, and the 1545 publication of the Grafton-Whitchurch primer. A primer was a personal prayer book meant for private devotions among members of the laity. As a private work, it was not authorized by the English church or the English government and did not necessarily conform to any rules or regulations that those bodies might have imposed on regular church services. Heretical infection could and did creep into private worship, with, so the king and others believed, detrimental effect on the English congregation as a whole.[3] A standard primer, authorized by the head of the English church, seemed advisable to insure conformity. The first steps toward such a work were taken in May 1544 with the appearance of the *King's Primer*, which was used for private devotions by the king himself but was not offered to the general public until May 1545.

The primer which preceded the *King's Primer* in common usage was written by John Hilsey, a Black Friar. It was dedicated to Cromwell and the Epistles and Gospels which appeared in it were from the Sarum Missal, that *Horae ad Usum Sarum* with which Catherine Parr had grown up. The *King's Primer* was published under the guise of being Henry's own work. He wrote a preface and an injunction, and in the latter, explained that the book's purpose was 'for the avoiding of the diversity of primer books, that are now abroad, whereof are almost innumerable sorts which minister occasion of contentions and vain disputations, rather than to edify, and to have one uniform order of all such books throughout all our dominion, both to be taught unto children, and also to be used for ordinary prayers of all our people not learned in the Latin tongue.'[4] The new primer has been judged by modern scholars as a outstanding piece of religious literature, far superior to any of its predecessors. 'The compiler, like his predecessors, makes use of old material, but he has mastered it, and can treat it with perfect freedom.'[5] That Cranmer wrote some or much of the primer is probable. His *Litany* is a central feature, and it contains prayers for the royal triumvirate – Henry, Catherine and Edward. God is requested to keep 'our noble queen Catherine in thy fear and love, giving her increase of all goodness, honour and children.'[6] Yet Cranmer was only one of the authors of the primer, and there is evidence to indicate that the queen may also have had a hand in its creation.[7]

Between May 1544, when Cranmer's new *Litany* appeared in the *King's Primer* and May 1545 when the primer was published by Grafton and Whitchurch, Cranmer's *Litany* had another publication. On 12 October 1544, it was published 'at London in Paul's Churchyard at the sign of the Maiden's Head by Thomas Petyt'.[8] Two points about this particular publication are of interest. The first point is that the sign under which Petit published, the maiden's head, was the queen's own personal emblem. Petit's use of it may have predated Catherine's but their joint use of that particular device is suggestive. The second point is that the *Litany* was not printed by itself alone but was issued as one half of a volume designed to be used as a 'mass book' during religious devotions. The second half of the volume consisted of Catherine's translation of *Psalms or Prayers*. Petit would hardly have undertaken to join Cranmer's work with that of the queen's without the express approval of both authors. An order for copies of the combined edition by the queen at the time of its publication indicates her involvement in its production.[9] From this joint publication then, it can be inferred that queen and archbishop were working together, 'adapting old forms to new uses.'[10] In the following year, 1545, Thomas Berthelet, who had first published *Psalms and Prayers* and *Prayers or Meditations*, published another version of both books bound in with Cranmer's *Litany*, and included a new prayer, presumably by the queen, for the forgiveness of sins, thus tacitly reiterating in print the common purpose of both authors' work.[11]

In May 1544, when the new primer first appeared at the king's devotions, the chamber accounts of the queen show that in that same month, her clerk of the closet, William Harper, recorded charges for 'a primer for her grace in Latin and English with epistles and gospels unbounden'.[12] Additional charges were made 'for the ruling and collating of the lessons of the said primer and of her grace's testament in French and for the gilding, convening and binding of the two books.' This was undoubtedly the same book as the king's, as was the primer which Catherine had with her at her death, 'Item, a primer in English covered with crimson velvet and garnished with silver and gilt.'[13] These books in the queen's possession suggest that she had an interest in the development of the new primer. This suggestion is confirmed by the choice of the primer's publishers.

On 29 May 1545, the *King's Primer* was issued under the king's name by Richard Grafton and his partner, Edward Whitchurch. Grafton was a new religionist publisher who under Cromwell's patronage and using Cromwell's own licence had published the English translation of the Bible, known as the Great Bible. After Cromwell's death in 1541, Grafton had gotten into trouble for publishing certain ballads defending his late master as well as Philipp Melanchthon's attack on the Six Articles. In 1542, Grafton published Nicholas Udall's English translation of Erasmus' *Apophthegmes*, which recorded the sayings of Greek notables such as Socrates and Diogenes and Roman notables such as Julius Caesar, Cicero and Demosthenes. Udall joined the queen's household a year or two after this publication and it was probably he who brought the radical publisher to the queen's attention.

With the publication of the primer in 1545, Grafton was given a special licence as 'printer and servant to our most dear son Prince Edward', and on 22 April 1547, after Edward's accession to the throne, Grafton was made king's printer with an annual stipend of £12 and the reversion of Thomas Berthelet's £4 annuity at Berthelet's death. It has been rightly pointed out that the author of Grafton's success was in all probability the queen.[14] Grafton's partner,

Edward Whitchurch, was chosen to publish both her *Lamentation of a Sinner* and the fruits of the project on which she laboured so many years, the English translation of Erasmus' *Paraphrases*.

The wide scope of the target audience for the new primer may reflect suggestions made by the queen. Like Cuthbert Tunstall's book on arithmetic, the *King's Primer* was not to be reserved to adults alone:

> Every schoolmaster and bringer up of young beginners
> in learning, next after their A.B.C., now by us also set
> forth, do teach this primer or book of ordinary prayers
> unto them in English, and that the youth customably or
> ordinarily use the same, until they be of competent
> understanding and knowledge to perceive it in Latin.[15]

The king's 'Injunction' states the two-pronged royal provisions for the education of children, a reading primer or ABC and a religious primer. Some obscurity attaches to the ABC, except that it was published at about the same time as the *King's Primer*, and its purpose was to teach children to read their own language as opposed to Latin or Greek, for which a number of grammar books, particularly the popular *Lily's Grammar*, already existed. The same group of new religionist writers who had provided the inspiration, impetus and text for the primer must have also been the group who encouraged publication of the *King's ABC*. This group almost certainly included the queen. For, after all, what good was a religious primer if the commonality could not read it? Literacy was the first step on the road to salvation, and the *King's ABC* probably took the form of a horn book or small wooden paddle to which was attached a sheet printed with the alphabet, followed by a list of numbers and the Paternoster. The sheet was covered with a transparent slice of horn to protect it and keep it clean. Recorded versions of the horn book date to as early as 1450 yet almost no actual samples survive.[16] Presumably they were used until they simply wore out. From this rudimental teaching tool, the student progressed to the intricacies of Latin as set out in books such as *Lily's Grammar*. An edition of this grammar book was reissued by the king's printer, Thomas Berthelet, in 1543–44, yet because the new publication to which the king refers is labeled an 'A.B.C.' and not a 'grammar', the reference seems to be to a basic form of the horn book.

This interest in the secular and religious education of the young was a major theme in the life of the queen. From her mother's will of 1529 leaving money for the founding of schools, to Lord Latimer's will of 1542 leaving money for the founding of a free school at Well, to Catherine's interest as queen in her grammar school at Clare and her involvement in the educations of her Neville stepdaughter and her two youngest Tudor stepchildren, to her patronage of Cambridge University, provision for the teaching of the young was a predominant concern. Standard government issued textbooks for 'young beginners' ABC's' and for their religious instruction covered an area with which the queen was particularly involved and material to which she was particularly committed.

The *King's Primer* was reissued on 6 September 1545, exactly two months before the publication of the queen's *Prayers or Meditations*, compiled from 'holy works'. Cranmer was thus not the only author of importance at court 'engrossed in liturgical studies' at this time.[17] Psalm CXIX is lauded in the preface to the Commendations in the primer, yet was demonstrably tedious to the archbishop. He would hardly have chosen to include it, yet it contains much that would have appealed to the queen, and was in fact echoed in works with which she was involved. 'And I will walk at liberty: for I seek thy precepts. I will speak of thy testimonies also before kings, and will not be ashamed,' sings the Psalmist. 'Remember the word unto thy servant, upon which thou hast caused me to hope. This is my comfort in my affliction: for thy word hath quickened me. The proud have had me greatly in derision: yet have I not declined from thy law. I remembered thy judgements of old, O Lord; and have comforted myself.'[18] If the queen actually did write some portion of the primer, such as any of the 'Certain godly prayers for sundry purposes', if would not be the only time that her work appeared under her husband's name. Her translation of *Psalms or Prayers* was published numerous times after 1556 as *The King's Psalms* and attributed to Henry's authorship. Whatever form the queen's contribution to the primer project took, the evidence implies that she did indeed have a hand in it, 'yet cared not that [it] should be known or spoken of.'

The most demanding project with which the queen interested herself from 1545 to 1548 was the English translation of Erasmus' *Paraphrases Upon the New Testament*. With the organization of the *Paraphrases* project, Catherine took an increasingly visible role in the arena of English vernacular Protestant propaganda, designed as it was to inform and enlighten minds of both sexes unequipped to deal with the intricacies of Latin but who sought a literary exegesis of spiritual truths defined by the Reformation and couched in England's own familiar tongue. The queen has been portrayed as a rather passive participant in this project, providing money to the assumed organizer, Nicholas Udall, and little else.[19] Yet Udall in his preface to the book of 'St. Luke', dedicated to the queen and dated 30 September 1545, remarks, 'I shall turn my style somewhat to treat of Luke, whom it pleased your highness to commit unto me to be translated. Which commandment, when it came first unto me in your grace's name, although I knew how little it was that I could do in this kind, yet was I glad that your commandment did so justly concur with the determination of mine own mind and purpose.'[20] Throughout the various dedications to the queen in the translation, written by Udall and by the translator of St. Mark, Thomas Key, who said prayers daily in her oratory, are remarks on the queen's personal organization of the project. It was she who selected the project at Udall's suggestion, decided to organize the massive undertaking by dividing the translation work among several translators, and selected who those translators were to be. Thomas Key recorded how one of the king's doctors, George Owen, encouraged him to volunteer to undertake the translation of St. Mark after all of the other books had been distributed, 'affirming that I should do a thing right acceptable unto your highness.'[21]

As translator for the 'Book of St. John', Catherine chose her stepdaughter, Princess Mary. The reasons for this may have been more than a desire to improve Mary's Latin. Having been highly successful in championing the king's inclusion of the princess in the line of succession, Catherine now sought to wean her from her more conservative religious convictions by drawing her into a major project for the reformed religion. Francis Mallet, who had been the queen's chaplain, joined Mary's household, charged perhaps with initiating and encouraging a trend toward reform in the princess.[22] As part of this effort, Catherine and Mallet both persuaded Mary to undertake the translation of the 'Book of St. John', and to win her stepmother's approval, Mary agreed to the project. She began to translate a book that later as queen she would order destroyed as heretical.[23]

Three of Catherine's appointed translators are known – Mary undertook the 'Book of St. John'; Udall, himself, translated the 'Book of St. Luke', and Thomas Key, the 'Book of St. Mark'. The work began in 1545 and continued into the fall of 1547, when the queen wrote to request Mary, who was ill, to have Mallet finish and polish the translation of 'St. John' so that it could be included in the final publication of 31 January 1548.[24] If the translators of Mark, Luke and John are known, who then were the translators of the 'Book of St. Matthew' and the 'Acts'? On this point, Strype in his *Ecclesiastical Memorials* remarks, 'But I am apt to think Queen Katharin herself might do one at least, and perhaps that upon St. Matthew.'[25] A close examination of the translation of St. Matthew and a comparison of this book with Catherine's other known writings indicate that Strype may have been correct. It is not impossible, indeed it is highly likely, that some or all of this work was done by the queen, herself.[26]

Udall includes Catherine and Mary among those noble ladies who possess the ability to translate books out of Latin into English in his preface to the 'Book of St. John'. In the introduction to the 'Book of St. Matthew', he also refers to the queen's 'incessant pains and travails'[27] in the cause of true religion, which may be an oblique reference to her work on the very book he was introducing to the reading public. Udall declares in the text that he has revised and checked the two gospels of St. Matthew and Acts against the Latin originals, something he does not mention having done for any of the other books. The implication must be that the translators of Matthew and Acts were not accepted Latinists of the scholarly community. Why else would Udall publicly acknowledge that he had proofed their text? An accepted scholar would have been insulted by such an announcement. Mary had Mallet to vouch for her translation but translations undertaken by other women, fluent though they might be in Latin, required in Udall's view, certainly in the king's, and probably in the queen's as well, a public stamp of approval by an accredited male scholar. This would prevent backbiting at court from those who knew what the queen was about and felt that she presumed too much in undertaking such a task. Of these, Stephen Gardiner, Bishop of Winchester, was certainly one.

A comparison of the language used in the English translation of 'St. Matthew', with that used in Catherine's own writings supports this thesis. The glosses on the 28 March 1548 edition of *Lamentation of a Sinner* show that the queen was widely read in Scripture. She paraphrases or quotes from no less than twenty-three books of the Bible with the 'Book of St. John', 'Romans' and 'Corinthians' being particular favourites. The most quotes, by far, however, over thirty-six in number come from the 'Book of St. Matthew'. The queen's familiarity with St. Matthew was extensive. Her familiarity with Erasmus' paraphrase on the meaning of the text was equally thorough. 'If men so greedily embrace a book,' states the paraphrase in words with which the queen would have fully concurred, 'which is set forth by the industry of man, concerning the preservation or restoring of health, or the way to increase husbandry, or touching any other faculty which maketh only for worldly commodities, with how much more fervent love and desire ought this book to be received of all men whose profit and commodity belongeth indifferently to all men.'[28] The comparison of verses below shows the parallel thought and word usage in the English translation of the St. Matthew paraphrase and in the queen's other work.

Paraphrase of St. Matthew	*Psalms or Prayers*
... for God by his secret counsel which man's wit is utterly unable to search out ...	O most mighty god of angels and of men: whose judgements be unsearchable ...

	Lamentation of a Sinner
(The Jews) signifying and showing before by divers dark figures and shadows ...	For (the Jews) lived under shadows and figures and were bound to the law.

The eternal verity doth not deceive,
God the promiser disappointeth not,
further man's law shall not now
perceive what is to be done, but
Christian charity shall plainly tell.

And, therefore, (the Lord) promiseth
and bindeth himself by his word, to
give good and beneficial gifts to all
them that seek him with true faith ...
(That same doctrine of Christ) which
never can be attained by human
doctrine, wit nor reason ... (but by knowing)
the loving charity of God.

Yea the more earnestly they laboured
to come unto innocency and felicity,
trusting to man's help, the more they
were entangled with vice and filthy desires ...

Christ was innocent and void of all
sin, and I wallowed in filthy sin and
was free from no sin.

Psalms or Prayers
Wherefore it is a vain thing, to trust
in man: For the true trust and health
of man, is only in thee.

Lamentation of a Sinner
... for I had a blind guide called
Ignorance who dimmed mine eyes ...
Christ despised the world with all the
vanities, thereof, and I made it my
god because of the vanities.

For many (don't believe in
Christ the Messiah) because their
eyes be blinded with desires of
worldly things ...

(Jesus is in the world) to overcome
the tyranny of death ... and the sore
provocations of concupiscence by the
sword of the spirit ...[29]

But let us know that Christ yet
fighteth in spirit in his elect
vessels and shall fight even to the
day of judgement. At which day
shall that great enemy death be
wholly destroyed and shall be no
more.[30]

'The evangelical faith,' states the paraphrase, '... is the heavenly seed of God's word.'[31] This was the core of the queen's own belief. A year or so later, when Catherine was writing clandestinely to her lover, Sir Thomas Seymour, she accused him of deliberately misinterpreting something she had said, remarking, 'I know not whether ye be a paraphraser or not. If ye be learned in that science, it is possible ye may of one word make a whole sentence, and yet not at all times alter the true meaning of the writer ...'[32] By the year the letter was written, 1547, the queen had had considerable experience of translations and paraphrasers.

One other piece of evidence that ties Catherine's work to the anonymously translated gospel is the virulent antipathy of Bishop Gardiner to the anonymous translator of the 'Book of St. Matthew'. Writing from his prison cell in the Fleet to the Lord Protector, the Duke of Somerset, in the autumn of 1547, Gardiner excoriated both the paraphrase of the book and the translator of St. Matthew. 'By the Paraphrase,' wrote Gardiner, 'the keeping of a Concubine is called but a light fault and that were good for Lancashire ... and when to have a concubine, it is called a light fault, methinks if the maid can read, it may serve well, lightly to persuade her ... [for] the Translator in English wanted speech, when he turned it thus.'[33] The immediate conjunction of the image of the literate concubine with a commentary on the translator is suggestive. Gardiner continues his letter in a rant against this person.

> And your Grace shall further understand that he (who it is I know not) who hath taken the labour to translate Erasmus into English, hath for his part offended some time, as appeareth plainly, by ignorance, and some time evidently of purpose, to put in, leave out, and change as he thought best, never to the better, but to the worse: with specialities whereof I will not encumber your Grace, but assure you it is so.

Modern commentary on Catherine's paraphrase of Thomas a Kempis in *Prayers or Meditations* makes many of the same comments but in a far less denigratory tone.[34]

As Somerset failed to respond in anything but a tepid manner to Gardiner's objections to translator and translation, the imprisoned conservative became more virulent. In November he continued his attack on 'the malice and untruth of much matter out of Erasmus' pen and also the arrogant ignorancy of the translator into English', who had shown himself 'ignorant in Latin and English, a man far unmeet to meddle with such a matter, and not without malice.' 'This translator,' he continued in another tirade, 'was asleep when [he] began, having such faults.'[35]

Gardiner's disavowal of all knowledge of the identity of the translator seems disingenuous, a guise allowing him the liberty of attack without being accused of a libelous vendetta against a particular individual. Neither Udall nor Key could be savaged in such a way on the grounds of their ignorance of English or Latin. Nor is it likely that Gardiner would have allowed himself a venomous tirade against the Princess Mary, translator of the 'Book of St. John', who after all had Mallet's expertise on which to rely. Gardiner had, however, already proven himself an enemy of the queen's and his opinions regarding her 'unmeetness to meddle with such a matter' as the tenants of religion were a matter of record. One facet of the translation that Gardiner particularly objected to was the way in which the Eucharist was treated. 'If this Paraphrase go abroad,' he wrote to Somerset, 'people shall be learned to call the Sacrament of the Altar holy bread, and a Symbol. At which new name many will marvel, and they be wanton words'[36] – the wanton words of a literate concubine. Significantly, it was this sensitive issue of the Eucharist which became the flashpoint for the persecution of the queen in 1546. Gardiner's attack of 1547 was a reprise of his attack on the queen in 1546. At the time Gardiner was writing to Somerset, Catherine, as queen dowager, was fighting an on-going war of attrition with the lord protector and his wife and was, as Gardiner must have been well aware, vulnerable to the sort of attack he was waging against the unknown translator. That it did not materially affect the distribution of the *Paraphrases* was due more to Somerset's own commitment to the reformed religion than any protective feelings he may have had for his royal sister-in-law.

Edward Whitchurch, partner of Grafton and Catherine's chosen publisher, brought out 'The 1st tome or volume of the Paraphrases upon the New Testament' on 31 January 1548. If the queen was the translator of the 'Book of St. Matthew', she had cause to feel satisfaction with her work. Despite the animosity of religious conservatives, the first volume of the *Paraphrases* had a circulation of some 20,000 volumes between 1548 and 1551. As patron or as patron/translator, her work reached during her lifetime a wide audience. Udall recognized Catherine's patronage of the entire translation project in his preface to Matthew:

> ... since the time of your first calling to the estate and dignity of espousal and marriage ... [you] hath never ceased by all possible means that in you might lie, to advance and to increase the public commodity and benefit of this commonweal of England ... to whose benefit and edifying in true religion, all these your incessant pains and travails do finally redound.[37]

The translation of the 'Book of St. John', Udall dedicated specifically to Catherine, touching those points he thought would please her:

> When I consider, most gracious Queen Katerine, the great number of noble women in this our time and country of England not only given to the study of human sciences and of strange tongues, but also so thoroughly expert in holy Scriptures, that they are able to compare with the best masters as well in endicting and penning of godly and fruitful treatises to the instruction and edifying of

whole realms in the knowledge of God, as also in translating good books out of
Latin or Greek into English, for the use and commodity of such as are rude and
ignorant of the same tongues: I cannot but think and esteem the famous learned
[of] Antiquity so far behind these times, that there cannot justly be made any comparison between them.[38]

With these words, Udall paid graceful homage to Catherine's efforts as Latin
translator (*Psalms or Prayers, Book of St. Matthew* (?)) and as author/paraphraser
(*Prayers or Meditations*).

Udall and Key dedicated each book in turn to the queen and in the preface
of 'Acts', Udall informed the queen that she:

deserveth no less than to be esteemed and called the chief patroness (to sew
abroad the word of God, and to plant true religion in all parts of his realms and
dominions), not only for diverse, most godly Psalms and meditations of your own
penning and setting forth to the great admiration of all people, [but] to the notable
example of other noble and public personages, and to the effectual stirring up and
enkindling of the reader's devotion.[39]

Three months prior to the publication of the *Paraphrases*, Catherine had
published yet another volume, *Lamentation of a Sinner*, dedicated to stirring
people up and enkindling their devotion. In it, the passionate outpouring of
her religious fervor found a unique and final voice.

The Lamentation of a Sinner, probably written in the winter of 1545–1546
shortly after the publication of *Prayers or Meditations*, was kept secret until after
Henry's death. The reasons for this were the queen's eroding position with
the king and the fear that had been instilled in her by accusations of heresy
and the plots against her life during the summer of 1546. *Lamentation* was a far
more personal work than any of its predecessors, although it had undoubtedly
been written for publication, and was not published until 5 November 1547 by
Edward Whitchurche. Even after Henry's death, it took the combined efforts of
William Cecil, the Duchess of Suffolk, and Catherine's brother, William, then
Earl of Essex, to convince the queen to allow her meditation to be made public.
Yet *Lamentation of a Sinner* as an expression of Catherine's religious views was
fairly typical of religious attitudes among the group of reformers to which she
belonged and who by November 1547 were in control of the government.

Roger Ascham voiced the scholarly reaction to it in January 1548, when he
wrote from St. John's College, Cambridge, to William Cecil: 'We have read the
most holy confessions of our Queen, together with your most eloquent letter.
I wish that you could find it in your heart to devote some of your time to the

cultivation of English, so that men might know how easily our language admits all the members of eloquence.'[40] Despite the eloquence of her English, the queen was reluctant to place herself once more on the public stage by allowing the book's publication. As Henry was dead, this reluctance must have stemmed from the notoriety that she had endured during the summer of 1547 when her secret and precipitate marriage to Sir Thomas Seymour became common knowledge. So ribald were the jests made at her expense that Seymour had attempted to get an act of Parliament passed condemning public slander against the queen. Royal lamentations by Catherine in November 1547 over sins she had committed would have had all too specific an interpretation for the backbiters at court and the wags in city taverns.

Fortunately for posterity she was persuaded to publication, for the last book the queen wrote carries the sound of her voice and the imprint of her mind as none before it had done. Throwing off the shackles of 'translated by' or 'collected by' or 'paraphrased by' which put the burden of doctrine purposefully on other shoulders, *Lamentation of a Sinner* belongs to the queen alone. The public voice and the private conscience have finally become one despite a cultural bias against the appropriateness of the female voice in published works. Mild-mannered Erasmeanism has given way to a proselytizing Lutheranism central to the queen's deepest convictions, yet fragments of the more radical thinking that would produce Calvinist Puritanism are also apparent. Ironically, the foundations for Catherine's last book bearing witness to the English Reformation have their roots in continental Catholicism.

In 1480, a Carthusian named Dionysius de Lewis de Rickel of Limbourg (1402–1471), known as Dionysius Carthusianus, published a book entitled *Speculum arrum anime peccatricia a quodam cartusiense*, or the 'Mirror of Gold to the Sinful Soul'. It was subsequently translated from Latin into French and published in Paris. In 1507, Lady Margaret Beaufort translated the work into English and had it published by Richard Pynson as *The Mirror of Gold to the Sinful Soul*. The second edition of Lady Margaret's translation, that of 1522, was issued simultaneously by the presses of Wynkyn de Worde and John Skot. The tone of the book and several of the themes – man as sinner, the emptiness of worldly things, false vanity, and fear of God's judgement – were carried over in each later incarnation of the work. Lady Margaret's purpose in presenting Dionysius' book to the English reading public was clearly stated:

> I have willed to make and accomplish this present treaty, gathering and assembling many diverse authorities of holy doctors of the church to the intent that the poor sinful soul troubled by the fraud of enemy and oft overcome ... May be addressed to the light of justice and truth ...[41]

Yet Lady Margaret's work, Catholic though it might be, issued from the emerging world of English humanism and attempted what Catherine Parr later attempted, to make a work of impeccable Roman Catholicism accessible to an audience soon to move in other religious directions. It is entirely possible, given the links between the Vaux-Parr menage and Lady Margaret, that a copy of her translation stood on the shelves of Catherine Parr's schoolroom.

Dionysius' religious beliefs were conservative in that, pre-dating the emergence of humanism, he failed to acknowledge the humanist insistence on God's loving mercy and the totality of faith. The Day of Judgement and eternal damnation for sinners were invoked upon an errant Christianity – the fist of God upraised in wrathful threats rather than the hand of God open and extended in charitable forgiveness. It remained for that French humanist 'pearl of the Valois', Marguerite of Navarre, to take Lady Margaret Beaufort's intent – 'that the sinful soul soiled and defouled by sin may in every chapter have a new mirror wherein he may behold and consider the face of his soul'[42] – and put it on a new humanist footing, focusing on God's love in such sensual and mystic images that the book was condemned for heresy by the University of Sorbonne.

Marguerite of Navarre's version of the work, *The Mirror of the Sinful Soul*, was originally published in rhymed French decasyllables as a long, graceful and ecstatic religious poem which first appeared in England in French in 1531, and in a second, more comprehensive edition in 1535. In her introduction to the reader, Marguerite asks, 'For what thing is a man (as for his own strength), before that he hath received the gift of faith: whereby only hath he knowledge of the goodness, wisdom and power of God ... '[43] It was not difficult to interpret this as a statement of the Protestant insistence on justification by faith alone, demonstrating one reason for the book's condemnation. Marguerite then went on to describe what was to become the standard opening statement in self-proclaimed confessional works of this type – her wretchedness as a miserable sinner and the greatness of the grace of God, which alone had the strength to break the chains from which no mortal man could deliver her. The similarity of language used in these self-abasing proclamations, found in the works of many female writers such as Marguerite of Navarre and Catherine Parr, underscores a psychological equivalence, particular to women, between religious masochism and female submission. Given the framework of an ideal Christian society as outlined both by patristic authors and by the religious writers of the Reformation, there was inherently little difference between the total obedience a woman owed to her husband, as authorized by the Church, and the total obedience she owed to God. 'Obedience is better than Sacrifice for nothing is more acceptable before God than to obey. Women are much bound to God to have so acceptable a virtue enjoined them for their penance.'[44] God was, after all, simply an extreme and omniscient form of the male demiurge whose power, significantly for all, extended into the afterlife.

The Mirror of the Sinful Soul is full of ecstatic assurances of God's forgiveness for every sin and mystical allusions to Marguerite's relationship in apposition to Him. In St. Theresian ecstasy, Marguerite's soul begets and is begotten by God simultaneously as her heart is pierced by the flaming arrow of love. Heavily influenced by the 'Song of Solomon', Marguerite wrote a love play between her soul and God. '[for] the soul which is in love with God ... commeth for to embrace her husband ... Now I have (through thy good grace) recovered the place of thy wife. O happy and desired place, gracious bed, throne right honourable, seat of peace.'[45] These same pseudo-religious, sexual images echo through Catherine Parr's early works. In *Prayers or Meditations*, the queen addresses Jesus Christ as 'my most loving spouse, who shall give me wings of perfect love, that I may fly up from these worldly miseries and rest in thee.'[46] In another sexually charged verse, she begs God to, 'Quicken my soul and all the powers thereof, that it may cleave fast and be joined to thee in joyful gladness of ghostly ravishings.'[47]

Princess Elizabeth had translated Marguerite's *Mirror* for her stepmother in December 1544 as a New Year's gift.[48] Whether Catherine was aware of the book prior to this is not known. She may very well have been and that was the reason that Elizabeth selected it for translation. Marguerite of Navarre, humanist queen, sister of Francois I, published author and erudite elitist, was a role model for many high-born English ladies. The daughters of the Duke of Somerset published a compendium of elegies upon Marguerite's death in 1549. Whenever Catherine became aware of Marguerite's book, she devoured it avidly and used many of its images, such as the sinful soul awakening to its wretchedness through the grace of God and finding a faith through that grace which engendered in the sinner perfect Christian charity. These images were becoming the common currency of Protestant works. Yet oddly enough, the open sensuality which is so apparent in Marguerite's writings and which Catherine embraced so eagerly in earlier works is largely missing from *Lamentation of a Sinner*. This may be due to the sex scandal involving Sir Thomas Seymour in which she was involved shortly before the book's publication. Publicly professing an appetite for ghostly ravishings after a unsettling scandal involving the real thing could have had little attraction for the queen.

Another aspect of this lack of female sexuality as religious metaphor lies in the conscious androgyny of the book. *Lamentation of a Sinner* is addressed to 'all Christians'[49] and adopts a male voice through almost the entire text. Only

Cecil's introduction and Catherine's aside on 'my most sovereign favourable lord and husband'[50] tell the reader that the author is a woman. The lack of self-constraint and exhibition of aggressive confidence in the language which addresses, for the most part, those who suffer from earthly lusts, 'the dregs of Adam', as well as those who call themselves the 'children of light',[51] and relegates women as a sex to a few paragraphs on their wifely duties according to St. Paul, demonstrates the mind of a queen who no longer saw herself as a woman like other women, but as Diana, half-male, half-female, particular, apart. Catherine's pronouns are almost uniformly masculine – 'Who understandeth his faults?' 'Yea, if men would not acknowledge and confess the same, the stones would cry it out.'[52] Her images deal with the world of men. 'And I, most presumptuously thinking nothing of Christ crucified, went about to set forth mine own righteousness, saying with the proud Pharisee, 'Good Lord, I thank thee, I am not like other men.'[53] 'Was it not a marvellous unkindness,' Catherine asks the reader, 'when God did speak to me, and also call me, that I would not answer him? What man so called would not have heard, or what man hearing, would not have answered?'[54]

Catherine points out in painful detail 'the faults of men, which be in the world'.[55] She has no hesitation in speaking directly and scathingly to 'the professors of the gospel', who although protesting their virtue, are 'contentious disputers ... foul gluttons, slanderers, backbiters, advowterers, fornicators, swearers and blasphemers.'[56] By such condemnation she has assumed a mantle of male identity, speaking to the sinful not as a mere woman, not even as an equal, but as a ruler chastising the guilty of both sexes who have deserved her chastisement. She does not hesitate to spell out the duty of all Christians. 'It were all our parts and duties to procure and seek all the ways and means possible to have more knowledge of God's words set forth abroad in the world,'[57] and by 'us', she means 'all men and women' under the spiritual captaincy of Christ.

The uncompromising androgyny of the text is underscored by Catherine's description of Christ as one who impersonated virtues commonly bestowed upon women. 'Christ,' proclaims the queen, 'was innocent ... obedient unto his father ... meek and humble in the heart ... [who] came to serve ... [and] despised worldly honour.' Catherine, on the other hand, describes herself as 'disobedient and most stubborn ... most proud and vainglorious ... I coveted to rule over [my brethren] ... [and] I much delighted to attain [worldly honour].'[58] This was a paradox which ran through most of the literature of the time. Jesus was proposed as the paradigm of Christian virtues – chaste, humble, meek, obedient, charitable, despising worldly things, submissive to his father's will, one who spoke only to a serious, divinely ordained purpose. Yet these were the virtues not of the ideal Christian man but of the ideal Christian woman. To imitate Christ, therefore, a duty enjoined on all Christians, was to imitate those qualities considered proper only for the naturally inferior sex. The courage to face death, particularly on the battlefield, a Christ-like quality enthusiastically arrogated to the male of the species, was uneasily recognized as a quality not dissimilar to the courage needed to face death in childbirth. The only difference being, seemingly, that there was greater merit for a man who chose to risk his life on the battlefield than for a woman who had no choice but to fulfil her natural function. This inversion of roles and attributes so forcefully expressed in *Lamentation*, granting the queen male characteristics in opposition to Christ's female ones, underscores Catherine's interpretation of her own self-image as one who was set apart by virtue of position and understanding from her sex in general and from those restrictions commonly imposed on that sex in particular. This was the image of queenship which the young Elizabeth took as her study.[59]

Patricia Crawford has commented on the ability of women at this period to 'both accept beliefs about their inferiority and transcend them.'[60] Yet in *Lamentation of a Sinner*, Catherine implicitly denies the notion of her own inferiority. It is she who speaks in the first person directly to God through the medium of the Holy Ghost and not through any male intermediary. 'I will first require and pray the Lord to give me His holy spirit'[61] has more the tone of masculine command than of female supplication. Regarding the hypocrites who pretend repentance for themselves but call for the persecution of others, the queen states that, 'I cannot allow, neither praise, all kind of lamentation but such as may stand with Christian charity.'[62] Throughout the book, then, Catherine speaks bluntly in the first person of an androgynized 'I am'. She tacitly recognizes this, explaining that her 'audacity and boldness' of speech are a gift from God, that 'marvellous man',[63] whose grace of spiritual salvation includes the liberation of tongues to speak truth boldly, an imperative outweighing the discrimination of gender and overriding the 'natural' inferiority of sex. If God's grace supersedes the law then, for Catherine and in her own case at least, woman's limitations decreed by that law must also be set aside.

The queen, however, stops short of a declaration of generic female equality. Her text declares her own liberation through grace but she was very much aware of her special status as Henry's queen. The generality of women are encouraged in *Lamentation*, indeed commanded, to play their traditional submissive role as outlined by St. Paul. Yet they are also encouraged on an equal footing with men to seek their own salvation through God's grace alone and not through any human intermediary, and to act in ways that would disseminate God's word. When the queen pronounces that: 'It were all our parts and duties to procure and seek all the ways and means possible to have more knowledge of God's word set forth abroad in the world, and not allow ignorance and discommend knowledge of God's word',[64] she is concentrating on the spread of vernacular literature and may perhaps still intend the proper sphere of women's work in the spreading of the word to be confined to children and servants. But she does not say this. Instead, Catherine defines the role of *all* Christians to spread the word by *all* means possible, implicitly enjoining them not to be bound by the traditions and constraints of a superseded human law. In such thought processes, it is possible to detect Catherine's affinity for the life and works of Anne Askew.

Another belief which found expression in *Lamentation of a Sinner*, and one which echoed Erasmus' own beliefs, was Catherine's distaste for torture and persecution of so-called heretics. This restraint in the face of religious excess resonates through the reign of her stepdaughter Elizabeth as well. In *Lamentation* Catherine denounces false ministers of God's word who rebuke other men's faults, yet themselves are 'an offence and a slander to the word of God'.[65] These hypocrites and self-appointed prophets, who 'be not able to maintain their own inventions and doctrine with any jot of the Scripture … most cruelly persecute them that be contrary to the same. Be such the lovers of Christ? Nay, nay.'[66] The queen's baptism of blood and fire during the Pilgrimage of Grace in Yorkshire had left in her mind an abhorrence of violence raised in the name of religious extremism. While understanding the occasional need for a Christian army to march off to battle in the name of Christ, she yet abhorred the shedding of any Christian blood. Catherine believed in the 'boke of the crucifix' but she also believed that a tolerant and loving guidance could and would bring a world full of sinners to that same understanding and belief which she, herself, had found. Diplomacy through grace and not destruction was the divinely authorized route to conversion. The sort of extremism found in religious persecution was not in her nature.

Lamentation is a remarkable book, one of the very few volumes of original prose published by an Englishwoman in the sixteenth century. In it, the queen sums up clearly and concisely her personal religious beliefs and her sense of mission to spread those beliefs. The eloquent imagery of her text gives evidence of the wide reading and intense study of Scriptures that has led to her embracing the religious tenets she enthusiastically endorses:

Therefore, inwardly to behold Christ crucified upon the cross, is the best and god-liest meditation that can be. We may see also in Christ crucified, the beauty of the soul, better than in all the books of the world.

St. Paul saith, we be justified by the faith in Christ, and not by the deeds of the law … This dignity of faith is no derogation to good works, for out of this faith springeth all good works. Yet we may not impute to the worthiness of faith or works our justification before God, but ascribe and give the worthiness of it wholly to the merits of Christ's passion, and refer and attribute the knowledge and perceiving thereof, only to faith whose very true only property is to take, apprehend and hold fast the promise of God's mercy, the which maketh us righteous, and to cause me continually to hope for the same mercy, and in love, to work all manner of ways allowed in the Scripture, that I may be thankful for the same.[67]

Here then finally is Catherine's open testament to her reformed faith.[68] The text is loosely divided into eight topics: the sin of the speaker, the universality of sin, remission and salvation through the free grace of God embodied in the life and death of His Son, progression by the true believer from the sin-infected wisdom of the world to the pure wisdom of Christ, a warning against false speakers of the gospel, spiritual knowledge versus secular knowledge, charity, and the Day of Judgement. Belief in justification by faith alone, salvation by God's grace, given as a divine gift and not earned by the merits of the receiver of the gift, God's mercy and grace revealed through Christ's passion as described in the Gospels, and the preparation of a place in bliss for God's elect, 'which was before the beginning of the world', are the central tenants of the queen's beliefs. Condemnation of false prophets, those so-called 'professors of the gospel',[69] is strongly emphasized, as are scathing attacks on the papacy and the futility of a sole dependence on the law of man and worldly wisdom. 'And where worldly wisdom most governeth, there most sin ruleth. For as the world is enemy to God, so also the wisdom thereof is adverse to God.'[70]

Catherine also embraces the Calvinist concept of the fellowship of the army of the cross, led by Christ, 'so valiant a captain of God'. 'We seeing then that the triumph and victory of our captain, Christ, is so marvellous, glorious and noble to the which war we be appointed. Let us force ourselves to follow him with bearing our cross, that we may have fellowship with him in his kingdom.'[71] Another Calvinist metaphor, the labyrinth or maze, also emerges in *Lamentation of a Sinner*:

If I should hope by mine own strength, and power to come out of this maze of iniquity and wickedness wherein I have walked so long, I should be deceived. For I am so ignorant, blind, weak and feeble that I cannot bring myself out of this entangled and wayward maze: but the more I seek means and ways to wind myself out, the more I am wrapped and tangled therein ... It is the hand of the Lord that can and will bring me out of the endless maze of death.[72]

In *Lamentation of a Sinner*, the queen publicly parts company with mainstream Erasmeanism, with its study of classical models and its attempt to balance reason and faith. Only by a subjective washing away of all self-will, all learned knowledge, all deductive logic, in a spiritual baptism of the Passion's miraculous mysteries from which flow the waters of everlasting life, and which both symbolize and embody God's divine mercy to an inherently evil mankind, can salvation be achieved. And this cleansing is made possible through the grace of God alone. 'For in Christ is all fullness of the godhead, and in him, are hidden all the treasures of wisdom and knowledge.'[73] This was the jewel beneath the 'cloddy earth' that Catherine had found, which had led to an awakening of faith, a re-energizing of intense personal passion focused in a realization of 'new' religious truths. Baptized through God's mercy in the blood of Christ, the queen describes herself as coming 'as it were, in a new garment before God.'[74]

Catherine deals with a series of ideas and topics of importance to her in *Lamentation of a Sinner*, and they flow seamlessly into each other in a monologue that by its very intimacy becomes a spiritual dialogue with the reader. The queen begins by stating her credentials for writing such a book – that she is a sinner who deserves damnation yet has been offered salvation through God's mercy and her faith in Christ. As a sinner, she is not alone. Although set apart in the world, in the spirit she walks in a community of equals, equals in their burden of offenses against God. She goes on to address release from this condition, the remission of sin and the acquiring of salvation through the free grace of God, embodied in the life and death of His Son. Yet how is this salvation to be realised? Not through the wisdom of the world nor through false speakers of the gospel nor through any accumulation of good works or secular knowledge but through the pure wisdom of Christ crucified.

How is that pure wisdom to be learned? Through vernacular translations of the Scriptures, so that all may study the words and works of God. Luther's doctrine of God, described in *The Bondage of the Will*, is a deity of two natures, the hidden, unknowable God of mystery and the God of grace, revealed by his word.[75] The hidden God judges man for election or damnation and there is no appeal. Only the complete acceptance of either fate, as determined by God alone, on the part of individual man demonstrates that quality of faith necessary for salvation. Catherine echoes this when she describes that in the chosen children of God, 'All fear of damnation is gone from them, for they have put their whole hope of salvation in his hands which will and can perform it, neither have they any past or pillar to lean to, but God and his smooth and unwrinkled church.'[76]

Yet if the hidden God decrees inexorable damnation for some, innocent and guilty alike, the revealed God offers salvation for all through an acceptance of his grace. Is the revealed word of God then not absolute but contingent on a divine whim? Luther never satisfactorily answered this question but Catherine's response to this seeming paradox was a resounding 'no!'. The unalterable truth of the 'boke of the Crucifix', the only absolute available within the human condition, is God's self-imposed and therefore unbreakable promise to mankind written with the blood of his son. In *Lamentation*, Catherine describes those of a Lutheran persuasion who say of their fellows, 'he that hath sinned may be one of God's elect; peradventure, the Lord hath suffered him to fall to the intent he may the better know himself.'[77] Yet there are others who chafe at such predetermined justice and others still who smugly accept it, saying, 'God is partial, because he hath elected some and some reproved. And, therefore, they say that the elected be sure of salvation, taking by that, occasion to do evil enough, saying, whatsoever God hath determined shall be performed.'[78] Acceptance of God's will as revealed by a study of God's word and not second guessing unknowable mysteries is for Catherine the only possible path through a deeply shadowed forest of rational paradox.

Human charity, for the queen, is counterpoised against divine retribution at the Day of Judgement. Justification by faith does not release the faithful from charitable works and acts, for by such acts shall the elect of God be known and the word of God be spread. God's grace is freely given yet it must also be earned by true repentance. ' ... Christ yet fighteth in spirit in his elect vessels and shall fight even to the day of judgement.'[79] The pure in spirit are not only captains in the army of the Lord, they are the clay in the hands of the potter. And their greatest reward will be to hear 'the happy comfortable and most joyful sentence ordained for the children of God, which is, 'Come hither ye blessed of my father, and receive the kingdom of heaven, prepared for you before the beginning of the world.'[80]

Another concept of importance to Catherine was that of the community and fellowship of Christ and that 'continual conversation in faith'[81] that can remove the scales of ignorance from the eyes of the blind and lead the world to dress itself in the new garments of evangelicalism:

> That as we have professed one God, one faith, and one baptism so we may be all of one mind, and one accord, putting away all biting and gnawing. For in backbiting, slandering, and misreporting our Christian brethren, we show not ourselves the disciples of Christ whom we profess.[82]

This sense of Christian community has been reinforced in Catherine's thinking by her intensive reading of St. Paul and his letters to nascent Christian communities all over Asia. Where Priscilla, Lois, Eunice, Prisca, Claudia and Apphia, women mentioned in the letters of Paul and lauded for doing the work of God, carried the Word of Truth established in Jesus Christ to their communities 1500 years before, so she, Catherine Parr, daughter of a Westmorland knight, exalted in rank beyond all expectation like Esther, was another Christian woman doing the work of God within the community of those engaged in His service. This was heady stuff and played on the queen's personal sense of mission.

One aspect of *Lamentation* which helps to illustrate why the queen hid the book away during the last six months of Henry's life, is the subversive quality of a number of its passages. The impotency of worldly princes when compared to the Prince of Princes, the worthlessness of human law and the willingness of evil men to subvert it, and the paucity of charity to be found among the mighty were points of view, which however valid they may have been in Catherine's life experience, would have enraged her dangerous and dying husband:

> The Princes of the world never did fight without the strength of the world. Christ contrarily went to war, even against all the strength of the world. He would fight as David did with Goliath, unarmed of all human wisdom, and policy and without all worldly power and strength. Nevertheless he was fully replenished and armed with the whole armor of the spirit. And in this one battle, he overcame forever, all his enemies.[83]

The conqueror of Boulogne would have ill appreciated such a comment, nor would he have relished Catherine's metaphor for controlling sexual desire as the appointment of subjects to rule over their former lords:

> When a prince fighteth with his enemies, which sometime had the sovereignty over his people, and subduing them, may kill them if he will, yet he preserveth and saveth them. And whereas they were lords over his people, he maketh them after to serve, whom they before had ruled. Now in such a case, the prince doth show himself a greater conqueror, in that he hath made them which were rulers to obey, and the subjects to be lords over them, to whom they served, then if he had utterly destroyed them upon the conquest.[84]

This sort of thinking, even in metaphor, when combined with statements that assured the reader that the coming of Christ 'hath cancelled the law, which was in evil men the occasion of sin',[85] were statements which would have opened the queen to scurrilous attack. Any earthly king, in Catherine's opinion, was inferior to the mercy and glory of Christ:

Is there any worldly prince or magistrate, that would show such clemency, and mercy, to their disobedient and rebellious subjects, having offended them? I suppose they would not with such words allure them except it were to call them, whom they cannot take, and punish them being taken.[86]

Given the queen's background of experience in civil war and Robert Aske's initial pardon and subsequent execution, this statement takes on a particularly potent meaning. While it is true that *Lamentation* was published nine months after Henry's death and could thus have been altered by the queen during that time, the homogeneity of the text, complete with praises of Henry as the new Moses, renders major revisions unlikely. Catherine must have been aware that 'such audacity and boldness' of speech, if published would take her into realms no Tudor queen had ever trod.[87]

As to such matters of moment as the sacrificial character of the mass, clerical celibacy, a belief in Purgatory or other remnants of Roman Catholic practice, Catherine was outspoken in her condemnation of former practices. Yet by the time the book was published in November 1547, the mass as Henry VIII had instituted it was a thing of the past. The lord protector was a declared Calvinist as were Catherine's brother, her friend, the dowager Duchess of Suffolk, and even her husband, Sir Thomas Seymour, an avid patron of Hugh Latimer. There was little need by that date for the queen to beat a dead horse. Lingering contradictions, however, float through Catherine's prose. She enthusiastically embraces the Lutheran position on predestination and the kingdom of God's elect, yet remarks: 'Christ hath made us free, setting us in a godly liberty. I mean not licence to sin, as many be glad to interpret the same, when as Christian liberty is godly entreated of.'[88] This owes far more to Erasmus than Luther and illustrates the tangled skein of religious ideas with which the queen was trying to weave a web of truth.[89]

In 1544, Parliament had passed an act allowing the dissolution of colleges. On 24 November 1545, Parliament granted Henry VIII sovereign power over colleges, chantries and hospitals, 'to alter and transpose and order them to the glory of God, and the profit of the commonwealth.'[90] The universities, nervous already after nearly ten years of full out royal assault on ecclesiastical prerogatives, stifled a secret groan. In accepting the gift, the king personally addressed Parliament, informing them: 'Doubt not I pray you, but your expectation shall be served, more Godly and goodly than you will wish or desire.'[91] This sent chills of terror down the body politic of the universities of Oxford and Cambridge. Facing possible dissolution and dispersal, dependent upon income from the chantry system and envisioning its eradication and the seizure of their lands, the notables of England's two great universities began to look around them for a patron powerful enough to intervene with the king on their behalf. They chose the queen. The University of Cambridge sent an official request to her, pleading for her intercession with Henry.

Taking advantage of this opportunity, Catherine wrote on 26 February 1546 a manifesto, ostensibly to allay the fears of the university. That this statement was of great importance to her is evidenced by the draft of the final letter written and corrected in her own hand.[92] In it she attacks ideas central to medieval Thomism, propounded by Thomas Aquinas and later scholastics, with its emphasis on Aristotle and the Greek philosophers and its required mastery of Logic, Rhetoric and Philosophy, study that she later called the 'subtle and crafty persuasions of Philosophy and Sophistry, whereof commeth no fruit but a great perturbation of the mind.'[93] She chastises the notables of Cambridge for using a dead language, both foreign and integrally linked to the Roman Church, in which to address her, rather than conveying their wishes 'familiarly in our vulgar tongue'. She goes so far as to deny even recognizing Latin at sight, a reformist pose which takes simplicity to an extreme limit.

In the place of the old and deceitful intellectual models, the queen proclaims Luther's 'theology of the cross'. The principal purpose of study, she asserts, should be the 'setting forth the better Christ's reverend and most sacred doctrine.' As she had in *Lamentation of a Sinner* dared to preach at the preachers who perverted Christ's message, and had once admonished Lady Wriothesley about her willful stubbornness against God's ordinances, the queen now admonished the university about theirs:

> That it may not be laid against you in evidence at the tribunal seat of God, how ye were ashamed of Christ's doctrine. For this Latin lesson I am taught to say of St. Paul, 'Non me pudet, evangelii'. The sincere setting forth whereof I trust universally in all your vocations and ministries, you will apply and conform your sundry gifts, arts and studies to such end and sort that Cambridge may be accounted rather an university of divine philosophy than of natural or moral, as Athens was.

Yet humanism still survives beneath the evangelical rhetoric. Still resonating through Catherine's text is the humanist view that man's role in the world should be as an active rather than contemplative creature, using a disciplined mind to absorb knowledge, secular as well as religious but religious above all, that might provide some future means of doing good for his fellows. She was after all at this time hard at work on the preparation of an English translation of Erasmus, and was known by reputation, as the university acknowledged, to be 'a maintainer and cherisher of the learned state'. The queen would prove, to the university's relief, to be scholarship's good servant, if God's first.

This is an astonishing letter, uncompromising, fearless and forthright. In it, the queen casts off the vocabulary of scholastic classicism, a shared given among the English intellectual elite, and strikes out with the hammer blows of Lutheran *sum eritis*. For a woman of Catherine's birth and background, who had spent most of her adult life in the ultra-conservative north, this letter is the manifesto of a one-woman social revolution. It has been discussed at length in recent scholarship that society's requirements for women at this time and in this place demanded a chaste, submissive and obedient silence.[94] Yet with this letter, addressed to the minds which a decade before Catherine had considered infinitely more knowledgeable than her own, the queen instructs, upbraids and openly criticizes their motives, their acts, and their failure to meet a Lutheran-defined ideal.

Catherine's remarks about English being the language 'aptest for my intelligence' are not an admission of faulty Latin scholarship but a statement of religious policy. In *Lamentation of a Sinner*, she comments on 'my simple and unlearned judgement', rhetorically identifying herself with the commons, 'we that be unlettered remain confused without God.'[95] This public self-identification by a Tudor queen with the illiterate commons rather than portraying herself as a royal thus remote patron of the needy is a startling innovation. Yet no matter how passionately felt the context, these were, in the end, political statements directed toward a political end; certainly they were not intended to be taken at face value by any who knew the queen. Religious re-evaluation, royal marriage and apprenticeship as Regent-General of England had freed 'the words of my mouth', and given the queen a sense of personal empowerment and a supreme confidence in herself almost unheard of in a woman of the sixteenth century. The queen's advocacy of the university took a form that the university did not expect:[96]

> I, according to your desires, attempted my lord the king's majesty for the stay of your possessions, in which nothwithstanding his majesty's property and interest through the consent of the high court of Parliament, his highness being such a patron to good learning, he will rather advance and erect new occasion therefore than confound these your colleges, so that learning may hereafter ascribe her very original, whole confirmation and sure stay to our sovereign lord, her only defence and worthy ornament.

The 'new occasion' which Henry erected three months later was Trinity College, Cambridge.

Henry may have already had some such plan in mind when he addressed Parliament in November, assuring them that 'your expectation shall be served, more Godly and goodly than you will wish or desire.'[97] Yet the queen's hand in the college's foundation may also be discerned. Roger Ascham offered the gratitude of the university in a letter of 1547, when he acknowledged to the queen that 'we would certainly be guilty of the greatest offense were we ever to forget either so great a favour in coming to our aid, or your extraordinary kindness in writing. And also your services have been so acceptable to us that except for them the welfare of the University could not have been preserved.'[98]

Shortly after the queen wrote to the worthies of Cambridge, the decision was made, probably in March, to incorporate the earlier foundations of King's Hall, Michaelhouse and the Physic Hostel into a new foundation to be called Trinity College. John Redman (1499–1551), the master of King's Hall, was named first master of Trinity. On 29 October 1546, the lands of the two colleges were officially surrendered and on 19 December, the charter of foundation of Trinity was issued.[99] Not everyone necessarily was pleased by the decision. Thomas Wriothesley, William Paget and Stephen Gardiner were all alumnae of King's Hall. Their feelings regarding its dissolution may not have been particularly sanguine. Another outstanding alumnus was Catherine's cousin, Cuthbert Tunstall, who had attended King's Hall during the 1490's. Its master in 1546, John Redman, was both his cousin and the queen's.

The Redmans and the Parrs of Kendal had a long history together. The Redmans of Levens Hall were an old Westmorland family, one member of which, William Redman, had been chosen by Westmorland's hereditary sheriff, Sir William Parr of Kendal, the queen's grandfather, to serve as knight for the shire in 1478. Another Redman, Edward, had been elected, together with the queen's grandfather, as knights of the shire for Cumberland in June 1483. In the fifteenth century, the Redmans served the Parrs in a gentry feudal relationship,[100] and they continued to serve them well into the sixteenth century. Another William Redman was in service with Maud Parr in the 1520's and in 1534 was one of her son's servants.[101] John Redman, a member of the prolific clan, had devoted himself to scholarship on the advice of Cuthbert Tunstall.[102] Made a fellow of St. John's College on 3 November 1530, he was appointed master of King's Hall in 1542. Redman was a close friend, too, of Matthew Parker's and together they were appointed commissioners to survey the property of the colleges on 16 January 1546, just a month before the queen's historic letter.[103] Another, more tenuous connection between the queen and King's Hall was the suit by Princess Elizabeth in 1545 to have John Huddleston, B.A., made a fellow of the college upon the next vacancy.[104] Elizabeth was probably at Ashridge when she put forward this suit for a man who may have been one of her tutors at the time. Like Redman, Huddleston came from a Cumbrian family with gentry feudal ties to the Parrs.[105]

Whatever the role Catherine played in the founding of Trinity College, her interest in and advocacy for the university itself is attested to both by herself and by Roger Ascham. The letter which the queen wrote to Cambridge demonstrates the confidence that she had acquired in the two and a half years since her marriage to Henry and how secure she felt her position to be. She had renounced a romantic love for Thomas Seymour for a religious rediscovery of Christ and had been amply rewarded not only by wealth and position but by the comforting reassurance of the ever-present grace of God. This God demanded personal sacrifice and a constant self-examination of motives and acts. He also demanded proselytizers unafraid to speak out publicly, and the queen did just that. Ultimately this exposure of Catherine's private religious thoughts in a public arena opened her to criticism by the conservative party and gave them a weapon they could use against her. It did not help Catherine in this struggle about to break over her head that, in her own mind, the double duty deity that she believed in, who offered both eternal damnation and eternal salvation, bore a striking resemblance to the dying, dangerous and unpredictable king to whom she was married. Her statements to Cambridge University were to prove the last religious commentary on which she embarked during Henry's reign. At the very moment that she felt herself secure enough to speak freely to the world, the Bishop of Winchester 'bent his bow to shoot at some of the head Deer'[106] and bring the reformers down. It is thus of profound significance that the day after her revolutionary letter was addressed by the queen to the University of Cambridge, imperial ambassador Van der Delft reported to Charles V that he had heard 'rumours of a new Queen',[107] rumours that were to prove the opening shots in a campaign designed to bring the newly empowered and now irrepressibly vocal Catherine to the block and silence her forever.

13

Fall From Grace

By the winter of 1545–46, Catherine had every reason to be confident. In the two and a half years since her marriage, she had acted as Henry's queen, companion, advisor and confidante. She had been made regent-general of the kingdom and had cultivated an unparalleled influence with the royal children. She had become a patron *par excellence* of the English Renaissance and openly published a variety of books intended to secure the foundations of the English Reformation. Her private chamber had become a hotbed of new religionists where forbidden books were read, private sermons preached and lively but dangerous discussions carried on. Her opinions and attitudes were no longer confided to intimates at court but were now trumpeted abroad in letters to the universities and in popular religious tracts sold cheaply to make them available to the general reading public. She had interested herself in nearly every aspect of politics, religion, the arts, and foreign affairs. The biologically determined, culturally condoned and religiously decreed 'place of women'[1] in society had since the summer of 1544 been largely and publicly ignored by the queen. She had taken to heart her uncle's teaching that, 'a well-managed boldness is the virtue of monarchical courts, and a discrete submission that of a republican.'[2] This maxim was undoubtedly intended for men only whose natural sphere was the political one and was quoted by a man who loathed republicanism. Yet socially endorsed sexual exclusivity relegating political boldness to the male preserve was an idea more or less abandoned by the energetic queen. This increasingly conspicuous public role which she was playing flew in the face of societal precepts which defined a forward woman as a wanton.[3]

Catherine's readiness to lecture the intellectual and religious establishments also called up echoes of that other strongly deprecated female stereotype, the shrew. Those critical of the queen might have quoted her own words: 'we run headling, like unbridled colts, without snaffle or bit,'[4] and felt that it would be better for the natural order of things if she were brought under control and returned to her stall. Yet the queen appeared to turn a blind eye to criticism which as long as she had the king's confidence and support could not have been very vocal. Catherine's impatience with cultural constraints on her activities must have been increasing in direct proportion to her willingness, indeed her desire, to voice her positions in public. Her enthusiasm for lecturing those she saw in need of her advice extended even to her husband. The muted quality of the criticism she had thus far been exposed to had led the queen to the fatal mistake of believing that she could play the androgynous Diana within the very constraints of her own marriage. 'But, alas,' Catherine wrote that winter, 'we be so much given to love and to flatter ourselves, and so blinded with carnal affections, that we can see and perceive no fault in ourselves.'[5] The queen's 'lively faith'[6] 'that maketh me bold'[7] had rendered her 'now very blind [who] seeth not how vain, foolish, false, ingrate, cruel, hard, wicked and evil the world is.'[8] This blindness was to nearly prove her undoing.

Ever since their wedding day, Henry had appeared eager to spoil his wife and to gratify her wishes. The course of the king's emotional attachments to his wives or to his favourites followed a predictable pattern. During the initial phases of the relationship, the king appeared to put all of his faith and trust in wife or favourite. With the wives, he doted. With the favourites, he confided. The recipient of all of this indulgent emotion invariably came to see it as evidence of his or her power over the king. Most, though not all – Cromwell seems to have been more cautious than most – were led to believe that the king was their creature whom they could use for their own advantage. A dozen heads upon a dozen necks had paid the penalty for this misreading of the king's character. Henry could and did turn upon a pin prick and the lavishly indulged favourite of today could find himself embracing the block tomorrow. ''Tis time to fear when tyrants seem to kiss,' muses Shakespeare's Pericles, Prince of Tyre. It was a lesson that should have been well learned by those at the court of Henry VIII.

Catherine had not been at court during the rise and fall of Cardinal Wolsey, Sir Thomas More, Bishop Fisher, Anne Boleyn or Katherine Howard. She must have heard stories from her brother and sister and from close friends but she, too, now fell into the trap of overestimating Henry's tolerant affection and underestimating his enormous capacity for sudden emotional shifts and capricious cruelty. She had married him, no doubt with a trembling heart, prepared for the worst. But the worst had not happened. Instead, Henry had proved as loving and kindly as a man chronically suffering from a variety of physical ailments could. 'And even such confidence I have in your majesty's gentleness,' Catherine wrote to her husband in July 1544, 'knowing myself never to have done my duty as were requisite and mete to such a noble and worthy prince, at whose hands I have found and received so much love and goodness, that with words I cannot express it.'[9]

The king had offered her the ultimate accolade of naming her regent of the kingdom in his absence, had listened to her advice in such weighty matters as the succession and foreign policy, condoned and encouraged her efforts as writer, translator and paraphraser, trusted her with the care of his children, and seemed to enjoy discussions of religion and those theological points which interested Catherine so much. This attitude lulled Catherine into a state of overconfidence. Her religious convictions had become outspokenly Lutheran at a time when the king was retreating further into conservatism. Henry in his last years seems to have been having second thoughts. Although he had no intention of relinquishing his supremacy over the church or of returning to former ties with Rome, neither did he intend for radical Protestants to dominate the English religious establishment. A sixteenth-century Dr. Frankenstein, he was in his own mind a man who had created a monster in the religious revolution he had set in motion in England, who now was not quite sure of what to do with it.[10]

Catherine's evolving religious vision was growing sharply away from the king's, as is patently apparent in *Lamentation of a Sinner*, on which she began to work probably at the beginning of 1546. Yet for political reasons, the queen had never openly challenged the conservatives, heretofore trying to maintain cordial relations with both religious camps even as she worked tirelessly in the cause of the English Reformation. The crisis of 1546 seems to have taken her completely by surprise. Nor does the queen ever admit, in print at least, that it was her zealous pursuit of religious goals not her imagined worldly vanity which were nearly her undoing with the king. A glimpse of the forceful missionary cast of Catherine's religious beliefs and her outspoken way of arguing them is evident from the queen's description in *Lamentation of a Sinner* of her role regarding:

> One of my Christian brethren who hath sinned. I will admonish, and rebuke him, and in case I find him desperate, I will comfort him, and show him the great goodness and mercy of God, in Christ: and with godly consolations I will see, if I can lift him up.[11]

This sense of mission, explained in her own words, helps to illustrate the queen's aggressive stance during religious debate.

Yet Catherine's voluble obsession with religious doctrine was typical of the time. The sixteenth century in Europe was an age of religious self-examination and revolutionary ideas. If the queen tended to go on at length about the subject, it was nothing more than most of her contemporaries, including the king, did as well. It was not only the quality and meaning of life on earth that were at stake but eternal salvation or infernal damnation. With all of eternity in the balance, it was no wonder that many people were obsessed with the rules and regulations required for achieving Heaven and ineffable bliss. It was not Catherine's preoccupation with religious matters that was at fault but her lack of sensitivity to time and place and particularly to her husband's moods. By attempting to move beyond the sphere of women enjoined upon her by society she risked coming to grief not as Anne Askew, at the hands of society, but at the hands of England's societal and religious arbiter, who was growing increasingly more arbitrary with age, and who also happened to be Catherine's husband. Success and enthusiasm had robbed the queen of her customary clear-sightedness and made her vulnerable. If in 1544, she had carefully cultivated 'the simplicity of the dove'[12] in her dealings with the king, a year and a half later, as Henry's health continued to decline, the queen came to see her husband as a toothless old lion, more growl than bite, dependent on her skills as a nurse and on her love as a wife. She grew overconfident of her power. 'There is no such remedy against flattery of a man's self,' her uncle had taught her, 'as the liberty of a friend.'[13] While the queen took ever greater liberties as a royal councillor, her irritable and ill husband, who far preferred flatterers, was growing increasingly restive and resentful. No friend apparently took the liberty of pointing this fact out to the queen.

The winter of 1545–46 marked a frightening change in Henry's relationship with his wife. As late as the autumn of 1545, their marriage seemed to observers to be a happy one.[14] 'Now the King and the Queen and their daughter are going to hunt,' reads a note written in September 1545 from Sir William Paget to Jacomo Zambon, the Venetian secretary in England, 'his Majesty invites you to accompany him.'[15] According to the reports of imperial ambassadors Chapuys and Van der Delft such lighthearted pleasures between the king and queen were typical. But by January 1546, things had begun to change. One reason for the change was the king's health which had taken a turn for the worse. He was in great pain and in no mood to have his will crossed in anything. That his death was only a matter of time, and not very much time at that, certainly must have occurred to many at court. Factions supporting both extremes of the religious spectrum began to count heads and plot strategies.

There has been some argument among scholars about the importance of Catherine Parr's role in the English Reformation. Was she indeed the first true queen of the new order or merely a cipher? The evidence hitherto discussed strongly supports the former interpretation. In the winter of 1545, the chief court apostles of the new religion were Thomas Cranmer, Archbishop of Canterbury, among the religious establishment, and Catherine Parr among the secular. The queen's chamber had become the royal clubhouse of the new religion. John Foxe reported that Catherine:

> Was very much given to the reading and study of the Holy Scriptures, and that she, for the purpose, had retained divers well learned and godly persons to instruct

her ... [and] every day in the afternoon, for the space of an hour, one of her said chaplains in her privy chamber, made some collation to her and to her ladies and gentlewomen of her privy chamber, or others that were disposed to hear; in which sermons they ofttimes touched such abuses as in the church then were rife.[16]

There seems nothing controversial in Foxe's claim. It fits the pattern of daily life which Goldsmith, Udall, Latimer and Ascham all attribute to the queen. Yet hearing – and discussing – sermons by preachers who denounced church abuses within Henry's own church came perilously close to violating the very tenants of that church. In the king's Christmas Eve speech of 1545 before Parliament, he had roundly condemned both clergy, who 'preach one against another, teach one contrary to another, inveigh one against another without charity or discretion', as well as those men and women who decided for themselves whether 'bishop or preacher erreth or teacheth perverse doctrine.' When they made such decisions, declared God's Vicar, they meddled in the king's business.[17] When in addition to such sermons and questionable discussions, the queen publicly linked herself with alleged purveyors of radical books like Stephen Cobbe, she was sailing deep into dangerous waters.[18] The importance of the increasing radicalism of her religious opinions, for friends and enemies alike, was compounded by her apparent power within the royal household. She appeared to her contemporaries to have profound influence over her aging husband and, just as importantly perhaps, with his heirs.

Edward's enthusiastic Protestant leanings found consistent encouragement in his stepmother. Were the king to die, it would not be fanciful to imagine that the queen would continue to have a significant influence on the religious direction of the next reign under a child king. This would be particularly true were she to be named regent as she had been two years before. Speculation about how much influence the queen might carry into a new reign ran high during 1546 until the king's death in the following year. The reformer, Richard Hilles, wrote to Henry Bullinger from Strasbourg in January 1547, stating that the queen was personally committed to pious doctrine and would take the Protestant viewpoint.[19] At the same time, Chapuys was assuring the Catholic regent of the Netherlands that Catherine had been encouraged by others (notably the Duchess of Suffolk, the Countess of Hertford and Lady Lisle) in heretical religious beliefs, implying that the queen might be brought back to the true religion by pressure and persuasion.[20]

Chapuys had misinterpreted Catherine's kindness to Princess Mary as a tendency to sympathise with Mary's religion. The political expediency of the middle way followed so cautiously by the queen in the early days of her marriage, he had interpreted as a lukewarm commitment to the new religion.

The kindness that the queen had shown him personally – 'the Queen, being anxious, as it seemed to me, that I should not suffer from having to stand too long'[21] – and her early interest in an alliance between her husband and the emperor, he had misread as sympathy toward the empire. International speculation about the queen's personal religious feelings underscores their potential importance to the political situation developing in England. The care Catherine had taken to keep her public voice and her private conscience separate prior to November 1545, when she first published under her own name, had reassured the one-time imperial ambassador, who had not after all been in England since the first week of May 1545, of the moderation of the queen's beliefs. Had Chapuys been privy to the pages of *Lamentation of a Sinner*, he would have been less sanguine about the queen's religious convictions. It was precisely because Catherine was of enormous significance to the party of the new religion, particularly were she to be named regent for the prince, that the Bishop of Winchester and his cohorts now sought to attack and destroy her.

The role of Stephen Gardiner, Bishop of Winchester, in the plots of 1546 against the queen has recently been called into question.[22] Three items are presented as evidence of Gardiner's innocency of ill intent – that the conspiracy was not mentioned at the December 1550 trial which led to the deprivation of his bishopric, that the account of Gardiner's complicity did not appear in print until 1563, and that no account of it occurs in John Bale's brief sketches of Gardiner or the queen. Yet the account of John Foxe, published in 1563 in his *Acts and Monuments*, is considered generally convincing by most scholars.[23] It has also been stated that Foxe gives no sources for his story, yet this is not entirely true. Foxe had at least one source among the women of the queen's household, 'as certain of her ladies and gentlewomen, being yet alive, who were then present about her, can testify.'[24] Robert Parsons, a Jesuit who wrote *A Treatise of Three Conversions* in 1603 in which he excoriated John Foxe, accepted the general outlines of the plot against Catherine, with the revision that in fact it was the king rather than the bishop who was the arch-conspirator.[25] If Gardiner did indeed initiate a plot against the queen, what reasons could there have been for not mentioning it at his trial, or for suppressing publication of an account of it until 1563?

On 24 December 1546, some months after the crisis, imperial ambassador Van der Delft wrote to his master, Charles V: 'Four or five months ago great enquiries and prosecutions were carried out against the heretics and sacramentarians, but they have now ceased ... As regards the diversity of religion, the people at large are to a great extent on [the new religion's] side ... They do not, indeed, conceal their wish to see the Bishop of Winchester and other adherents of the ancient faith sent to the Tower to keep company with the Duke of Norfolk.'[26] The implicit involvement of Stephen Gardiner, Bishop of Winchester, with the prosecutions of 1546 was thus noted both by 'the people' and by Van der Delft, himself.

Six months before, on 6 July 1546, Van der Delft had written: 'I had several conversations with [the Bishop of] Winchester and [Sir William] Paget, whom I found very favourable to the public good, and to the interests of his Majesty [Charles V]. As these are the councillors most in favour with the king, I doubt not that they will be good instruments for maintaining the existing friendship and for preventing the Protestants from gaining footing or favour here. [Winchester and Paget] have confidently promised this.'[27] Most in favour with the king in July, Gardiner had conspicuously lost that favour by October. And capricious as Henry could be, Gardiner's disgrace was hardly a whim. The link between Gardiner and Paget, too, is suggestive. Paget came from a modest background and had studied under Gardiner at King's Hall, Cambridge. Gardiner subsequently sent the promising student to Padua to study and afterward made him his protégé at court. His later reputation among the blue bloods at court held that he was 'no gentleman of blood, neither in his father's side nor mother's side,' yet this snobbery did not stop his rising career.[28] Knighted on 18 October 1537, clerk of the Privy Council by 1540, Paget had risen to become one of Henry's secretaries of state by April 1543 and a privy councillor. He owed his rise to his own abilities and to the patronage of Stephen Gardiner. The two men maintained a very close relationship over the years, reinforced by a lively correspondence when either was away from court. In the minds of many, including the Spanish ambassador, Paget was Gardiner's lieutenant. Yet only a few months after the July 1546 dispatch, Paget, so long the bishop's right hand man, deserted Gardiner's sinking ship and threw in his lot with the very group that up until that time he had so vigorously opposed – the new religionists. Barely six months after he promised Van der Delft to hold England against the heretics, Paget became 'the principal instrument in setting up [the Duke of Somerset as] Protector',[29] and making Calvinism the religion of choice at court.[30]

In any plot against the new religionists, Gardiner, Paget and Wriothesley, another King's Hall man, religious chameleon, and contemporary of Paget's, would rightly be the natural suspects. Sir Richard Rich, whose perjured testimony had sent Sir Thomas More to the block, makes an unlovely fourth in this quartet of conspirators. There seems no reason to doubt that accusations against Gardiner, Wriothesley and Rich are true. During the arrest and torture of Anne Askew in June–July, discussed below, the soon-to-be executed woman, herself, charges Gardiner with complicity in the 1546 conspiracy and

Wriothesley with turning the wheel of the rack on which she was broken. Paget is mentioned in the more benign role of attempting through argument to persuade Anne to recant her heretical views. 'Then came Mr. Paget unto me with many glorious words, and desired me to speak my mind unto him. I might, he said, deny it again if need were.' Paget then counselled her to talk in 'common with some wise men.'[31] Anne's manuscript account of these confrontations was smuggled out of England immediately after her death by a Dutch merchant and handed over to John Bale in Germany who published it in 1548 while all parties to it were still alive. No credible evidence has been raised impugning the manuscript's veracity nor was it so raised at the time.

On the evidence, then, it appears clear that Gardiner, who together with Paget were 'the councillors most in favour with the king', was the agent of a conspiracy, to which Wriothesley and Rich were also party, whose purpose was to compromise and destroy the queen and as many of the coterie of new religionists around her as possible. Paget's complicity to some extent in the actions of his mentor and close associate, Gardiner, would go a long way toward explaining the curious omission of charges of conspiracy being brought against the bishop at his trial four years later. Paget, Wriothesley and Rich were men without much personal religious conviction and since all three had active careers after Gardiner's fall, it is probably safe to assume that Gardiner and his religious fervency took the lead in a conspiracy to ensure that the power of the radicals was broken before the king's death. Gardiner acknowledged in a letter to Paget that, 'ye told me once ye love no extremities and the mean is best ... who [ever] could hit it.'[32] Paget, himself, in a memorandum of worldly advice, wrote: 'Speak little. Care less. Desire nothing. Never earnest [promise].'[33] Paget was too intelligent and too privy to the goings on of Gardiner's inner circle not to have known the purpose of singling out Anne Askew for persecution, particularly as he was involved to the extent of questioning the woman, herself, in her prison cell.

Whatever the level of Paget's involvement in the conspiracy against the queen, the extremity of it must have caused in this lover of the mean a profound revulsion. The scandal and horror felt by many at the treatment of Anne Askew, coupled with a careful cultivation of his own political survival, may have been the deciding factor in Paget's sudden abandonment of his old friend and mentor, Stephen Gardiner. Six months later, Paget became the oracle of Henry's alleged deathbed bequest of lands and titles to the new ruling clique around the Duke of Somerset. Paget was a crucial political architect in the construction of Somerset's protectorate, and his subsequent importance to Somerset in 1550, during the latter's vicious internecine war with the Earl of Warwick for control of the council, would have made the suppression of any former sins of commission on Paget's part imperative. No mention would have been made of the attempts on the queen at Gardiner's trial because of Somerset's fear that Paget's crucial position on the Privy Council would be compromised.

John Bale, who was out of the country until after the death of Henry VIII, never mentioned the plots of 1546 in his 1548 *Illustrium Majoris Britanniae Scriptorum*, published in Wesel, because no one had told him about them. Nor were his biographical sketches anything but that, the meticulous detailing of his subjects' lives was not his intent. Paget, himself, conveniently omitting details of his own part in the conspiracy, was in all probability one source of Foxe's story, either directly or through an intermediary such as Bale's patron, the dowager Duchess of Suffolk. Certainly no one in power had anything to gain by contradicting his version. Nor could his co-conspirators protest. Wriothesley had died in 1550 and Gardiner in 1555. The great secrecy with which the conspirators had gone about to collect evidence against the queen kept the number of people who knew the entire story to a minimum.[34] Not until Paget's death in 1563, did Foxe feel free to publish the details he had been told and unlike history, itself, Paget played no part in the retelling.

If the conservatives, led by Gardiner, had been biding their time, waiting for the most opportune moment in which to attack the queen, Catherine's sudden vulnerability during Henry's bout of illness early in 1546 gave Gardiner the opening for which he had been waiting. If Catherine were to be destroyed and many of her supporters with her before Henry's death, the political power of the new religion would suffer a tremendous set-back, leaving a power vacuum that Gardiner felt confident he and his own supporters could fill. The bishop, Sir William Paget, the Duke of Norfolk and Wriothesley, the Lord Chancellor, could then position themselves to move forward into the next reign where a child king might be easily persuaded to follow their lead in matters of both religion and politics.

Gardiner, whom Catherine's brother, William, referred to as that 'willful and heady man', was no stranger to witch hunts for heretical schismatics. He had tried unsuccessfully on several occasions to destroy Archbishop Cranmer but had failed for a number of reasons, the most important of which was Henry's recognized need for his archbishop's talents. The king had once referred to Cranmer as the greatest heretic in Kent but he had no plans for dispensing with his services. Gardiner and his creature, Dr. John London, had made a last assault on the archbishop's position just prior to Henry's marriage to Catherine. The assault had backfired resulting in London's own incarceration and subsequent death in the Fleet.[35] 1546 saw a sudden upsurge in prosecutions for heresy, evidence of the retrograde religious tendencies of the king, whom Sir Geoffrey Elton has noted 'was losing that single and ultimate control over English policy which he had exercised since Cromwell's fall.'[36] Gardiner, chief instigator of these prosecutions, judged the time and the temper of his master right for another assault on the bastions of heterodoxy.

One activity which could possibly be used against her was Catherine's skill at healing. Witchcraft and healing had uncomfortably close associations in the minds of many and traditionally female practices of compounding remedies and treating illness could prove dangerous to the practitioner. Although helping to cure the sick 'was part of the charity of godly women of higher social status', nevertheless, a knowledge and use of herbs could be 'construed as conjuring.'[37] As for Catherine, she continued both her habitual daily visits to the king, her medical advice and her now perilous discussions of religion without realizing the danger into which she was putting herself. 'They leap at me as it were so many dogs,' the queen had written in 1544. 'The companies of the wicked bark at me. They beset my hands and feet round about.'[38] For Catherine, the howling of wolves was growing nearer.

In a mood of overconfidence, Catherine played into Gardiner's hands. Henry had fed his wife's sense of self-importance for three years and Catherine had taken this indulgence seriously. She continued not to discuss but to argue with the king about religion. She dared to contradict and instruct him. It was no more than she had always done and Henry had always accepted, but in the king's deteriorating condition it was too much. According to John Foxe, an abrupt change of subject by the king during one of his wife's energetic perorations on religion gave Gardiner the idea that the time was right to strike. 'A good hearing it is when women become such clerks,' Henry is supposed to have said irritably to Gardiner, after his wife had left the room, 'and a thing much to my comfort, to come in mine old days to be taught by my wife.'[39] Gardiner suddenly saw the way in which he might destroy the queen.

At the same time that the queen was admonishing the elders of Cambridge University for their failure to stress religious priorities, Gardiner began an anonymous smear campaign against her. On 27 February 1546, imperial ambassador Van der Delft wrote to Charles V: 'I hesitate to report there are rumours of a new Queen. Some attribute it to the sterility of the present Queen ... Madame Suffolk is much talked about and is in great favour; but the King shows no alteration in his behaviour to the Queen.'[40] Catherine's attitude was reported as being neither frightened nor worried by the rumours, but 'much annoyed'. She apparently had no sense of the danger that threatened and was reported to be in a mischievous mood, teasing Princess Mary about a proposed marriage between the princess and the Polish king.[41] But Gardiner was still feeling his way. The opening shots of the campaign against the queen were directed at her inability to give Henry another heir. No mention was made of heretical beliefs and her rumoured successor, the Duchess of Suffolk, was as staunch a supporter of the new religion as the queen herself. For this reason, it is probable that Henry's sharp words to Gardiner concerning Catherine, it they occurred as Foxe described, took place sometime after Van der Delft's letter. The king's remarks altered Gardiner's plan from an attack on Catherine's sterility, with perhaps hints at the black sorcery she used to avoid motherhood, to an attack on her religious beliefs.

If in February Catherine was publicly annoyed by the rumours of her imminent demise, there are indications in her chamber records that privately the queen had begun to feel uneasy about the slander campaign and even about her own position. In the middle of this month, around the time of Van der Delft's February dispatch, Catherine ordered new coffers for her chamber, with new locks, metal hinges, corner bands and handles with nails.[42] If, as she was later accused, she had forbidden books in her possession, this was a wise move to protect her possessions from prying eyes. By mid-March her unease appears to have increased, and between then and mid-April, the queen began to draw a defensive group of supporters closely about her. Her uncle, who was in ill health and had been living in quiet retirement at his manor of Horton in Northamptonshire, suddenly reappeared at court to take up once more his official duties as his niece's chamberlain. Letters went out from the queen in abundance – to Catherine's brother, who was staying at Baas manor in Essex, to Lady Anne Grey, her friend and supporter, at Mote Park in Kent, to Sir Anthony Denny, to the Countess of Hertford, and to Lady Margaret Douglas, the king's niece, at Stepney. There is an implication both in the queen's sudden concern for security and, although we cannot be certain of the contents of the letters, in this flurry of letter writing, of a shoring up of palisades, a securing of outer defenses. If Catherine felt that she was under siege, she had reason to feel so.[43]

One adjunct of the persecution of heretics in England during the spring and summer of 1546 was the international ramifications that English religious policy had on English political interests abroad. After the debacle of the 1544 invasion of France, Henry was attempting to renegotiate his position with Charles V and the empire, but radical changes in English religious practices such as Cranmer and the queen both supported, changes to the liturgy, and a prohibition against the veiling of religious images and making obeisances to the crucifix, would not go down well with Charles. Gardiner, who had been on the continent as the king's ambassador, drove this point home, reiterating 'how noxious such changes must be to the prospects of friendship with the emperor.'[44] Burdened with an empty treasury and the enormous expense of maintaining the garrison at Boulogne, Henry needed a peaceful conclusion to imperial negotiations.

That this need gave Gardiner another weapon to use against eager reformers coincided felicitously for the conservatives with the maturation of Gardiner's plan to destroy the queen.

By May the rumour mill began to concentrate on the queen's supposed heresies but Gardiner with great subtlety focused the attacks on members of the queen's inner circle at first rather than on the queen herself. In conjunction with a significant increase in government prosecutions for religious transgressions, Gardiner now brought the witch hunt for heretics into the heart of the court. On 2 May 1546, Lord Thomas Howard, the outspoken second son of the Duke of Norfolk, eager supporter of the reformed religion and familiar of the queen, was summoned before the Privy Council. He was charged with 'disputing indiscreetly of Scripture with other young gentlemen of the court.'[45] On 7 May, he was examined again and offered clemency, 'if he would confess what he said in disproof of sermons preached in Court last Lent and his other talk in the Queen's chamber and elsewhere in Court concerning Scripture.'[46] The fact that the council specified the queen's chamber as the scene of the indiscreet disputation was significant and ominous. Howard confessed that he had been at fault but when pushed to 'confess particulars', undoubtedly to give damaging testimony against members of the queen's household, he would not confess 'those particulars which the Privy Council would have had him confess.' It is possible, however, that Howard let something slip about the sort of books available in the queen's privy chamber because the next step the council took toward the prosecution of heretics at court was to send a letter to the mayor of London concerning the illegal import of heretical books by John Bale, 'lately brought in a hoy of Flanders'.[47]

The methods by which heretical books, smuggled illegally into England, were distributed and reached places as remote as the recesses of the queen's garderobe is roughly indicated by the Privy Council's investigations. Books smuggled in from the Continent in boats such as the 'hoy of Flanders' would then be passed on to a sympathetic port official, such as 'Hollande, the searcher', who, in turn, distributed them to such couriers as 'Morton, the grocer's apprentice of Bucklersbury', boys and young men who moved a great deal about the city. Apprentices like Morton came from a group with a reputation for free-wheeling rebellion. Religiously sympathetic members of the great fraternity of apprentices could carry the books throughout the city and make contact with traditional messengers for the royal household, such as the page named Worley, accused of making heretical statements at court and questioned before the council at the same time as Lord Thomas Howard. From a royal page, it was a quick passage through the hands of a gentlewoman of the chamber to the queen's secret book chest. Then, too, the queen may have had a tenuous connection with John Bale, writer of the heretical books indicted by the Privy Council, who two years later found a loyal patron in Catherine's confidant, the dowager Duchess of Suffolk.

Bale, a former monk known for his vitriol as 'Bilious Bale', was an outspoken and zealous proponent of the reformed religion. In the late 1530s, under Cromwell's protection, he had written propaganda plays such as, *A Brief Comedy or Interlude of John the Baptist's Preaching in the Wilderness, opening the crafty assaults of the hypocrites with the glorious baptism of the Lord Jesus Christ*, an exhaustively titled attack on the community of friars to which he had once belonged. His plays were not the sleek court comedies that Nicholas Udall put on but unsubtle and aggressive attempts to sway general public opinion to the support of radical religious reform. After Cromwell's death, Bale was forced to take refuge on the continent and continued to bombard England with his caustic writings, smuggled across the Channel from his sanctuary in Germany. The queen's interest in the writers of the English Reformation must have led her to at least a familiarity with Bale's work by 1546. In January 1547, she secured for one Philip Bale, the presentation of the parsonage of Pyworthy or Pury in Devonshire.[48] Philip Bale is described as being one of the king's chaplains and may or may not have been related to the radical writer. Yet also in the following year, John Bale published at Marburg, *The Examination of Anne Askewe*, a work detailing the terrors of 1546 in which Catherine was to be so deeply involved.

Tenuous as this connection with a notorious heretical writer seems, the chamber accounts of the queen provide evidence that she was indeed reading forbidden literature. These supposedly heretical books were hidden in her garderobe and as prosecutions for heresy intensified, Catherine gave the books to her uncle to smuggle out of the palace. After Henry died, the queen retrieved the hidden books, sending her trusted agent, Richard Aglionby, in April 1547 from St. James to Greenwich, 'concerning books of the garderobe had to the Lord Chamberlain.'[49] The knowledge that the queen was in possession of forbidden literature would alone have been enough for Gardiner to push forward his case against her. Prosecution for the possession of proscribed books must have sent a cold chill down the spine of Catherine and her ladies. Long memories at court would certainly have recalled the queen's role in the affair of radical publisher Stephen Cobbe.

All during May, the investigations concerning supposed heresies and heretics at court continued. On 8 May, not only Lord Thomas Howard but with him Sir Edward Warner, another of the queen's supporters and the man who had secured Cobbe's release in 1544, were called before the council and forced to promise, 'to reform their indiscreet talking of Scripture matters.'[50] On 11 May, Dr. Edward Crome, radical theologian, '*enfant terrible* of the London clergy',[51] and a friend of the caustic Calvinist Hugh Latimer, was called before the Privy Council, one of a series of command appearances he made during these months. Crome had preached a sermon before the congregation of the Mercers' Chapel on Passion Sunday, 11 April, denying the existence of Purgatory and the efficacy of prayers by the living for the souls of the dead. Chastised by the council, he was ordered to recant in another sermon to be given at St. Paul's Cross. Crome opened his supposed recantation at St. Paul's by announcing belligerently, 'I came not hither to recant, nor God willing, I will not recant.'[52] The Privy Council took great exception to Crome's second sermon. 'Our news here,' wrote one London merchant to his brother, '[is] of Dr. Crome's canting, recanting, decanting, or rather double canting.'[53] Heresy as a joke did not amuse Gardiner and company.

At the same time more supposed heretics were hauled in for questioning. A page of the Pallet Chamber named Worley was imprisoned 'for unseemly reasoning of Scripture.' Dr. William Huicke was committed under the Six Articles Act, 'for erroneous opinions' and his support of Dr. Crome. On 16 May, Johan Bette was condemned to death for violation of the Six Articles Act.[54] All of these men appear to have had links to members of the queen's household. Richard Worley was a yeoman of the queen's chamber, and John Worley was one of her sumptermen.[55] Dr. William Huicke was almost certainly related to the queen's physician, Dr. Robert Huicke. Richard Bette was one of the queen's couriers and his kinsman Adam Bette was a yeoman of her chamber.[56] Howard, Worley, Huicke and Bette were interviewed minutely but none of these interviews gave Gardiner the weapon he needed to bring about the downfall of the queen. And then on 13 June, a self-proclaimed religious prophet from Lincolnshire, Anne Askew, was arraigned by the mayor of London for preaching sacramentarianism, a belief that the sacraments in the Eucharist were symbolic not corporeal manifestations of Christ, a view considered damning and heretical by English conservatives and moderates alike.

Anne Askew was the daughter of a Lincolnshire knight, Sir William Askew or Ayscough. She had been born in 1521 at Stallingborough near Grimsby, only eighteen miles from Kirton-in-Lindsey, where Catherine Parr came to live as the bride of Edward Borough in 1530. Anne Askew's father, Sir William, was a close friend of Sir Thomas Borough of Gainsborough, Catherine's first father-in-law, and served with him and his nephew Sir Robert Tyrwhit, now Catherine's master of the horse, during the Pilgrimage of Grace.[57] At a very young age, Anne found herself married off to the considerably older Thomas Kyme. The Kyme family originally lived on a manor once owned by the maternal grandfather of Sir Robert Tyrwhit. The newly-married Kymes made their home in Kelsey, barely six miles from Kirton-in-Lindsey. It is not known whether Catherine Parr actually knew the precocious Anne Askew in Lincolnshire, and Anne herself was only twelve years old when Catherine left Kirton-in-Lindsey for good. Yet despite her youth, Anne may already have been married and living at Kelsey when Catherine lived with Edward Borough at Kirton-in-Lindsey, and despite the difference in their ages, the two women shared a mutual passion for learning and biblical studies. It is not beyond the realm of possibility to suppose that when Anne left Lincolnshire, she chose to go to London in order to recommend herself to a previously sympathetic neighbour who now happened to be queen.

Anne Askew and her husband, Thomas Kyme, were an incompatible couple from the first. Anne was a woman for whom the age provided no role suited to her gifts. Her fate like all girls of her class and position, particularly after the mass closure of the religious houses, was to marry and bear children. Accused by a London priest near the end of her life for reasoning 'against the order of schools', Anne replied with curtness. 'I told him, I was but a woman, and knew not the course of schools.'[58] It little mattered that she could read and write, that she could reason and respond, holding her own in religious disputations or academic argument. No one cared very greatly about her mind, her attitudes or her viewpoint and when she pressed them, her husband reacted with violence. Anne dutifully bore Kyme two children but her spirit was irrepressible. With no sanctioned social outlet for her abilities, Anne's temper turned to religious zealotry. She became outspoken to the point that the much tried Thomas Kyme threw her out of his house for insulting the priests. Anne decided to take her mission and her message to London and soon found herself in trouble for her advanced, mostly heretical views.

The dyspeptic Jesuit, Robert Parsons, described her as 'a coy dame, and of very evil fame for wantonness: in that she left the company of her husband, Master Kyme, to gad up and down the country a gospelling and gossiping where she might, and out not. And this for diverse years before her imprisonment; but especially she delighted to be in London near the court.'[59] Anne had friends in London who attempted to protect her. When a warrant was issued for her arrest in 1546, she managed to hide for nearly a month before being caught. But her own need to preach the gospel of her beliefs finally entrapped her in the meshes of heretical prosecution.

In March 1545, she was closely questioned about her beliefs before Christopher Dare, the lord mayor of London, and on 13 June Anne Askew was arraigned for heresy. Since no witnesses appeared against her, she was subsequently released. The following year she was not so lucky. On 18 June 1546 she was once more arraigned for heresy at the Guildhall. Anne, it was stated in the records of the Privy Council, 'refused [Thomas Kyme] to be her husband

... [and] she was very obstinate and heady in reasoning of matters of religion, wherein she showed herself to be of a naughty opinion, seeing no persuasions of good reasons could take place, she was sent to Newgate to remain there to answer to the law.'[60] One interesting black mark raised against Anne was the fact that, like the queen, she continued to use her maiden name.

What made Anne's professed heretical views of such importance to Bishop Gardiner were her rumoured close connections with the highest circles at court. According to her nephew, writing after her death, she was captured when a letter she was trying to send was intercepted.[61] Parsons declares that the letter was part of an organized letter-writing campaign on Anne's part 'to enter [into discourse] with the principal of the land, namely with Queen Katharine Parr herself.'[62] In prison, Anne had received money both from the Countess of Hertford and from Lady Denny, members of the queen's inner circle, as well as visits from the queen's own cousin, Nicholas Throckmorton. Then there was the tenuous connection with Sir Robert Tyrwhit and his wife, Elizabeth, both servants and close confidants of the queen. For Gardiner and his allies, there was every likelihood that if sufficient pressure were brought to bear on Anne, 'so unarmed, naked, given up and alone',[63] she could be made to implicate other ladies-in-waiting and perhaps even the queen herself. But Gardiner, Paget, Wriothesley and Rich reckoned without Anne Askew's prodigious strength of character and physical courage.

Put repeatedly to the rack – the wheels of which, Anne herself reported, were turned by Wriothesley and the wretched Sir Richard Rich – the tortured woman refused to implicate anyone. Gardiner mocked her steadfastness and told her that 'she was a parrot',[64] quoting theology that she did not and could not understand.[65] It was suggested to her, no doubt repeatedly, as her bones were cracked, her flesh torn and her joints dislocated that she name the Countesses of Hertford and Sussex, the Duchess of Suffolk, and the Ladies Denny and Fitzwilliam as her patrons and fellow heretics at court. Anne Askew's reputed first-hand account of the scene illustrates the determination of her torturers to extract information that would compromise the queen's inner circle.

Then they said, there were of the council that did maintain me. And I said, no. Then they did put me on the rack, because I confessed no ladies nor gentlewomen to be of my opinion, and thereon they kept me a long time. And because I lay still and did not cry, my lord Chancellor [Wriothesley] and master Rich, took pains to rack me [with] their own hands, till I was nigh dead.

Then the lieutenant caused me to be loosed from the rack. Immediately I swooned, and then they recovered me again. After that I sat two long hours reasoning with my lord Chancellor upon the bare floor, where as he with many flattering words,

persuaded me to leave my opinion. But my lord God (I thank his everlasting goodness) gave me grace to persevere, and will do (I hope) to the very end.[66]

That all of the women named to Askew were of the queen's inner circle is
of particular significance. If it was in fact the husbands of these women that
Gardiner had in his target sights rather than the queen, herself, then the targets
were strangely chosen. The Duchess of Suffolk was a widow, and neither Sir
Anthony Denny nor Sir William Fitzwilliam[67] were of such importance that
their fall would be a fatal blow to the reformed religion group. Only the
disgrace of Edward Seymour, Earl of Hertford, or the Earl of Sussex could be
considered a real prize if Gardiner's actual intent was to destroy the spouses of
these women rather than their royal mistress. All the versions of the story given
in the years immediately following Anne Askew's death point to Catherine Parr
as the principal 'deer' at whom the Bishop of Winchester 'had bent his bow to
shoot'.

The horror of the Anne Askew's torture was especially appalling to her
contemporaries at court. Charles Wriothesley in his *Chronicle*, commented that
'Anne Askewe alias Keme, was had to the Tower of London and there set on
the rack where she was sore tormented, but she would not convert for all the
pain.'[68] To rack a woman, gently born, and already condemned to death set up
waves of revulsion among those privy to the story. 'She hath been racked since
her condemnation (as men say), which is a strange thing in my understanding.
The Lord be merciful to us all,' Otwell Johnson, London merchant, wrote to
his brother on 2 July 1546.[69] It was not only inhumane, it was patently against
the law, as Gardiner and his cohorts knew.

On 8 July, five days before the torture of Askew, a proclamation for the
discovery of heretical books was made, requiring that 'from henceforth no man,
woman, or other person, of what estate, condition, or degree he or they may be,
shall, after the last day of August next ensuing, receive, have, take, or keep in his
or their possession the text of the New Testament of Tyndale's or Coverdale's.'[70]
Catherine, who took Coverdale into her household as her almoner upon
Henry's death, almost certainly had a copy of his translation in her possession.
This proclamation, originating as it did with the conservative faction on the
council, put the queen in the unenviable position of either publicly confessing
to the ownership of heretical books or concealing them and risking search
and prosecution. Were Catherine to allow a member of her household to
confess the books, precedent had been set for torture to extract the name
of the real owner from them. Yet even with the queen exposed to possible
legal prosecution, Gardiner still needed some sort of compromising statement
from Anne Askew to initiate an investigation. Anne refused to give it to him

and the knowledge that he was treading far beyond his brief by torturing a woman to such extremity that she had to be carried to her execution made the desperation of the gallant little band of conservative conspirators particularly vicious. Frantic for some admission that would let them plead that the end had justified the means, Wriothesley and Rich put their own arms to the wheel of the rack but managed to extract nothing.

Two members of the council in a particularly uncomfortable position were William Parr, Earl of Essex, the queen's brother, and John Dudley, Lord Lisle, husband of Jane Guildford, the queen's cousin and another of her intimates. Overseen by Gardiner, who must have had a twisted sense of humour, Essex and Lisle were selected to question Anne during another session of torture. They begged the suffering woman to recant her heresies and to admit that the Sacrament did indeed become flesh. Anne answered without hesitation that 'it was great shame for them [Essex and Lisle] to counsel contrary to their knowledge.' This implication that she had already spoken to the two men on religious topics and therefore knew what they believed made the uncomfortable lords even more uncomfortable. 'Whereunto, in few words, they did say that they would gladly all things were well.'[71]

On 16 July, Anne Askew was sent to the stake without having compromised either the queen or her circle. It is possible that she said nothing under torture because there was nothing to say, that she had in fact never met the queen. However it should be noted that truth had never in the past stopped victims of extreme torture from perjuring themselves, and Anne's words to Essex and Lisle imply some degree of familiarity with the inner circle's religious discussions. Whether Anne refused to lie or whether in fact she refused to tell the truth, she refused in either case to play Gardiner's game and went to her death with an awesome degree of self-possession and courage.

Frustrated for the moment of their quarry, the bishop and the lord chancellor stepped up the rumour mill. 'Dangerous prophecies' of a new queen and the imminent demise of the present one were repeated in the streets during June and July.[72] By now Catherine was certainly more than just 'annoyed'. 'They rejoice and be glad of my fall ... They be assembled together against me. They strike to kill me in the way before I may beware of them. They gather themselves together in corners,' she had written in 1544. 'They curse and ban my words everyday, and all their thoughts be set to do me harm ... They watch my steps, how they may take my soul in a trap ... They do beset my way, that I should not escape. They look and stare upon me ... I am so vexed that I am utterly weary... '[73] Her enemies had not abandoned the hunt. Gardiner had one more arrow in his quiver and he released it around the time that Anne Askew went to the stake.

It was probably during the last two weeks of July, shortly after Askew's death, that Gardiner made his final attempt to bring down the queen. A window of opportunity opened during those two weeks for the conservatives. The leading new religionists among the courtiers were all away from court which was then at Westminster. Edward Seymour, Earl of Hertford, had left on a military mission to the Pale and Boulogne and did not return to the Privy Council until 1 August. John Dudley, Lord Lisle, after the very uncomfortable episode with Askew on the rack in the Tower, decamped immediately afterward to Oxford and then left England altogether on a royal commission to France. He did not return to England until the beginning of August. Catherine's other protector, Cuthbert Tunstall, Bishop of Durham, left London at the end of the first week in July for France and did not return to the council until 1 November. The queen's brother, too, decided to absent himself from London.[74] No one on the council, which had shrunk to the core of the conservative party, now stood between Gardiner and the queen and, according to John Foxe, he seized the opportunity offered.

The king's health and humour, too, favoured Gardiner's plans. On 6 July, Van der Delft wrote to Mary of Hungary, that 'the King has continued melancholy. Certainly although dressed to go to mass, he did not go that day, nor did he go into his gardens as his habit is in summer.'[75] Van der Delft made the ominous observation: 'Here is great examination and punishment of heretics, no class being spared.' Despite the fact that Catherine, 'with all painful endeavours [applied] herself, by all virtuous means, in all things to please [the king's] humour.',[76] yet her spirited arguments about religion and her efforts to push forward the reformed church and eradicate all vestiges of popery were getting on Henry's nerves. Henry had a secretive and dissimulating nature which enjoyed playing two opposing forces against each other. 'If my cap knew what I was thinking,' he is supposed to have exclaimed, 'I would throw it in the fire.' When Gardiner and his group had sought to arrest Archbishop Cranmer and send him to the Tower shortly before Catherine's marriage in 1543, the king had made no attempt to stop them but had instead turned Gardiner's gambit into a game for his own amusement. Henry sent secretly for the archbishop and gave him a ring which Cranmer could produce at the appropriate moment, forcing a hearing before the king and so confounding his enemies. The mystified archbishop took the ring and when faced with arrest shortly thereafter, produced it, to the king's huge enjoyment. Henry took delight in causing discomfiture in those who had irritated him and now he was to play the same game with Catherine, Gardiner and Wriothesley.

In Foxe's account, the story plays like the first two acts of *Othello* followed by the final act of *The Taming of the Shrew*.[77] Gardiner whispered in his royal master's ear that Catherine expressed herself of views that under his own laws would be judged heretical. What is more, promised the bishop, 'he, with others of his faithful councillors, could within short time, disclose such treasons cloaked with this cloak of heresy, that his majesty could easily perceive how perilous a matter it is, to cherish a serpent within his own bosom.' Once before such an offer of heinous revelations had been made to Henry, revelations regarding Katherine Howard's infidelities. Convinced of her innocence, the king had allowed the investigation to go forward and the results had broken his heart, wounded his pride, and led to the execution of his queen. Henry could not bear to think of himself as either a fool or a cuckold. The ailing king told Gardiner to proceed with his investigations into the queen's beliefs.

The Bishop of Winchester made plans to have the private closets of the three women closest to Catherine – Anne Herbert, Maud Lane, and Elizabeth Tyrwhit – searched for forbidden books. It is not clear whether he actually put this plan into effect or was foiled by the quick action of the ladies in question, who, warned in advance, hid the proscribed books before the searchers could find them. Gardiner next began to 'suborn accusers, as otherwise to betray [the queen] in seeking to understand what books, by law forbidden, she had in her closet.' Gardiner may have tried this with the queen's clerk of closet, William Harper. A passage with which Catherine was very familiar, St. Matthew 10:36, warns: 'And a man's foes shall be they of his own household.' Harper's duties gave him access to many of the secret recesses of the queen's chamber. Responsible for such personal attentions to her as the ordering of her books and the organizing of linen laundering, Harper must have known what the queen was reading and where the books were kept. Then, too, his sympathies seemed to be with Gardiner's party. While vicar of Writtle in Essex and under the patronage of the queen's brother, Harper was prosecuted for 'Popish practices'.[78] The queen's policy of employing servants regardless of their religion was one of long-standing.[79] On 18 October 1546, Harper was instituted by the queen to Sampford Courteney in Devon, a living she held by virtue of the manor.[80] This would appear to be a reward given after the terrors of the summer, possibly for loyalty in the face of great pressure brought to bear on Harper to betray his mistress. Although Harper seems to have remained loyal, others may have been willing to lay information for money or principal. Whatever proof was presented to the king, it was enough to convince Henry to have a warrant made out for Catherine's arrest: 'the poor queen,' lamented Foxe, 'neither knew, nor suspected anything at all, and therefore used, after her accustomed manner, when she came to visit the king, still to deal with him touching religion, as before she did.'

Only a few days before her scheduled arrest, Henry in a fit of (calculated?)

garrulousness, confided the whole plan to one of his physicians, possibly Dr. George Owen or Dr. Thomas Wendy but also possibly Dr. Robert Huicke, swearing him to secrecy. Whether the doctor immediately broke his word or whether, as Foxe relates, the warrant for the queen's arrest was providentially dropped by accident and found its way into her hands, she was somehow made aware of her extreme danger. Catherine may have written only a few months before that she no longer feared death and that 'now we be bold through the spirit, for the sure hope of the resurrection, that we receive it with joy. It is now no more bitter, but sweet, no more feared but desired.'[81] Yet when faced with death's sudden imminent possibility her response was more human than saintly.

Terrified and nearly hysterical, 'as certain of her ladies and gentlewomen, being yet alive, who were then present about her, can testify', Catherine was not so paralyzed with fear that she refused now to heed the doctor's sage advice. She took at once to her bed, giving it out that her health was in a dangerous state, which was hardly a lie under the circumstances. It was well known at court that Henry avoided the company of wives that he intended to arrest. Catherine's convenient illness was a ploy to bring him to her and it worked. Hearing of her illness, the king came to visit her and Catherine blurted out all her fear that somehow unintentionally she had displeased her dear husband. Mollified by her eagerness to remedy her wrong, the king allowed her to visit him the next day, her speedy recovery from dangerous illness no doubt explained by Henry's personal concern for her health.

Having ordered her ladies to destroy any proscribed books they might still have hidden, Catherine visited the king at night alone. Sitting on his lap, she lavished him with loving enticements, calculated to defuse Henry's anger. If Catherine's beliefs had displeased him, perhaps her body could buy back Henry's favour. Although he happily accepted the offer, the king was not ready to forgive and forget quite yet. He tried to lure Catherine into another compromising religious argument. Shrewder this time, the queen was not to be bated and in a speech worthy of Shakespeare's own Katharina,[82] she spoke fulsomely on a wife's duty to submit her hand beneath her husband's foot and all her own footling opinions to the superior wisdom of her lord. She was, Catherine declared, but 'a silly poor woman', while Henry was 'my only anchor, supreme head and governor here in earth, next unto God, to lean unto.'

Henry was still not convinced of the genuineness of her submission. "Not so by St. Mary', quoth the king; 'you are become a doctor, Kate, to instruct us (as we take it), and not to be instructed or directed by us." Catherine hurriedly explained that if she had argued with the king or seemed to dispute him, it was in order to take his mind off of his pain. 'I have not done it so much to

maintain opinion,' she told him, 'as I did it rather to minister talk, not only to
the end your majesty might with less grief pass over this painful time of your
infirmity, being attentive to our talk, and hoping that your majesty should reap
some ease thereby; but also that I, hearing your majesty's earnest discourse,
might receive to myself some profit thereby.' Catherine had learned well how
to dissemble and touched her querulous husband on those points where he was
most vulnerable, his health and his vanity. "And is it even so sweet heart!' quoth
the king, 'and tended your arguments to no worse end? Then, perfect friends
we are now again, as ever any time heretofore." – and pulling her into his lap,
he began to kiss her.[83] The Bishop of Winchester had lost the battle and was
shortly to lose the war as well.

The Earl of Hertford and Lord Lisle, duel pillars of the new religion, both
returned from France the first week in August and reclaimed their seats on
the Privy Council. In that week, too, the king and queen moved to Hampton
Court, where they remained during the rest of the month.[84] The denouement
of the on-going drama for the life of the queen must thus have taken place
during that week. Henry's love of confounding people whom he felt were
plotting against him was given full play when Wriothesley and forty guards
appeared one afternoon in the palace gardens, where the king and queen
were together, to arrest Catherine and carry her off to the Tower. Wriothesley
should have been forewarned by Henry's presence among the queen and her
ladies, for the king always made it a point to be elsewhere when his wives were
arrested. But overly sure of himself, Wriothesley did not stop to consider and
his appearance put the king into a fury. It is just barely possible that Henry
had actually forgotten about the appointed hour for the queen's arrest in the
pleasure of her submission and the renewal of conjugal relations between
them. Or perhaps he wanted to press home his point one more time with his
outspoken wife. Whatever the circumstances, the unfortunate Lord Chancellor's
arrival aroused all the royal ire. The king pulled Wriothesley aside none too
gently and was heard to yell at him, 'Knave! arrant knave! beast! and fool!'
Henry brusquely ordered Sir Thomas out of his sight.

As the confused, frightened and no doubt infuriated Wriothesley took
himself off, Catherine exhibited her own brand of dissimulation and 'with as
sweet words as she could utter, she endeavoured to qualify the king's displeasure,
with request unto his majesty in behalf of the lord chancellor, with whom he
seemed to be offended.' Touched by her seeming concern for a man who was
her enemy, Henry responded: 'Ah! poor soul, thou little knowest how evil
he deserveth this grace at thy hands. Of my word, sweet heart! he hath been
towards thee an arrant knave and so let him go.' Bishop Gardiner's attempts to
bring down the queen and her supporters with her had failed.

The king never forgave the conservatives for their attack on Catherine. It was not a liberalising of Henry's religious views but this failed personal vendetta against his queen that drove the conservatives from favour until the end of his reign. Both Paget and Wriothesley continued to serve the king but deserted Gardiner, a fact conspicuously brought home to the bishop at Henry's death. The king, as was his wont, continued to use all tools at hand, including the Bishop of Winchester, but the favour that Gardiner had enjoyed with his royal master at the beginning of summer had melted away by fall. John Dudley, Lord Lisle, the husband of Catherine's persecuted lady-in-waiting, Jane Guildford, and first-hand witness to the racking and torture of Anne Askew, felt secure enough of his position to strike the bishop in the face at a council meeting in November.[85] Henry, on his death bed, refused to include Gardiner in his will though begged to do so surprisingly, so Foxe relates, by the very group he had tried to destroy. 'If he were one of you,' Henry informed them, 'he would cumber you all and you would never rule him, he is of so troublesome a nature. Marry, I myself could use him and rule him to all manner of purposes, as seemed good unto me; but so shall you never do' – a singularly percipient observation. That other arch-conservative, the Duke of Norfolk, found himself under sentence of death by December. As a New Year's present to her fellow religionist, Edward Seymour, Earl of Hertford, Catherine chose a gift that symbolized her victory over her enemies – a double portrait of herself and Henry as King and Queen of England.[86]

Henry was as implacable in his hate as he was importunate in his love. Nine days after Anne Askew died at the stake, he set himself to make lavish amends to his wife for his former suspicions. Between 25 July 1546 and early December, when his health began to fail for good, Henry issued no less than five licenses for French, Flemish and Italian jewelers to bring to England 'all manner of jewels, pearls, and precious stones ... of skins and sable furs ... clothes and new gentlenesses of fashion ... as he or they shall think best for the pleasure of us [and] our dearest wife, the Queen.'[87] As another gesture of trust, Prince Edward was given into Catherine's care from mid-summer until the beginning of winter. The followers of the new religion had cause to rejoice. The machinations of Bishop Gardiner and his cohorts had failed to displace them. Lord Lisle and the Earl of Hertford, the most powerful lords on the council as the winter of 1546–1547 drew on, were also two of the most outstanding supporters of the queen. Catherine Parr had defeated her enemies. She had proven herself by conviction, by influence and by actions the first true queen of the English Reformation.

'Very Shadows and Dreams'

The reason for the absence of so many of Henry's councillors in France during the month of July 1546 was the finalization of negotiations between Henry and Francois I over the fate of Boulogne. Henry fully intended to keep this trophy of war and Francois, not unsurprisingly, wanted it back. Mending fences with his fellow monarchs on the Continent, as he had been forced to do since the 1544 French invasion, Henry agreed to a treaty that would return Boulogne to the French in eight years upon the payment of an indemnity of two million crowns. When Van der Delft commented to the English king that the French would never be able to raise such a sum to ransom the town, Henry just smiled. He never intended that they should.[1]

The official ratification of the treaty in England was scheduled to take place in July but delays by the French postponed the arrival of Francois' emissary, Admiral Claude d'Annebaut, until the middle of August. The reception for d'Annebaut and his entourage and the festivities that surrounded the signing of the treaty were the last official orchestrations of Tudor magnificence in Henry's reign. The king was determined that the French should be dazzled by English splendor. He ordered caches of jewels from the royal collection sent to his wife and to his daughter, Mary.[2] To complement her new jewellery wardrobe, Catherine gave orders to one Mark Mylloner in London for 625 aiglettes of gold set in purple ribbon and two pairs of perfumed gloves of crimson velvet and purple, trimmed with buttons of diamonds and rubies, to match the twenty-seven pairs of golden aiglettes set with diamonds and rubies that she had ordered in June.[3] Having avoided being done away with by her husband by the narrowest of margins, Catherine was now called upon to impersonate the full glory of the Tudor monarchy. If clothes and jewels maketh the man, how much more do they maketh a queen? Behind the glittering façade, festooned in red and purple velvet and cascading aiglettes of gold, diamonds and rubies, Catherine's emotions must have been in turmoil. To add to the emotional strain, Sir Thomas Seymour had returned to court, fresh from fabulous naval exploits with three galleys of pirates who had put him in such danger of his life that in order to escape being shot, he had had to row a shallop himself out of firing range.[4]

In deference to the queen, Henry prominently featured her brother, the Earl of Essex, in the arrangements for the festivities to welcome Admiral d'Annebaut. Essex was fluent in French and knowledgeable on the subjects of French protocol and custom. It was the first of a number of ceremonial meetings and negotiations with French ambassadors, both in England and on the continent, at which Essex was to be of use to his monarch over the next 25 years. On 19 August, the French admiral's 'twelve fair galleys, well-trimmed and decked', were received by the Earls of Essex and Derby at Greenwich.[5] All of London had been called out to welcome the French deputation. Mayor, aldermen, guilds, apprentices and populace lined the streets. The Tower was furnished with an ample supply of ordnance (Thomas Seymour was the master of the ordnance) to fire a salvo of deafening salutes, and the river was covered with barges gallantly accoutered, with brilliantly coloured flags and pennants waving in the sunlight. Over a thousand people made up the French deputation and the English had spared no expense or detail for their entertainment and simultaneous indoctrination into English court splendor. Orders were even given for it to be ascertained secretly 'whether the Admiral useth to sit abroad with the number of his train or to sit apart privately with a few,' so that the tables could be made up for his pleasure.[6]

Essex received and entertained d'Annebaut at Greenwich Palace and the following day brought him on board the king's barge and proceeded to Limehouse where the mayor, aldermen and guild barges awaited to accompany the riverine procession to Tower Wharf. All along the route, 'on all the banks by the waterside, lay pieces of ordnance which shot off, but especially the Tower of London, where was shot a terrible peal of ordnance and from thence [d'Annebaut] rode though London, in great triumph, the Mayor and the crafts standing in the streets in good order, to the Bishop's Palace of London, where he lodged.'[7] It was regretted that the admiral could not be the guest of Cuthbert Tunstall at Durham House but fire had recently damaged the structure and so he was forced to put up in the less magnificent apartments of Edmund Bonner, Bishop of London.

On the eve of St. Bartholemew's Day, the French travelled by water to Hampton Court where the king and a party of 2,000 men on horseback rode out to greet him. The Earl of Essex, as master of the pensioners, and the men under his command, both Seymour brothers, all the esquirie, and evidently everyone else present, all dressed in great array, welcomed the party to Hampton Court. 'And at the outer gate of the Court, the Lord Chancellor, and all the King's council received [the admiral], and brought him to his lodging.'[8] Presents were showered on the French, plate, horses, greyhounds, and wine. Henry could afford to be generous, secretly nursing the fine joke that despite the treaty, Boulogne would never be ransomed and would continue, as he intended, in English hands. The following day, the king, dressed with great richness, met with Admiral d'Annebaut in the chapel where the treaty between the two kings was sworn and signed.

One enigmatic item leading to much scholarly debate over the centuries is a remark that the king made to the French admiral in the presence of Archbishop Cranmer.[9] Standing in one of the temporarily erected pavilions in the gardens of Hampton Court, 'after the banquet was done the first night,' Cranmer later told his secretary Ralph Morice a curious tale. 'The King was leaning upon the ambassador and upon me,' explained Cranmer. 'If I should tell what communication between the King's Highness and the said ambassador was had, concerning the establishing of sincere religion then, a man would hardly have believed it; nor had I myself thought the King's Highness had been so forward in those matters as then appeared.'[10] Surveying the scene while leaning on the shoulders of Cranmer and d'Annebaut, the king amazed his archbishop by referring to the joint intention of himself and the King of France to mutually abolish the sacrifice of the mass from religious services and institute a simple communion service in its place. After the persecutions, torture and burnings for heresy that had taken place only weeks before, Cranmer had every reason to doubt his hearing. Yet he stated later that he had clearly understood the king to say that he and Francois I 'were so thoroughly and firmly resolved in that behalf' to institute this sweeping reform in their respective kingdoms within the next six months, 'that they meant also to exhort the Emperor to do the like in Flanders and other his countries and seigniories, or else they would break off from him.' What Henry actually meant by this astounding confidence to d'Annebaut was then as now a matter for much speculation. He could hardly have believed that either Francois I or Charles V would countenance the implementation of such a proposal. That Henry, speaking thus before the French king's representative, was testing political waters for some ulterior motive may be imagined. As Professor Scarisbrick has so aptly remarked: 'What precisely Henry's diplomatic intentions were during the months which ran from the conclusion of the Anglo-French treaty in June 1546 to his death at the end of the following January only Heaven and Henry know.'[11]

Around the solemn ceremony of treaty signing and disconcerting royal confidences, the pageantry of Tudor England continued to flow in glittering, well-organized performance for the benefit of the French:

> To tell you of the costly banquet houses, [confides Hall], that were built, and of the great banquets, the costly masques, the liberal huntings that were shewed to [d'Annebaut], you would much marvel, and scant believe. But on Friday following, he being rewarded with a cupboard of plate, to the value of £1,200, [the admiral] returned to London and on Sunday took his galleys and departed.[12]

The queen's impersonation of a submissive wife and decorative consort pleased Henry, and after the French had left, he took Catherine on a progress that was a sort of second honeymoon. From Hampton Court they travelled to Oatlands, where Henry had recently lavished a good deal of money on the house and added a new processional staircase to the queen's apartments.[13] From there the royal pair travelled on to Guildford to be entertained by Catherine's brother, and from thence to hunt at the Lodge at Chobham in late August, where much of the court had to be put up in tents as the house was not large enough to contain them, and finally to Windsor. This rather ghastly echo of the queen's triumphant progress with the royal children two years earlier, after her sterling performance as regent-general, could not have been easy for Catherine. There was a great deal of hunting, at least on the part of the queen, who sent the gift of a buck to Mr. Bush, one of her goldsmiths in London, a stag to Anne of Cleves and half a stag to Lord Lisle.[14] She spent her spare time studying Spanish and continued to play her role of submissive wife.[15] All work by her on religious projects stopped.

The Pauline prototype of a Christian wife, chaste, obedient, silent, had taken the place of the outspoken social and religious rebel. *Lamentation of a Sinner* was buried at the bottom of a locked chest. The English translation of Erasmus' *Paraphrases* was shelved. No more admonishing letters were dispatched to institutions of higher learning. By December, the king was preoccupied with arranging the executions of the Duke of Norfolk and his son, the Earl of Surrey, both in the Tower under sentence of death for treason. Catherine must have privately shuddered at their fate, the more so as Surrey had been a close friend and schoolmate of her brother's. But for a quirk of chance that had shown her in time the danger in which she stood, it would have been she who prepared to receive the last rites and the headman's ax instead of the Howards. As her cousin, Sir Nicholas Throckmorton, is said to have described the situation:

> We wished to please, we feared to offend,
> We saw the Prince's wrath brought heavy end.[16]

There must have been in Catherine's mind no guarantee that at any moment, on a sudden whim, should she fail to please him, her husband might not decide to send her to the Tower as well to keep company with the condemned.

Catherine spent October at Windsor with the king, moving back to Oatlands in the middle of November and from there to the king's playhouse, Nonesuch,[17] in the first week of December.[18] Realizing that continued proximity to her husband was her best guarantee of a continued existence, the queen remained close to the king through the first week in December, but when Henry left Nonesuch for London to keep Christmas, Catherine went by herself to Greenwich. This last Christmas of her reign she spent apart from the king, 'although,' according to Van der Delft, 'she has never before left him on a solemn occasion.'[19] That this was Henry's decision and not Catherine's is certain. With the king ill and the future unsure, absenting herself from her husband's immediate vicinity would have been the last thing the queen would have chosen to do. Catherine spent the holidays with the court at Greenwich while the king, 'who keeps himself secluded from all but his Councillors and three or four gentlemen of his Chamber', rode on Christmas Eve from Westminster to Hampton Court.[20] By 10 January both he and the queen were back at Westminster, but according to the French ambassador, Henry would not allow either the queen or Princess Mary to see him.[21]

On 21 January, Henry Howard, Earl of Surrey, was executed for treason. By the time of Surrey's death it was open knowledge that the king's health was failing dramatically. Diplomatic dispatches were full of the news. Mary of Hungary, Hapsburg regent of the Netherlands, was informed by her agents that the king had had an attack just before Christmas at Windsor.[22] Francois I received news from his informants that the king was very ill, and that the ulcers on his legs had had to be cauterised.[23] After parting from the king shortly before Christmas, there is no evidence that Catherine, although she seems to have tried on more than one occasion, ever saw her husband alive again. This point is important as it bears on the make-up of the subsequent regency council.

When Henry made his will in 1544, shortly before departing for France, he created his queen at the same time regent-general of his kingdom. According to the statute of 1536, an heir, if left a minor at the king's death, was to govern under the guidance of his mother and a regency council. Although Catherine was not technically Edward's mother, it is probable that the will of 1544 made provision for a regency council that included the queen. This was a royal decision which Catherine seems to have actively lobbied to keep in place between July 1544 and February 1546. All of her letters to the king while he was in France tended to a reassurance of Henry of her ability to manage the kingdom while he was away. In 1540, the erudite courtier Sir Thomas Elyot had published a book entitled, *The Defence of Good Women*, and dedicated it to the queen of the moment, Anne of Cleves. Yet a careful analysis of the text indicates that it may have been written some years earlier as veiled encouragement to the beleaguered Catherine of Aragon to oppose the marital machinations of her husband militarily and proclaim herself regent in her daughter's name.[24] By 1540, however, the politics of the work were obsolete and what remained was special pleading on behalf of a qualified woman's right to act as regent for the royal heir.

Significantly, Elyot's book was given its only reissue in the sixteenth century in the year 1545, during the two and a half year period when Catherine believed herself to be the nominated regent for any future regency involving her stepson. The book was reissued by its original publisher, Thomas Berthelet, who in that same year was busy preparing the queen's own work, *Prayers or Meditations*, for publication. The reissuance of a work arguing for the regency of a woman as mother of the king during this period cannot be overlooked as merely coincidence. It is of value to examine Elyot's regent and her similarities to the character and situation in which Catherine now found herself.

The Defence of Good Women is a dialogue in the Platonic tradition between the misogynist Caninius and his opposite, the philogynist Candidus. The core of the dialogue involves a discussion of the historical Queen Zenobia of Palmyra, a friend of Candidus, who ruled as regent for her young sons after her husband's death. Recipient of a humanist education, Zenobia is characterized as a learned woman, who had pretensions to scholarship and yet was modest and dutiful as a wife. She is also characterized as a woman courageous enough to believe that the obedience she owed to her husband extended only so far as his intents were benevolent and ended when his desires or actions 'may turn them both to loss or dishonesty.'[25] A woman is, in Elyot's parable, impelled by a cosmic moral order to exercise her own judgement and to offer true and wise counsel to her husband, disguised with sugar-coating if she feels that counsel to be unwelcome or provocative. As regent, Zenobia had proven to be an admirable ruler, using her familiarity with the efficient running of a royal household as a model for the efficient running of an empire. She even found success as a military leader by familiarising herself with the defensive fortifications of Palmyra and by adding to her empire, 'not so much by force, as by renown of just and politic governance.'[26] In this dialogue, Zenobia's sterling example of the virtuous female ruler is too much for the arguments of the misogynist Caninius to deny, and he concedes her value to the State.

A comparison of Zenobia's virtues and activities with those of Catherine Parr elicit some startling parallels. The requirement to provide wise counsel to one's husband, even if he did not care to hear it, was certainly something that Catherine took to heart. She had been given a humanist education and had a reputation for dutifulness and modesty. Yet she was also demonstrably learned and had already proven her mettle and her courage under trying circumstances as regent during her husband's absence. She had even studied some of England's modern fortifications at Leeds Castle with the king upon his return from France in October 1544 and had visited the munitions factories set up at Syon and Mortlake. In the text of Elyot's book, Queen Zenobia informs Caninius that, 'in women is both courage, constancy and reason,' and that 'without prudence and constancy, women might be brought lightly into error.'[27] It would undoubtedly have struck a chord with the court – and no doubt was intended to do so – that Constance was a courtly nickname for Catherine, and another chord with the commons that virtue and prudence were the two characteristics mostly commonly attributed to the queen.[28] With so many similarities, it is difficult not to suspect that Catherine, herself, was the instigator of Berthelet's second edition of Elyot's work, and that it became part of her on-going campaign with the king to ensure her appointment as regent for her stepson. That Catherine was aware of the terms of the king's 1544 will and fully expected to reclaim the regency at Henry's death would account for the two documents bearing her signature as 'Kateryn the Quene-Regent, KP', signed shortly after Henry's demise. What Catherine could not have foreseen was that Zenobia's captor and jailer, the Roman Emperor Aurelius, would have a contemporary counterpart in her own life, effectively disbarring her from any exercise of power – Edward Seymour, Duke of Somerset. Did the king change his mind about the regency, and if so, why? Or was Seymour the architect of Catherine's continuing exclusion from any decision-making capacity?

The affair of Henry's will and the testamentary disposal of his kingdom is a tale of many theories. One school of thought preaches the theorem of Ockham's razor – all things being equal, that which seems to be the simplest explanation is the true one.[30] Henry made out his will in the way he wanted and passed on the rule of his kingdom to his heir under a personally selected regency council, which the king intended from the beginning should be led by the Earl of Hertford. Another school of thought invests Sir Anthony Denny, Sir William Paget and Sir William Herbert with Machiavellian intentions and confers upon them the honour of not only rigging the will and the composition of the council on Hertford's behalf but of masterminding the fall of Gardiner and the execution of the Earl of Surrey for the same reason.[31] This conspiracy theory flies in the face of the evidence that Henry was in control of what he was about until nearly the last hours of his life. That far from behaving like an impaired puppet behind the protective palisade of plotting courtiers who controlled access to the king on their own authority, Henry received both the French and the imperial ambassadors on 16 January, the former reporting to his master that the king seemed recovered in health and in full command both of his faculties and of his servants.[32]

Although this is indisputably so, Henry was a dying man whose abilities must certainly have been less than they had been. It is true, too, that Denny and Paget controlled access to the king's privy chamber, but hardly against the king's express will, and that during the month of December, Privy Council meetings had taken place not at Westminster but at the Earl of Hertford's Somerset

House. So it might be argued that if Henry had summoned the queen to him, his courtiers would have obeyed him, but if the queen herself tried to gain access to the king, she might have been, unknown to Henry, denied. Another curious item used by conspiracy theorists is that the final production of the king's will after Henry's death, signed by dry stamp and not by the king's own hand, was registered a month late in the official records. This certainly leaves room for speculation, if not unarguable evidence, that perhaps the will was tampered with in some way after all.[33] If it was altered during the three days that Henry lay dead while the Privy Council *in caucus* produced a version more compatible with their own ambitions than with the dying king's intentions, there is little doubt that any role the king may have assigned to his consort would have been ruthlessly erased by Hertford and his colleagues. Despite the fact that the queen was of the same mind on matters of religion as the soon-to-be lord protector and his supporters, to have their actions dependent upon the approval of a woman, especially an assertive woman who less than four years before had been merely Lady Latimer of Yorkshire, was antithetical to all the prejudices and prerogatives of the male ruling establishment. Catherine's moral sense too might have acted as an impediment in the acquisition of Crown lands with which the council rewarded itself soon afterwards.[34] The queen's disapproval of the dispersal of these, an act she considered little better than theft, was made very clear when Sir Robert Tyrwhit testified in 1549 that Catherine had said to him: 'Mr. Tyrwhit, you shall see the king, when he cometh to his full age, he will call his lands again, as fast as they be now given from him.'[35] The enraged presence of a mother defending her son's inheritance from the depredations of his omnivorous council would have been the last thing the lord protector or the council wanted.

Yet despite all of this, the responsibility for the queen's exclusion from the regency council lies in all probability with the king. Henry's opinions on female rule were quite clearly expressed when he turned the English religious establishment inside out to secure both Anne Boleyn and a son as an heir. When in early 1546, the Earl of Surrey had requested from Boulogne that the king dispatch his wife to him, Henry had replied sharply that the situation in Boulogne was 'unmeet for women's imbecilities'.[36] This was not simply a compliment to the countess but a fairly complete comment on the king's considered judgement regarding the entire sex. If the French ambassador is to be believed, and there seems little reason why he should not be, that Henry had kept himself apart from the women in his family for nearly a month before his death, it was in order to avoid lamentations and fuss and any pressure that those women might have brought to be included in the rule of the kingdom after his death. The queen's desire to be near Henry during the final month of his life was no doubt motivated in part at least by such political considerations.

Catherine's influence with the king, so paramount during the first two and a half years of her marriage, had floundered against the combined forces of Gardiner's animosity, Hertford's ambition and Henry's neurotic suspicions and ill health. It was one thing after all for the king to make use of his wife as an unofficial councillor during his lifetime; it was quite another to entrust the keeping of the kingdom to a woman after he was gone. Henry had not wanted a wife to tell him what to do in matters of religion and he certainly did not want one in the final days of his life to tell him how to dispose of his crown. That he did not bother to inform Catherine of this fact and left her to suppose that she would head the regency council after his death, was Henry's last bitter gift to his much tried queen.

In the early hours of Friday, 28 January 1547, Henry VIII died, leaving a nine and a half-year-old boy as his heir under the protection of a hand-picked council dominated by the supporters of the reformed religion. News of the king's death was kept secret for three days. The Spanish ambassador reported that during those three days, 'not the slightest signs of [the king's death] were to be seen at court, and even the usual ceremony of bearing in the royal dishes to the sounds of trumpets was continued without interruption.'[37] Closeted in the king's secret lodgings at Hampton Court, to which Sir Anthony Denny as first gentleman of the bed chamber controlled access, behind a cleverly constructed facade of attending to the needs of the suffering monarch, an intense period of negotiation and power brokering took place among the more prominent members of the council as they jockeyed for position and pulled the final settlement of the regency together for public inspection. In this Sir William Paget was a key player. According to Paget, himself, the dying king 'devised with me apart (as it is well known he used to open his pleasure to me alone in many things).'[38] Armed with this alleged secret knowledge of the king's final devises, Paget was able to play the hold card on the lord protector's behalf. He reassured the council 'concerning the late king's alleged intentions of conferring honours, offices, and lands upon them, as communicated on his deathbed ... For these agreeable revelations the Council were stated to be under obligations to Paget and to hold him in great esteem.'[39] Thus, at the end of three days, on Monday, 31 January, with the majority of the council behind him, Edward Seymour, Earl of Hertford, made himself Duke of Somerset and Lord Protector of the realm. Parliament was dissolved after Sir Thomas Wriothesley officially announced the king's death and Sir William Paget read out Henry's will. Under any circumstances, there was little likelihood that the new protector would look kindly on Catherine's participation in power, and Somerset effectively shut the door of the council chamber in her face. All that was left for the moment for the new queen dowager to do was to bury yet another husband.

Catherine sent her jewels off to the Tower for safekeeping and once again donned widow's weeds and mourning jewellery – '11 buttons of gold enamelled black whereof one is round; a brooch of gold enamelled black upon the border with a table diamond, a table ruby and a very small rock ruby; a habiliment of gold enamelled black containing xli pieces; a pair of bracelets of gold enamelled black; two little hoops of gold enamelled black; and a ring of gold with a death's head'.[40] The death's head of Christian lamentation on her finger and in deepest mourning, the queen secluded herself while preparations were made for her late husband's funeral.

For ten days the king's embalmed body lay in his privy chamber in a huge chest lit by flaring tapers. On 8 February, recognition of the king's passing was made throughout his kingdom as every parish church tolled its bell and offered up a solemn Dirge. Requiem masses for the king's soul were held the following morning. Despite the controversy over the existence of Purgatory, Henry would have expected no less. Five days later, on 14 February, the funeral procession formed. Like Henry, himself, it was bigger than life and equally impressive in death.[41] Seven stories high, the king's great hearse, decorated with a carefully crafted effigy of the late monarch, moved down the road from Westminster to Windsor, stopping for the night at the lord protector's new mansion of Syon on the way. The road itself had to be repaved to bear the weight of this beast and trees cut back to allow its passage. The funeral cortege was four miles long and made up of a thousand men on horseback, 250 paid mourners, the children, clerks and priests of the Chapel Royal, the yeomen of the guard, dressed in black, three abreast, their halberds pointed toward the ground, the henchmen, gentlemen pensioners, household officers, Privy Council, mayor and aldermen of London and foreign ambassadors. All the world, it seemed, had turned out to bid farewell to a king who for better or worse had left his mark on an age.[42]

Henry had ordered that his final resting place should be in Edward IV's great chapel of St. George's, Windsor, next to Jane Seymour, the only queen who had managed to provide him with a son. Even in death, the king could not sleep alone. As the king's own monument, begun for himself by Cardinal Wolsey, was not yet complete – and indeed never would be – Henry's huge and bulging coffin was lowered into Jane's crypt. One legend has it that the great box burst open while being carried into the chapel and some stray dogs appeared to lick at the salty fluid that leaked out, thus fulfilling a hostile prophecy concerning the heretic king that after his death, dogs would gnaw his bones. Whether or not this element of horror was introduced into the proceedings, the ceremony for those present was memorable enough. It took sixteen of the yeomen and the help of 'four strong linen towels' to lower the massive box into Jane's grave. 'Then the Lord Chamberlain, the Lord Great Master, Mr. Treasurer, Mr. Comptroller and the Sergeant Porter, breaking their white staves [of office] upon their heads in three parts, as did likewise all the Gentlemen Ushers, threw them into the grave.' The Garter King of Arms proclaimed the accession of the new king, and an echo of '*Vive le noble Roy Edward*' sounded from the throats of some of the multitude, who were then drowned out by trumpet flourishes from the rood loft announcing a new king and a new age.[43]

Dressed in blue velvet lined with purple, the queen watched the proceedings from the Queen's Closet above the choir. It was the final act of a drama that had begun for Catherine over four years before. It had raised her to the heights of unimagined power and had nearly brought her to the depths of ignominious death. What her thoughts were in that moment at Windsor, it would be interesting to know. No doubt, a disbelief in Purgatory notwithstanding, she said at least one prayer for her husband's soul. Whatever else she may have thought about in the cramped little closet where she watched and waited as that most majestic, quixotic, capricious and ruthless representative of the House of Tudor ever to sit on the throne was laid to rest, she may have spared at least one thought for the new lord protector's brother, Sir Thomas Seymour, so recently returned to court from his travels. Understandably furious at being excluded from the regency council, the queen might have raised more of a protest if her thoughts and emotions had not been otherwise occupied. For if the new Duke of Somerset had wasted little time in getting himself named Lord Protector of England, his brother, Sir Thomas Seymour, wasted equally little time in getting Catherine Parr into his bed. Within weeks of the king's death, the dowager queen had taken him as her lover.

15

'Requests and Desires'

Sir Thomas Seymour has been given short shrift by history. His reputation, motives and habits have come down to us mostly from the testimonies of his enemies and the transcripts of his trial for treason, all of which paint him in the worst possible light. 'A good name,' he is quoted as saying, 'is the embalming of the virtuous to an eternity of love and gratitude among posterity.' Unfortunately for Seymour, his embalming and hence his good name was left to the tender ministrations of individuals who despised him. In the tomb of history, he smells less than sweet. He has been habitually included in that group of men whom Catherine called 'the most furious, unbridled, carnal men.'[2] As a rogue, a ruffian, a blackguard and a pirate, he has plagued the annals of Catherine Parr's life in the role of yet another highly unsatisfactory husband. This is a skewed and unbalanced portrait of the man for Seymour led an interesting, varied and highly adventurous life and was far from being the complete villain that his enemies pictured him. By the time he was twenty-one, before his sister's marriage with the king, Seymour had achieved a knighthood, been made an alderman of London and joined the entourage of Sir Francis Bryan, ambassador to France.[3] Seymour was a restless man and much of his adult life was spent traveling to and from the continent, either on government missions or simply for the sheer adventure of it. He craved danger, fought the Turks under the emperor's brother, and racked up an impressive military record both on land and at sea against the French and pirates of all persuasions who haunted the Channel. He was an intelligent man if not a scholarly one, and if he had an unfortunate habit of making enemies in high places, he had the knack, too, of inspiring a deep loyalty in the men who served under him. He had no use for political subtleties. For him, the shortest route between two points was always the line drawn by the edge of a sword.

The consummate man of action, Seymour had a full complement of skills necessary to a courtier. He wrote poetry and set it to music. He had a superb singing voice which he used to advantage. His sartorial vanity was legendary. '[If] at times he found it difficult to behave like a gentleman, he always contrived to look like [one].'[4] He was not a religious man and had earned Archbishop Cranmer's enmity by volunteering in hope of reward to prove 'that the archbishop of Canterbury kept no hospitality or house correspondent unto his revenues and dignity, but sold his woods, and by great incomes and fines maketh money to purchase lands for his wife and his children.'[5] The Seymours, who were great gamblers, had, as the king was quick to perceive and point out, 'consumed some [of their revenue] with superfluous apparel, some at dice and cards and other ungracious rule, and now you would have bishop's lands and revenues to abuse likewise.'

Seymour, accuses Cranmer's secretary, Ralph Morice:

> Blasted [the slander against Cranmer] abroad in the court, insomuch that (mine eldest brother [Sir William Morice], being one of) the gentlemen ushers, and he fell out for the same, my brother declaring that his report was manifest false ... This nothwithstanding, Mr. Seymour went through with his said information, and declared unto the king as is before declared.

An impromptu visit to Cranmer at Lambeth, who treated him with great courtesy and lavish hospitality, disabused Seymour of his part in the plot. He went to the king and:

> Kneeled down and sought the king's majesty of pardon. 'What is the matter?' (said the king). 'I do remember (said Mr. Seymour), that I told your highness that my lord of Canterbury kept no hospitality correspondent unto his dignity; and now I perceive that I did abuse your highness with an untruth, for, besides your grace's house, I think he be not in the realm of none estate or degree that hath such a hall furnished, or that fareth more honourably at his own table.' 'Ah! (quod the king), have you espied your own fault now?' 'I assure your highness, (quoth Mr. Seymour) it is not so much my fault as other men's who seemed to be honest men that informed me hereof, but I shall henceforth the worse trust them while they live.

This anecdote throws a clear light on Seymour's character. Always daring and willing to take on any challenge, when proven wrong, the error was rarely allowed to be his own. The fault lay with other men who had played him false and he would not trust them again.

If Seymour was not overfond of Cranmer, he was fascinated by Hugh Latimer. This seems to have been more a fascination with the vitriol of the man than a concurrence of religious beliefs, for Seymour's nature was far from being in tune with the rigors of Calvinism. Latimer had preached the funeral sermon of Jane Seymour and from that time on, the preacher found a patron in her brother. Sir Thomas advised Edward VI on the amount of money to present to Latimer after a sermon; Seymour requested that Latimer visit him to administer the last rites when he was in the Tower on charges of treason, and he left as a last request that Latimer preach his funeral sermon.[6] Latimer was not grateful for this attention and turned spiteful toward his erstwhile patron after the latter's death, excoriating his memory in a number of sermons. These sermons became part and parcel of history's evaluation of the man while the mournful memorial 'sonnet' by his servant, Sir John Harington, is rarely quoted.

> Of person rare, strong limbs, and manly shape;
> Of nature framed to rule on sea or land;
> Of friendship firm in good state and ill hap;
> In peace head wise, in war heart great, bold hand
> On horse, on foot, in peril or in play;
> None could excel though many did essay.
> A subject true to king, and servant great;
> Friend to God's truth, enemy to Rome's deceit;
> Sumptuous abroad, for honour of the land;
> Temperate at home; yet kept great state withstay
> And noble house; and gave more mouths more meat
> Then some that climbed on higher steps to stand.
> Yet against Nature, Reason and just Laws,
> His blood was split, guiltless without just cause.[7]

Seymour's gifts to posterity were not merely a mishmash of apocryphal stories related to his pursuit of various royal women, most of which are demonstrable fabrications by such inventive manufacturers of Tudor fiction as Grigorio Leti, but his contributions to the English navy and the founding of the English munitions industry. As master of the ordnance, Seymour took a small ordnance factory in the Sussex Weald founded in the early 1540s by the Duke of Norfolk, and greatly expanded it to include an annual production of well over 200 tons. In 1549, the value of the stock was more than £2,000 and more than fifty workmen and a large number of woodcutters were employed at the foundry.[8] The establishment of a viable English fleet was as much on Seymour's mind in the 1540s as the establishment of a source of ordnance to fire from the decks of English ships. One of the charges made against Seymour in January 1549 was that he had used extortion to secure large sums of money for the buildings of ships.[9]

Unlike his predecessor as Lord Admiral, John Dudley, Lord Lisle, Seymour was not a fairweather sailor whose military competence ended where the sea began. He was made a temporary admiral of Henry's fleet in October 1544 after the fall of Boulogne, and upon his appointment, Seymour wrote down for the edification of the king and council, a battle plan for bringing the scattered ships of the English navy into an effective fighting unit and turning them loose on France.[10] His flagship was a 500-tonne, 400-man galleon called the *Peter Pomegranite*, or just *The Peter*. From it, he would, he claimed, 'endeavour himself to endommage th'enemies by all wayes and meanes possible.'[11] Seymour took into account all contingencies of action by the French and included in his report a list of all the ships then under his command as acting admiral with the names of their owners, their captains, their total tonnage and men. It was a masterful report but it did not secure Seymour what he undoubtedly hoped it would, the office of Lord Admiral of the English navy. He had to wait two and a half more years for that.

During Catherine's marriage to Henry, Seymour had spent much of his time out of the country. This decision to send him on his travels appears to be both Seymour's own choice as well as the king's. It was probably safer, both for Catherine and her erstwhile lover, that he spend as little time near her as possible to prevent tongues from wagging at court. When he blew back into London in August 1546 to attend the festivities for French Admiral d'Annebaut, with sea stories of ships sunk beneath him and a reputation for 'notable damage done' by the fleet under his command, Catherine could hardly help but compare his swashbuckling life to her Machiavellian one.[12] For four years she had had to suppress her feelings for Seymour. By her own statement, she sincerely thought that she had succeeded in excising him from her heart. Her faith had sustained her, she declared. 'This is it that maketh me bold. This is it that comforteth me. This is it that quencheth all despair.'[13] For the queen, the battle of the flesh had been a hard-fought one, but one that she believed she had finally won:

> Christ hath left in us these concupiscences to the intent they should serve us to the exercise of our virtues, where first they did reign over us to the exercise of our sins. And it may be plainly seen, that whereas, first they were such impediments to us that we could not move ourselves towards God, now by Christ, we have so much strength that, notwithstanding the force of them, we may assuredly walk to heaven.[14]

In the privacy of her oratory Catherine may have comforted herself with the knowledge that she had exchanged the lusts of earthly love for the divine salvation of the spirit, but with Henry dead, the entire situation now changed and the comforts of religion quickly proved less satisfactory than the comforts of Sir Thomas Seymour's arms.

For Seymour, the queen-dowager would be a valuable asset in his quest for greater influence on the council. She was still in love with him and to his experienced eye, ripe for seduction. Seymour was an omnivorous lover and his taste in women seems to have been thoroughly eclectic. Shortly before Catherine became queen, 'a lewd woman, that had lived an unclean life, and was condemned with some of her comrades for a robbery, as she went to execution, declared that Thomas Seymour had first of all debauched her.'[15] Within weeks of her widowhood, Catherine had become Seymour's mistress. But Seymour was not interested in a clandestine affair; he began to press Catherine to marry him.

That the queen realized the precariousness of her position is evident in surviving letters which she and Seymour exchanged during these months. At first she tried to put him off, telling him that she could not possibly consider remarrying before she had passed a two-year period of mourning. He pleaded with her to turn the two years into two months. Catherine's own inclination, starved for years by weak, sickly or tyrannous old men, argued on Seymour's behalf. The sensual, experienced Seymour played on an appetite that in Catherine had had little exercise. Using those ecstasies in her character that he knew to be well-developed, her religious emotions, Seymour cleverly gave them another face, that of sexual ecstasy. In the back of one of Catherine's religious books, among the paraphrased Beatitudes and religious maxims, Seymour scrawled a love poem urging the queen to 'And sith beside if/Ye licence give withal/Set doubts aside/And to some sporting fall.' Addressing her as his 'fair nymph', he urges her to spare her blushes and terrors and surrender herself to him: 'thence nymph/Doth terrify/And bless/Thou will be down/I only suspicionless.'[16] This sort of flowery sexual word play and its implications, planted among the cabbages and potatoes of religious dogma, seems to have excited and terrified Catherine. But there was no doubt in her own mind that she still wanted Thomas Seymour as she had wanted him four years earlier – before friends, relations and circumstances had pressured her into becoming Henry's queen. And there was little doubt that a committed and experienced lover like Seymour would find no insuperable barrier between himself and the queen's bed.

Another circumstance that urged Catherine on was the Duke of Somerset's rather surprising approval of such a match. The capture of the queen in bonds of marriage for the Somerset clique would be a major move on the political game board. It was early days yet and the brothers Seymour had not yet entered into the bitter internecine feud that was to have such deadly consequences for both of them. Like Sir Thomas, Somerset was well aware of Catherine's potential as a marriage pawn and apparently wasted little time in informing her that her goodwill toward his brother would be most acceptable to him. Catherine told Seymour of her conversation with the protector and Sir Thomas advised her to speak plainly, telling Somerset that it would be Seymour or no one if she did marry again. He did not want the world to say that the protector had arranged the match and so take all the credit for it, 'beseeching your highness that I may not so use my said strength that they shall think and hereafter cast in my teeth that by their suit I sought and obtained your good will.'[17] 'I do well allow your advice in that my Lord your Brother should not have all the thanks for my good will in this matter,' the queen replied in a letter to her lover. 'For I was fully bent before ye wrote, so to frame mine answer to him, when he should attempt the matter, as that he might well and manifestly perceive my fantasy to be more towards you for marriage than any other.'[18] She begged Seymour to believe that her feelings for him were not a sudden whim, nor her 'goodness to him' lightly given. He answered her that he was sure that her favours were not lightly bestowed and that he would prove it to her at their next meeting to both their satisfactions.[19] The notion that, in the eyes of the world, the lord protector would certainly take all of the credit for his alliance with the queen chaffed Sir Thomas Seymour mightily. He wanted it known that it was Thomas Seymour's prowess not Edward Seymour's influence that captured this particular queen. He need not have worried. The initial acceptance by Somerset of such a match in theory later crumbled before its enactment in fact.

For awhile they kept their affair very circumspect. 'I think to see the King one day this week,' Catherine wrote to Seymour, 'at which time I would be glad to see you, though I shall scarce dare ask or speak ... When you be at leisure let me hear from you. I dare not desire to see you for fear of suspicion.'[20] This arrangement soon became unsatisfactory for both of them as desire overwhelmed caution. Catherine moved into her dower house at Chelsea, a place of which she was particularly fond. It may have reminded her of her childhood on the Lea River at Rye House in Hertfordshire or it may simply have been that at Chelsea, Catherine was removed from the prying eyes of the court and Seymour could visit her at night without arousing suspicion. 'I pray you be not offended with me,' Catherine wrote to him, 'that I send sooner to you than I said I would ... [for] the time is well abbreviated, by what means I know not, except the weeks be shorter at Chelsea than in other places.'[21] Orchards of cherry, peach and filbert trees and beds of fragrant herbs, lavender and rosemary, had been planted between hedges of privet and white thorn at Chelsea. Damask roses bloomed beneath the blossoming trees of spring as Catherine waited for Seymour's clandestine arrivals.[22]

Letters were carried back and forth by trusted messengers with feverish regularity between Catherine at Chelsea and Seymour in London or wherever he happened to be. Catherine's joy at receiving a letter from Sir Thomas can be judged by the huge sum of five shillings that she rewarded a servant of his, 'for bringing a letter'.[23] John Grove, Catherine's faithful yeoman of the chamber, was sent from Hanworth near Richmond down into Kent,[24] with letters for Seymour.[25] 'If I knew by what means,' wrote Seymour, 'I might gratify your highness for your goodness to me, showed at our last being together, [I] should not be slack to declare mine to you again ... wishing that my hap [luck] may be one so good, that I may declare so much by mouth at the same hour that this was writing, which was twelve of the clock in the night.'[26] Catherine quickly replied, 'My Lord, where as you desire to know how ye might gratify my goodness showed to you at your being here, I can require nothing for the same more than ye say I have which is your heart.'[27]

Yet the queen still had realistic fears about the perils of discovery. When Seymour wrote to her: 'I met with a man of my Lord Marquis [Catherine's brother] as I came to Chelsea, whom I knew not, who told Nicholas Throckmorton that I was in Chelsea fields',[28] Catherine replied in some agitation: 'When it shall be your pleasure to repair hither, ye must take some pain to come early in the morning, that ye may be gone again by seven o'clock. And so, I suppose, ye may come without suspect. I pray you let me have knowledge overnight at what hour ye will come, that your portress may wait at the gate to the fields for you.'[29] She begged him to burn all of her letters to him. '[Your] letter being finished and my hand thereat,' Seymour answered, 'I remembered your commandment to me, wherewith I threw it into the fire, be minding to keep your requests and desires.'[30] The survival of so many of both Catherine's and Seymour's letters shows that neither was always so punctilious. Where Catherine was careful, Seymour was careless, even reckless. The queen might have fallen in love with his swashbuckling qualities, but they were to cause her no end of trouble in the coming months.

The queen's impetuosity in beginning an affair so soon after the king's death was fraught with danger. In Henry's will, the succession to the throne had been left first to Edward and then, should Edward die without heirs, to any child of Catherine's that she might bear the king. Catherine knew very well that she was not pregnant by Henry when he died. Had she become pregnant by Seymour at the king's death, and had she given birth prematurely, Seymour might have been tempted to pass his own child off as a royal heir. This possibility was raised against him at his trial for treason after Catherine's death.

Another inherent danger in the relationship was the fact that Catherine, as a member of the royal family, could be accused of treason for marrying without the king's permission. Both of the Seymour brothers, Sir Thomas and the Duke of Somerset, were very much aware of Catherine's influence with the new king and had factored Edward's affection for his stepmother into their future plans. Sir Thomas hoped that the queen would be able to help him gain control of Edward. His brother grew increasingly concerned about the very same thing. But Edward VI, a secretive, cold and judgemental child who showed genuine fondness for very few people, was still a minor. Although he was technically king, he could not successfully oppose decisions made by a council momentarily united under the control of his uncle. Catherine's influence on Edward, directed as it would soon be against Somerset, himself, was never therefore put to the test. Only when circumstances and fluctuating power cliques offered the boy king an opportunity for making decisions could Edward act, proving himself a stern arbiter of family matters and quite willing to execute both of his uncles if the situation demanded it. As it turned out, Catherine and Seymour's subsequent attempts to trick Edward into approving an affair already several months old had the effect of alienating the young king and neutralizing his stepmother's original influence with him. When it was revealed during the summer of 1547 that Catherine and Seymour had formed a relationship so soon after Henry VIII's death, both Edward and his sister, Princess Mary, were reported to be seriously displeased. Edward's displeasure was not something to be treated lightly even if he was still a child.

Catherine managed to keep secret her affair from everyone, even her sister, who, as Seymour remarked, 'knowing how well you trusted her',[31] could not have been easy. When Catherine finally let Anne into the secret, 'she did not a little rejoyce.'[32] Anne proceeded to tease Seymour, who was unaware Catherine had told her about the affair. As Seymour reported back to his royal mistress: 'she [Anne] waded further with me touching my lodging with your highness at Chelsea, which I denied ... till at last, she told me further tokens, which made me change my colours, who, like a false wench, took me with the manner ... by her company, in default of yours, I shall shorten the weeks in these parts, which heretofore were four days longer in everyone of them than they were under the plumet [duvet] at Chelsea.'[33] But the pursuit of a clandestine affair did not conform either with Seymour's plans or with Catherine's notions of how a queen and a Christian behaved herself. In addition, a growing number of friends were being taken into the secret. Seymour wrote to Catherine from the Palace of St. James:

> I wrote to you of this yesterday, taking the letter to my brother Herbert to be
> delivered to his wife who, I think, knows of our matter, but not by me ... None
> shall, save those you appoint, until it is further forth. I perceive I have my lady of
> Suffolk's good will touching my desire of you: she told my friend, Sir William
> Sharington she wished me to be married to their mistress – as would I.[34]

Even the Princess Elizabeth's servant, Katherine Ashley, had heard the rumours. When she happened to run into Seymour in St. James Park, she challenged him

with his marriage plans. As Katherine Ashley later related, Seymour told her 'he
would prove to have the queen, which I said was past proof as I had heard he
was already married to her.'[35]

By late spring Seymour had had his way and had married the queen-dowager
in a secret ceremony. The ceremony may have taken place at Baynard's Castle,[36]
part of Catherine's jointure and, by her gift, the home of her sister, Anne, and
Anne's husband, William Herbert. During the frustrating and frightening weeks
prior to the king's death, when Catherine was prevented from seeing her
husband, she had taken refuge with her sister in Baynard's Castle and was in
the habit of visiting there.[37] Within its walls could be found privacy and family
support. If the marriage did take place here, it was solemnized during the last
two weeks in May. By 12 May Seymour was signing his letters, 'From him who
is your loving and faithful husband during his life', which were answered by
Catherine's, signed, 'By your humble, true and loving wife in her heart', but five
days later, Catherine was still insisting that they wait to marry. 'Notwithstanding
I am determined to add thereto a full determination never to marry, and break
it when I have done, if I live two years.'[38] Sometime between 18 May and
the beginning of June, Catherine's resolution crumbled and a secret marriage
ceremony was celebrated for her and Seymour. Yet neither was eager to make
the marriage public. Since Catherine had married without the knowledge and
consent of the king and council, both she and Seymour were only too well
aware that such a hasty and clandestine union would be greeted with general
disfavour and possibly even with charges of treason. The situation was further
complicated by the growing disaffection between the queen and Seymour and
Seymour's brother, the lord protector.

At Henry VIII's death, Sir Thomas Seymour had every reason to expect a
dramatic increase in position and possessions. He had been made a member of
the Privy Council only days before the king's death but had been listed as an
'assistant' not a councillor in Henry's will. If Somerset and his supporters had
actually tampered with the will and had left Sir Thomas in such a subsidiary
role, Seymour's grudge against his brother may have begun with such a slight.
His admission to the Privy Council under Somerset was an admission that
Somerset held the reins of his career, not the unalterable will of the late king.
Yet as the uncle of the new king and brother of the lord protector, Sir Thomas
anticipated nothing less than a suitable outpouring of titles and grants. He was
to be sadly disappointed. His brother, while still Lord Hertford, put it about
that just before the old king's death, Henry had intended to elevate some of his
more important courtiers to higher ranks and bestow grants of land on them to
support their new dignities. Less than three weeks after Henry's death, Hertford
had himself named Duke of Somerset and added the offices of Treasurer of the

Exchequer and Earl Marshal of England to his achievements. He also began to indulge his greed for land acquisition with an appetite worthy of a fifteenth-century Neville. To ensure the loyalty of other key members of the council, the new duke saw to it that John Dudley, Lord Lisle, became the Earl of Warwick and High Chamberlain of England. William Parr, Earl of Essex since December 1543, was now raised to the dignity of the Marquessate of Northampton.

For his brother, Sir Thomas Seymour, the new Duke of Somerset provided a title and land, but nothing as impressive as a dukedom, marquessate or earldom. Instead the uncle of the king was made a mere baron and created Lord Seymour of Sudeley, with the castle, manor, park and other lands of Sudeley in Gloucestershire, lately held by Winchecombe monastery. For the new Lord Seymour, remembered by some without affection as one of the greediest men of his generation, it was simply not enough. Not even his election to the Order of the Garter and his elevation in February 1547 to the office of Lord Admiral of England had deterred him from passionate feelings of resentment and persecution. The lord protector soon began to regret this appointment but although he tried to convince Sir Thomas to relinquish the position, the new Lord Admiral refused. 'Why marry, now I shall have the rule of a good sort of ships and men,' he remarked meaningfully to Sir William Sharington, 'and, I tell you, it is a good thing to have the rule of men.'[39] Seymour proved quickly how little he knew of discretion or compromise and refused to ingratiate himself in any way with his brother.

Catherine might have been able to persuade her secret bridegroom to a course of common sense if she, too, had not had cause to be furious with both the Duke of Somerset and his outspoken duchess. The Somersets had been two of Catherine's closest supporters during her last difficult year as queen. They were as evangelical about the new religion as she was herself. Yet now Catherine and the Somersets fell into a succession of bitter disagreements, private quarrels, and public social slights. The loss of the regency had been a bitter blow that Catherine tried briefly to fight. Taking on herself the style of 'regent', she had consulted legal counsel as to 'whether a certain oath taken by the King's servants, and sent for their consideration, is invalidated by his Majesty's decease.' The legal experts thought not and 'touching certain other questions submitted to them, they have delivered their opinions to Sir Anthony Cope, her grace's vice-chamberlain.'[40] Yet legal experts and alleged royal intentions apart, Catherine was forced to live with Somerset's protectorate. But this was only the beginning.

With a conspicuous lack of tact not to mention an obvious breech of the law, Somerset refused to give Catherine the jewels that Henry VIII had not only bought for her – including her wedding ring – but had specifically left to her in his will, claiming that they were the legal property of the State.[41]

Somerset may have been technically right in judging that certain jewels which had belonged to a goodly number of Henry's queens might be considered to be State property, but as Henry was the State and, as witnessed by his will, he had certainly intended them as gifts to his wife and not as mere loans, Somerset was certainly on shaky legal ground. Henry had had an assortment of jewellery made up for the queen to wear during Admiral Claude d'Annebaut's visit in August 1546 and had also given jewellery to Mary to wear at the same time. Not unnaturally both the queen and the princess considered these jewels as gifts. There is certainly no record of Mary's ever having returned hers to the king once the French admiral had gone home, and Catherine still kept hers at Henry's death in a jewel chest or coffer 'having written upon it 'The Quene's Juelles".[42] In this jewel box, together with the gifts of August 1546, were other pieces, obviously the queen's personal property, such as her wedding ring, the king's gift of a crown-headed brooch, and a jewel in the shape of the initials 'H' and 'K' made expressly for her. Unfortunately for Catherine, the protectorate was working with a desperately depleted treasury and in need of bullion reserves in any form it could get them.[43] Unfortunate, too, was the fact that at the time of Henry's death, the queen's jewel chest was locked up for safekeeping in the King's Jewel House in the Tower. And there it remained. Try as she might, Catherine never managed to pry the coffer loose from the acquisitive grasp of the lord protector. Seymour threatened publicly to sue his brother for 'certain jewels which the late king gave the queen, including her wedding ring, which he thought legally hers.' But Somerset would not give up the jewels which only added fuel to the escalating family civil war.

The Duke of Somerset also refused to hand over certain property, possibly a cross of gold, 'containing ten fair diamonds of sundry making and three fair pearls pendant', left to Catherine by her own mother, an act calculated to enrage Maud Parr's daughter.[44] And he began granting leases on Catherine's dower lands without her knowledge or consent. Catherine's commands to the servants on her estates began to be ignored and growing fury is apparent in the written orders that reiterated these commands time and again but to no avail. 'A warrant signed by our hand,' she wrote curtly to her keeper of the park at Hundon in Suffolk, 'shall be your sufficient discharge in that behalf. [Orders] to you to the contrary notwithstanding.'[45] Oddly this letter was written from the Duke of Somerset's own house at Shene. Whether the queen had immediately discerned Somerset's hand behind the problems she was having in controlling her servants and had gone to Shene to confront him or whether, still ignorant of his intentions, she was on a visit hoping to enlist his support is not immediately apparent. Somerset, with a fine disregard of her feelings, continued the assault on her lands and the suborning of her servants. One contested lease in particular, that of Fausterne Park in Wiltshire, Catherine deeply resented. Somerset had leased it to Sir Henry Longe, who refused to allow the queen any rights in her own property. Catherine wrote to her new husband in fury:[46]

> This shall be to advertise you that my Lord, your brother, hath this afternoon made me a little warm. It was fortunate we were so distant, for I suppose else I should have bitten him ... [He] hath so used the matter [of Fausterne] with giving Master Longe such courage that he refuseth to receive such cattle as are brought for the provision of my house. And so, in the meantime, I am forced to commit them to farmers.[47]

Somerset's agent in this was his secretary, Sir John Thynne, formerly a member of Catherine's own household, a fact that did not sit well with the queen either. Besides leasing Catherine's land without her consent, Somerset also began to grant to himself and his supporters the reversion of large chunks of her dower. Between the summer of 1547 and the summer of 1548, Somerset assumed the reversion of much of Catherine's land in Gloucestershire, Dorset and Wiltshire. The new Lord Seymour of Sudeley might not unnaturally have expected a share in the reversion of his wife's estates but he received nothing even after their marriage had been made public.

In addition to such disputes over property which arose between Somerset and the queen, another matter concerning court protocol galled Catherine's pride to the core. Her former lady-in-waiting, Anne Stanhope, now the Duchess of Somerset, insisted that as wife of the lord protector she took precedence over Catherine at all court functions. Anne Stanhope had begun her court career as one of Catherine of Aragon's maids-in-waiting. Known familiarly to the Princess Mary as 'my Good Gossip' and 'my good Nann', Stanhope was less popular with others of the court and her sudden elevation as wife of the lord protector seems to have gone to her head. The appointment of her half-brother Sir Michael Stanhope as governor to Edward VI increased her arrogance and her unpopularity. It also increased the animosity between the duchess and her brother-in-law, Sir Thomas Seymour, who had coveted the position for himself.[48]

It has not been sufficiently appreciated, perhaps, just how much influence the duchess brought to bear on her husband's protectorship. In 1549, when imperial ambassador Van der Delft questioned Sir William Paget about the reasons for the lord protector's political difficulties, Paget replied succinctly, 'He has a bad wife.' Van der Delft remarked shortly, this 'amounted to a confession of his unworthiness, since he allowed himself to be ruled by his wife.'[49] As Erasmus had once cogently stated, 'an evil wife is not wont to chance but to evil husbands.'[50] Just how bad a reputation the duchess was earning for herself can be seen from a document dated 19 February 1549 listing items pilfered from the royal stores at

Westminster Palace by her and her brother, Sir Michael. A long list of silks and coifs, coverpanes and pillows richly wrought with silk and gold, 'and other things [were] taken trussed in a sheet from the silk house by the [Duchess] of Somerset and Sir Michael Stanhope [and] carried to her chamber.'[51] Items from the jewel house also went missing, to end up in Anne Stanhope's coffers. When Sir William Sharington was arrested for treason in January 1549, together with Sir Thomas Seymour, all of Lady Sharington's jewellery ended up in the hands of the Duchess of Somerset, who refused to return it. It is no wonder then that the queen, whose own jewels had been appropriated by the Duke of Somerset, perhaps at his wife's behest, had little love for her former lady-in-waiting.

The duchess was reputed to have slandered the queen as a nobody, a jumped-up country housewife, the former Mistress Latimer, unequal in dignity to herself. If her brother-in-law was unable to teach his wife better manners, the duchess is reported to have proclaimed, 'I am she who will teach her.'[52] '[She is] a devilish woman,' Sir John Hayward had heard the Duchess of Somerset described, and 'a woman for many imperfections intolerable, but for pride monstrous.'[53] Catherine, having been Queen of England for nearly four years, having served as Regent-General in 1544, and having been first lady in the kingdom long enough to have become accustomed to it, was now forced to jockey for position with an arrogant and unreasonable former servant. 'What cause have they to fear,' she wrote bitterly to Seymour, 'having such a wife? It is requisite for them continually to pray for short dispatch of that hell.'[54] Catherine's anger may be judged by the fact that the Tudor use of the slang phrase 'that hell' was the equivalent of a pejorative expletive based on female genitalia.[55] Matters were not made any easier by the fact that the duchess detested her brother-in-law, Sir Thomas, who fully agreed with his wife's estimation of the duchess' character. Relations between the two of them were every bit as acrimonious as those between Catherine and the duke.[56]

With such bad feelings between the Somersets and the Seymours, Catherine was increasingly concerned about breaking the news of her marriage to the world. 'I wish the world was as well pleased with our meaning as I am well assured [of] the goodness of God's,' she wrote wistfully to Seymour, 'but the world is so wicked that it cannot be contented with good things.'[57] With the circle of those who knew of their secret marriage growing larger and rumours running rife, it was only a matter of time before news reached the ears of the council. It was Catherine who decided that the best way to approach the problem was to approach Henry's children — 'I would desire ye might obtain the king's letters in your favour' Catherine urged Seymour.[58] She went on to suggest that he secure from Edward and from the Princess Mary their good will toward the match. Seymour was to persuade them to act as matchmakers by writing to their stepmother, urging her to accept Seymour as her husband. This would remove the onus of their hasty match and present it to the world as a royal command.

Seymour could be very persuasive but Mary, at least, was skeptical of his motives. 'God sends often times to good women evil husbands,' Mary remarked many years later, when not only her own father but perhaps Sir Thomas Seymour may have been in her thoughts. On 4 June 1547, in answer to Seymour's request for her blessing on his union with the queen, Mary replied: 'I have received your letter wherein, as me thinketh, I perceive strange news concerning a suit you have in hand for the queen for marriage, for the sooner obtaining whereof you seem to think that my letters might do you pleasure.' Mary was obviously displeased by the very suggestion of Catherine's marriage so soon after the king's death and wrote that she was not eager 'to be a meddler in this matter.' 'If she be minded to grant your suit,' the princess told Seymour repressively, 'my letters shall do you but small pleasure ... [but] if the remembrance of the king's majesty my father [whose soul God pardon], will not suffer her to grant your suit, I am nothing able to persuade her.'[59]

Catherine, too, appears to have begun a letter writing campaign, presumably to lay the groundwork for the announcement of her marriage to Seymour. From mid-May until mid-June, her messengers, particularly Robert Bourgoyne and John Grove, were kept busy carrying letters to the Princess Mary, the Earl of Warwick, the Duchesses of Suffolk and Somerset, Sir Anthony Denny, and Catherine's brother and sister.[60] Whatever the queen was urging in her letters and in whatever terms, Seymour was, as usual, less discrete. News of the Lord Admiral's letter writing campaign began to find its way into diplomatic dispatches. On 16 June, Van der Delft wrote to Charles V: 'I have been informed from a secret source [Princess Mary?] that a marriage is being arranged between the Queen Dowager and the Lord Admiral, brother of the Protector.'[61] Seymour realized that he had to act quickly, before the lord protector found out his plans and tried to prevent a marriage that had already taken place.

Having failed with Mary, Seymour now turned his attentions to the boy king. Through John Fowler, a servant in Edward's household whom Seymour had bribed, the Lord Admiral began to campaign for royal approval of his courtship and marriage to the queen. Fowler later swore under oath that:

At St. James, the Lord Admiral called me to his chamber ... and asked me, if I had communication with the king soon, to ask [Edward] if he would be content [the Lord Admiral] should marry, and if so whom. I agreed, and that night when the king was alone I said I marvelled that the admiral did not marry. [The king] said nothing. I asked him if he was content [his uncle] should do so and he agreed. I asked him whom [Seymour should marry] and he said Lady Anne of Cleves, and then he said no, but [Seymour] should marry his sister Mary, to turn her opinions. So [the king] went away. Next day the admiral came again to St. James's and called me to him in the gallery. I told him all the king had said. He laughed and asked me to ask the king if he would be content for him to marry the queen and if he would write in his suit. I agreed and did so that night.[62]

The next day, Fowler went on, 'the admiral came to the king; I cannot tell what communication they had, but the king wrote a letter to the queen and the admiral brought one back from her.'

According to one report, Catherine had "merrily written' requiring help against 'the Lord Admiral" and both the queen's letter and the Lord Admiral's suit 'were represented to the King [by Seymour] as a matter of mirth.'[63] Joking Edward into playing the part of Cupid with his stepmother for his uncle overcame whatever scruples Edward may have had on the unseemly brevity of Catherine's period of mourning for his father. Seymour's suit to the king was successful and on 25 June, Edward wrote to his stepmother, telling her benevolently that: 'ye shall not need to fear any grief to come or to suspect lack of aid in need, seeing that he, being my uncle, is of so good a nature, that he will not be troublesome any means unto you ... provide that he may live with you ... and I will so provide for you both, that if hereafter any grief befall, I shall be sufficient succour in your godly or praiseable enterprises.'[64] Edward did not know that he pleaded for the accomplishment of an act already consummated. With a becoming but feigned show of reluctance that the king would later deeply resent, his stepmother acceded to his wishes and agreed to marry his uncle.

The news of their marriage became public shortly after Edward's letter was written and was greeted generally with surprise, disgust and anger. Although the match was not an unsuitable one, both partners being relatives of the king, yet the haste and secrecy of the marriage led people to believe the worst, particularly of the queen's personal conduct. With the announcement of her marriage and the unseemly haste with which it had been accomplished, Catherine's former forwardness as queen consort now provided additional evidence for some of that other recognized biological female failing – wantonness.[65] Perceived sexual misconduct on the part of women produced cultural murmurs of 'whores and fornicators'. The queen, whose supporters had been so insistent on the purity of her virtue while Henry VIII was still alive, were for the moment outshouted by detractors who now accused the queen dowager of sexual license and audibly quoted St. Jerome's proverb on the 'insatiability of the barren womb.'[66] A woman whose chastity had been impugned and who had little defence for it, public or private, could hardly hope to maintain her influence with the Privy Council or with the king. In fact, the queen's reputation suffered so much that, according to Lord Clinton, Seymour angrily sought an act in Parliament 'that men should not have liberty to speak against the queen.'[67] Crude jests began to make the rounds and although, according to the Lord Admiral, the Duchess of Suffolk might have wished him to marry the queen, it did not prevent her from naming a black stallion in her stable 'Seymour' and a bay mare, 'Parr'.[68] Catherine and her husband – but particularly Catherine – became the targets of scorn and ribaldry in the gossip at court and in drunken jests in city taverns. Any potential influence that the queen might have commanded with the king and council died a stillbirth in Thomas Seymour's bed.

The Duke of Somerset, who had broached the subject of the queen's marriage with his brother shortly after the death of Henry VIII, had in three short months reversed his position on the matter. The Lord Admiral's blustering, head-strong, overbearing attempts to wrestle power from the lord protector and gain a stronger voice on the council had done irremediable damage to the two men's relationship. Coupled with Somerset's own greed and obstinacy over the queen's jewels and lands and his duchess' implacable hatred of her former mistress and that mistress' new husband, family wars expanded into the realm of national politics. Thus Catherine's marriage to Sir Thomas was not only a political affront to Somerset, it was a personal insult. The duke greeted the news of his brother's secret marriage to the queen with undisguised fury. In his journal, Edward VI noted without comment: 'The Lord Seymour married the Queen whose name was Catherine with which marriage the lord protector was much offended.'[70]

By her affair and precipitate marriage with Sir Thomas Seymour, Catherine relinquished whatever political influence she might have exerted on the members of the council. She alienated the king by deceiving him about the state of her relationship with the Lord Admiral and by manipulating him into approving a *fait accompli*. She offended the Princess Mary by foregoing any form of mourning period for Mary's father. All the influence which she had worked so hard to attain during her four years of union to Henry VIII, Catherine had sacrificed on the altar of her fourth marriage. That she feared just such an outcome in part explains her reluctance, first to marry Seymour and then to expose that marriage to the world. Catherine had wed Henry VIII only months after her second husband, Lord Latimer, died. Now she repeated the procedure with Seymour. No one had dared raise an objection in the first instance; few raised anything but objections in the second. Praised by friends and relations for one over-hasty marriage, the queen found herself condemned at court for another. Her new husband's emotional instability and bitter antagonism toward his brother did not ease the public stigmatism of their marriage. Through Catherine, the consequences of this marriage were to reverberate in the lives of her stepchildren, bringing one of them, the Princess Elizabeth, into danger of her life.

Lord Seymour of Sudeley

Gradually the wave of displeasure in the council and gossip in the court incurred by the queen's marriage to the Lord Admiral began to subside. Catherine divided her time between her dower manors of Chelsea and Hanworth (two and a half miles south of Hounslow), and Seymour's London house, Seymour Place, which neighboured his brother's ambitious Italianate palace of Somerset House under construction to the east. The queen dowager continued to pursue her various quarrels with the lord protector, supported her husband in his various quarrels and tried between battles to make a home for herself and her husband. Seymour was determined that Catherine should maintain a royal estate. It was important for his consequence with the council, for his wife's consequence at court, and it announced to a world dominated by the Somersets that Catherine Parr was still the only queen in England.

> Her house was term'd a second Court of right,
> Because there flocked still nobility.
> He [Seymour] spared no cost his lady to delight
> Or to maintain her princely royalty.[1]

So did Sir Nicholas Throckmorton describe his cousin's establishment. Seymour, himself, described their household as one suitable for a queen, large enough to include 'not only the gentlewomen of the Queen's Highness' Privy Chamber, but also the maids which waited at large and other women being about her Grace … with 120 gentlemen and yeomen, continually abiding in the house together.'[2] This was a large and costly household, certainly one fitted for royalty.

Catherine's nesting instinct was strong and her desire to have a family around her was made the more poignant by the fact that after three traumatic marriages she had no living child to show for her efforts. In June 1544 when Catherine's sister Anne Herbert gave birth to her younger son, Edward, Catherine lent her sister her own manor of Hanworth for the lying-in. The queen also sent regular messengers to Hanworth for news of Anne's health and provided a large delegation (five yeomen, two grooms and Henry Webbe) from her household to attend the child's christening. In July, messages were still being sent between the queen in London and her sister at Hanworth. Soon after, Anne travelled the short distance to the Hertfords' new home, Syon House, to visit Anne Stanhope, Countess of Hertford and her new baby. Then in August the queen paid for a barge to bring Anne by river from Syon House to Westminster.[3] To be surrounded by so much fertility would have made the queen's own barren state that much harder to bear. Catherine's involvement in the birth and christening of her nephew led to her taking him into her household as a toddler about the time of her marriage to Thomas Seymour. While it was usual to place young children in aristocratic households to learn social skills and develop important political and dynastic connections, young Edward's age made it unlikely that this was the principal reason for his entry into his aunt's household. Catherine's surviving privy chamber accounts show purchases for clothes for the child from June through December 1547. His nurse, Dorothy Savage, wife of the queen's servant, William Savage, was that very Dorothy Fountain, who had been the nurse of the queen's late stepdaughter, Margaret Neville. Catherine's adoption of Edward Herbert was only one piece of evidence of her desperate desire for a child of her own.[4]

This longing for a family was aided and abetted by Thomas Seymour's desire to control as many future claimants to Henry's throne as possible. Shortly after Henry's death, Seymour borrowed £500 from Sir William Sharington to buy the custody of Lady Jane Grey from her father, the Marquis of Dorset. Lady Jane, it would appear, lived under Seymour's guardianship at his London house of Seymour Place for most of 1547. She was the oldest surviving child of Frances Brandon, and granddaughter of Henry VIII's sister, Mary Tudor, and her second husband, Charles Brandon, Duke of Suffolk. According to the terms of Henry's will, Jane was now third in line for the throne after the Princesses Mary and Elizabeth. Jane had the advantage over both of her royal cousins in that there was no stigma of illegitimacy, potential or declared, attendant upon her birth. If for any reason despite their father's will, questions of Mary and Elizabeth's legitimacy were to be used politically to make them ineligible for the throne, Jane Grey would be, in the absence of Edward VI's own children, the next ruler of England. Thomas Seymour had known Jane's father, Henry Grey, Marquis of Dorset, since Dorset was one of the child companions of the Duke of Richmond in Yorkshire. Seymour now convinced Dorset to grant him custody of Jane, promising to do great things for her, specifically to arrange a marriage between her and his nephew, Edward VI. The ambitious, easily swayed, not overly bright Dorset gave Seymour his full support.

Jane's custody, however, was not enough for the calculating Seymour. The young King Edward could hardly live with his stepmother, although Seymour cherished dreams of becoming his 'governor'. Mary, after years of deep friendship and affection for her stepmother, was angry at the queen's precipitate fourth marriage and saw it as a slight to her father's memory. But to Catherine's and undoubtedly Seymour's delight, they managed to secure custody of the fourteen-year-old Princess Elizabeth. Together with her tutor, William Grindal, and a small household which included the two servants closest to the princess, her nurse, Katherine Ashley, and Thomas Parry, Elizabeth joined the establishment of the queen. Catherine and Elizabeth were genuinely fond of each other. Certainly Catherine was the only mother Elizabeth would ever know. What Seymour's plans for the princess were, he was probably not yet certain of himself.

There was a story told in the following century, principally by a creative historian named Grigorio Leti, of letters purporting to prove that Thomas Seymour had tried to persuade the Princess Elizabeth to marry him shortly after Henry VIII's death. The letters no longer exist and probably never did, and two facts weigh heavily against Leti's story. The actual surviving letters between Seymour and the queen demonstrate Seymour's passionate courtship of her almost from the moment Henry was laid to rest in St. George's Chapel, Windsor. No mention of Elizabeth was ever made by the gossips at court at the time. All talk was of Seymour and the queen, and the Lord Admiral by word and deed proved that his emotions and ambitions were totally engaged in his pursuit of Catherine. After Seymour had been arrested for treason in January 1549, Elizabeth testified that she had never been approached by Seymour with offers of marriage – a dangerous perjury if Leti's alleged letters had actually been written and preserved.

> Kat Ashley told me [Elizabeth stated], after that my Lord Admiral was married to the Queen, that if my Lord might have had his own will, he would have had me, afore the Queen. Then I asked her how she knew that: Then she said she knew it well enough ... she hath spoken to me of him many times ... [5]

Yet Katherine Ashley testified that shortly after Henry's death, Seymour had told her his desire was to the queen. Ashley also confessed that, 'I said [Elizabeth] should [marry Seymour] if the council agreed, for he was the noblest man unmarried in this land, but she always said no.'[6]

Elizabeth testified that after the queen's death, her nurse had coyly suggested that Seymour would now come to woo her because he had originally preferred marriage with her to marriage with the queen. The princess told her nurse skeptically that if that had been so, then he would have proposed it at the time: 'if he had his own will, he would have had me, [as] I thought there was no let, but only the Council of his part.'[7] Elizabeth's statement shows her actively discouraging Kat Ashley's romantic matchmaking. 'About All Hallowtide [the last day of October],' Ashley confessed, 'I asked leave to go to London to speak with the admiral. Her Grace refused it for it would be said I did stud her.'[8]

If as is probable Elizabeth had a crush on Seymour, Kat Ashley had one as well. Seymour had taken the time to exercise his charms on Ashley in order to gain an ally in whatever plans he might formulate for Elizabeth's future. When Elizabeth's servant, Thomas Parry, met with the Lord Admiral in London, he delivered a message from Elizabeth's nurse. "Sir,' quoth I, 'Mistress Ashley commends her unto you; and hath bidden me to tell you, that she is your Friend as she was.' 'Oh,' quoth he, 'I know she is my Friend."[9] But Seymour, on the evidence, had not used this friendship with Elizabeth's nurse in the pursuit of marriage with the princess before his marriage to the queen. Kat Ashley related that, 'I told the Admiral in St. James's park that I had heard he should have married my lady. He denied it, saying he loved not his life to lose a wife, and it could not be.'[10] It was Elizabeth's nurse who was fascinated by the handsome Lord Admiral and who foolishly tried to act as matchmaker between him and her mistress, almost from the moment of their joining the queen's household.

In her testimony at the time of Seymour's trial, Kat Ashley admitted having been rebuked not only by the queen but by the Duchess of Somerset on the subject. Even her husband had warned her to be more discrete. When Thomas Parry confided to Ashley that he fancied there was good will between Elizabeth and Seymour, she replied, 'Oh, it is true, but I had such a charge in this, that I dare nothing say in it, but I would wish her his wife of all men living.'[11] Ashley admitted that 'diverse times she hath had talk, and had communication of that matter with the said Lady Elizabeth, and hath wished both openly and privily, that they two were married together.' The story of Seymour's early marriage proposals to the princess, thus, seem to grow out of Katherine Ashley's romantic daydreams rather than Seymour's actual intentions. Elizabeth may well have had a crush on the dashing Seymour, encouraged by him, the better for her compliance in any future plans he might concoct. But Elizabeth at fourteen was unlikely to ever succeed to the throne and at least two of Seymour's intimates, Sir William Sharington and William Parr, Marquis of Northampton, albeit hardly unbiased witnesses, nevertheless swore that Seymour had said several times that he had no personal designs on the princess.[12] Seymour certainly was reckless but the seduction of the king's favourite sister would have been more than reckless, it would have been high treason.

Elizabeth lived with Catherine Parr at Chelsea, Hanworth, and Seymour Place, where Jane Grey was apparently permanently established, as there is no mention of her being with the Seymours at Catherine's two dower houses. Probably for the first time in her life, Elizabeth had a taste of personal freedom and she revelled in it. When the Duchess of Somerset found out that the teenage princess had gone out at night 'in a barge upon the Thames', presumably without her stepmother in attendance, and other 'light parts', she gave Katherine Ashley a blistering lecture, threatening to remove her from Elizabeth's household.[13] The duchess had made it her business to oversee the queen's conduct in her guardianship of her stepdaughter and her suspicions that Elizabeth was being given too much freedom were soon confirmed. With the combination of the Lord Seymour's arrogant disregard of the conventions, Elizabeth's teenage crush, and Kat Ashley's garrulous meddling, affairs in the queen's household soon got out of hand. The court, which at the beginning of the year had found plenty of food for gossip about Catherine and Thomas Seymour, now found just as much to gossip about Seymour and Elizabeth. The tittle-tattle quickly found its way to hostile ears on the Privy Council. There seemed to be enough and more to fuel the rumours of impropriety and indiscretion.

Seymour's informality with Elizabeth was given an evil interpretation. While the queen's household was at Chelsea, Kat Ashley later swore that Seymour:

> Would come many mornings into the said Lady Elizabeth's chamber, before she were ready, and sometime before she did rise. And if she were up, he would bid her good morrow, and ask how she did, and strike her upon the back or on the buttocks familiarly, and so go forth through [to] his lodgings ... and sometime go through to the maidens, and play with them.[14]

When Ashley spoke with Seymour about his behaviour toward Elizabeth, he was angry and ignored her warnings. 'I could not make him stop,' she later explained, 'and at last told the queen; who made little of it and said she would come with him, and did so ever after.'

Initially Catherine seemed to see in Seymour's behaviour nothing more than a playful surrogate father teasing his young foster daughter and engaging her in innocent games:

> At Hanworth [continued Kat Ashley], [Seymour] would likewise come in the morning unto her Grace; but as [I] remembereth, at all times, she was up before, saving two mornings, the which two mornings the Queen came with him ... and they tytled [tickled] my Lady Elizabeth in the bed ... At Seymour Place, when the Queen lay there, he did use awhile to come up every morning in his nightgown, barelegged in his slippers, where he found commonly the Lady Elizabeth up at her book: and then he would look in at the gallery door, and bid my Lady Elizabeth

good morrow, and so go his way. Then [I] told my Lord it was an unseemly sight
to come so barelegged to a maiden's chamber; with which he was angry, but he
left it.

Catherine continued to join in these frolics. Seymour had refused to allow the
queen two years of mourning for the late king and, as described by Kat Ashley,
he now playfully attacked Elizabeth's own mourning for her father:

> Another time at Hanworth, in the garden, he wrated with her, and cut her gown
> in an hundred pieces; being black cloth; and when she came up so trimmed, [I]
> chid with her and her Grace answered, She could not do withal for the Queen
> held her, while the Lord Admiral did so dress it.

As long as the queen seemed to condone Seymour's behaviour toward
Elizabeth, gossip, although inevitable, was kept more or less under control. But
little things continued to fuel the flames. Elizabeth's bedchamber at Chelsea was
small and her nurse's bed, usually placed in her charge's room, was moved into
another chamber for lack of space.[15] Elizabeth thus lay alone in her bedroom
where Seymour was in the habit of wandering about in his nightclothes in the
early morning, a fact that fed the rumours at court. When the queen found out
that Elizabeth's nurse was spinning fantasies for her charge about marriage with
Catherine's own husband, she was angry and upset. But sending Kat Ashley
packing, reproaching her husband openly or upbraiding her stepdaughter for
unseemly conduct was not easy. Seymour was hot-headed and jealous and
violently resented being criticised for his behaviour. Sir Thomas Perry confessed
that he 'had heard much evil report of the Lord Admiral, that he was not only
a very covetous man, and an oppressor, but also an evil jealous man, and how
cruelly, how dishonourably, and how jealously he had used the Queen.'[16] Kat
Ashley denied such slander but did allow the admiral to be a jealous man:

> And as for that jealousy of my Lord Admiral, I will tell you: As he came upon a
> time up a stairs to see the Queen, he met with a groom of the chamber upon the
> stairs with a coal basket, coming out of the chamber; and because the door was
> shut, and my Lord without, he was angry and pretended that he was jealous.[17]

Ashley's opinion that Seymour was only pretending jealousy may be laid to her
conviction that he never loved the queen and cherished designs on Elizabeth.
Meticulous in his deference to Catherine during their brief courtship, Seymour
proved less willing to play the courteous knight after their marriage. Jealous and
'homely with the queen', the Lord Admiral was in the habit of so far forgetting

himself toward the king's sister as to send her such messages by his servants as 'whether her great buttocks were grown any less or no?'[18] Such rough and public jests, as well as Seymour's boasting familiarity with Elizabeth's body, shocked his well-wishers and put weapons into the hands of his enemies. Once more, Kat Ashley tried to remonstrate with him and caused a violent scene for her pains:

> And then in the gallery [at Chelsea], [I] told my Lord that these things were com-
> plained of, and that my Lady was evil spoken of: The Lord Admiral swore, 'God's
> precious soul!' he would tell my Lord Protector how it slandered him, and he
> would not leave it, for he meant no evil.[19]

Seymour, who lacked imagination and was 'bold' to a fault, was apparently indifferent to the position in which he was placing Elizabeth as well as his wife, just as he had been indifferent to the censure to which he had exposed the queen by his hasty marriage with her. In his own eyes, his motives, no matter how it might look to others, were above reproach and above discussion.

To Seymour's reckless behaviour with the king's sister and his jealous rages at his wife (feigned or not) were added his outspoken attitude toward religion and unwillingness to pay even lip service to its rules and rites. Evangelical preacher Hugh Latimer proclaimed that he had been told Seymour had denied the immortality of the soul. While this is perfectly in keeping with Seymour's blustering, care-for-nothing behaviour, it was an unwise statement at best:

> He shall be Lot's wife to me as long as I live [Latimer stated grimly] … I have heard
> say, when [the queen] ordained in her house, daily prayer both before noon, and
> after noon, the admiral gets him out of the way like a mole digging in the earth.[20]

Such behaviour would have been dangerous the year before, while Henry VIII was still alive, and in the light of other rumours coming from the queen's household it was not particularly politic in 1547. This was especially so as Seymour's hated brother, the Duke of Somerset, became increasingly fixated on his religious mission to the nation. Religious laxity, let alone the heresy of denying the soul's immortality, would do little to mend the growing feud between the brothers and Seymour's questionable attentions to Elizabeth could only worsen the situation.

According to Kat Ashley, Catherine tried to warn her stepdaughter and her nurse in a subtle way, probably to avoid arousing Seymour's considerable ire:

> At Hanworth, the Queen told [me] that my Lord Admiral looked in at the gallery

window, and [saw] my Lady Elizabeth cast her arms about a man's neck. The which hearing [I] inquired for it of my Lady's Grace, who denied it weeping and bade ask all her women: They all denied it: and [I] knew it could not be so, for there came no man but Grindal, the Lady Elizabeth's schoolmaster. Howbeit, thereby [I] did suspect, that the Queen was jealous betwixt them, and did but fain this, to the intent that [I] should take more heed, and be, as it were, in watch betwixt her and my Lord Admiral.[21]

Then in December of 1547 the situation changed. The queen and her husband had kept Christmas with the king at Enfield, trying perhaps to recapture their former influence with Edward. It was at that time that Catherine Parr became pregnant with Thomas Seymour's child. After four husbands and twenty cumulative years of marriage, the queen was at last about to fulfil what she perceived to be the primary duty of marriage. Yet the emotional strain of ongoing quarrels with the lord protector and his wife, morning sickness,[22] worry about Elizabeth, and her husband's temper and lack of discretion must have made these early months of pregnancy very difficult. Two cramp rings for use against the pains of childbirth and three pieces of unicorn horn, sovereign remedy for stomach pains, found in a chest of Catherine's personal possessions in 1549 were probably talismans given to the queen by her husband and friends to alleviate the nausea and anticipated pangs of childbirth. Catherine was almost thirty-six, an advanced age to begin what may have been her first pregnancy and the emotional strain in her household could hardly have helped. Kat Ashley told Thomas Parry a story which has been accepted without question ever since describing the crisis which caused the queen to remove Elizabeth from her household. Some two months into Catherine's pregnancy, during the festivities of Twelfth Night, 6 January 1548, Seymour allegedly overreached the bounds of propriety with the princess yet again. According to Ashley's story:

The Queen, suspecting the often access of the Admiral to the Lady Elizabeth's Grace, came suddenly upon them, where they were all alone, (he having her in his arms:) wherefore the Queen fell out, both with the Lord Admiral, and with her Grace also … and, as I remember, this was the cause why she was sent from the Queen.[24]

A close examination of this dramatic moment seems to offer more of Kat Ashley's incessant gossip-mongering than it does of unbiased reportage. Elizabeth did not leave the queen's household for nearly five months after this supposed confrontation and a mere few weeks before Catherine herself left for Sudeley Castle. If Seymour had been in the habit of groping the princess in doorways, more than one witness would have made certain that the fact was known at court, and Elizabeth would have left the queen's household in a far speedier manner than she did.

Torn between the affection she held for both her husband and her stepdaughter, the jealousies caused by their thoughtless behaviour, and Kat Ashley's matchmaking, Catherine's state of mind may be imagined. What Seymour's intentions were toward Elizabeth is unclear. Certainly at this date marriage was not on his mind. Casual seduction of an heir to the throne in his wife's house seems fantastic even for the obstinately reckless Lord Admiral. Whatever was in his mind, his over-familiarity with Elizabeth and his constant flaunting of convention caused his wife great alarm.

Elizabeth was under more than usual emotional stress at this time. Besides the complicated state of affairs in her family, her beloved tutor, William Grindal, died at the end of January, leaving a gaping rent in the fabric of her existence. Her stepmother wanted to install Francis Goldsmith, a loyal retainer, in Grindal's place but Elizabeth was not overly fond of Goldsmith and preferred Grindal's former teacher, Roger Ascham, for the position. When informed of this fact, Ascham wrote to the princess, 'I shall believe it my greatest happiness, if that time come when my services can be of use to your Highness.'[25] Ascham counseled Elizabeth to defer to her guardians' wishes, perhaps aware of the turbulent state of affairs that obtained in the queen's household. To John Cheke, Ascham confided on 12 February that the princess had told him 'how much the Queen and my Lord Admiral were labouring in favour of Goldsmith. I advised her to comply with their recommendations; I commended Goldsmith to her and urged her as far as I could to follow your judgement and advice in the matter; and entreated her to set aside all her favour toward me and to consider before all else, how she could bring to maturity that singular hope in her awakened by Grindal's teaching.'[26] But Elizabeth was determined to have her own way and informed Ascham that when she come to London to join her stepmother, she would discuss the matter with Catherine and Sir Thomas, and depended upon Cheke to back her up in her choice. In the end she was successful in engaging Ascham as her tutor. But emotional conflict continued to simmer in the Seymour household.

By the spring of 1548 the gossip had grown too damaging for Catherine to ignore any longer and the situation too dangerous for her to allow it to continue. Not only was Seymour risking a charge of treason for himself, and by implication his pregnant wife, but he was placing Elizabeth in mortal danger. It had been, after all, alleged sexual misconduct that had brought both Elizabeth's mother, Anne Boleyn, and later her stepmother, Katherine Howard, to the block. It was probably not as much jealously as fear and a desire to protect herself, her husband, and their unborn child, as well as her heedless stepdaughter, that caused Catherine to make alternative living arrangements for Elizabeth while she, herself, travelled to her husband's manor of Sudeley in Gloucestershire to await the birth of their child. In May, a week after Whitsuntide, the queen sent Elizabeth into Hertfordshire to live in the household of Kat Ashley's sister, Joan Denny, and her husband, Sir Anthony Denny, at Cheshunt. She was never to see her stepdaughter again.

This abrupt removal into Hertfordshire caused a sea change in Elizabeth, who now became fully sensible of the danger into which Seymour, Ashley and her own conduct had put her. The Lord Admiral was, she later remarked, 'a man of much wit and very little judgement.' Upon her arrival at her new home, the princess wrote to Catherine:

> Although I could not be plentiful in giving thanks for the manifold kindness, received at your highness' hand at my departure, yet I am something to be borne withal, for truly I was replete with sorrow to depart from your highness, especially leaving you undoubtful of health; and albeit I answered little, I weighed it more deeper when you said you would warn me of all evils that you should hear of me, for if your grace had not a good opinion of me you would not have offered friendship to me that way.[27]

The emotional wrench of parting from Catherine is apparent in Elizabeth's letter but if her stepdaughter was suitably chastened, Catherine's husband was not. He now brought the ten-year-old Lady Jane Grey from Seymour Place in London and installed her in Elizabeth's place in his wife's household. The Lord Admiral seems to have charmed Lady Jane with much the same panache that he had used on Princess Elizabeth, but because of Jane's age, there could hardly be new imputations of sexual impropriety. 'You have been towards me a loving and kind father,' Jane wrote to Seymour in the fall of 1548. 'I shall be always most ready to obey your godly monitions and good instructions as behooveth one on whom you have heaped so many benefits.'[28] But Jane Grey was to become only a footnote in Seymour's plots to tip the scales of power against his brother and gain the upper hand in the council and with the king. With his wife's pregnancy, the Lord Admiral's hopes for redress of his real and imagined wrongs came increasingly to revolve around his unborn child.

17

'The End of Summer'

The gossip which finally forced the Princess Elizabeth's banishment from the queen's household was only one of the scandals in which Catherine found herself embroiled during the early of months of 1548. Her brother, William, now Marquis of Northampton, had been separated from his wife, Lady Anne Bourchier, since Anne's elopement in 1541. His affair with Elisabeth Brooke, the daughter of Lord Cobham, had gone on for five years and Northampton desperately wanted to marry his beautiful *paramour*. Elisabeth Brooke's position could hardly have been an easy one. If she were to bear Northampton's child, it would be illegitimate under the law and thus incapable of succeeding to its father's lands and titles. Unless Northampton made Elisabeth his legal wife, he had no way of securing for himself a legal heir, as all of Anne's children, by act of Parliament, had been disbarred from inheritance. With Henry VIII's death, the marquess had more freedom to pursue a second marriage, and he decided to initiate legal proceedings in an attempt to annul his first wife while maintaining his rights to her inheritance. In April 1547, Northampton petitioned for the formation of a commission to examine his marital status and legally dissolve his first marriage so that he might make a second.[1]

The marquess had every reason to expect sympathy for his efforts from the lord protector, whom he had known since childhood. Somerset's own first wife, Katherine Fillol, had suffered the same fate as Anne Bourchier. She had been accused of adultery and set aside by the duke. Although there was no marital irregularity on Somerset's part, as apparently Katherine died before Somerset's remarriage to his present duchess, nevertheless Northampton fully expected Somerset's understanding and support in the matter of his divorce. The lord protector, unfortunately for Northampton, had rather puritanical and myopic views when it came to other people's marital problems. An investigating commission which the marquess had requested was duly convened but dithered on through the spring and into the summer of 1547, unable to reach any decision. Northampton was forced to the expedient of trying to bribe one of the commissioners. His sister had been granted the manor of Yarlington in Somerset as part of her dowry from the late king, and in order to her help her brother, Catherine granted him the reversion of the manor in August 1547. Three months later Northampton sold the reversion to Thomas Smith, one of the most influential men among the commissioners, at the preferential price of £285.[2] Bribery had as little effect as bullying on the prodigiously slow commission deliberations. A man of volatile temper, Northampton soon ran out of patience. His sister's affair with Thomas Seymour had been regularized, why should not his own with Elisabeth Brooke be as well? Risking a charge of bigamy for himself and one of adultery for Elisabeth, Northampton took the matter into his own hands and had a marriage service secretly performed for the two of them near the end of the summer of 1547.[3]

If Northampton had expected Somerset's understanding and forgiveness for his actions, he was to be severely disappointed. This second irregular marriage in the Parr family in less than a year brought out all the worst characteristics of the lord protector. When news of Northampton's marriage became public in January 1548, Somerset exploded. The scandal rocked the court. Called to explain himself before the Privy Council, Northampton tried to brazen it out with an appeal to religious solidarity, directed no doubt at the lord protector. Northampton believed himself, so it was reported, 'justified in the step he had taken by the word of God, and that the indissolubility of the marriage tie was merely part of the law of the Romish church, by which marriage was reckoned a sacrament.'[4] Such desperate reasoning did nothing to impress Somerset. It did not help either that the gossips claimed that Catherine Parr and her new husband had been the chief conspirators in encouraging the marriage. Ambassador Van der Delft wrote to Charles V in February 1548, that:

> With regard [to the Marquis of Northampton], I have been told in strict confidence that by means of his sister, the Queen, and of the Duchess of Suffolk, he recently took for his wife the daughter of the Deputy of Calais, and that 8 or 9 days afterwards he was obliged by the command of the Council to put her away and never speak to her again on pain of death ... he is only spoken of secretly and does not show himself at Court.[5]

Forbidden to see Elisabeth on pain of death, expelled from his natural element at court and on the council, Northampton quickly realized that the stumbling block in his road to happiness was the lord protector himself. Elisabeth Brooke was sent in disgrace from court back to live with the queen, in whose household she had once resided. Newly pregnant and in the midst of her own problems with her husband and stepdaughter, Catherine hardly needed this complication. An additional quarrel with the lord protector by Catherine's brother and sometime wife sharpened all of the queen's former resentments against Somerset. The year before she had written to Thomas Seymour:

I supposed my Lord Protector would have used no delay with his friend and natural brother in a matter which is upright and just, as I take it. What will he do to other[s] that be indifferent to him? I judge not very well. I pray God he may deceive me, for his own wealth and benefit more than for mine own. Now I have uttered my choler, I shall desire you, good my lord, with all heart not to unquiet yourself with any of his unfriendly parts, but bear them for the time as well as ye can.[6]

Catherine probably gave similar advice to her brother, but her choler was not lessened by William's expulsion from the council nor by the presence of Elisabeth Brooke in her household.

This in-fighting among the group of new religionists who had gained control of the council at Henry VIII's death was a battle that would continue throughout the seven years of Edward VI's brief reign. Personality conflicts, rampant ambition, greed, and sexual desire were now to accomplish between 1547 and 1553 what Stephen Gardiner and a conspiracy of conservatives had not been able to do. Within seven years of Henry VIII's death, the chief players for the new religion in the 1546 drama for the life of the queen had either been executed or were in prison. The former Bishop of Winchester, sitting in his cell in the Tower observing the self-destruction of his enemies, might be forgiven for concluding that God was indeed on his side.

As Catherine's pregnancy progressed, her involvement in politics, if not her interest, diminished. She viewed her approaching motherhood with delight despite the knowledge that death in childbirth was a very real possibility.[7] In June she wrote to her husband from Hanworth: 'I gave your little knave your blessing, who like an honest man stirred apace after and before. For Mary Odell being abed with me had laid her hand upon my belly to feel it stir. It hath stirred these three days every morning and evening so that I trust when ye come it will make you some pastime.'[8] Seymour, also well aware of the potential perils of childbed to both mother and child, replied from Westminster: 'I do desire your highness to keep the little knave so lean and gaunt with your good diet and walking, that he may be so small that he may creep out of a mousehole.' Seymour, whose attitude toward his brother was beginning to verge on paranoia, had plans for his unborn son. 'I hear my little man doth shake his poll [head], [and] trusting if God should give him life to live as long as his father, he will revenge such wrongs as neither you nor I can.'[9]

Seymour had decided that Catherine should be confined as far away as possible from the press of business and turmoil of court as well as from the summer plagues of London. To that end he had spent £1,000 having rooms prepared for her in his newly acquired house at Sudeley in Gloucestershire.[10]

The nursery for the expected heir was done up in crimson velvet and taffeta, with furniture and plate enough for a royal birth. In Seymour's eyes, the child would be a member of the royal family as Catherine was still officially the only queen in England. After his daughter's birth, Seymour was overheard to tell Sir William Sharington that, 'it would be strange to some when his daughter came of age, taking [her] place above [the duchess of] Somerset, as a queen's daughter.'[11] Catherine's rank and state were still of utmost importance to the Lord Admiral even if her position had thus far done little to further his own.

Catherine depended on her husband to accompany her down to Sudeley the second week in June but a crisis at sea with the French looked as if it might force the Lord Admiral to postpone his departure from London. 'I am very sorry for the news of the Frenchmen,' Catherine wrote from Hanworth on 9 June, where she was waiting for her husband to join her. 'I pray God it be not a let to our journey. As soon as ye know what they will do, good my lord, I beseech you let me hear from you, for I shall not be very quiet till I know.'[12] The council had received word that the French meant to attack Pevensey Castle in Sussex but the Lord Admiral had no intention of altering his own plans for a rumoured French invasion. 'I spake to [the Lord Protector] of your going down into the country on Wednesday,' he answered Catherine from Westminster the same day he received her letter, 'who was sorry thereof, trusting that I would be here all tomorrow to hear what the Frenchmen will do. And on Monday dinner, I trust to be with you. As for the Frenchmen, I have no mistrust that they shall be any let of my going with you [on] this journey, or any of my continuance there [at Sudeley] with your highness.'[13]

Just before he left Westminster for Hanworth to join the queen, Seymour pushed his suits for Catherine's lands and jewels once more. Having been successful in coaxing Edward to write a letter in support of his marriage, Seymour now attempted to coax the king to write a letter to the lord protector ordering the release of the queen's jewels.[14] When the king demurred, Seymour enlisted the venal John Fowler as his public relations man with the king while he was away at Sudeley with the queen. Seymour called Fowler to his chamber in Westminster Palace and told him that he planned to sue his brother for his wife's jewels. Seymour urged Fowler not to let the young king forget him and 'desired remembrances from the king'. Fowler was to have Edward write to his uncle frequently while he and Catherine were in the country and Seymour paid Fowler well for his services:

> I procured the king to write several times [Fowler later testified], but only two or three lines of recommendation to him and the queen. Sometimes I wrote myself with them for money, and once had answer to receive £40 of [Anthony

Bourchier], the queen's receiver and so did. Many other times I had answer that if I lacked money I should have £40 of Mr. Locke at London, for [Seymour] had caused Bowcher [*sic*] to write to him to deliver me as much as I sent for.[15]

Having briefed Fowler, the Lord Admiral 'called for boats to Hanworth, bidding me send to him and nobody else if the king lacked anything. He often wished me to remind the king of him.'

On Wednesday, 13 June 1548, Seymour accompanied his wife, who was now six months pregnant, and his young ward, Lady Jane Grey, from Hanworth to Sudeley Castle in Gloucestershire. In the mellow, honey-coloured stone castle, Catherine spent the last three months of her pregnancy and the last summer of her life. She was attended by her old friend and doctor, Robert Huicke, and surrounded by other old friends, Miles Coverdale, her almoner, John Parkhurst, her chaplain, Sir Robert Tyrwhit, and the ladies who had been with her over the years, such as Elizabeth Tyrwhit and Mary Woodhull. Seymour had been good to Catherine's household, taking many of them, such as Sir William Sharington, Nicholas Throckmorton, Nicholas Pygot and Walter Erle, into his service. For the more important of the queen's servants, such as John Parkhurst, Seymour secured the rich living of Bishop's Cleve near Sudeley.[16] This carefully cultivated body of subordinate well-wishers, however, could not compensate for the powerful enemies Seymour had made at court.

In spite of his duties as Lord Admiral, Sir Thomas seems to have spent most of that summer with his wife. Those who wanted to confer with him on political matters were forced to the necessity of traveling down to Sudeley to do so. Arguments with the lord protector, together with admiralty business, pursued Seymour into Gloucestershire. When, in a letter to the lord protector, Seymour recommended a suit for his servant, Francis Agard, and complained at the same time about criticisms of his handling of the Admiralty, Somerset's answer was brusque and high-handed. He refused Agard's suit and as for the criticism he informed his brother that, 'We have no time to reply to your long letter of August 27. We are sorry that just complaints have been made against you, which it is our duty to receive. [You should] avoid extreme judgements. If the complaints are true, redress them.'[17] Such haughty pronouncements in the royal third person from his brother were unlikely to have been accepted with good grace by the Lord of Sudeley. Seymour informed Somerset ominously, that, 'It is better to be prepared against a suspicious [suspect] friend.'[18]

While her husband brooded on his wrongs, Catherine whiled away the summer days overseeing the education of Seymour's young ward and preparing for the birth of her baby. Catherine's affection for her husband seemed as strong as ever, as was her belief that in the final analysis, Seymour would make the moral choice over the immoral one. Sir Robert Tyrwhit remembered that:

> One day at Sudeley, walking in the park, amongst many communications, the
> Queen's grace said thus: Master Tyrwhit, you shall see the king when he cometh
> to his full age, he will call his lands again, as fast as they be now given from him:
> Mary, said I, then is Sudeley Castle gone from my Lord Admiral. Mary (said she),
> I do assure you, he intends to offer them to the King, and give them freely to him
> at that time.[19]

To add to the queen's comfort, she had reconciled with Princess Mary, who
wrote to her stepmother on 9 August: 'I trust to hear good success of your
Grace's great belly; and in the meantime shall desire much to hear of your
health, which I pray almighty God to continue and increase to his pleasure as
much as your own heart can desire.'[20] Princess Elizabeth wrote, too, answering
a letter of Catherine's in which the queen described the beauties of Sudeley
and wished the princess with her once more:

> Although your Highness' letters be most joyful to me in absence, yet consider-
> ing what pain it is to you to write, your Grace being so great with child, and so
> sickly, your commendation were enough in my Lord's letter. I much rejoice at
> your health with the well liking of the country, with my humble thanks, that your
> Grace wished me with you, till I were weary of that country. Your Highness were
> like to be cumbered, if I should not depart, till I were weary being with you; also
> it were in the worst soil in the world your presence would make it pleasant ... God
> send you a most lucky deliverance.[21]

On Thursday, 30 August, Catherine was brought to bed of a healthy baby
girl named Mary in honour of her stepsister, the princess. Disappointed
briefly that the son and avenger he had hoped for had turned out to be a
girl, Seymour rallied quickly and announced his daughter's birth to the lord
protector in glowing terms and with an effusive description of her beauty. The
father of twelve children, Somerset was amused by his brother's enthusiasm
for fatherhood. Somerset wrote in congratulation on 1 September from Syon
House:

> We are right glad to understand by your letters that the Queen your bedfellow hath
> had a happy hour; and, escaping all danger, hath made you the father of so pretty a
> daughter. And although (if it had so pleased God) it would have been both to us, and
> we suppose to you, a more joy and comfort if it had been this the first a son; yet the
> escape of danger, and the prophecy and good hansell [promise] of this to a great sort

of happy sons, the which as you write, we trust no less than to be true, is no small joy and comfort to us, as we are sure it is to you and to her Grace also.[22]

But Seymour's joy in his child's birth was followed by fear at his wife's worsening condition. Unfortunately for Catherine, Dr. Huicke, so advanced in matters of diet and exercise for proper prenatal care, was a man of his times in matters of hygiene. Having survived disease, civil insurrection, mob violence, charges of heresy and treason, four husbands including Henry Tudor, and the vicissitudes of life in sixteenth-century England for thirty-six years, Catherine Parr succumbed to puerperal or childbed fever contracted from her doctor's dirty hands.

Lady Elizabeth Tyrwhit left an eyewitness account of Catherine's last hours, but it should be remembered that Lady Tyrwhit was one of the few women who had not fallen under the spell of Seymour's charm and who gave evidence against him when he was arrested for treason. Her account therefore is not an unbiased one although the facts as she describes them seem true enough:

> Two days afore the death of the Queen, at my coming to her in the morning, she asked me where I had been so long, and said unto me, she did fear such things in herself, that she was sure she could not live: Whereunto I answered, as I thought, that I saw no likelihood of death in her. She then having my Lord Admiral by the hand, and divers others standing by, spake these words, partly, as I took it, idly [deliriously], 'My Lady Tyrwhit, I am not well handled, for those that be about me careth not for me, but standeth laughing at my grief, and the more good I will to them, the less good they will to me:' Whereunto my Lord Admiral answered, 'why sweetheart, I would you no hurt.' And she said to him again aloud, 'No, my Lord, I think so'; and immediately she said to him in his ear, 'but my Lord you have given me many shrewd taunts.' Those words I perceived she spoke with good memory, and very sharply and earnestly, for her mind was far unquieted. My Lord Admiral perceiving that I heard it, called me aside, and asked me what she said; and I declared it plainly to him.[23]

Lady Tyrwhit's animosity toward Seymour is obvious and she assumes that Catherine's accusations, which her lady-in-waiting first claims were spoken in delirium and then claims were spoken 'with good memory', were aimed solely at him. But even through Lady Tyrwhit's hostility, Seymour's tenderness toward his wife at this moment is apparent:

> Then he [Seymour] consulted with me, that he would lie down on the bed by her, to look if he could pacify her unquietness with gentle communication; whereunto I agreed. And by that time he had spoken three or four words to her, she answered

him very roundly and shortly, saying, 'My Lord, I would have given a thousand
marks to have had my full talk with Huicke, the first day I was delivered, but I
durst not, for displeasing of you': And I hearing that, perceived her trouble to be so
great, that my heart would serve me to her no more. Such like communication she
had with him the space of an hour; which they did hear that sat by her bedside.[24]

Catherine died on Wednesday, 5 September, 'between two and three of the clock
in the morning'.[25] She had once written to Henry VIII, that, 'I make like account
with your majesty, as I do with God, for his benefits and gifts heaped upon me
daily; knowledging myself always a great debtor unto Him ... In which state I am
certain to die, but yet I hope in His gracious acceptance of my goodwill.'[26] Her
own goodwill toward Seymour, she expressed in a dictated disposition of her
property, which the testators, Huicke and Parkhurst, signed just hours after her
death. In it, the queen bequeathed to her husband all of her possessions, 'wishing
them to be a thousand times more in value than they were ... but most liberally
gave him full power, authority, and order to dispose of the same goods, cattle and
debts at his own free will and pleasure to his most commodity.'[27] This testament
appears to discount a feeling of open hostility on Catherine's part toward Seymour
at the end. Significantly, even though it was an oral and not a written will, there is
no extensive protestation of faith recorded, reaffirming what other evidence seems
to imply, that passion for Seymour had taken the edge off Catherine's ecstatic need
for God and that during her marriage to Thomas, the majority of her time and
attention had centred on her husband.

While preparations for his wife's funeral services were put in hand, the Lord
Admiral seems to have left Sudeley immediately after Catherine's death. The
queen was buried in the manor chapel, without stone or monument, and with
the diminutive Jane Grey as her chief mourner, the child's 'train borne up by a
young lady.' Catherine's funeral service was a solemn affair as befitted a queen:

> When the corpse was sent within the rails, and the mourners placed, the whole
> choir began and sung certain psalms in English, and read three lessons; and after
> the third lesson, the mourners, according to their degrees and that which is accus-
> tomed, offered into the alms-box ... the offering done, doctor Coverdale, the
> queen's almoner, began his sermon which was very good and godly, and in one
> place thereof he took occasion to declare unto the people 'how that they should
> none there think, say, or spread abroad that the offering which was there done, was
> done anything to benefit the dead, but for the poor only; and also the lights, which
> were carried and stood about the corpse were for the honour of the person, and
> for none other intent nor purpose'; and so went through with his sermon, and
> made a godly prayer, and the whole church answered and prayed the same with

him in the end. The sermon done, the corpse was buried, during which time the choir sung *Te Deum* in English. And this done, the mourners dined, and the rest returned homeward again. All which aforesaid was done in a morning.[28]

Catherine was buried in a way she would have approved – to the sound of psalms, with a sermon preached in English, and with various admonitions against such popish devices as offerings to the dead and ritual candles. Her body was left beneath the floor of Sudeley chapel and forgotten and although the children she had helped to raise would rule England for nearly half a century more, Catherine Parr's own reign as Queen of England was finally over.[29]

His wife's sudden death left Thomas Seymour stunned. With Catherine gone, he lost control completely. All his ambitions lay in the dust; his affairs at court drifted. His mother, Marjorie Wentworth, Lady Seymour, arrived at Sudeley to take care of the baby, and Seymour sent Jane Grey back to her father, writing to Dorset that he was 'so amazed [by] my great loss' that he planned 'to have broken up and dissolved my whole house.'[30] Even the garrulous Kat Ashley was struck by Seymour's grief at his wife's death and remembered that: '[I] spake with one Edward [Rous], servant to the Lord Admiral, who told [me] that my Lord Admiral was an heavy man for the Queen.'[31] Ashley urged the Princess Elizabeth to write Seymour a letter of condolence, 'but she would not lest she be thought to woo him.' So lost was Seymour that he even visited the detested lord protector briefly at Syon House near Brentford, where Somerset made an attempt to end their differences by 'making very much' of his brother in his time of grief.[32] But Seymour's feelings for Somerset remained unaltered and grief soon turned to rage. Within weeks of Catherine's death, he had reclaimed custody of Jane Grey and launched himself on a frantic, ill-advised course of conspiracy and intrigue against his brother.

Returning to court, the Lord Admiral began to gather allies who shared grievances against the lord protector, and threatened to make 'the blackest Parliament that ever was in England.'[33] Seymour's brother-in-law, the Marquis of Northampton, related that:

> When the admiral first came to court after the queen's death, he showed me suits he had to the protector touching the queen's servants, jewels and other things which he claimed to be hers, for which he would remain at court. If he did not speed well, he would return to the country, which life he liked well. He was very friendly in deed and word, promising money or anything he had, and gave me a valuable specialty.[34]

Sir Richard Cotton reported that Seymour had been overheard to say, that 'he would wear black for one year, and would then know where to have a wife.'[35]

Seymour was now entertaining ideas of marrying one of the royal princesses and he began to drop hints of his plan to members of the Privy Council, testing the waters of their reaction. None of it was very favourable. Lord Russell, the Lord Privy Seal, stated that:

> I told the admiral I was sorry to hear rumours that he made means to marry Mary or Elizabeth, which would be his undoing. I told him I had heard this from some of his near friends, he denied attempting any such thing. Two or three days later, riding from the protector's house to parliament, he said I was very suspicious of him and asked who had told me of the marriage he should attempt. I declined [to tell him], but advised him against it. He replied that it was convenient for them to marry, and better within the realm than abroad, and why might not he or another made by their father marry one of them. I told him that it would be the undoing of anyone, particularly him who was so near the king.[36]

As with his behaviour toward the Princess Elizabeth in 1547, Seymour refused to listen to good advice, or to any advice at all. He began to draw up lists of men he could count on to back what he now intended to be a *coup* against the lord protector. 'He had the names of all the lords,' Fowler later swore, 'and totted those whom he thought he might have to his purpose to labour [lobby] them.'[37] When the Earl of Warwick requested that Seymour swap lands with him because Warwick wanted to add the manor of Stratford-upon-Avon to his nearby estates, Seymour refused, alienating the earl, whom he did not like. He informed the affronted Warwick that 'he would not part with [the manor], [as] it was a pretty town and would make many men.'[38] Seymour numbered the men and ships under his command and encouraged his friends, the Marquis of Northampton, the Marquis of Dorset, and the Earl of Rutland, to go into the country and visit their estates and count the number of men that they could depend on for support in a crisis.

Seymour tried to win over former enemies who had influence on the council, such as Thomas Wriothesley, Catherine Parr's old enemy and now Earl of Southampton, and men with little liking for him, such as Lord Clinton, and attach them to his cause. He even tried to enlist the support of Sir Robert Tyrwhit and his wife, Elizabeth, who hated him. The Lord Admiral went to visit them at their manor of Mortlake Park. Tyrwhit later recalled that, 'after supper, [Seymour] talked with my wife. And passing by him, he called me and said these words: 'Master Tyrwhit, I am talking with my Lady your wife in Divinity': I made him answer that my wife was not fine in divinity, but she was half a Scripture woman.'[39] But Seymour's attempts to woo Elizabeth Tyrwhit with discussions of religion did not succeed, anymore than did his attempts with Southampton or Clinton.

It very soon became obvious to more than a few observers that the Lord Admiral was planning to instigate a *coup* aimed at the overthrow of the lord protector. Seymour asked Lord Clinton rhetorically why his brother had been made protector in the first place, 'for there was no need of one.'[40] This not so subtle reference to the closed-door machinations regarding the late king's will that had gone on in camera for three days after Henry VIII's death, may have been Sir Thomas' attempt to blackmail his brother. But to make any public revelations about the power brokering on the council at that time would be to expose more than Somerset to public criticism. Seymour's friends and even his enemies warned him of his folly but impatient as ever of criticism, Seymour refused to listen. He ordered his servant, Edward Rous, to prepare his manor of Bewdley in Shropshire, where he intended 'to keep household from the beginning of May for most of the summer ... saying he would keep as great a house there as he did in the queen's life, despite the charge, in order not to be bullied out of his own.'[41]

Sir George Blagge, who in 1546 had avoided being burned at the stake as a heretic by a whisker, warned the Lord Admiral that if he did not moderate his speech and behaviour, the lord protector would be within his rights to have him put under arrest.[42] Seymour answered that Somerset would not dare. According to Lord Clinton, shortly before Seymour's arrest, he had 'said to my Lord Marquis [of Northampton] he would take his fist from the best of their ears from the highest to the lowest: saying, that he would not spare my Lord Protector's Grace. My Lord Marquis answered, that these words should not need; he trusted that all should be well, and that my Lord's Grace and he should be friends and persuaded [Seymour] to pacify himself.'[43] Yet Northampton and his friend, the Earl of Rutland, privately sympathised with the ire behind the words and, as events were to indicate, had undoubtedly discussed secretly with Seymour the best way in which to encompass Somerset's downfall. To his fellow conspirators' great unease, however, Seymour had no idea of how to conduct an effective conspiracy. He talked too much and too loudly and had run well out of anyone's control. Far more dangerous than angry blustering, Seymour was remembered to have mentioned to John Fowler shortly after the Princess Elizabeth left the queen's household, that, 'he would be glad to have the king in his custody ... and thought [the king] might be brought through the gallery to his chamber and so to his house [Seymour Place].' At the time, Fowler swore, Seymour had spoken in jest, 'meaning no harm'.[44] Jests about kidnapping the king by the sworn enemy of the lord protector failed to amuse the members of the Privy Council. When the Earl of Rutland ventured to mention to the Lord Admiral, 'how I thought his power was much diminished by [the queen's] death: He answered, 'Judge, Judge: the Council never feared me so much as they do now.'[45]

A loose cannon in a far from secure government, Seymour's headstrong and violent humours had lost Catherine's steadying hand. 'Truly, charity maketh men live like angels,' she had written only three years before. 'And of the most furious, unbridled, carnal men, maketh meek lambs.'[46] But without his wife, charity for Seymour had turned stone cold. Reckless, ruthless, bombastic and deluded, the Lord Admiral pursued the illusive phantom of power straight to the block. Arrested on 17 January 1549 by Sir Thomas Smith and Sir John Baker at Seymour Place, which ironically stood just next door to his brother's London home of Somerset House, the Lord Admiral was taken to the Tower. There he refused to answer any of the charges brought against him or to defend himself or to request clemency from his brother or from his nephew, the king. If Seymour had intended suicide, he had chosen an effective means. Found guilty of piracy for his intrigues with known pirates, of embezzlement on a grand scale and of conspiracy to marry the Princess Elizabeth, denounced for his precipitate marriage to the late queen, who, it was hinted, might have died by Seymour's orders if not by his hand, Thomas, Lord Seymour of Sudeley, was condemned to death. The lord protector later claimed that if Thomas had thrown himself on his brother's mercy, he could never have signed the death warrant.[47]

Seymour met his death on Tower Hill on the chilly morning of 20 March 1549, his bravado and self-deception apparent to the very end as he called upon his friends to avenge him. The first blow did not kill the former Lord Admiral. It took two strokes of the headsman's axe to sever Seymour's head from his body and for a short time, his bungled execution became a metaphor at court for brutality. 'And some because he seemed to die boldly, were apt to suppose him to die innocently.'[48] Hugh Latimer, Bishop of Worcester, was under no such illusion. The viper-tongued Latimer had visited Seymour in the Tower before his execution and commented extensively on Seymour's death in his sermons. 'And when a man hath two strokes with an axe who can tell but that between two strokes he doth repent? It is very hard to judge. Well, I will not go so nigh to work [speculate]; but this I will say, if they ask me what I think of his death, that he died very dangerously, irksomely, horribly.'[49]

Up to the end, Seymour insisted on viewing his brother as his worst enemy and plotted against him. Latimer, an eye witness, self-righteously informed the court of Seymour's conspiracies:

The man [Seymour] being in the Tower wrote certain papers which I saw myself. There were two little ones, one to my Lady Mary's grace, and another to my Lady Elizabeth's grace, tending to this end, that they should conspire against my Lord Protector's Grace … when he was ready to lay his head upon the block, he turns me to the Lieutenant's servant, and saith, 'Bid my servant speed the thing that he wots [knows] of.' Well, the word was overheard. His servant confessed these two papers, and they were found in a shoe of [Seymour's]: they were sewed between the soles of a velvet shoe. He made his ink so craftily and with such workmanship, as the like hath not been seen ... He made his pen of the aiglet of a point, that he plucked from his hose, and thus wrote these letters so seditiously ... surely he was a wicked man.[50]

Latimer's obvious personal hatred for the resourceful if wrong-headed Seymour caused talk at court and he 'was severely censured for the reflections which he made upon that bad, but ill-treated man.'[51]

The deluded Seymour, thinking Latimer his friend, made a last request, that the bishop preach his funeral sermon. Latimer had nothing good to say about the late Lord of Sudeley. 'he was a man the furthest from the fear of God that I ever knew or heard of in England ... surely he was a wicked man, and the realm is well rid of him.'[52] If Seymour had expected Latimer to preach a kindly sermon for the late queen's sake, he was in this, as in so much else, mistaken. Others were kinder – his brother-in-law, the Marquis of Northampton, Sir John Harington, Sir Nicholas Throckmorton. Throckmorton's epitaph read:

> But th'Admiral, my spokesman, was at home,
> Who stay'd, his Nephew's safety to regard.
> He was, at all essays, my perfect friend,
> And patron, too, unto his dying end.[53]

Seven months old and already an orphan, baby Mary Seymour was, at another of her father's final requests, transferred from the lord protector's household at Syon House to that of Katherine Willoughby, dowager Duchess of Suffolk's, at Grimsthorpe in Lincolnshire. Involved in her own romance with her master of the horse and with her own children to care for, the duchess was not overly eager to take on the added responsibility of Mary Seymour, her nurse, her governess, Elizabeth Aglionby, and her large retinue of attendants. The Duke of Somerset, who had custody of the baby while her father was in the Tower, had made certain that Mary was given an income to pay for her household. On 17 March 1549, Catherine Parr's daughter was granted for her maintenance for a year and a half, an income by the Privy Council from the receiver of the Court of Wards of just under £500 a year.[54] Evidently when custody of Mary and her retinue were transferred to the Duchess of Suffolk, custody of her income was not.

In the summer of 1549, the Duchess of Suffolk wrote to her good friend, William Cecil, secretary to the lord protectorlord protector, requesting money for Mary and her household. 'I have so wearied myself with letters to [the Duke and Duchess of Somerset],' she complained on 24 July, 'that I have none for you.'[55] The baby's household was an establishment as elaborate as her father had commanded it should be, because Mary Seymour was the daughter of a queen, but neither of the Somersets had any interest in supporting its members. Unimpressed with the late Lord Admiral's pretensions, and out of patience with the Somersets' indifference, as well as the cost, noise and nuisance of the retinue, the duchess would have liked to send the baby to the Marquis of Northampton, 'but,' she wrote to Cecil, 'he has a weak back for such a burden as I, and would receive her, but more willingly with the appurtenances.' Restored in blood on 22 January 1550, Mary Seymour was made legally eligible to inherit any family property to which she might subsequently fall heir.[56] Lands formerly owned by her parents, forfeited at her father's death, had already been snapped up by new owners. Mary Seymour disappears from the records shortly after this. As her maintenance grant was not renewed on 17 September 1550, when the original eighteen-month grant would have expired, Catherine Parr's 'so pretty a daughter', almost certainly died at Grimsthorpe sometime around her second birthday, and she is probably buried somewhere in the parish church at Edenham, which still contains memorials to the family of her guardian, the Duchess of Suffolk.

List of Abbreviations

APC	Acts of the Privy Council
BIHR	Bulletin of the Institute of Historical Research
BL	British Library
CAL. IPM	Calendar of Inquisitions Post Mortem
CCR	Calendar of Close Rolls
CFR	Calendar of Fine Rolls
CPR	Calendar of Patent Rolls
CSP	Calendar of State Papers
CW1	Transactions of the Cumberland and Westmorland Antiquarian and Archaeological Society, Old Series
CW2	Transactions of the Cumberland and Westmorland Antiquarian and Archaeological Society, New Series
EHR	English Historical Review
HMC	Historical Manuscripts Commission
L&P	Letters and Papers, Foreign & Domestic of the Reign of Henry VIII
PCC	Prerogative Court of Canterbury
NA	National Archives, London
ROT. PARL.	Rotuli Parlimentorum (Rolls of Parliament)
SP	State Papers
TRHS	Transactions of the Royal Historical Society
V&A	Victoria and Albert Museum
VCH	The Victoria History of the Counties of England

Notes

Introduction

1. The majority of the religious beliefs of Anne Boleyn, the first queen to reign after the separation of the English Church from the church of Rome, were still firmly and understandably rooted in Roman Catholicism. Although she believed in the separation and supported the publication of religious works in the vernacular, she desired the reformation of abuses in monasteries and not their wholesale dissolution. In 1536 as queen, Anne refused to support the publication of a work which 'approved of justification by faith and communion in both kinds.' Justification by faith was a central and pivotal tenant of Protestant belief and Anne's reluctance to support such a tenant shows a reluctance to enter into the full spirit of the Reformation. For a discussion of Anne Boleyn's religious beliefs, see Retha M. Warnicke, *The Rise and Fall of Anne Boleyn: Family Politics at the Court of Henry VIII*, Cambridge, 1989, 153–162. While technically a Protestant, Anne of Cleves' impact on the Henrician settlement was so slight and the duration of her marriage so short that her claims to the title must be considered negligible.

Chapter 1

1. CPR: Henry VII, 1494-1509, 565.
2. The principal Parr holdings in the northwest, primarily in southern Westmorland, consisted of over 5,000 acres of land, only 700 of which were arable. This also included 12 manors, 46 tenements in Kendal, and other lands in 13 Westmorland hamlets, as well as smaller holdings in Cumberland and Lancashire. These holdings brought in an estimated income of about £150 per annum. Maud Parr's inheritance included a moiety of the manor of Green's Norton and some subsidiary lands in Northamptonshire, the manors and towns of Stonegrave, Nunnington and Ness in Yorkshire, the two manors of Kegworth and Long Clawson overlapping the Leicestershire–Nottinghamshire border, and lands in Lincolnshire. The latter were clustered in two areas. One area was between Sleaford and Boston and included the manor of Beesby, with rents in Heckington, Helpringham, Hale and Folkingham. The second area was on the coast, east of Louth, and included the manor of Maltby, with land in Mablethorpe, Theddlethorpe, Great Carlton, South Reston, Gayton, Markby, Asserby and Huttoft that formed a chain running roughly southeast from Louth to Skegness.
3. Apart from one example of her signature as a child in which she spelled her name *Katheryn*, Catherine Parr always signed her name *Kateryn Parr, KP*. Modern convention spells the name 'Catherine' and that has been used here for convenience of reference.
4. Susan E. James, 'Sir William Parr of Kendal: Part I, 1434–1471', *CW2*, XCIII (1993), 100–114, and Susan E. James, 'Sir William Parr of Kendal: Part II, 1471–1483', *CW2*, XCIV (1994), 105–120.
5. *York Civic Records*, A. Raine (ed.), III, in *The Yorkshire Archaeological Society Record Series*, CVI, 1942, 49–51, and L&P, 2, i, no.1861, and ii, p.1472.
6. L&P, 1, i, no.132(41) and (86).
7. L&P, 1, ii, no.2684(64) and L&P, 1, i, no.257(1).
8. CPR: Henry VII, II, 163; L&P, 1, i, no.218(55).
9. L&P, 2, ii, p.1490.
10. The closeness of Sir Thomas and Lady Parr to the king and queen is illustrated in their wills. In his will, Sir Thomas mentions 'my signet that the king's grace gave me' (NA: PROB 11/19; Image Reference 45/34), and in her will, Maud mentions 'my beads of lacquer allemagne dressed with gold which the said Queen's grace gave me', and 'a tablet with pictures of the king and queen' and 'a Katherine wheel of diamonds with

four pearls set in it' (NA: PROB 11/24; Image Reference 149/110), which may also have been a gift from Catherine of Aragon.

11. Kirkoswald was a manor belonging to Thomas, Lord Dacre, and held by Sir Thomas Parr as a feoffee of Dacre's mother, Mabel, Lady Dacre (d.1503). Lady Dacre was Parr's paternal aunt.

12. L&P, 1, i, no.438; L&P, 2, ii, no.2932.

13. Parr's partners in this venture were his stepfather, Sir Nicholas Vaux, his brother-in-law, Sir Thomas Cheyney, his stepbrother, John Colt, and Sir William Saye, the father-in-law of the Earl of Essex. CPR: 1494–1509, no.228.

14. The tomb was destroyed together with the church at the Dissolution. For a sketch of its appearance, see BL: Addit. MS 45,131 f.109b.

15. Dakota Lee Hamilton (*The Household of Queen Katherine Parr*, D.Phil. thesis, Oxford, 1992, 3, quotes a wardrobe bill in the Public Records Office (NA: E101/423/12, f.6v) as being issued, 'For the Maundy ... for livery cloth to thirty-one poor women, each for one year of the queen's life', which would place Catherine's birthdate in 1513. Apart from the difficulty Maud Parr would have experienced in producing Catherine in the same year in which she gave birth to William on 14 August, this date is incorrect as the bill has been misquoted and actually reads: 'For the Maundy: Mr. Bartholemew ... for lxxvij elles d of linen cloth for xxj poor women for the Maundy, every one of them having ij elles at price the elle xd.' On 14 July 1523, Maud Parr stated in a letter to Lord Dacre (BL: Addit. MS 24,965, f. 23) that her daughter had not yet reached her twelfth birthday. She also offered on that date to pay fifty marks a year in a marriage contract until Catherine turned twelve, implying that at least a year would elapse before that day. As Catherine's burial record of 5 September 1548 declared that she had passed her thirty-sixth birthday, the likeliest date of her birth is between late July and the end of August 1512.

16. Joseph Nicolson and Richard Burn, *The History and Antiquities of the Counties of Westmorland and Cumberland*, London, 1777, 44.

17. J. Nicolson & R. Burn: 1777, 45–46, and the archaeological findings during the excavation of Kendal Castle by Barbara Harbottle as published in Abbot Hall *Quarto*, V, no.4 (January 1968); VI, no.4 (January 1969); VII, no.4 (January 1970); X, no.1 (August 1972), Kendal.

18. In 1504, Parr purchased from his cousin, Thomas Tunstall of Dowcra, two tenements in Finkle Street and one in Stramongate in the town of Kendal. These he probably used as lodgings during his visits in the area. William Farrer, *Records Relating to the Barony of Kendal*, John F. Curwen (ed.), 3 vols, Kendal (1923–26), I, 54.

19. Great Kimble had belonged to Richard Empson, Henry VII's hated councilor. The manor was forfeited at Empson's death to the Crown. The Parrs lost their grant of the manor when Thomas Empson, Richard's son and heir, was restored to his father's lands by act of Parliament in November 1512.

20. L&P, 2, ii, no.2932.

21. L&P, Addenda, 1, i, no.196.

22. Parr leased Rye House from its owner, his cousin Andrew Agard.

23. The Fitzhugh holdings which Parr inherited included twenty-three manors plus farmlands and woodland in the North Riding of Yorkshire and the palatinate of Durham. These tended to cluster in the river valleys of the Tees, the Swale and the Ure. The most important of these were the lower Uredale manors of West and East Tansfield, Askrigg manor in Wensleydale, Sedbergh and Dent on the Dee River in Dentdale, as well as Ravensworth Castle, the Fitzhughs' principal seat. Parr leased out Ravensworth during his lifetime and apparently never lived there. From the Fitzhugh estate, too, Parr inherited the sponsorship of Jervaulx Abbey, one of the most important religious foundations in the north. The Fitzhughs had been among the abbey's lay founders and Jervaulx was their chief burial place.

24. At the death of Lord Fitzhugh, Parr began to style himself 'Thomas Parr, Lord Fitzhugh'. His cousin, Lord Dacre of the South, took exception, maintaining that by legal inheritance and seniority the title belonged to him. The king made no move to interfere and Dacre kept the title.

25. Sir Thomas Lovell (d.1524) was a staunch supporter of Henry VII, who created him Chancellor of the Exchequer for life on 12 October 1485. That same year, he was elected speaker of the House of Commons. Lovell also served as treasurer of Henry VII's household and was involved with Empson and Dudley in the prosecution of *prerogativa regis*. He did not however suffer their fate and under the new king, Henry VIII, he found favor and was reappointed chancellor of the Exchequer.

26. After Parr's death, Lovell acquired another associate master in Sir Richard Weston. Weston then acquired the mastership and held it jointly with Sir Edward Belknap until 1521. H.E. Bell, *An Introduction to the History and Records of the Court of Wards and Liveries*, Cambridge, 1953, 6–10.

27. The bill is a grant to William Boughton of the wardship of the female heirs of John Danvers of Wiltshire, an area outside of Parr's sphere of influence thus eliminating the possibility of a feodary interest as the reason

for Parr's signature. The date of 11 May 1519 (a year and a half after Parr's death) has been inserted on the bill and by a different hand (NA: C82/476, f.20). As the disposition of the wardship of the various Danvers heirs extended over some time (see, L&P, 1, i, no.381(25) and L&P, 2, ii, p.1490), this would probably account for the later date entered on the signet bill.

28. Susan E. James, 'Parr Memorials in Kendal Parish Church', *CW2*, XCII (1992), 99–103.

29. NA: PROB 11/19; Image Reference 45/34. The provision was made out of land he had inherited from the Fitzhugh estates that had once belonged to the Scropes of Masham. The fourth Lord Scrope had sold them in 1443 to Lord Fitzhugh for £2,000 and Scrope's descendants were trying (unsuccessfully) to recover them. H.H.E. Craster, *A History of Northumberland*, IX, Newcastle-on-Tyne & London, 1909, 80.

30. Tunstall was Parr's cousin, Sir William Parr of Horton, Parr's younger brother, and Dr. Melton was in all probability Parr's chaplain.

31. Parr's inquisition post mortem gives the date of his death as 12 November but the chantry in the church of St. Anne's, Blackfriars, which was endowed for prayers to be said for his soul, celebrated these masses on 11 November, and this, together with the inscription on his tomb, establish the correct date beyond doubt.

32. Anne Green had been married at the age of eighteen to Sir Nicholas Vaux of Harrowden, a widower nearly three times her age and stepfather of Sir Thomas Parr. Anne was the second wife of Sir Nicholas and the mother of his only son and heir, William.

33. In Alison Plowden's words: 'Whatever her private inclinations, it took an exceedingly strong-minded lady to face the difficulties of life on her own, especially if she had young children to think of, or to withstand family pressures and the deeply-ingrained prejudices of society against the independent single woman.' Alison Plowden, *Tudor Women: Queens and Commoners*, New York, 1979, 117.

34. Catherine Parr to Sir Thomas Seymour, 1547, Dent-Brocklehurst MS, Sudeley Castle.

35. Ruth Kelso, *Doctrine for the Lady of the Renaissance*, Urbana, 1956, 78.

36. Katherine Usher Henderson and Barbara F. McManus, *Half Humankind: Contexts and Texts of the Controversy About Women in England, 1540–1640*, Urbana & Chicago, 1985, 27.

37. Diane Willen, 'Women and Religion in Early Modern Europe: Public and Private Worlds', in *Women in Reformation and Counter-Reformation Europe*, Sherrin Marshall (ed.), Bloomington & Indianapolis, 1989, 149, quoting William Gouge, *Of domesticall duties*, London, 1622, 259, and Wendy Wall, *The Imprint of Gender: Authorship and Publication in the English Renaissance*, Ithaca & London, 1993, 280–281.

38. 'The ability to make a will constitutes one of the significant legal rights that historians identify in determining the gendered power relations within the culture.' W. Wall: 1993, 295.

39. For a discussion of 'the controversy about women' in sixteenth-century England, see, K. Henderson & B. McManus: 1985, and *The Renaissance Englishwoman in Print: Counterbalancing the Canon*, Anne M. Haselkorn and Betty S. Travitsky (eds), Amherst, 1990, 3–41; D. Willen: 1989, 140–165; Retha M. Warnicke, *Women of the English Renaissance and Reformation*, Westport, 1983.

40. John Strype, *Ecclesiastical Memorials of Henry VIII, Edward VI, and Mary I*, 3 vols, London, 1822, II, i, 132.

41. This attitude is apparent in William's letters from the mid-1530s commenting on his mother's disposition of family monies and lands in her will. NA: SP1/74, f.97 and NA: SP1/79, ff.148–49.

Chapter 2

1. NA: PROB 11/24; Image Reference 149/110

2. L&P, 4, i, no.1939.

3. NA: E/314/22, ff.11, 40.

4. CUL:Inc.4.J.1.2 (3570), *Horae ad Usum Sarum*, 19b.

5. Elizabeth's husband, Thomas, Lord Vaux, may have had something to do with this. Although a poet of some ability, Vaux was stubborn, spoiled and improvident, as well as ultra-conservative in religion, opposing the establishment of the English Church. His mismanagement of his estates caused his wife numerous problems and forced the sale of much of their lands. Catherine's brother, however, maintained a good relationship with the Vauxs. William made Thomas Vaux one of his trustees upon reaching his majority in June 1535 (L&P, 8, no.962(30)), and sent his poet cousin a book in the fall of the same year (L&P, 9, no.697). For the Vauxs' troubles with Cromwell, see Chapter 5 in this volume.

6. *Renaissance Englishwoman*: 1990, 20–22.

7. For a discussion of the negativist approach to women in sixteenth-century England's inherited tradition, see K. Henderson & B. McManus: 1985, 4–11, and W. Wall: 1993, 279–283. Even such noted sixteenth-

century educators as Juan Luis Vives and John Aylmer temporized their enthusiasm for female education with admonitions that 'in company [a woman should] hold her tongue demurely, and let few see her, and none at all hear her.' Quoted in Wall (281). Women, like children, should be seen and not heard.

8. K. Henderson & B. McManus: 1985, 12–13. John Knox found primacy in women in any form 'monstrous'.

9. Catherine Parr, *The Lamentation of a Sinner*, London, 28 March 1548, f. Fviib.

10. John N. King, 'Patronage and Piety: The Influence of Catherine Parr', in *Silent but for the Word*, Margaret Patterson Hannay (ed.), Kent, OH, 1985, 44–49; James K. McConica, *English Humanists and Reformation Politics under Henry VIII and Edward VI*, Oxford, 1965, 215–280; C. Fenno Hoffman, Jr., 'Catherine Parr as a Woman of Letters', in *Huntington Library Quarterly*, 23 (1959), 349–367, for the mainstream view.

11. Maria Dowling, 'The Gospel and the Court: Reform under Henry VIII', in *Protestantism and the National Church in the Sixteenth Century*, Peter Lake and Maria Dowling (eds), New York & Sydney, 1987, 59–71; David Starkey, *The Reign of Henry VIII, Personalities and Politics*, London, 1985, 140–1; William P. Haugaard, 'Katherine Parr: the Religious Convictions of a Renaissance Queen', in *Renaissance Quarterly*, 22, 1969, 350–1, for the minority viewpoint.

12. Geoffrey Anstruther, *Vaux of Harrowden*, Newport, 1953, 7.

13. John Fisher, Bishop of Rochester, 'A Morning Remembrance, A Sermon on the Death of Margaret, Countess of Richmond', and Charles Henry Cooper, *Memoir of Margaret, Countess of Richmond and Derby*, Cambridge, 1874, 113–14.

14. C. Cooper: 1874, 43.

15. Henry Percy, 4th Earl of Northumberland, had four sons – Henry Algernon (1478–1527), who later became the fifth earl in 1489 under the cognomen 'Henry, the Magnificent' for his lavish collecting propensities, Sir William Percy, Alan Percy, who entered the church, and Josceline Percy. Just which son was educated at Colyweston is not clear.

16. S. James: 1994, 105–06.

17. Maurice Addison Hatch, *The Ascham Letters: An Annotated Translation of the Latin Correspondence*, unpublished Ph.D. thesis, Cornell University, New York, 1948, 153.

18. CUL:Inc.4.J.1.2 (3570), *Horae ad Usum Sarum*, 58b, 77b–78a.

19. M. Hatch: 1948, 151.

20. Jane's father, John Colt, and Thomas Parr were stepbrothers who despite the difference in their ages maintained a brotherly relationship. Thomas' father, Sir William Parr, had married in 1467 as his first wife, the widow of Thomas Colt, Joanna Trusbut, mother of three-year-old John and his two small sisters. Sir William was their guardian and raised them at Netherhall in Essex, a Colt property. When John was twelve, Sir William Parr sold his wardship and marriage to Sir John Elrington, treasurer of the royal household, who married him to his daughter. Two years later, in 1478, John's stepbrother, Thomas Parr, was born to Sir William's second wife, Elizabeth Fitzhugh. Although John Colt was fourteen years older, he and Thomas Parr behaved in the manner of brothers, maintaining a close relationship. They were business partners as well in the venture in the English Pale at Guisnes and Hammes.

21. D. Hamilton: 1992, 311–12.

22. NA: PROB 11/24; Image Reference 149/110

23. Maud Parr appears to have used her husband's Latin *Horae ad Usum Sarum*, but beyond that and Lord Dacre's comments on her linguistic abilities, no other measure of Maud's abilities in Latin has survived.

24. BL: Addit. MS 24,965, f.134b.

25. D. Hamilton: 1992, 311–12. According to Hamilton, 'it would be something of a feat to use the More household as a model and to leave out Latin!'

26. Hilda L. Smith, 'Humanist education and the Renaissance concept of woman', in *Women and Literature in Britain, 1500–1700*, Helen Wilcox (ed.), Cambridge, 1996, 21.

27. H. Smith: 1996, 26.

28. Anthony Martienssen, *Queen Katherine Parr*, London, 1973, 21–28.

29. H. Smith: 1996, 16.

30. NA: PROB 11/24; Image Reference 149/110

31. BL: Addit. MS 24,965, f.103 (formerly 201).

32. CSP: Venetian, 1534–1554, no.116, Cardinal Pole to Cardinal Giovanni Matteo Giberti of Verona, 10 August 1536.

33. For this and the following quotes of Tunstall, Erasmus and More, Charles Sturge, *Cuthbert Tunstal*, London, New York & Toronto, 1938, 23–30, 52–55, and 72–78.

34. C. Parr: 1548, f. Fviia.

35. CUL: Inc.4.J.1.2 (3570), *Horae ad Usum Sarum*, 44b, 58b, 80b.

36. CUL: Inc.4.J.1.2 (3570): 20a.

37. Catherine Parr, *Prayers or Meditations*, 6 November 1547, f. Diib.

38. M. Hatch: 1948, 223.

39. BL: Cott. MS Nero C.x.f.8.

40. BL: Cott. MS Vespasian F.3.f.37.

41. While the date of this letter has been somewhat in doubt, it was almost certainly written on 20 September 1547 at Catherine's dower manor of Hanworth. It concerns not a request to the Princess Mary to begin an English translation of Erasmus' *Paraphrase of St. John*, as has been so often stated, but a request to polish an already existent, nearly complete translation, presumably in preparation for its publication the following January. Catherine rarely if ever stayed at Hanworth before Henry's death. However, a letter written to Sir Edward North on 14 September 1547 in the queen's own hand (NA: E101/426/3) from Hanworth, proves that she was in residence there during that month. As Elizabeth was under Catherine's guardianship at the time and living in her household and Mary was quite ill (a fact mentioned in the letter) in September 1547, the dating of the letter to this year seems to be secure.

42. BL: Harleian MS 5087.

43. See Chapter 12 in this volume.

44. C. Parr: 1548, ff. Fviiib-Gia.

45. M. Hatch: 1948, 154.

46. Joan Simon, *Education and Society in Tudor England*, Cambridge, 1967, 103.

47. J. A. Giles, *Six Old English Chronicles*, London, 1848, 314–17.

48. Although written nearly 300 years later, Jane Austen's comment in *Persuasion* on the pervasive prejudice of received literature is apt. When Anne Elliot argues with Captain Harville for woman's faithfulness, Harville replies: 'Well, Miss Elliot,' (lowering his voice) 'as I was saying, we shall never agree I suppose upon this point. No man and woman would, probably. But let me observe that all histories are against you, all stories, prose and verse … I do not think I ever opened a book in my life which had not something to say upon woman's inconstancy. Songs and proverbs all talk of woman's fickleness. But perhaps you will say, these were all written by men.' Anne answers: 'Perhaps I shall. – Yes, yes, if you please, no reference to examples in books. Men have had every advantage of us in telling their own story. Education has been theirs in so much higher a degree; the pen has been in their hands. I will not allow books to prove any thing.' (Jane Austen, *Persuasion*, The World's Classics edition, Oxford, 1971 (for 1817), 220–221.)

49. BL: Addit. MS 46,348, f.208a.

50. BL: Addit. MS 46,348, f.208a and *Literary Remains of Edward VI*, J. G. Nichols (ed.), London, 1857, cccxxvi.

51. NA: E315/161, f.32b.

52. BL: Addit. MS 46,348, f.208a.

53. C. Sturge: 1938, 56.

54. C. Parr: 1548, f. Gva.

55. Richard Eales, *Chess, The History of a Game*, London, 1985, 71–76.

56. Catherine's apothecary bill for the first six months of her marriage to Henry VIII contains twenty-three closely written, double-sided folios (NA: E315/161, f.22 following).

57. 'Item a Testament of Mr. Neville's under the Bishop's seal,' given Mr. Neville's religious conservativism was probably in Latin. Society of Antiquaries MS 129 pt. A, f.219b.

58. NA: E101/424/12, f.189.

59. BL: Addit. MS 46,348, f.208b.

60. M. Hatch: 1948, 153.

61. The Middletons were a family linked by gentry feudalism to the Parrs. Edward Middleton served under Sir Thomas Parr as parker of Ravensworth in Yorkshire, a property inherited by Sir Thomas from the Fitzhugh family (NA: PROB 11/19; Image Reference 45/34) and Thomas Middleton served his son, William, in the latter's household in 1553 (NA: E101/520/9). From 1520 until he came of age in 1522, Sir William Parr of Horton held the wardship of Gervase Middleton, the younger son and eventual heir of Thomas Middleton of Beetham and his wife, Joanna Strickland of Sizergh in Westmorland (L&P, 3, i, p.1541). Joanna was the daughter of Agnes Parr, Parr of Horton's aunt. Whether or not Reginald Middleton was a member of this family is not certain, but he may well have been thus earning Anne's interest in his career.

62. M. Hatch: 1948, 153.

63. *Privy Purse Expenses of Princess Mary*, Frederick Madden (ed.), London, 1831, 144.

64. D. Hamilton: 1992, 338–339.

65. John Venn and J. K. Venn, *Alumni Cantabrigienses*, Cambridge, 1927, part I, vol. III, 312–313.

66. NA: DL 42/133, ff.83a, 96b, 120a, 164a, 175a. Of Parr, Thomas Fuller wrote: 'Much was he given to music

and poetry.' (Thomas Fuller, *The History of the Worthies of England*, II, London, 1660, 535).

67. L&P, 21, i, no.963(155–6).

68. Roger Ascham, *The Whole Works*, Dr. Giles (ed.), 3 vols, London, 1864, I, i, 77–78. The original inscription is in the Folger Shakespeare Library in Washington, D.C.

69. J. Venn & J. K. Venn: 1927, part I, vol. I, 150; Charles Henry Cooper and Thompson Cooper, *Athenae Cantabrigienses*, II, Cambridge, 1858, 527; HMC: 2nd Report, 85, No. 28; STC 3059.4 (1586).

70. M. Hatch: 1948, 318.

71. BL: Lansdowne MS 1236, f.11.

72. See Chapter 12 in this volume.

73. C. Parr: 1548, f. Bviiia. For skeptical opinions on Catherine Parr's intellectual capacities, see Maria Dowling, *Humanism in the Age of Henry VIII*, 66, 211, and footnote 11 above.

74. BL: Cott. MS Otho C.x.231.

75. John Bale, *Illustrium Majoris Britanniae Scriptorum*, Wesel, 1548, f.238a.

76. Nicholas Udall, Preface to the translation of the 'Book of Luke', D. Erasmus, Paraphrases, 31 January 1548, ff.cciii/a–cciiii/b.

Chapter 3

1. NA: E101/426/3, f.21

2. NA: Star Chamber Proceedings 2/32/16; NA: SP1/80, ff.22–23; NA: SP1/85, f.76; W.T. Mellows, 'The Last Days of Petersborough Monastery', *Publications of the Northamptonshire Record Society*, 12, LX, lxxxi, for some examples of Sir William Parr of Horton's dealings in the county.

3. NA: SP49/2, ff.11–12.

4. Parr had served very briefly as 'knight and chamberlain to the Queen' during the journey of Henry VIII's sister, Margaret, the dowager Queen of Scotland, from the Scottish border to London during the spring of 1516. A. Raine: 1942, 49.

5. Frequent requests to Wolsey for a resident physician for the duke imply perhaps that Richmond was not always in robust health (L&P, 4, i, no. 1540; L&P, 4, ii, no. 4305).

6. Parr's salary was £26 13s 4d per annum, but most household officials in noble or royal households found supplemental ways of enriching themselves. One of the most important was through influence peddling.

7. Parr dutifully appeared at most meetings of the northern council between August and November 1525. His name does not appear again until November-December 1526 and then only briefly. During 1527 Parr began to appear at meetings once more on a fairly regular basis, probably the result of the household civil wars that had broken out, but after that year he attended only two more sessions – May 1528 and May 1530.

8. NA: SP1/35, ff.232-33. Although Richmond travelled from London to Rye House in a litter due to ill health, by the end of his journey, in late August, he had recovered and was reported to be in good health. His illness may have had something to do with the sudden separation of a six-year-old child from those who had attended his nursery and all surroundings familiar to him, although he did take his nurse with him. She was pensioned off in 1530. L&P, 4, i, no.1540, no.1596, no.1954; L&P, 4, ii, no.4305; L&P, 5, no.1799(23).

9. J. Hurstfield, 'Political Corruption in Modern England', *History* , LII (1967), 16–34; Lawrence Stone, *Family and Fortune*, Oxford, 1973, 56.

10. BL: Sloane MS no.1523, f.37b.

11. L&P, 9, no.427.

12. The fact that George Throckmorton's brother, Michael, was a member of Cardinal Pole's household did not improve the Throckmorton family's fortunes. This fact and the fact that two of George and Catherine's sons, John and Robert, remained staunch Roman Catholics has been used to connect Catherine Parr with their convictions (Diarmaid MacCulloch, *Thomas Cranmer, A Life*, New Haven & London, 1996, 313–14, 326). However, Nicholas, Clement, Kellam and George Throckmorton, the younger, all broke with their parents' religious position, becoming supporters of the English Reformed Church. And these, not their Catholic brethren, were taken into Catherine's household when she became queen.

13. *The Legend of Sir Nicholas Throckmorton*, John Gough Nichols (ed.), Roxburghe Club, V, London, 1874, 3, 6. Although composed by his nephew, this poem recounts Nicholas Throckmorton's no doubt oft-told memories of his career.

14. L&P, 4, i, no.1947. One comment on the chain of command in Richmond's household a few years later is found in a letter written to Cromwell by Anthony Dryland, who was on his way to join the household in 1532. 'I hear he [Parr] is good to me … but all lies in Mr. Magnus, to whom I have spoken … by him all is ruled.' Thomas Magnus (d.1550) was the Archdeacon of East Riding and treasurer of the wars in the north. L&P, 5, no.981.

15. *Wolsey Correspondence*, Camden Miscellany, III, 78, lxxi.

16. L&P, 4, i, nos 1141, 1142, 1143.

17. The Cottons were friends and 'playfellows' of the king. In June 1531, for instance, George Cotton won £7 2s by outshooting Henry, and in the same month the king was defeated in three sets of tennis by both brothers in Greenwich Park. L&P, 5, no.1799. Ten years after Richmond's death, they joined the household of Edward, Prince of Wales. L&P, Addenda, I, i, no.1636.

18. Parr is quoted as saying, 'If you do the common sort of people nineteen courtesies together, yet you may lose their love, if you go but over the stile before them.' David Lloyd described Parr as 'no man being more beloved by the vulgar, no man less in love with them.' David Lloyd, *State Worthies*, London, 1670, 203.

19. L&P, 4, i, no.1954.

20. L&P, 4, ii, no.1954. Palsgrave later struggled to refine the poor quality of Latin that Richmond had been taught in order to say his prayers.

21. L&P, 4, ii, no.3135.

22. For examples of Parr's involvement in various quarrels, L&P, 6, nos 9, 1337, 1463.

23. L&P, 4, ii, no.3135.

24. L&P, 4, i, no.1596.

25. Somewhat ironically, he was hired fifteen years later, in May 1544, by the queen, Catherine Parr, to copy out a few of her dower patents and given as payment ten shillings and a doublet of crimson satin for the privilege (NA: E315/161, f.35).

26. NA: SP1/55, ff.14-15.

27. *The Correspondence of Sir Thomas More*, Elizabeth Frances Rogers (ed.), Princeton, 1947, 405.

28. E. Rogers: 1947, 403–04.

29. Provision for Palsgrave's retirement may have been arranged by the Parrs. On 7 November 1545, he was given the rectory of Wadenhoe in Northamptonshire where he resided until his death in 1554. Wadenhoe, on the edge of Rockingham Forest, was located in the heart of the Parr sphere of influence in Northamptonshire. William Parr of Horton succeeded his stepfather, Sir Nicholas Vaux, as keeper of Rockingham Castle and of the surrounding forest in 1523 where he had been ranger since April 1511.

30. E. Rogers: 1947, 404–05.

31. NA: SP1/50, ff.197-98, a letter from Thomas Magnus, whose own part in the royal displeasure over the state of Richmond's household is implied by the tone of the letter.

32. L&P, 4, ii, no.3069.

33. L&P, 4, ii, no.4536.

Chapter 4

1. *Renaissance Englishwoman*: 1990, 10.

2. BL: Addit. MS 24,965, f.230b (formerly f. 200).

3. BL: Addit. MS 24,965, f.23 and f.24 (formerly f.57 and f.58).

4. Besides having another daughter to provide for, Maud Parr had recently had the additional expense of one thousand marks in the form of a forced loan to the king.

5. BL: Addit. MS 24,965, f.173 (formerly f. 59).

6. BL: Addit. MS 24,965, f.38 (formerly f. 68).

7. This was Thomas Howard, Earl of Surrey, and later third Duke of Norfolk, who succeeded his father as Lord Treasurer on 4 December 1522 and held the office until February 1547.

8. BL: Addit. MS 24,965, f.200b (formerly f. 165).

9. Dacre had married a northern heiress, Elizabeth Greystoke, granddaughter of Ralph, Lord Greystoke, and had benefited substantially from the match as Elizabeth had, due to the death of her father, become her grandfather's sole heir.

10. BL: Addit. MS 24,965, f.103 (formerly f. 201).

11. BL: Addit. MS 24,965, f.230b (formerly f. 200).

12. Lord Scrope managed a good match for his son and heir, John, with Catherine Clifford, the daughter of Henry Clifford, Earl of Cumberland.

13. Sir William Fitzwilliam went on to become Lord High Admiral of England (1536) and first Earl of Southampton (1537). His wife, Mabel Clifford, sister of the first Earl of Cumberland, was a gentlewoman to Catherine of Aragon and thus well known to Maud Parr. Fitzwilliam had been a friend and business associate of both Sir Thomas and Sir William Parr (BL: Addit. MS 21,481, f.289). After Sir Thomas Parr's death, Fitzwilliam remained a good friend to the Parrs. He not only helped Lady Parr engineer her son's marriage in 1527, and lent her money for that purpose, but some years later, in 1536, his influence was crucial in saving Catherine Parr's second husband, Lord Latimer, from the block during the Pilgrimage of Grace.

14. Chief Justice Sir Edward Montague was an influential member of Northamptonshire society. He was a close friend of Sir Thomas Parr's but quarreled continually with Sir William Parr of Horton, especially over Parr's alleged mishandling of the office of ranger for Rockingham Forest. Sir Harris Nicholas, *Proceedings and Ordinances of the Privy Council of England*, VII (1540-1542), 223. Parr's pestering of Montague about his rights and the peccadilloes of his neighbors may have gone a long way toward alienating the man. HMC: Buccleuch, I, 221.

15. *The Letters of Stephen Gardiner*, James Arthur Muller (ed.), Cambridge, 1933, 161, a letter written 5 November 1545 from Gardiner to Sir William Paget: 'the olde Erle of Essex, Bowser ... '; L&P, 16, no. 878(26), 'William, Lord Parr, and Dame Anne Bowser, his wife (16 February 1541)'; NA: PROB 11/24; Image Reference 149/110, 'to my lady Bowser ... when she lieth with my son.'

16. The Saye lands were concentrated mostly in Hertfordshire, including the manors of Benington, Sawbridgeworth, Broxbourne, Hoddesdon and Baas. Sir William Saye had been a friend of Sir Thomas Parr's and was one of Parr's partners in the leasehold of Hammes Castle in the English Pale of Calais in 1510. CPR: 1494–1509, no. 228.

17. Essex owned two manors in Buckinghamshire, four in Cambridgeshire, six in Suffolk. Cal. IPM, Richard III, 415.

18. *Letters of ... Gardiner.* 1933, 161–2.

19. On 16 March 1534, Essex wrote to Cromwell complaining of Richard Stannesby, former bailiff of Essex's land in Bildeston, Suffolk. Stannesby was trying to claim the earl's stream as his own freehold, which, Essex declared to Cromwell, was outrageous as Stannesby had 'made the covenant between my lady Parre and me, and is himself one of the feoffees' for the earl's ownership of both property and stream. The letter also describes how Essex was legally bound not to 'diminish' the holdings that were to descend to his daughter and her husband. L&P, 7, no. 332. For similar examples of Essex's legal and financial problems, NA: SP1/141, ff.218–19; NA: SP1/82, ff.289-90; L&P, 10, no. 1057; L&P, 14, i, no. 411.

20. NA: PROB 11/24; Image Reference 149/110.

21. L&P, 4, iii, no. 5508.

22. *Allegations for Marriage Licences issued by the Bishop of London (1520–1610)*, I, Harleian Society, XXV, London, 1887, 5.

23. Susan E. James, 'A Tudor Divorce: The Marital History of William Parr, Marquis of Northampton', *CW2*, XC, (1990), 199-204.

24. In this she was at odds with her own parents who had supported Anne Boleyn and the establishment of the new religion. On Thursday, 15 July 1529, the Countess of Essex made a deposition swearing that Prince Arthur and Catherine of Aragon had slept together. In 1536 when Princess Mary made her submission to her father, Essex is reported to have told the king that this 'was a game that would cost him his head, for the injurious language he had used against the Princess.' L&P, 4, iii, no. 5778; L&P, 11, no. 5 (p.8).

25. If William did indeed attend Cambridge as Venn claims, it was sometime between 1527, the year of his marriage, and 1534, the year of his majority. J. Venn & J. Venn: 1927, part I, vol. III, 312-13.

26. That William Parr visited Richmond frequently after his marriage is indicated in letters written by him while staying with Richmond in his household. W. Farrer: 1923–26, I, 62–63. He seems to have been on excellent terms, too, with Richmond's wife, Mary Howard, and he stayed with her at Kenninghall in Norfolk the autumn after Richmond's death. L&P, Addenda, 1, i, no. 1097.

27. NA: PROB 11/24; Image Reference 149/110.

28. L&P, 1, i, no. 563(10).

29. See the discussion in M. E. James, 'Obedience and Dissent in Henrician England: The Lincolnshire Rebellion, 1536', *Past and Present*, 48 (August 1970), 3–78. Also, L&P, 2, i, no. 1363. The Roos family apparently contained the genetic seeds of insanity which incessant intermarriage spread through the Lincolnshire gentry. Lord Roos of Hamlake was a confirmed lunatic, (M. E. James, 49), as was Lord Borough and Sir George Tailboys, all of whom had Roos ancestry.

30. Edward Borough served as a feoffee for Thomas Kiddall. L&P, 5, no. 1694, and L&P, 11, no. 943(7).

31. Maud Parr, still by her own statement in good health, made her will on 20 May 1529 (NA: PROB 11/24; Image Reference 149/110). The wording of the will implies that Catherine's marriage had only recently taken place and the making of the will itself may have been inspired by the recently concluded marriage of Lady Parr's elder daughter.

32. His erstwhile daughter-in-law, Elizabeth Owen, daughter of Sir David Owen and his wife, Anne Devereux, complained that her husband was a pawn in his father's hands, too terrified of him to defy him, and she was reduced to petitioning Cromwell for an income with which to feed her children. L&P, 18, i, no. 66 (p.46); L&P, 7, no. 56; L&P, 8, no. 597-8; L&P, 12, ii, no. 1073-74; L&P, 13, i, no. 311. For Catherine's pension to Elizabeth, NA: E315/340, f.66a.

33. L&P, 12, ii, nos 704, 1492.

34. L&P, 6, p.241.

35. L&P, 6, no. 601.

36. D. Willen: 1989, 148-152.

37. NA: PROB 11/24; Image Reference 149/110. To ensure that Borough had repayment of the debt, Maud named him a trustee for her son's estates until young William should come of age (L&P, 8, no. 962(30)).

38. Maud Parr's travels, including the journey into Lincolnshire, are indicated by the bequests which she left in her will to three churches attached to manors which she owned. Maltby in Lincolnshire was close to Catherine at Gainsborough; Nunnington manor was only eight miles from Sheriff Hutton, where Maud's son, William, was living in the household of the young Duke of Richmond during the late 1520s; and Kegworth manor was used by the Parrs as a hunting box for excursions into nearby Charnwood Forest. To each of these manors, singled out in her will, Maud left furnishings for their churches, an indication of her visits to them.

39. A soke was a district over which jurisdiction was granted to hold court and to collect certain fines or fees connected with the prosecution of that court. Borough was granted this on 1 September 1518. Borough also held a lease of the markets and fairs of Kirton-in-Lindsey, granted 15 March 1524. L&P, 2, ii, no. 4410; L&P, 4, i, no. 213; L&P, 4, iii, no. 6803(19).

40. For Chaucer's patient Griselda as a paradigm of the perfect wife, see K. Henderson & B. McManus: 1985, 10-11.

41. Oxsted and Westcliff in Surrey (both of which lay on the main road between Guildford and Sevenoaks) and Alington Cobham in Thurnham, Kent (east of Maidstone and north of Leeds Castle). L&P, 12, ii, no. 187(6).

42. One subsequent event which lends credence to a close relationship between the two women was the appointment of Catherine's third husband, William Kynyatt of Colyweston, whom she married on 9 March 1535, to the post of auditor of the queen's household when Catherine Parr became queen. Daniel Scott, *The Stricklands of Sizergh Castle*, Kendal, 1908, 82, 84, 88-89; L&P, 4, iii, no. 680(10).

43. On 10 May 1534, John Lyngfield was presented to the living at Oxsted in Surrey by 'Katherine Burgh, widow' (L&P, 7, no. 761(19)). She married Lord Latimer shortly afterward.

44. Charles Ross, *Edward IV*, London, 1974, 70.

45. On 7 December 1535, Latimer took out a loan of a 100 marks from the monks of London's Charterhouse (L&P, 8, no. 614). By the end of 1538, Latimer had repaid the debt to the now dissolved house and was owed £30 from its income, for which he held 'a mitre and a cross' as security (Gerald S. Davies, *Charterhouse in London*, London, 1922, 328).

46. L&P, 7, no. 438.

47. Bigod (1508-1537) had some pretensions to scholarship. He attended Oxford and although he took no degree, he translated some works out of the Latin. Unfortunately for his longevity, he also wrote against the Supremacy and participated in the Pilgrimage of Grace.

48. L&P, 7, no. 134.

49. L&P, 8, no. 135.

50. Sir Richard Gresham (c.1485-1549) was sheriff of London and Middlesex. Lodge may have been Thomas Lodge, later Sir Thomas, who became warden of the Grocer's Company in 1548 and was later mayor of London, although he would seem to have been too young in 1535 to have posed much of a threat to Bigod.

51. L&P, 4, iii, no. 6776.

52. L&P, 5, no. 1679.

53. APC: IV, 1552-1554, 256. HMC: Rutland MSS, i, 68. On 16 April 1557, Thomas Edwards wrote to the Earl of Rutland: 'I heard within these four days my good lord Latimer would have ravished the wife of the house where he lay, and, I trow, struck the goodman there. There was such an outcry, as I heard, that the

constables and street rose and set him out of his house, and brought him through Cheapside to the mayor's and forty boys at his heels [taunting] him, and should have gone to the Counter, but he went to the Fleet, too great a villainy for a noble man, my thought.' John Neville, 4th Lord Latimer, married Lucy Somerset, daughter of Henry, 2nd Earl of Worcester, in 1545 in a marriage probably arranged by his stepmother, the queen, who established a close relationship with her new daughter-in-law. John died at Snape Castle on 22 August 1577 and was buried at Well. Of his four daughters, born between the years 1546-1549, Catherine, goddaughter of the queen, married Henry Percy, 9th Earl of Northumberland; Dorothy married Thomas Cecil, Earl of Exeter; Lucy married Sir William Cornwallis; and Elizabeth married first Sir John Danvers and secondly the son of Lord Hunsdon, Sir Edmund Carey.

54. Lawrence Stone, *The Crisis of the Aristocracy*, Oxford, 1965, 243.

55. NA: PROB 11/29; Image Reference 292/208, will of John Neville, Lord Latimer.

56. C. Parr: 1548, ff.Fiib-Fiiib.

57. Although Margaret does not appear on the official list of the queen's maids-in-waiting (NA: LC2/2, f.45a), yet from chamber accounts, she would seem to have filled such a position before her death (NA: E101/423/12, ff.3a-b; NA: E315/161, ff.112, 132.). The reason that she does not appear on the list of the maids is no doubt because it was compiled after her death in 1546.

58. NA: E315/161, ff.112, 132 and L&P, 19, ii, no. 794.

59. Among her personal books which Catherine Parr had with her in a chest of valuables at her death was 'a Testament of Mr. Neville's under the Bishop's seal', which had belonged to her husband. Society of Antiquaries MS 129 Part A, f. 219b.

Chapter 5

1. At the christening of the Princess Mary on 21 February 1516, Sir Thomas Parr and his stepfather, Sir Nicholas Vaux, were two of the courtiers chosen to carry the canopy over the infant princess.

2. J. J. Scarisbrick, *Henry VIII*, Berkeley & Los Angeles, 1968, 207.

3. L&P, 4, iii, no. 6248(20).

4. Jane Vaux married twice. Her first husband, whom she married in 1489, was Sir Richard Guildford, who died while on pilgrimage to the Holy Land in 1506, leaving a widow and three children. Lady Guildford's son, Sir Henry Guildford, became comptroller of the royal household in 1523. He was a favorite of Henry VIII and rose quickly in his service, being elected to the Order of the Garter in 1526, and serving as master of the horse (1515–1522) and chamberlain of the Exchequer (1526). Sir Henry had a sister, Philippa Guildford, who married Sir John Gage, and a brother, Edward Guildford, whose daughter, Jane, was married to Sir Henry's ward, John Dudley, the future Duke of Northumberland.

5. NA: SP1/74, f.97.

6. NA: SP1/79, ff.148–49.

7. NA: SP1/84, ff.231–32.

8. L&P, 8, no. 1144.

9. There was a third conflict in 1538 when Archbishop Cranmer asked Cromwell to intercede with Parr and secure the vicarage of Roydon, Essex, for his client, Thomas Lawney. Parr's own chaplain, Osias Le Moyne, was in possession of the living and Cranmer wanted Parr to replace him with Lawney. This Parr refused to do. Although he wrote protesting his goodwill to both Cranmer and Cromwell, he made no move to replace Le Moyne to satisfy Cranmer. It is likely that since the original request came from the archbishop rather than from Cromwell, Parr was not put under as much pressure to comply and felt free to stall Cranmer indefinitely as he had not felt free to do with Cromwell. L&P, 13, i, no. 892 and no. 1072.

10. For Parr's grudging acquiescence to Cromwell's will, he received token patronage. In 1539, Cromwell secured a joint patent in survivorship for William Parr and his uncle, Parr of Horton, making the younger William heir to his uncle's office of keeper of the park at Brigstock with its herbage and pannage. The younger Parr also was made heir to some other minor offices held by his uncle, dealing with the royal forests of Northamptonshire. Cromwell lent young Parr money, too, in small sums. But these modest favors certainly were less important to Parr, himself, than the accommodations he had to make with Cromwell to achieve them.

11. The only public office that Thomas, Lord Vaux, ever held was the governorship of the Isle of Jersey in which he succeeded Sir Arthur Darcy in January 1536 but then sold the following August to Sir Edward

Seymour for £150. G. Anstruther: 1953, 53.

12. NA: SP1/239, f.239.

13. Pempole went to Cromwell's kinswoman, Susan Tregian. G.Anstruther: 1953, 52.

14. M. James: 1970, 4.

15. It is important to remember that especially in Lincolnshire, the commons who rose did not consider themselves to be rebels against the king. As Sir Geoffrey Elton expresses it: 'All through they declared themselves to be loyal to the crown, and perhaps the most remarkable thing about the whole rising was the confidence of these deluded men that the king was on their side, and they on his.' G.R. Elton, *England Under the Tudors*, Cambridge, 1962, 146.

16. L&P, 12, i, no. 131.

17. L&P, 11, no. 759.

18. L&P, 12, i, nos 6, 29, 337.

19. L&P, 12, i, no. 131. He wrote in much the same vein to Sir William Fitzwilliam two days later, thanking him for his good report 'of me in my being among the commons against my will ... ' (L&P, 12, i, no. 173).

20. NA: SP1/107, f.115.

21. NA: SP1/107, ff.147–48.

22. L&P, 6, no. 1513 and L&P, Addenda, I, i, no. 1065.

23. 'Your rents and others cannot yet be levied, but I trust soon shall be. Mr. Parr, amongst others, can get none in many places, and I dare not yet send him to Kendal, Dent or Sedbergh.' Duke of Norfolk to Henry VIII, 7 February 1537, from York. L&P, 12, i, no. 362.

24. L&P, Addenda, 1, i, no. 1097. William Thornborough died in 1552. An inquisition post mortem of his lands is printed in W. Farrer: 1923-26, I, 243–244.

25. It was Sir James Leyburne who suppressed the local rebels in Kendal. Leyburne had been intimidated by the commons into a brief complicity with them at Lancaster. A local vicar had 'persuaded the people that they should go to heaven if they died in that quarrel', and had so aroused the commons that they 'spoiled' Leyburne's house in Kendal and threatened worse if he did not join them. Appearing with the rebels briefly at Lancaster, Leyburne soon took the opportunity to turn the tables on John Atkinson, captain of the Kendal insurgents. Leyburne and his son-in-law, Richard Ducket, were credited by the Duke of Norfolk with capturing Atkinson, who was betrayed to Parr's servants by his own nephew.

26. There had been recent enclosure riots in Cumbria as well as in Yorkshire. Sir James Leyburne, William Parr's steward, had had to deal with one in Kendal in July 1535 which indicates that William Parr may have been involved in local acts of enclosure. L&P, 8, no. 1133.

27. L&P, 12, i, no. 16; L&P, 12, ii, no. 665.

28. L&P, 12, i, no. 632.

29. L&P, 12, i, no. 789; *The Coronation of Richard III, the Extant Documents*, Anne F. Sutton and P.W. Hammond (eds.), Gloucester & New York, 1983, 331.

30. NA: PROB11/29; Image Reference 292/208. They may also have been two of the vast progeny of William Layton of Dalmain in Cumberland, one of whose thirty-two children, Richard, was one of Cromwell's most hated northern commissioners.

31. L&P, 11, nos 615, 619, 621, 658, 725, 808, 883, 888.

32. L&P, 11, no. 1174.

33. L&P, 12, i, no. 29.

34. R.B. Smith has stated that Latimer was a client of the Earl of Westmorland, who interceded with the king on Latimer's behalf. But the influence of Fitzwilliam and the Duke of Norfolk seems to have been far more decisive. R.B. Smith, *Land and Politics in the England of Henry VIII*, Oxford, 1970, 172.

35. L&P, 12, i, no. 173.

36. SP: Henry VIII, I, 534.

37. L&P, 12, ii, no. 14.

38. Norfolk's opinion of William Parr is indicated in a letter to Cromwell in which the duke states that Parr 'is a proper man and handled himself wisely and discretely in all this business as ever I saw (a) man of his age.' NA: SP1/117, f.106.

39. L&P, 12, ii, no. 101.

40. These were Wingrave manor in Buckinghamshire, which Latimer was forced to sell to Cromwell for £280 in January 1538, and Renhold manor in Bedfordshire, which Cromwell forced Latimer to sell to John and Joan Gostwyk the following year. L&P, 12, i, no. 913 and L&P, 13, nos 312, 812.

41. BL: Cott. MS Vespasian Fxiii 236, f.131, vol. II, article 183.

42. NA: PROB11/29; Image Reference 292/208.

43. Latimer undoubtedly continued to visit Snape periodically to oversee his affairs. In April 1542, his

brother-in-law, Lord Parr, helped him to secure the office of steward and master of the game within the forest of Galtries in Yorkshire. This was probably for the sake of the fees attached as well as to satisfy a desire to hunt in the forest. NA: DL42/133, f.124a.

44. It is described as 'a mansion and tenement at the east end of the churchyard with stables and gardens between the cloisters and priory and the house and garden of Ralph Warren, alderman.' BL: Cott. MS Vespasian Fxiii 236, f.131.

45. William Seymour, in *Ordeal by Ambition*, New York, 1972, 214, claims that Catherine owned a house in Wimbledon during these years. Although Catherine was made Lord of the Manor of Wimbledon in 1543, the house in question, the Old Rectory, was owned by the Crown after 1536 and was leased first to Sir John Jennings in 1540 and later to Sir Robert Tyrwhit, Catherine's master of the horse. 'So the Latimers certainly never lived in Wimbledon.' I am indebted to Richard Milward, M.A. (Oxon.) for the information on Wimbledon.

Chapter 6

1. BL: Addit. MS 8219, f.114 and 'Narrative of the Visit of the Duke of Najera', *Archaeologia*, XXIII (1831), 348–357.

2. For this and subsequent quotes, *The Second Book of the Travels of Nicander Nucius of Corcyra*, Rev. J.A. Cramer (ed.), Camden Society, vol. 17, London, 1841, 8-18. Nucius visited London in 1545 during the period that Catherine Parr was queen.

3. L&P, 17, nos 779, 815, 886.

4. NA: PROB11/29; Image Reference 292/208.

5. L&P, 18, i, no. 443. Had this been a bill for Catherine's stepdaughter, Margaret Neville, as has been suggested, it would have been paid, as all Margaret's bills were paid, through the queen's chamber accounts. That it was not suggests rather conclusively that the bill was for Mary. Skutt submitted it to the Crown for payment while Lord Latimer was still alive, five months before Catherine married Henry VIII. Latimer was, however, quite ill and it is highly unlikely that Catherine would have ordered such an elaborate wardrobe for her stepdaughter at a time when both women would soon be expected to go into mourning.

6. David Loades, *Mary Tudor: A Life*, 1989, 113, 117.

7. Three of these dolls are described in 1542 as 'Itm: one great baby lying in a box ... gown of white cloth of silver and a kirtle of green velvet. Itm: two little babies, one in crimson satin and one in white velvet.' V&A: MS 86.cc.49, f.196b.

8. On 3 February 1537, only six months after Richmond's death, Seymour had asked Cromwell's secretary, Ralph Sadler, to secure Cromwell's consent to the marriage. Over a year later, Seymour's pursuit of the match was still going forward. On 14 July 1538, Sadler wrote to Cromwell that Seymour's 'heart is most inclined' toward the widowed Duchess of Richmond. The king had remarked 'merrily (on the proposed match) that if (the Duke of Norfolk) were so minded to bestow his daughter on the said Sir Thomas Seymour, he should be sure to couple her with one of such lust and youth, as should be able to please her well at all points.' Eight years later, in December 1546, Norfolk wrote from the Tower to the Privy Council that 'on Tuesday in Witsun week last, I begged the King's help for a marriage between my daughter and Sir Thomas Seymour ... ' Evidently both he and his son, the Earl of Surrey, had been charged with trying to obstruct the match. SP: Henry VIII, I, 577-78, and L&P, 21, ii, no. 554.

9. BL: Sloane MS no. 1523, f.37b.

10. L&P, 16, nos 808, 809, 811, 835.

11. L&P, 17, nos 459, 488, 504, 583, 626, 748, 877, 941, 1192, 1242, 1246, for correspondence related to Seymour's travels.

12. L&P, 17, no. 701.

13. L&P, 17, no. 1247.

14. Susan E. James, 'Two Holbein Miniatures', *Apollo*, (May 1998), 15–20.

15. Dent Brocklehurst MS, Sudeley Castle.

16. Sir John Hayward, *The Life and Reign of King Edward VI*, London, 1630, 196.

17. *Nicholas Throckmorton*: 1874, nos 74, 19.

18. See Chapter 16 in this volume.

19. L&P, 12, ii, no. 1060 (p.374).

20. NA: Stowe MS 559, f.55a.

21. Anne ultimately relinquished control of Katherine's jewels on 27 February 1542 following the queen's execution in the Tower. L&P, 17, no. 283(35).

22. 'The malice borne me by both my nieces whom it pleased the King to marry is not unknown to such as kept them in this house [the Tower], as my lady Herbert.' L&P, 21 ii, no. 554 (letter written in December 1546 by the Duke of Norfolk, Anne Boleyn's uncle). For Christmas 1539, Anne was given 50s by the king. Honor, Lady Lisle, kept close tabs on Anne's marital status between 1537 and 1538, hoping to snap up her vacated position as maid for one of her own daughters. *The Lisle Letters*, Muriel St. Clare Byrne (ed.), Chicago, 1981, 4, 198.

23. M. M. Reese, *Master of the Horse*, London, 1976, 148.

24. On 9 March 1535, Herbert was granted denization as he had been born a subject of the King of France (L&P, 8, no. 481(14)). Since William Herbert spoke no French ('Master Herbert ... who knows no other language but his native English' [CSP: Spanish, XI, 18-19]), it is likely that his family left France while he was still quite young.

25. L&P, 6, no. 1656.

26. L&P, 7, no. 587(29).

27. L&P, 21, ii, no. 648(34).

28. L&P, 12, ii, nos 167, 424. Although there were rumors of a marriage for Anne during the summer of 1537, she was still unmarried in November and is listed among the maids at Jane Seymour's funeral in November. Her marriage to Herbert took place shortly after that date.

29. S. James: 1990, 199–204.

30. Parr was created Lord Parr on 9 March 1539 at Westminster, 'after the sacring of the King's high mass', in the same ceremony that made Sir William Paulet, Lord St. John (later Marquis of Winchester), and Sir John Russell, Lord Russell (later Earl of Bedford). Parr's robes were carried by 'Norrey, in default of a baron' from the pages' chamber and he was led into the hall by his lifelong friend, Thomas, Lord Wentworth. Together with Paulet, Russell, and their supporters, the men 'then proceeded to the Chamber of Presence, where they were commanded to put on their robes and from that in due order to the King and received their patents not read. Their styles were proclaimed afterwards at the second course as they sat at dinner.' BL: Harl. MS 6074, f.56b and L&P, 14, i, no. 477.

31. L&P, 14, i, no. 651(20). He was created Baron Parr but not, as many later authors have it, Baron Parr of Kendal. The 'of Kendal' was added perhaps in the literature to distinguish him from his uncle, Baron Parr of Horton, although Parr of Horton was created a baron on the same day (23 December 1543) that his nephew was finally elevated to the earldom of Essex and this presumably would have eliminated any confusion between them. There is, in fact, a seemingly scrupulous effort to keep Parr's northern estates from appearing in his successive titles.

32. L&P, 18, i, no. 66 (Cap. xliii, 47) and no. 67(4), and George Baker, *History and Antiquities of the County of Northamptonshire*, 1822–41, ii, 60.

33. L&P, 7, no. 761(19).

34. Parr would appear to have been sterile. He consummated three marriages without begetting a child. Yet two of his wives, his first, Lady Anne Bourchier, and his third, Helena Snakenborg, both had children by other men.

35. Bodleian: Rawlinson MS A.112, ff.66b-67b.

36. H. W. King, 'Inventories of Church Goods, 6 Edward VI', *Transactions of the Essex Archaeological Society*, 1873, V, 132.

37. L&P, 16, no. 1339, and Lacey Baldwin Smith, *A Tudor Tragedy*, London, 1961, 159.

38. Elisabeth's aunt, also Elisabeth Brooke, married Wyatt but he separated from her on the grounds of her infidelities.

39. BL: Harl. MS 283, f.175 Lord Cobham's anxieties must have been heightened by the scandal arising from his sister's adultery and separation from Sir Thomas Wyatt.

40. By the terms of Latimer's will, Catherine was to receive a third of his estate, 'whether of right she ought so to have or not'; all his goods 'now within her lying Chambre,' two gilt standing cups with covers; two gilt goblets, one with a cover; 'my best basin and ewer of silver and my two silver flagons'; the manor of Stowe in Northamptonshire with 'my churches and little Stowe with all appurtenances' for life, and £60 in rents from the manor of Beoley north of Redditch, 'in full satisfaction and recompense of her whole dower ... over and beside her jointure and feoffement'. NA: PROB11/29; Image Reference 292/208.

41. William Dugdale, *History of St. Paul's Cathedral*, London, 1716, 48, and John Weever, *Antient Funeral Monuments*, London, 1631, 371. According to Weever, Latimer's funeral monument was all broken to pieces by 1631.

42. L&P, 17, no. 1128.

43. For a discussion of the Earl of Hertford's reluctance to accept and Lord Lisle's relief at relinquishing the wardenship, see M. L. Bush, 'The Problem of the Far North, A Study of the Crisis of 1537 and Its Consequences', *Northern History*, IV (1971), 50–52.

44. L&P, 18, ii, no. 623(71). Within six months of Catherine's wedding, Herbert had received both his knighthood and, together with his wife, the grant of the monastic lands of Wilton in Wiltshire which subsequently became his seat.

45. John Crawford Hodgson, *A History of Northumberland*, V, Newcastle-on-Tyne, 1899, 59.

46. L&P, 18, i, no. 741.

47. L&P, 18, i, no. 964

48. The Duke of Suffolk's paternal feelings toward Parr were expressed in September 1543 when he requested Parr be appointed captain of the horsemen, and in February 1544 when he wrote to the king that if Lord Lisle could not be spared in the north, 'will [it] please your majesty that I may have my Lord Parr.' L&P, 18, ii, no. 118; *The Hamilton Papers: Letters and Papers illustrating the Political Relations of England and Scotland in the XVIth Century*, Joseph Bain (ed.), Edinburgh, 1890–92, ii, 268–69.

49. SP: Henry VIII, V, 299–300, 330

50. SP: Henry VIII, V, 300.

51. SP: Henry VIII, V, 301.

52. L&P, 18, ii, no. 297.

53. CSP: Scotland (1509–1603), I, 45; *The Hamilton Papers*: 1890–92, i, 579, 599.

54. CSP: Scotland (1509–1603), II, 80

55. L&P, 18, ii, no. 740.

56. L&P, 18, ii, no. 308.

Chapter 7

1. The Queen's Closet was located next to the King's Closet above the west end of the Chapel Royal and provided a room for private worship with a clear view of the chapel altar, measuring roughly 10 x 14 meters. See Simon Thurley, *The Royal Palaces of Tudor England*, New Haven & London, 1993, plan 7.

2. Sir Thomas Heneage, the elder, uncle of Elizabeth I's vice-chamberlain, was gentleman usher to Cardinal Wolsey and gentleman of the privy chamber to Henry VIII. Sir Thomas Darcy was a younger son of Thomas, Lord Darcy, who had been beheaded in 1537 for his participation in the Pilgrimage of Grace. Sir Edward Baynton was married to Anne Boleyn's half-sister and served as vice-chamberlain for three of Henry's queens. Sir Henry Knyvet was the grandson of the second Duke of Norfolk and was married to Anne Pickering, a member of the family who had long been clients of the Parrs. Sir Anthony Denny, known for his support of both the new religion and the new learning, subsequently served under William Parr, Marquis of Northampton, during Kett's Rebellion. His wife, Joan Champernowne, had a reputation as a lady of great beauty and learning and was a close friend of Catherine Parr's. Sir Thomas Speke and Sir Richard Long were gentlemen of the king's privy chamber. Speke owned lands in Somerset, and Long later became captain of Hull and had ties to the London commercial community through his wife, Margaret.

3. The selection of the conservative Gairdner as officiating clergyman has been offered as proof of the bride's own conservative beliefs (D. MacCulloch: 1996, 313–14, 326). Not only is it far more likely that the king made the selection of officiating clergyman rather than Catherine, but evidence of the bride's reformist tendencies date from the first days of her marriage.

4. L&P, 18, ii, no. 873.

5. J. F. D. Shrewsbury, 'Henry VIII: A Medical Study', *Journal of the History of Medicine*, VIII (1952), 55–106.

6. L&P, 17, no. 1212.

7. There has been some discussion of late regarding Henry's potency or lack thereof. (See especially E. W. Ives, *Anne Boleyn*, Oxford, 1986, 236–39, and Retha M. Warnicke, *The Rise and Fall of Anne Boleyn*, Cambridge, 1989, 216-17, 231, 235.) While the evidence detailed by Ives may have impaired Henry's sexual performance on occasion, his concern to create a marital relationship which could produce a second male heir argues against any chronically debilitating problem. It argues instead a deep-seated need for psychological sexual stimulation. Had the king been unable to perform with Katherine Howard, his honeymoon humour would have been far shorter-lived than it obviously was. The evidence seems rather

to indicate a low sperm count than a chronic lack of potency. On this issue, the Tudor family as a whole were profoundly unprolific. Henry VII, Edmund Tudor's only child, and Elizabeth of York produced four children who survived to adulthood, only three of whom reproduced. The third generation produced seven viable heirs, who in the fourth generation produced seven more. By the fifth generation, only five surviving descendants were born. Using a twentieth-century generational base increase of 2.5 children (undoubtedly lower than that which obtained in the sixteenth century), by the fifth generation, a family of average genetic make-up should have produced an incrementation of thirty-nine descendants. Even with the high mortality rates of the sixteenth century, compared with other families such as the Howards or the Nevilles, the Tudor output of babies seems abnormally small.

8. J . Strype: 1822, II, ii, 339–40. Imperial ambassador Chapuys, retailing court gossip, reported that Henry had no hope of issue with Catherine as she had had none with her two former husbands. But as both of these marriages had occurred in the north, far from court, it is unlikely that Chapuys had any real knowledge of Catherine's gynecological history and was simply describing the present state of her childlessness. L&P, 18, i, no. 954.

9. BL: Lansdowne MS 76, article 81, f.182.

10. L&P, 18, ii, no. 740.

11. *Catalogue of the Library of Henry Huth*, 5 vols, London, 1880, V, 1695–96.

12. Scarisbrick concludes that in private Henry was becoming increasingly liberal in his religious views in his last years. Yet despite Cranmer's story of a conversation with the French ambassador illustrating this trend, one that certainly stunned Cranmer, Henry's actions give little indication of any consistent move toward a radicalization of thought. J. Scarisbrick: 1968, 472–78.

13. J. Strype: 1822, II, ii, 339–40; *The Letters of Richard Scudamore to Sir Philip Hoby, September* 1549-*March* 1555, Susan Brigden (ed.), Camden Miscellany, XXX, 4th Series, London, 1990, 78.

14. Dent-Brocklehurst MS, Sudeley Castle.

15. Ironically Catherine became queen just as the 'pamphlet wars' were heating up, debating the nature of women and the desirability of their education and their performance in public arenas. In 1541, a pamphlet called *The Schoolhouse of Women* appeared, which denounced women in general as peacocks, portraying them as vain, lustful, prodigal, deceitful, scolding, willful, wicked and destructive. Another pamphlet, *Mulierum Paean*, published at much the same time, attempted to exculpate the sex from the multitude of crimes laid at her door over the ages. The author of *Mulierum Paean* describes how he agreed to denounce the wholesale condemnation of *The Schoolhouse of Women* when a group of women awakened him and begged him to:

'Consider our grief and how we be blamed,
And all by a book that lately is passed
Which by report by thee was first framed,
The school of women, none author named.
In print it is passed, lewdly compiled;
All women whereby be sore reviled.'

The plea illuminates the cultural biases of the time when women were rarely allowed to speak for themselves and had to beg a male author to do so in their name. See, K. Henderson & B. McManus: 1985, 11–20, 137–170.

16. BL: Lansdowne MS 76, article 81, f.182.

17. *Henry Huth*: 1880, V, 1695–96.

18. SP: Henry VIII, IX, 472.

19. BL: Lansdowne MS 97, f.43 and L&P, 18, ii, no. 531.

20. SP: Domestic, V, 323 (20 July 1543) and A. J. Slavin, *Politics and Profit: A Study of Sir Ralph Sadler*, 1507–1547, Cambridge, 1966, 138.

21. NA: SP1/180, f.69.

22. The olfactory sense seems to have been highly developed in the king and one of the most important aspects of his sexual arousal. This would explain in part his violently adverse and sexually inhibiting reaction to the smell of Anne of Cleves' body.

23. NA: E315/161, f.22.

24. NA: E101/423/13, f.10.

25. S. Thurley: 1993, plan 7.

26. A second wardrobe for the queen, the wardrobe of the beds, where furnishings pertaining to the beds were stored, was located in 1536 beneath the king's presence chamber. Simon Thurley, 'Henry VIII and the Building of Hampton Court: A reconstruction of the Tudor Palace', *Architectural History*, 31 (1988), 24.

27. S. Thurley: 1993, 138–139.

28. These noises and smells so bothered Queen Elizabeth some years later that she had another privy kitchen built elsewhere. S. Thurley: 1988, 35.

29. For a discussion of the demise of the great hall and the evolution of stacked lodgings into a less layered layout of rooms, divided into separate chambers for public functions and for private living, see S. Thurley: 1993, 135–161.

30. S. Thurley: 1993, 139.

31. S. Thurley: 1993, 140.

32. S. Thurley: 1988, 40–41, and S. Thurley: 1993, 156, fig. 199.

33. L&P, 4, i, no. 1939.

34. S. Thurley: 1988, 11.

35. NA: E315/161, ff. 63, 194.

36. This does not hold true regarding gifts for her closest intimates however. In an early list of chamber payments (NA: E101/423/12, 18 July 1543-21 March 1544), the queen purchased black damask, black silk, russet worsted and russet silk velvet for gowns for her stepdaughter, Margaret Neville, still in mourning for her father who had been dead less than five months, black velvet and blue velvet for gowns for Anne Herbert, black double jean velvet for gowns for Maud Lane and Elizabeth Tyrwhit and black satin for a (night?)gown for her brother, William Parr. There were also presentation gifts such as cloth of silver for kirtles for Princesses Mary and Elizabeth and Lady Anne of Cleves, purple velvet and purple cloth of gold for Princess Elizabeth and a long list of clothing especially made for Prince Edward.

37. NA: E315/161, f.32b.

38. NA: SP1/217, f.54.

39. Nearly all of the important artists of this period either began their careers as goldsmiths or came from families who earned their living by that trade. Peter Richardson was born in Haarlem, c.1505–07, possibly near 'the greate woode bridge' and the Hospital of St. Elizabeth, both of which he refers to in his will. His original surname may have been other than Richardson, and indeed, Richard may have been his father. In 1536, Richardson had established himself as a successful jeweller in Holland, but decided (possibly on religious grounds) to seek a position at the English court. Henry VIII, who had just buried Anne Boleyn and married Jane Seymour, granted a licence to the Dutch goldsmith on 15 September 1536 to keep six servants or journeymen (native or foreign) and to make 'jewels, works and divises' for Queen Jane (L&P, 11, no. 519, p.209). Richardson worked continuously for Henry's wives and later for his daughters until his death in April 1586. In 1544, he and his two servants were living in St. Martin's-le-Grand, Aldersgate Ward, and by 1549, he had moved to St. Leonard's Parish in Foster's Lane (*Return of Aliens in the City and Suburbs of London, from Henry VIII to James I*, R. E. G. Kirk & E. F. Kirk (eds), London, 1900-07, 10, i, 83, 172). In 1544, he appears in Catherine Parr's chamber accounts on 20 June, 'for the making of spangles for her grace's footmen's coats', for which he charged £20 (NA: E315/161, f.18). In December 1544, £30 was delivered to him by the Princess Mary 'to make the king's New Year's gift' (*Privy Purse*: 1831, 170). On the queen's household list, Richardson is listed as 'Peter, the goldsmith' (NA: LC 2/2, f.45b). Another royal notice of Richardson appears in January 1547, a writ to Mr. Peckham to 'deliver to John Andewarpe (Jan or Hans of Antwerp) and Peter Richardson, goldsmiths, for your use, 80 oz of crown gold, worth 47s the oz = 188 li' (L&P, 21, ii, no. 770 p.405). During the reign of Elizabeth I, Richardson leased out his East Smithfield property to an English bricklayer named Johnson and his Netherlandish wife, Kattelyne (Katlijne), their two children Frances and Sarah, and a Dutch smith named Francis Franke, his wife, Barbara, and son, Francis, Jr., all of whom were born in Antwerp (*Return of Aliens*, 10, iii, 421). The successful Richardson married Anne Wilson, the daughter of Robert Wilson, and moved into a home near the Savoy. The Richardsons had no surviving children and on Peter's death in 1586, he left his wife as sole executor of his will, with legacies to her, her father and two sisters, a widow Mary Southill, wife of the late Peter Southill (Richardson's godson?), and her young children, as well as to an assortment of hospitals, prisons and charitable groups for distribution among the poor.

40. Susan E. James, 'Lady Jane Grey or Queen Catherine Parr?', *The Burlington Magazine*, CXXXVIII (January 1996), 20-24.

41. Janet Arnold, *Queen Elizabeth's Wardrobe Unlock'd*, Leeds, 1988, 139.

42. NA: 101/423/12, ff.3a, 6a.

43. BL: Addit. MS 46,348, f.207b.

44. Bl: Addit. MS 46,348, f.206a.

45. NA: E314/22, ff.7, 10; E315/161, f.18; SP1/195, f.180b.

46. BL: SL 5308.43.

47. NA: E101/520/9 (29 April 1553).

48. BL: Addit. MS 46,348, f.6b.

49. BL: Addit. MS 46,348, f.208b.

50. BL: Addit. MS 46,348, ff.169b, 170a.

51. NA: E101/423/13, f.6.

52. Scholars have raised the argument that medieval literary attacks on a woman's body, as a perceived cesspit of sin, produced a cultural 'repugnance for the female body' in the Middle Ages, remnants of which filtered through to the consciousness of the early Renaissance. The human body in Christian doctrine as something to be ashamed of, repressed and controlled, held many philosophical equivalencies in the English Renaissance with the female sex, also in need of repression and control. Freud might happily conjoin a love of cleanliness with a sense of physical shame, a sense of trying to purify that which was by definition corrupt, but as Catherine has left no record of her feelings on the matter of baths, her motives for frequent bathing must be left open to subjective interpretation. K. Henderson & B. McManus: 1985, 15.

53. BL: Addit. MS 46,348, f.206b.

54. BL: Addit. MS 46,348, f.208a.

55. *The Letter Book of John Parkhurst*, R.A. Houlbrooke (ed.), Norfolk Record Society, vol. 43, Norwich, 1874–75, 83.

56. BL: Cott. MS Vespasian III, f.16b (29–37).

57. BL: Addit. MS 46,348, f.206a.

58. NA: E101/424/12, f.14.

59. L&P, 21, i, no. 802.

60. BL: Addit. MS 8219, f.114 and ' Duke of Najera': 1831, 348–57.

61. See Chapter 9 in this volume.

Chapter 8

1. CSP: Spanish, VI, pt. 2, 459.

2. *Privy Purse*: 1831, 185.

3. Cecil MS 147, f.6, Hatfield House, dated 3 June 1544.

4. CSP: Spanish, VIII, 2.

5. L&P 19, i, no. 118; CSP: Spanish, VII, 120–21.

6. CSP: Spanish, VII, 70.

7. CSP: Spanish, VIII, 2.

8. CSP: Spanish, VIII, 2.

9. CSP: Spanish, VIII, 104-05.

10. CSP: Spanish VIII, 105.

11. L&P, 20, ii, no. 149.

12. NA: LC2/2, f.45a and L&P, 20, ii, no. 909(47).

13. L&P, 20, ii, no. 900.

14. L&P, 21, ii, no. 756.

15. M. Hatch: 1948, 155.

16. L&P, 21, i, no. 968.

17. L&P 19, i, no. 118; CSP: Spanish, VII, 120–21.

18. Katherine Champernowne was the daughter of Sir Philip of Modbury, Devon, and the sister of Elizabeth, Lady Denny. She came to court in 1532, joined the royal household through Cromwell's influence and was made governor of the Princess Elizabeth in 1536. She married John Astley, the younger, about 1545–6 and died July 1565. Her married name is habitually spelled 'Ashley' in contemporary records and that spelling is followed here.

19. NA: SP10/2, f.25 (84c). This letter is frequently misquoted, 'that all men judge the contrary,' being misread as, 'that all men urge the contrary'.

20. BL: Cott. MS Otho C.x. 231; *The Letters of Queen Elizabeth*, G. B. Harrison (ed.), London, 1968, 4–5.

21. See Chapter 12 in this volume.

22. L&P, 19, ii, no. 794.

23. Scottish Records Office: RH 13/78 and BL: Royal MS 7.D.x. Also see, Margaret H. Swain, 'A New Year's Gift from the Princess Elizabeth', *The Connisseur*, (August 1973), 258–66.

24. BL: Cott. MS Nero C.x.f.8.
25. NA: E101/424/12, f.189.
26. L&P, 21, i, no. 968.
27. J. Strype: 1822, II, i, 60.
28. M. Dowling; 1987, 59-71.
29. L&P, 20, ii, App. 2.
30. NA: E315/161, f.40.
31. NA: E101/424/12, f.15.
32. NA: E101/426/3, f.31.
33. M. Hatch: 1948, 285.
34. L&P, 19, i, no. 1035(78).
35. *Sir Nicholas Throckmorton*: 1874, 8.
36. M. Hatch: 1948, 155.
37. R. Ascham: 1864, Parr-Ascham correspondence.
38. M. Hatch: 1948, 280, 283–86.
39. BL: Harl. MS 5087.
40. W. K. Jordan questions Cooke's having been a tutor to Edward VI yet cites the reference where Cooke was granted a £100 annuity 'for having provided 'training in good letters and manners' to the King (NA: E315/221/131).' Jordan also quotes Bishop Hooper's explicit statement in a letter of March 1550 that Cooke was a royal tutor and Bale's comments in *Index britanniae scriptorum* that Cooke was 'one of the royal preceptors'. These three contemporary pieces of evidence would seem to take Cooke's employment as a tutor beyond the realm of doubt. W. K. Jordan, *Edward VI: The Threshold of Power*, Cambridge, MA, 1970, 406, note 4.
41. NA: PROB 11/31; Image Reference 94/72.
42. BL: Cott. MS Nero C.x.f.6.
43. M. Hatch: 1948, 218.
44. M. Hatch: 1948, 223.
45. L&P, 20, ii, no. 418(78); Leonard Howard, *A Collection of Letters from the Original Manuscripts*, London, 1753, 190–91; HMC: 77 De L'Isle and Dudley, I, 273-274.
46. L&P, 20, ii, no. 418(78).
47. *Sylloge Epistolarum*, Thomas Hearne (ed.), London, 1716, 165–66.
48. L&P, 21, i, no. 650(17).
49. NA: LC2/2, f.45a; L&P, 20, ii, no. 909(47).
50. Catherine and Mary also shared servants. 'Mistress Barbara' and Jane Fool served in both of their households as did Mary Finch, who prior to 1543 was one of Mary's gentlewomen and keeper of her jewels. After Henry VIII's death, Edward VI awarded Mary Finch an annuity for her services to his stepmother. *Privy Purse*: 1831, xii and 233; CPR: Edward VI, 1547-48, I, 208.
51. SP: Henry VIII, IX, 570.
52. L&P, 19, ii, no. 4.
53. For Elizabeth's return to court at this time see Chapter 10 in this volume.
54. NA: SP1/195, ff.177-83.

Chapter 9

1. NA: E101/426/3, f.22.
2. NA: E314/22, f.42.
3. NA: E315/340, ff.38a-39b; L&P, 19, ii, no. 688.
4. NA: E315/161, f.31.
5. As in the king's household, the queen's household servants were required to swear an oath of loyalty to their mistress upon taking up their duties. 'July 1543. Item to Mistress Barbara, when she was sworn the queen's woman … 7s 6d;' (*Privy Purse*: 1831, 123); 'The oath of the queen's councillors ministered to Anthony Bourchier by Sir Edmund Walsingham, the queen's vice-chamberlain (December 1544);' (L&P, 19, ii, no. 798); D. Hamilton: 1992, 20.

6. Carew used his position to borrow money but on one occasion at least left scrupulous records of repayment. NA: E101/424/3, ff.5, 7-10, 16.

7. Although the chief officers of her household formed the queen's great council, for all practical purposes a considerably smaller one functioned as a quorum council. An early reference to business transacted by the queen's council lists Sir Thomas Arundell, Walter Bucler, and Sir Robert Tyrwhit, with Hugh Aglionby as clerk, as participants (NA: E315/161, f.97).

8. NA: E101/423/12, f.5a.

9. L&P, 21, ii, no. 199(75).

10. NA: PROB11/31; Image Reference 94/72.

11. Lord Parr of Horton died before 14 September 1547 (NA: E101/426/3, f.21), probably sometime at the end of the summer of 1547. During his tenure as his niece's chamberlain he seems to have been unwell and, except for a turn on Catherine's regency council during the summer of 1544 and the early months of 1546, seems to have spent most of his time at home. Catherine's accounts (NA: E315/161) refer to several payments made 'for riding into Northamptonshire to Mr. Pare' (ff.117, 165), or for 'riding into Northamptonshire upon the queen's grace's affairs' (f.196), which may have come to the same thing. Her grief at his death may be deduced from a letter of recommendation she wrote for his former clerk. NA: E101/426/3, f.21.

12. Conversely and intriguingly, Catherine's own cousin, Francis Agard, served Thomas Seymour, although whether or not this service began when Catherine was queen is uncertain. CSP: Edward VI (1992 edition), no. 148.

13. NA: LC2/2.

14. The Aglionbys were typical of a family who made their careers in an evolving civil service that still included personal service to the royal household as one of its adjuncts. Edward Aglionby had been a gentleman usher of Henry VIII's chamber in 1534 and a client of Cromwell's. Hugh Aglionby was appointed banker and assayer of the money and coinage in the Tower of London and comptroller and clerk of the same on 5 March 1542. On 21 May 1544, Aglionby resigned these offices in exchange for a £20 annuity and became Catherine Parr's clerk of council. Richard Aglionby, possibly Hugh's brother, was Catherine's clerk of the wardrobe (NA: E101/426/2). A 'Mistress Eglaby', presumably another member of the family, was one of Catherine's maids (NA: E101/426/2). At Henry VIII's death, Hugh continued in the queen-dowager's household as her secretary (NA: E315/479, f.5; NA: E101/426/2 and E315/161, f.97). His wife served as a gentlewoman of the queen's privy chamber (NA: E314/22, f.7). At the birth of Catherine's daughter, Mary Seymour, she became the baby's governess. Later Mistress Aglionby succeeded Katherine Ashley as Queen Elizabeth's mother of the maids.

15. Dorothy Fountain had risen to the position of chamberer by 1547. NA: E101/426/2.

16. Cal.IPM: Henry VII, no. 165, p.77.

17. NA: PROB11/29; Image Reference 292/208.

18. L&P, 19, i, no. 812(41). This was another member of the extensive Layton clan of Yorkshire, two of whom, Robert and John, had been employed by Lord Latimer at Snape and one of whom, Dr. Richard Layton (d. June 1544), had featured so prominently in the 1536 Pilgrimage of Grace.

19. CSP: Domestic, Henry VIII, V, p.309.

20. By 1547, Mary Woodhull had been promoted to the position of gentlewoman of the queen's chamber with a five shilling salary (NA: E101/426/2). The Woodhull family served the Parrs throughout the sixteenth century. Lord Parr of Horton's son-in-law and Mary's father, Nicholas Woodhull, was sheriff of Northamptonshire from 1525-7. Maud Parr left a bequest to Woodhull's wife, Elizabeth Parr, in 1529 and Lord Parr of Horton left £100 to his granddaughter Mary Woodhull in 1547, together with £20 to 'my cousin (grandson) Fulke Woodhull'. In the 1572 survey of the lands and holdings of the late William Parr, Marquis of Northampton, Fulke Woodhull is once again named.

21. The upper gentry did not enjoy the sort of income that the nobility could command thus could not afford to buy supporters and well-wishers with fees and annuities. But they could offer a modified patronage in the form of favors – of legal support, offices secured, trusteeship duties in enfeoffment to uses, intercession with the king or important magnates, dispute arbitration, military aid in local quarrels, and help in promoting advantageous marriages. The clients within this network were frequently but not always tenants of the patron. Occasionally, they were related by blood as well, and as in bastard feudalism, one family tended to invest its loyalty in another family over a period of generations if not centuries. The Parrs of Kendal had made full and frequent use of gentry feudalism from the time of Catherine's great-grandfather, Sir Thomas Parr of Kendal (1407–1461). S. James: 1993, 104–05.

22. For a discussion of the use of female networking as a strategy to overcome cultural and geographic isolation, see D. Willen: 1989, 151–52.

23. Dr. Robert Huicke, B.A. 1529, was a fellow of Merton College, Oxford, and a close friend of Merton

fellow, John Parkhurst. He served in the Duchess of Suffolk's household prior to Catherine's marriage to Henry. Huicke was medical advisor to the king as well as the queen's personal physician, and was one of the signatories of Henry's will in its function as a certificate of death. On 4 July 1550, he was granted an annuity of £50 for services rendered to both Henry VIII and Catherine Parr. His wife was also a member of the queen's household. CPR: Edward VI, I, 1547-48, 299 and *Letter Book*: 1974-75, 20–21.

24. Frances B. Rose-Troup, 'Two Book Bills of Katherine Parr', *The Library*, January 1911, 6, also in *Six Pamphlets on the History of Books*, Bodleian 2581.d.73(4).

25. L&P, 20, i, no. 441.

26. L&P, 20, i, no. 904; L&P, Addenda, I, ii, no. 1742. Warner also functioned as one of the two 'servers for the mouth' in Catherine's household.

27. CSP: Spanish, VIII, 130.

28. L&P, 20, i, no. 628; L&P, 20, ii, nos 570, 601; L&P, Addenda, I, ii, no. 1662, nos 1683, 1739, 1788, 1791.

29. L&P, Addenda, I, ii, no. 1693.

30. NA: SP1/196, f.40b.

31. L&P, 20, i, no. 1335(34). The queen's generosity to other relatives included the grant of the reversion of the manor of Sudbury to her cousin, Bridget Vaux's husband, Maurice Walsh, and the grant of four Hertfordshire manors to Clement's brother, Nicholas Throckmorton.

32. BL: Cott. MS Caligula E.4., f.55; M. Byrne: 1968, 365-68.

33. L&P, 20, ii, no. 570.

34. Anne's closeness to her sister is exemplified by her surrender of her young son Edward into Catherine's care when he was still a toddler. See Chapter 16 in this volume.

35. NA: E101/423/12, f.6b.

36. D. Willen: 1989, 150.

37. The king's lack of enthusiasm for some of the queen's ladies can be seen in a letter he wrote to her on 8 September 1544 while he was in France. 'And, whereas you desired to know our pleasure for the accepting into your Chamber of certain ladies in places of others that cannot well give their attendance by reason of sickness; albeit we think those whom you have named unto us as unable almost to attend by reason of weakness as the others be ... ' BL: Cott. MS Caligula E.4, f.55; M. Byrne: 1968, 365-68.

38. Anne Calthorp, Countess of Sussex, had a miserably unhappy marriage. Wed prior to 21 November 1538, she was divorced by the earl in 1555 and censured as 'unnatural and unkind', a charge which might indicate her lack of enthusiasm for marital relations with her husband. After her separation from Sussex, Anne's attempts to marry Sir Edmond Knyvett were thwarted. Charges of sorcery were also made against her. Thrown into the Tower in 1552 and committed to the Fleet in 1557, barred from dower or jointure, she finally fled to France.

39. For further discussion, see D. Willen: 1989, 140-65.

40. Betty S. Travitsky, 'The possibilities of prose', in *Women and Literature in Britain, 1500-1700*, Helen Wilcox, (ed.), Cambridge, 1996, 239, and Pearl Hogrefe, 'Anne Cooke, Lady Bacon', in *Women of Action in Tudor England*, Ames, IA, 1977, 39-56.

41. NA: PROB11/65; Image Reference 189/151.

42. NA: E101/520/9/11 March 1553.

43. Barbara E. Harrison, *The Bassanos, Italian Musicians at the English Court, 1531- 1664*, privately published, 1991, 1-20.

44. Catherine may have known the Bassano family before she became queen. They were leased rooms by the Crown in the old cells of the Carthusian brothers at Charterhouse from 1542 to 1552. The Latimers' townhouse was built directly against this monastery. NA: C66/752, m.6, and David Knowles & W. F. Grimes, *Charterhouse: The Medieval Foundation in Light of Recent Discoveries*, London, 1954, 38, 78-79, 81, 84-85.

45. NA: DL42/133, ff.83a, 96b, 120a, 164a, 170b, 175a. Also, Andrew Ashbee, *Records of English Court Music, VII (1485–1558)*, London, 1993, 84–86.

46. Susan E. James, 'Nicholas Lanier, Part I (1588-1612)', in *Journal of the Greenwich Historical Society*, vol. I, no. 2, (1993), 53–56.

47. For a detailed discussion of the queen's portraits, see, Susan E. James, *The Feminine Dynamic in English Art, 1485–1603*, to be published in 2008.

48. NA: E315/340, f.23b.

49. Giles Gering, stranger, was granted an annuity of £20 on 8 October 1545, possibly at the queen's request. He worked as a 'moldmaker' or stucco artist on Nonesuch Palace.

50. L&P, 21, ii, no. 475 (101). Also, Erna Auerbach, *Tudor Artists*, London & New York, 1954, 51.

51. V&A: MS L.30-1982 Pembroke Inventory (12 December 1561), f.92a.

52. HMC: Salisbury, I, 1306-1571, 131.

53. S. Thurley: 1993, 214–15.

54. *Literary Remains*: 1857, cccxxvi.

55. E. Auerbach: 1954, 68.

56. *Holbein and the Court of Henry VIII*, catalogue, The Queen's Gallery, Buckingham Palace, 1978-1979, no. 70 (R.L. 12256; Parker 48).

57. V&A: MS L.30-1982 Pembroke Inventory (12 December 1561), f.85a.

58. D. Hamilton: 1992, 338-39.

59. NA: E101/520/9/10 February 1553 and Susan E. James, 'A New Source for Shakespeare's *The Taming of the Shrew*', *Bulletin of the John Rylands University Library of Manchester* (Spring 1999), 49-62.

60 *The History of the King's Works*, H. M. Colvin (ed.), IV, 1485-1660 (part II), London, 1982, 52.

61. S. Thurley: 1993, 50.

62. S. Thurley: 1993, 217, fig. 284, and Otto Kurz, 'An Architectural Design for Henry VIII, *The Burlington Magazine* , LXXXII (1943), 82 and 233.

63. S. Thurley: 1993, 220, figs 291 a and b.

Chapter 10

1. NA: E314/22, f.22, 29; L&P, 21, i, no. 969.

2. G. E. Cokayne, *The Complete Peerage* ,VII, London, 1929, 599, note c; CSP: Spanish,VIII, part 1, 206.

3. L&P, 19, i, 487.

4. Catherine's keen interest in the Scottish situation was a family trait derived from the days when the Parrs' income came solely from their northern estates. Her grandfather, Sir William Parr of Kendal, had been one of the chief advisors and negotiators on all things Scottish under Edward IV, a fact of which she must have been well aware.

5. G. R. Elton, *Reform and Reformation England, 1509-1558*, London, 1977, 307.

6. J. Scarisbrick: 1968, 450.

7. D. L. Potter believes that Henry 'played a poorish hand with considerable skill', yet the poorish hand was one he dealt himself by his decision to invade France in the first place. D. L. Potter, 'Diplomacy in the Mid-Sixteenth Century: England and France, 1536–1550', unpublished Ph.D. dissertation, Cambridge, 1973.

8. Catherine Parr stood godmother to Petre's daughter, Catherine. F. G. Emmison, *Tudor Secretary: Sir William Petre at Court and Home*, Cambridge, MA, 1961, 53–55.

9. SP: Domestic, Henry VIII, I, 1518–1547, 763–4. 'Lord Parr of Horton shall be used in council with them, for all such matters as concern the realm.' Parr's health was not robust and his signature does not appear on any of the council minutes.

10. For a pertinent discussion, particularly by such 'liberal' minds as John Aylmer and John Jewel, see Carole Levin, 'John Foxe and the Responsibilities of Queenship', in *Women in the Middle Ages and the Renaissance: Literary and Historical Perspectives*, Mary Beth Rose (ed.), Syracuse, 1986, 113–133.

11. *Tudor Royal Proclamations: Volume I: The Early Tudors (1485–1553)*, Paul L. Hughes and James F. Larkin (eds), New Haven & London, 1964, 336–340.

12. L&P, 19, i, no. 937.

13. L&P, 19, ii, nos 207, 231, 332.

14. L&P, 19, ii, no. 302.

15. *Tudor Royal Proclamations*: 1964, 339–340.

16. L&P, 19, ii, no. 324.

17. BL: Cott. MS.Caligula E.4, f.55.

18. In a sense, the gentlemen pensioners were the inheritors of the special position about the king's person which the fifteenth century knights for the body had held under Edward IV. They were members of families anxious to place them in advantageous positions within the king's household. Competition for these places was keen but the appointment was more of a sinecure than Edward IV's knights for the body had been. Henry VIII's grandfather had used his knights for the body for all manner of tasks. Henry's own gentlemen pensioners were more decorative and less functional.

19. Essex's salary was £66 13s 2d per annum prior to 1545 and £133 6s 8d after that, the increase in salary possibly attributable to the queen's influence.

20. BL: Lansdowne MS 1236, f.9.

21. L&P, 18, ii, no. 873.

22. The only record of any monies being expended for repairs on Ashridge by the Queen's Works is in 1564 when £67 10s 7d were allowed in preparation for a royal progress into Hertfordshire. In 1575 the house was sold. NA: E351/3202 and *History of the King's Works*: 1982, IV, 47-48.

23. BL: Cott. Otho C.x.231. The Prince of Wales spent part of this period with his sister at Ashridge. In January 1544, Catherine sent her yeoman John Grove with a present of venison for 'my lord prince'. NA: E315/161, f.99.

24. NA: E101/423/12, ff.7a, 8a.

25. BL: Cott. Otho C.x.231.

26. Derek Wilson, *Hans Holbein, Portrait of an Unknown Man*, London, 1996, 280–281.

27. NA: E315/161, ff.112, 132.

28. L&P, 19, i, nos 927, 937, 943, 954.

29. L&P, 19, ii, no. 688.

30. BL: Cott. Otho C.x.231.

31. L&P, 19, ii, no. 41.

32 . BL: Cott. MS.Caligula E.4, f.55.

33. J. Scarisbrick: 1968, 447-8.

34. CSP: Domestic, Henry VIII, I, 1518-47, 767.

35. BL: Cott. MS.Caligula E.4, f.55.

36. L&P, 19, ii, no. 1957.

37. L&P, 20, ii, no. 910(45).

38. NA: SP1/191, f.52 (6 August 1544).

39. BL: Lansdowne MS 1236, f.9.

40. NA: SP1/195, f.180b.

41. J. Strype: 1822, II, i, 132.

42. Nicholas Udall, *Ralph Roister Doister*, William Durrant Cooper (ed.), printed for the Shakespeare Society, London, 1847, act 1, scene 1.

43. G. Scheurweghs, *Materials for the Study of the Old English Drama*, vol. 16, Louvain, 1939, lviii–lix.

44. *Tudor Royal Proclamations*: 1964, I, 372–373.

45. G. Scheurweghs: 1939, xxxviii.

46. Nicholas Udall, *A New Enterlude Called Thersytes*, f.Eia. In 1533, Udall composed verses for several pageants held in celebration of the coronation of Anne Boleyn (L&P, 6, no. 564).

47. N. Udall: 1847, act 2, scene 4.

48. N. Udall: 1847: act 2, scene 4.

49. N. Udall: 1847: act 4, scene 3.

50. S. James: 1999, *Rylands*, 49-62.

51. N. Udall: 1847: act 3, scene 4.

52. N. Udall: 1847: act 4, scene 3.

53. N. Udall: 1847: act 3, scene 4.

54. N. Udall: 1847: act 3, scene 3.

55. N. Udall: 1847: act 4, scene 3.

56. N. Udall: 1847: act 1, scene 2.

57. C. Levin: 1986, 121.

58. N. Udall: 1847: act 5, scene 3.

59. C. Parr: 1548, f.Eiiib.

60. BL: Cott. MS.Caligula E.4, f.55.

61. *Hall's Chronicle: Containing the History of England (1548–1550)*, H. Ellis (ed.), London, 1809 edition, 862.

62. L&P, 19, ii, no. 251.

63. CSP: Spanish, VII, no. 148 (p.243).

64. L&P, 19, ii, no. 688.

65. *Tudor Royal Proclamations*: 1964, 339.

66. L&P, 19, ii, no. 44.

67. Jasper Ridley states that Cranmer 'was in constant attendance upon the Queen' at this time but in fact, Cranmer, together with Wriothesley, Petre and the Bishop of Westminster, remained at Woking while the queen and the royal children were on progress during September. Jasper Ridley, *Thomas Cranmer*, London, 1962, 248.

68. Mortlake was one of Catherine's dower houses and together with Syon House was being used as the site of a munitions factory for 'ingens and habyliments of warre'. *History of the King's Works*: 1982, 272.

69. L&P, 19, ii, no. 688.

70. L&P, 19, ii, no. 688.

71. BL: Cott. MS.Caligula E.4, f.55.

72. SP: Domestic, Henry VIII, 1518–1547, I, no. 767.

73. NA: SP 1/195, f.182a.

74. L&P, 19, ii, no. 726.

75. L&P, 19, ii, no. 688.

76. NA: E315/161 ff.129, 136, 139.

77. J. Strype: 1824, I, ii, 495.

78. *Renaissance Englishwoman*: 1990, 15–17.

79. BL: Lansdowne ME 1236 , f.9.

80. L&P, 19, ii, no. 332.

81. CSP: Spanish, VII, no. 148 (p. 243).

82. CSP: Domestic, X, 278-83.

83. L&P, 20, i, no. 971.

84. CSP: Spanish, VIII, 130; CSP: Domestic, X, 278-83. On 5 May 1546, Catherine's servant, Cornelius Van Den, received a passport to travel to Germany. Could this have been connected in some way with Bucler's previous mission? L&P, 21, i, no. 744.

Chapter 11

1. L&P, 2, i, no. 1153. In March 1530, after his fall from grace, Wolsey spent his second night on the road toward his northern exile at York with Lady Parr at Rye House (W.T. Mellows, 'The Last Days of Peterborough Monastery', *Publications of the Northamptonshire Record Society*, 12, 1947, xviii).

2. Andrew Pettegree, *Foreign Protestant Communities in Sixteenth Century London*, Oxford, 1986, 9-22.

3. CUL: Inc.4.J.1.2 (3570), *Horae ad Usum Sarum*, 58b, 116b.

4. C. Parr: 1548, ff.Aviia-b.

5. C. Parr: 1548, f.Aviiib.

6. C. Parr: 1548, f.Dvb.

7. L&P, 13, i, nos 704, 1492.

8. W. Farrer: 1923-26, 235.

9. C. Parr: 1548, ff.Aiiib-Aiva.

10. C. Parr: 1548, f.Eib.

11. C. Parr: 1548, f.Dia.

12. C. Parr: 1548, ff.Eiib-Eiiia, Eiiiia-b.

13. NA: E315/161, ff.101, 117; NA: E101/424/12, f.43.

14. L&P, 12, i, no. 700; L&P, 12, ii, no. 489.

15. Agnes Strickland, *Lives of the Queens of England*, III, London, 1851, 198, where Strickland gives Lawrence Echard, *The History of England*, London, 1707, as a source. Echard states that Catherine Parr 'was a secret favourer of the Reformation: yet could not divert a Storm, which at this time fell on some of her Party at Windsor, particularly Person, Testwood, Filmer and Marbeck, all but the last of whom were burnt alive ... (p.709).'

16. J. McConica: 1965, 215–80, argues for Catherine's early familiarity with these men. W. Haugaard: 1969, 350–51, argues against it.

17. C. Parr: 1548, f.Aiiia.

18. BL: Lansdowne MS 97, f.43. Hoffman questions the dating of the letter which was written by Goldsmith to thank the queen for employing him in her household, but there seems to be nothing inconsistent with dating it to the early days of her marriage when her household was being formed nor does that timing appear to be too early a date for Catherine's reformist sympathies to be generally known (C. Hoffman, Jr.: 1959, 356).

19. William Cecil, the *Preface* to C. Parr: 1548, f.Ava.

20. C. Parr: 1548, ff.Dvb-Dvia.

21. BL: Lansdowne 76, art. 81, f.182. Anthony may be the baby born to Jane Cheyney in May 1544 as an item in the queen's chamber accounts records allowance for Henry Webb, the queen's servant, to represent her at the 'christening of Lord Wriothesley's child'. The bill is docketed in May in the 1543-44 accounts

(NA: E315/161, f.81). However, as the Wriothesleys had several daughters as well, it is equally possible that Anthony was born in the spring of 1543, died shortly after Catherine's marriage to Henry, and that the child born in May 1544 was a daughter. The Wriothesleys' next child, Henry, was christened in April 1545.

22. APC: 1558-1570, 174.

23. G. E. Cokayne: 1929, XII, i, 127, note b.

24. John Fisher, *Psalms or Prayers*, Catherine Parr (trans.), London, 1544, ff. Dviib- viiia, Dvib-viia.

25. Maria Dowling seems to be of this opinion (M. Dowling: 1987, 59-71).

26. C. Parr: 1548, f.Gviib.

27. C. Parr: 1548, f.Aiib.

28. C. Parr: 1548, f.Fviia.

29. Nicholas Udall, *Preface* to Desiderius Erasmus, *Paraphrase on St. Luke*, London, 31. January 1548, f.CCIIIb.

30. William Cecil, *Preface* to C. Parr: 1548, f.Aivb.

31. C. Parr: 1548, ff.Dvb, Bvia.

32. C. Parr: 1548, ff.Bviia-b.

33. BL: Lansdowne MS 1236, f.11.

34. M. Hatch: 1948, 221-23.

35. T. More: 1947, 404.

36. J. Fisher & C. Parr: 1544, 'The First Psalm: For the obtaining remission of sins'.

37. J. Fisher& C. Parr: 1544, f.Aiiiib.

38. J. Fisher & C. Parr: 1544, ff.Biiiia-b, Cva-b, Cva, Dviia, Ciiib, Ciiia, Ciia.

39. BL: Lansdowne MS 76, art. 81, f.182; C. Parr: 1548, ff. Aiiia, Aviia, Biib, Dvia, Dvib-Dviia; Catherine Parr, *Prayers or Meditations*, London, 6 November 1547, f.Cviiib.

40. J. Fisher & C. Parr: 1544, ff.Eviiib, Hiib.

41. J. Fisher & C. Parr: 1544, ff.Hiia-b.

42. C. Parr: 1548, f. Eva.

43. Patrick Bronte, 1818, quoted in Juliet Barker, *The Brontes*, London, 1995, 76.

44. Suzanne Trill, 'Sixteenth-century women's writing: Mary Sidney's Psalmes and the 'femininity' of translation', in *Writing and the English Renaissance*, William Zunder and Suzanne Trill (ed.), London & New York, 1996, 140-58. Trill deals with attitudes towards translation several decades later, however, and it should be noted that male translators far outnumbered female ones in the 1540s and that the alleged stigma later attached to such work, as discussed by Trill, seemed not to exist as this earlier date.

45. W. Wall: 1993, 280, note 3.

46. *Renaissance Englishwoman*: 1990, 21.

47. K. Henderson & B. McManus: 1985, 23.

48. Strype attributes the *Psalms or Prayers* to the queen's authorship (J. Strype: 1822, II, i, 204ff).

49. Nicholas Udall, the *Preface* to Desiderius Erasmus, *Paraphrase on Acts*, London, 1548, f. CCCCCXXb.

50. F. Rose-Troup: 1911, and Bodleian 2581.d.73(4), 3-6.

51. NA: E315/161, f.46.

52. NA: E315/161, f.46.

53. NA: E315/161, ff.185, 201, 206.

54. A letter written on October 24, 1932, from Sotheby's to the librarian of Exeter College (on file at the college), describes three copies of *Psalms or Prayers*, one of which the college had recently purchased. Of the other two, one was owned in that year by Miss Jane Seymour of Moyle in Wiltshire, who was a direct descendent of Edward Seymour, Duke of Somerset, whose presentation copy this may have been. The third copy was found in 1931 in the library of the late Earl of Carysfort at Elton Hall and sold by Sotheby's to an unnamed buyer. According to Sotheby's, 'This contains the name of Catherine Parr with presentation inscription from [crossed out] to [written in] her to [crossed out] from [written in] the King ... ' Given the amount of evidence that Catherine was the presenter of the copy, it would seem that the author of the letter had his 'from's' and 'to's' correct in the first place and erred in the alterations.

55. John Bale, *Illustrium Majoris Britanniae Scriptorum*, Wesel, 1548, f.238b.

56. NA: E314/22, f.17.

57. BL: Addit. MS 46,348, f.206a.

58. Udall's translation was marked, 'Transtulit ad reginam Catherinam' (G. Scheurweghs: 1939, xxxviii, note 3). On 23 February 1548, Imperial Ambassador Van der Delft wrote to Charles V that, '[Bernardino Ochinus] grows less and less esteemed, and I sincerely hope that at last he will have no auditors at all, unless it be the Duchess of Suffolk and [William Parr] the Marquis of Northampton ... ' (CSP: Spanish, vol. 9, Edward VI, 1547-1549, 253-54).

59. J. Strype: 1822, II, i, 204ff. In 1539, the work was published in London by Robert Redman, bound in with Savonarola's *Meditation of Psalme of Inte Domine speraui*. In 1540 a new edition came out also published in London by J. Herforde for R. Toye.

60. J. Bale: 1548, f.238b.

61. J. Fisher: 1544, ff. Aviib, Bviiia, Ciiib.

62. Ps 51:2, 5, 6, 11.

63. STC 4818, Bodleian Library, Oxford.

64. C. Parr: 1548, ff. Aiiiia-b, Ava, Eib.

65. See Chapter 12 in this volume.

66. Diane Willen writes of religious radicalism among women being constrained 'within the context of family religion', the family acting as the sponge which prevented the seepage of female religious radicalism into society at large, and so operating as a catalyst for social radicalism. Yet Catherine Parr's 'family' was the ruling one, a fact which offered her far greater exposure of her religious views and consequently far greater opportunity for instigating social change. D. Willen: 1989, 142–43.

67. *Renaissance Englishwoman*: 1990, 25–26, and Margaret L. King, *Women of the Renaissance*, Chicago & London, 1991, 208–09. King's assertion that, 'With the exception of the descendants of the More circle, the classically trained women of England nearly all derived from families who moved in the circuit of royalty,' makes Catherine Parr's achievement even more unique.

68. Elaine V. Beilin, *Redeeming Eve: Women Writers of the English Renaissance*, Princeton, 1987, xxi.

69. The later Elizabethan period produced a handful of original writers who also happened to be women such as Amelia Bassano and Mary Sidney, but they never became a commonplace.

70. BL: Lansdowne MS 1236, f.9.

71. Paul Althaus, *The Theology of Martin Luther*, Robert C. Schultz (trans.), Philadelphia, 1966, 274–86. I am indebted to Pastor James Kniseley of the Lutheran Church in the Foothills, La Canada, California, for bringing this work to my attention.

72. Now at Sudeley Castle, Gloucestershire.

73. STC 14639, Huntington Library 82485.

74. STC 14639, ff. Avb-via.

75. BL: Lansdowne MS 1236, f.9.

76. C. Parr: 1548, f.Eiib.

77. NA: E101/424/12, f.15, a book bill dated 4 June 1547 for two works by Erasmus, the *Enchiridion* and 'the book called the Preparation to Death'.

78. C. Parr: 1548, ff. Bviiib-Cia.

79. NA: PROB11/31; Image Reference: 94/72. The date on the will is 'the 28th day of March in the 45th year of our lord', obviously a clerical error. As the will was probated 27 March 1546, Margaret died the following year.

80. C. Parr: 1548, f.Divb.

81. For a discussion of these points, C. Hoffman, Jr.: 1959, 349–67, and qualifying comments in Janel Mueller, 'Devotion as Difference: Intertextuality in Queen Katherine Parr's *Prayers or Meditations* (1545)', *Huntington Library Quarterly*, 53, 1988, 171–97.

82. C. Hoffman, Jr.: 1959, 355, note 21.

83. J. Mueller: 1988, 177.

84. C. Hoffman, Jr.: 1959, 354.

85. J. McConica: 1965, 229–30, and John N. King, 'Patronage and Piety: The Influence of Catherine Parr', in *Silent But for the Word: Tudor Women as Patrons, Translators and Writers of Religious Works*, Margaret Patterson Hannay (ed.), Kent, OH, 1985, 50.

86. C. Parr: 1547, ff. Bviia, Bvb.

87. C. Parr: 1547, f.Biiib.

88. C. Parr: 1547, f.Bviiia.

89. J. Mueller: 1988, 177.

90. C. Parr: 1547, f. Ciia.

91. C. Parr: 1547, f.Aiiiia.

92. C. Parr: 1547, f.Aiiib.

93. NA: SP 10/4, no. 14 (35).

94. Goldsmith compares her to Esther and Sheba, Udall to Esther, Susanna, Mary, mother of James, Johanna, wife of Chusa, and Mary Magdalene. Ascham compares her to 'famous ladies out of Jerome and Augustine', Bale to Sheba and Esther and Parkhurst to Penelope.

95. Although the handwriting in the manuscript is quite close to the queen's own hand and may indeed

have been written by her, it is also very similar to that of her clerk of the closet, William Harper, and may in fact have been copied out by him.

96. J. Mueller: 1988, 190-91.

97. M. Hatch: 1948, 285.

98. NA: E101/426/3, f.3.

99. BL: Lansdowne MS 1236, f.11; M. Hatch: 1948, 221–23.

100. L&P, 21, i, no. 650(17).

101. *Morning and Evening Prayers With Diverse Psalms, Hymns and Meditations, Made and Set Forth by the Lady Elizabeth Tyrwhit*, was published in 1574 and reissued in 1582 in Thomas Bentley's *Monument of Matrons*. Lady Tyrwhit's work is less philosophical and less sophisticated than her mentor's, Catherine Parr.

102 L&P, 21, i, no. 790.

103 NA: LC2/2, f.45a.

Chapter 12

1. J. Strype: 1822, II, i, 203.

2. One avenue by which the queen could have come into possession of literature from Venice was through her household musicians, the Bassanos, who during her time as queen, made several licensed journeys to their home there. NA: E179/69/37, 31 May 1545 and 13 March 1546. The queen's book of Petrarch was published in Venice in 1534 by Gabriel Giolidi of Ferrara.

3. H. Maynard Smith, *Henry VIII and the Reformation*, London, 1948, 394-99.

4. *The Primer in English and Latin set forth by the King's Majesty and his Clergy*, 6 September 1545, f.Bivb.

5. H. Smith: 1948, 398.

6. *The Primer:* 1545, ff.Giiib-iva.

7. H. Smith: 1948, 398-399.

8. STC 300.2 Huntington Library, San Marino, California.

9. L&P, 19, ii, no. 688.

10. H. Smith: 1948, 396.

11. STC 4818 Bodleian Library, Oxford.

12. NA: E315/161, f.69.

13. BL: Addit. MS 46,348, f.208a.

14. E. J. Devereux, 'The Publication of the English Paraphrases', *Bulletin of the John Rylands Library*, 51 (1968–69), 354.

15. *The Primer:* 1545, f.Bivb.

16. William Tuer, *The History of the Horn Book*, vol. 1, London, 1896, 5–18.

17. H. Smith: 1948, 399.

18. Psalms 119:45–46, 49–51.

19. M. King: 1991, 208–09, and J. King: 1985, 48.

20. N. Udall, *Preface* to the *Paraphrase of St. Luke*, f.ccvi.

21. Thomas Key, *Preface* to the *Paraphrase of St. Mark*, f.ccix.

22. If this was the intent, Mary had more influence on Mallet than he on her. On 29 April 1551, he was sent to the Tower for saying mass. APC: III, 267.

23. E. Devereux: 1968-69, 365, and Philip Hughes, *The Reformation in England*, II, London 1954, 243.

24. BL: Cott. MS Vespasian, F.3, f.37.

25. J. Strype: 1822, II, i, 48.

26. S. Trill: 1996, 140-58.

27. N. Udall: 1548, *Preface* to the *Paraphrase of St. Matthew*.

28. Desiderius Erasmus, *The 1st Tome or Volume of the Paraphrases upon the New Testament*, London, 31 January 1548, f.Aia.

29. D. Erasmus: 1548, ff.Aia-b, Aiiia-b, 21a.

30. C. Parr: 1548, ff.E3a-b, Bviib, Bivb, Aviib, Aiiiib, Divb; C. Parr: 1547, f.Bviiia.

31. D. Erasmus: 1548, f.Aiib.

32. Bodleian: Ashmolean MS, no. 1729, 4.

33. John Strype, *Memorials of Thomas Cranmer*, London, 1694, 80.

34. J. Mueller: 1988, 175-78.

35. E. Devereux: 1968-69, 365-67, and *Letters of ... Gardiner:* 1933, 133-35.

36. J. Muller: 1933, 135.

37. N. Udall: 1548, *Preface* to the *Paraphrase of St. Matthew*.

38. N. Udall, Preface to the *Paraphrase of St. John*, f.cccxcix.

39. Nicholas Udall: 1548, *Preface* to the *Paraphrase of Acts*, f.ccccxx.

40. M Hatch: 1948, 278.

41. Lady Margaret Beaufort, the *Preface* to *The Mirroure of Golde to the Synfull Soule*, 1522.

42. M. Beaufort: 1522, *Preface*.

43. Marguerite of Navarre, *Mirror of the Sinful Soul*, translated into English by Princess Elizabeth Tudor (1544), Percy W. Ames, *Introduction*, London, 1897, 40.

44. Esther Sowernam, *Esther Hath Hanged Haman*, 1617, quoted in K. Henderson & B. McManus: 1985, 27.

45. Marguerite of Navarre: 1897, 39ff and *Introduction*, 40.

46. C. Parr: 1547, f.Aviia.

47. C. Parr: 1547, f.Bvb.

48. In 1548, John Bale published what he claimed to be Elizabeth's translation, but was probably in reality his own version of the book. He retitled it *A Godly Meditation of the Inward Love of the Soul*, and it is this title which was subsequently used for all later English editions. Bale's version is what might be described as a fleshed out version of the book constructed on the bare bones of Elizabeth's prose. In 1570, another version was published, again claiming to be Elizabeth's work. Its florid, rhetorical style is typical of much popular devotional literature of the period. For a commentary on Elizabeth and Marguerite of Valois, see Anne Lake Prescott, 'The Pearl of the Valois and Elizabeth I', in *Silent But for the Word: Tudor Women as Patrons, Translators and Writers of Religious Works*, Margaret Patterson Hannay (ed.), Kent, OH, 1985, 61-75.

49. C. Parr: 1548, ff.Aia-b.

50. C. Parr: 1548, f.Eia.

51. C. Parr: 1548, ff.Cvib, Giia..

52. C. Parr: 1548, ff.Aib-iia.

53. C. Parr: 1548, f.Avia.

54. C. Parr: 1548, ff.Aiiia-b.

55. C. Parr: 1548, f.Gviiib.

56. C.-Parr: 1548, ff.Fvb-vib.

57. C. Parr: 1548, f.Fviiia.

58. C. Parr: 1548, f.Aviib.

59. Plowden comments that Catherine Parr's influence on Elizabeth had 'incalculable consequences for England.' A. Plowden: 1979, 104.

60. Patricia Crawford, *Women and Religion in England, 1500–1720*, London & New York, 1993, 1, and Suzanne Trill, 'Religion and the construction of femininity', in *Women and Literature in Britain, 1500–1700*, Helen Wilcox (ed.), Cambridge, 1996, 32.

61 . C. Parr: 1548, f.Biib.

62. C. Parr: 1548, f.Evb.

63. Catherine Parr to Sir Thomas Seymour, 1547, Dent-Brocklehurst MS at Sudeley Castle.

64. C. Parr: 1548, f.Fviiia.

65. C. Parr: 1548, f.Fvia.

66. C. Parr: 1548, f.Eva.

67. C. Parr: 1548, ff.Ciia, Bva-b.

68. It has been suggested that the queen's *Lamentation of a Sinner* circulated in manuscript form at court before Henry's death and that it was part of a package of suspect books sent by Sir William Paget to Stephen Gardiner, while the latter was on the continent (Janel Mueller, 'A Tudor Queen Finds Her Voice: Katherine Parr's Lamentation of a Sinner', in *The Historical Renaissance: New Essays on Tudor and Stuart Literature and Culture*, Heather Dubrow and Richard Strier (eds), Chicago, 1988, 28, and Anthony Martienssen, *Queen Katherine Parr*, London, 1973, 201). An examination of the text of Gardiner's letter to Paget, dated 5 November 1545, however, makes no mention of the queen or of her book (L&P, 20, ii, no. 733). The *Lamentation* mentioned in the letter is a work (probably written in 1543), entitled *The Lamentation of a Christian Man against the City of London*, by Henry Brinklow, who died that same year, under the pseudonym Roderyck Mors. This volume may have been known to the queen as Brinklow's widow subsequently married Stephen Vaughan, the king's financial agent in Antwerp, whose first wife was Catherine's silkwoman. It is highly unlikely that Catherine's *Lamentation of a Sinner* was written before 1546, or that, having escaped arrest by a hair's breadth in that year, she would have risked further peril by circulating what was a far more radical religious work than any she had so far published.

69. C. Parr: 1548, f.Fvb.

70. C. Parr: 1548, f.Diia.
71. C. Parr: 1548, f.Dva.
72. C. Parr: 1548, ff.Biia-b.
73. C. Parr: 1548, f.Dvib.
74. C. Parr: 1548, f.Bvia.
75. P. Althaus: 1966, 274-286.
76. C. Parr: 1548, ff.Giva-b.
77. C. Parr: 1548, f.Fia.
78. C. Parr: 1548, f.Fva.
79. C. Parr: 1548, f.Divb.
80. C. Parr: 1548, f.Hiib.
81. C. Parr: 1548, f.Ciiib.
82. C. Parr: 1548, f.Gvb.
83. C. Parr: 1548, f..Civb.
84. C. Parr: 1548, ff.Cvib-viia.
85. C. Parr: 1548, ff.Cvia-b.
86. C. Parr: 1548, ff.Biiib-iva.
87. C. Parr: 1548, ff.Biiia-b.
88. C. Parr: 1548, f.Eiiib.
89. Jean Bellemain, Edward VI's French tutor, translated *Lamentation of a Sinner* into a French poem for the king, including Cecil's preface. Two copies of Bellemain's translation are known to exist. One is in the British Library, and the other is among the Cecil Papers at Hatfield House (BL: Royal MS 16 Exxviii and Cecil Papers no. 314). The gift of a copy of the poem to Cecil as co-sponsor of the original project would have been a politic gesture. In addition to French, *Lamentation* was translated into Latin, an irony that would not have been lost on the queen, by John Radcliffe of Cleeve, the son of Robert Radcliffe, first Earl of Sussex (BL: Royal MS 7D.IX).
90. *Hall's Chronicle*: 1809, 864-65.
91. *Hall's Chronicle*: 1809, 865.
92. BL: Lansdowne MS 1236, f.11.
93. C. Parr: 1548, f.Fviiia.
94. See J. Mueller: 1988, 191-97, particularly notes 9 -11.
95. C. Parr: 1548, ff.Eivb, Eia-b.
96. Diarmaid MacCulloch comments on the important role Catherine played in lobbying for Cambridge University (D. MacCulloch: 1996, 326).
97. *Hall's Chronicle*: 1809, 865.
98. M. Hatch: 1948, 221.
99. I am indebted to Jonathan Smith, manuscript cataloguer of Trinity College Library, for pertinent information regarding the founding of the college.
100. S. James: 1993, 104.
101. L&P, 5, no. 951 and L&P, 7, no. 432.
102. *Dictionary of National Biography* , XVI, Sir Leslie Stephen & Sir Sidney Lee (eds), London, 1917, p.825, article on John Redman.
103. Other members of the Redman clan, John Redman and Robert Redman (active 1517–1540) and his wife, Elizabeth Pickering, were printers in London. Robert, whose press was near Greyfriars, died in 1540 and his widow continued the business under her own name until she remarried a year later. John Redman was active between 1534–1541 in Southwark. Katharine F. Pantzer, *Short Title Catalogue*, III, London, 1919, 143.
104. L&P, 20, ii, no. 909(50).
105. The Huddlestons were an ancient Cumberland family related to both the Parrs and the Redmans. Sir John Huddleston of Millom, Penrith and Blennerhasset, died in 1493, leaving as his heir, his seventeen-year-old grandson, Richard, under the guardianship of his uncles, Sir John Huddleston, the younger, and William Huddleston, and Edward Redman, among others. Richard eloped before 1497 with Elizabeth Dacre, daughter of Catherine Parr's great-aunt, Mabel Parr, Lady Dacre, and sister of Thomas, Lord Dacre, who in 1523-4 tried unsuccessfully to arrange Catherine's first marriage. Princess Elizabeth's fellowship candidate was a member of this family. Susan E. James, 'Henry VII and the Prerogativa Regis: The Case of Mabel Dacre', *CW2*, XCIX (1999), 1777-84.
106. J. Strype: 1694, 109.
107. L&P, 21, i, no. 289.

Chapter 13

1. *Renaissance Englishwoman*: 1990, 5.
2. BL: Sloane MS no. 1523, f.37b.
3. K. Henderson & B. McManus: 1985, 36.
4. C. Parr: 1548, f.Gvia.
5. C. Parr: 1548, ff.Gviiia-b.
6. C. Parr: 1548, f.Ciib.
7. C. Parr: 1548, f.Bva.
8. C. Parr: 1548, f.Ciiia.
9. BL: Lansdowne MS 1236, f.9.
10. Henry's promulgation in 1539 of the Six Articles was a public affirmation of his efforts to prevent the English Church from evolving any further toward what he perceived as heretical radicalism.
11. C. Parr: 1548, f.Fia.
12. C. Parr: 1548, f.Eviia.
13. BL: Sloane MS no. 1523, f.37b.
14. Redworth claims that a 'rift between the royal couple was widely talked about well before Gardiner left the Low Countries.' He gives no reference for this and all the evidence supports the contrary. Glyn Redworth, *In Defence of the Catholic Church*, Oxford, 1990, 233 and note 10.
15. CSP: Venice, 6, iii, p. 1632.
16. J. Foxe: 1866, V, 553-61, for Foxe's version of the Stephen Gardiner-Thomas Wriothesley conspiracy against the queen and for all subsequent Foxe quotes.
17. P. Hughes: 1950/1963, II, 63.
18. Susan Brigden, *London and the Reformation*, Oxford, 1989, 359.
19. L&P, 21, ii, no. 752.
20. L&P, 21, ii, no. 756.
21. CSP: Spanish, VIII, p.104.
22. G. Redworth: 1990, 231-38.
23. In James Gairdner's opinion, 'nothwithstanding (Foxe's Protestant) bias (for which it is not difficult to make allowance), no doubt it is true at least in substance ... Strange as it is, however, we cannot say that what is known of Henry VIII's personal history makes it at all inconceivable, and we have seen already that Foxe vouches for its truth by the evidence of witnesses living when he wrote. Moreover, Parsons, the Jesuit, in his comments on Foxe, accepts it all as true, except that he maintains the Queen was saved, not by her submission and renewed favour in the King's eyes, but by the King's mortal illness and death; for the date, as he infers from Foxe, was the very last year of the King's reign.' James Gairdner, *Lollardy and the Reformation in England*, II, London, 1908, 455, 460. Another biographer of Stephen Gardiner's, James Arthur Muller, believes that: 'After we discount Foxe's animus toward Gardiner, and his desire to put the King's proceedings in the best light possible, there is nothing inherently improbable in the story.' J. Muller: 1926, 139.
24. J. Foxe: 1866, V, 558.
25. *Narratives of the Days of the Reformation*, John Gough Nichols (ed.), Camden Society Papers, 77, London, 1859, 308-11.
26. CSP: Spanish, VIII, 1545-1556, 533.
27. CSP: Spanish, VIII, 1545-1556, 425.
28. *Literary Remains*: 1857, ii, 410.
29. CSP: Spanish, IX, 1547-1549, 428-29.
30. Shortly after Henry's death, Van der Delft gave it as his opinion that the Duke of Somerset and Paget 'would split the rule (of council and kingdom) between them.' CSP: Spanish, 1547-1549, 153.
31. L&P, 21, i, no. 1181.
32. L&P, 21, i, no. 661.
33. G. Cokayne: 1929, X, 280, note d.
34. According to Foxe, the plan was to arrest the queen and her principal ladies and accomplices in heresy – Anne Herbert, Maud Lane and Elizabeth Tyrwhit – and convey them quickly and quietly by barge at night to the Tower. J. Foxe: 1866, V, 557.

35. For a description of Gardiner's attempts on the privy chamber, see, *Letters of ... Scudamore*: 1990, 67-148.

36. G. Elton: 1977, 310. Scarisbrick disagrees with this, concluding that Henry had to the end, a firm hand on the helm of state (J.Scarisbrick: 1968, 458).

37. P. Crawford: 1993, 105.

38. C. Parr: 1544, f.Jiiia.

39. J. Foxe: 1866, V, 555.

40. L&P, 21, i, no. 289. Charles Brandon, Duke of Suffolk, died 22 August 1545.

41. L&P, 21, i, no. 289.

42. NA: E314/22, f.44.

43. NA: E314/22, ff.22, 29, 47-48, 51-53.

44. P. Hughes: 1950/1963, 64.

45. APC: I, 1542-1547, 400.

46. APC: I, 1542-1547, 408, and L&P, 21, i, nos 732, 744, 759, 790.

47. L&P, 21, i, no. 769.

48. L&P, 21, ii, no. 770(71).

49. NA: E101/424/12, f.157.

50. L&P, 21, i, no. 769.

51. J. Scarisbrick: 1968, 473.

52. L&P, 21, i, no. 1180.

53. J. Gairdner: 1908, II, 465.

54. L&P, 21, i, no. 845.

55. NA: E315/161, f.3 and E314/22, ff.6, 10.

56. NA: E101/426/2 and E101/424/12, f.124.

57. L&P, 11, no. 533.

58. E. Beilin: 1987, 39, 43.

59. *Narratives*: 1859, 309.

60. APC, I, 1542-1547, 462

61. Edward Ascu, *A Historie contayning the Warres & Etc.*, London, 1607, 308.

62. Robert Persons, *A Treatise of Three Conversions of England*, II, London, 1976, 493.

63. C. Parr: 1548, f.Cvb.

64. L&P, 21, i, no. 1181.

65. For a discussion of Anne Askew as a woman expected to learn from religious ideology but not to contribute to it, see D. Willen: 1989, 143-44.

66. J. Gairdner: 1908, II, 453.

67. This was Sir William Fitzwilliam of Milton in Northamptonshire.

68. L&P, 21, i, p.586, note.

69. L&P, 21, i, no. 1180. Also see P. Hughes: 1950/1963, 68, and J. Gairdner: 1908, II, 453-54.

70. *Narratives*: 1859, 307, note b.

71. L&P, 21, i, no. 1181.

72. L&P, 21, i, no. 1027.

73. C. Parr: 1544, ff.Hiia-Hiiib.

74. William Parr, Earl of Essex, was absent from council meetings during 1-12 July. He reappeared 13-15 July, was absent 16-19 July and returned 20 July, attending more or less regularly until the council moved to Hampton Court during the second week in August.

75. L&P, 21, i, no. 1227.

76. J. Foxe: 1866, V, 554.

77. J. Foxe: 1866, V, 556-60.

78. F. Rose-Troup: 1911, and Bodleian 2581.d.73(4), 6.

79. Robert Cooch is an example of this. Bishop Parkhurst wrote in 1574: 'Robert Cooch is a very accomplished man, and well skilled in music. When I was preacher in Queen Catherine's household, he was steward of the wine cellar. When King Edward was alive, that most famous physician and very learned divine Master William Turner wrote a book against him in which he refuted his opinion on original sin. At that time he likewise held erroneous opinions on the baptism of infants. He dreamed up strange things about the Lord's Supper. He very often troubled Coverdale and myself with these controversies, so much so that we wearied of him. He was extremely verbose. When Jewel and other learned men came to the court to visit me, he instantly began to discuss these subjects with them, nor could he make an end of his talking (*Letter Book*: 1974-75, 83).' That the queen allowed such liberties

of thought and speech in her wine steward illustrates the general freedom with which her household was treated by its mistress.

80. I am grateful to John Brunton, Senior Archivist at the Devon Record Office, for information regarding this manor.

81. C. Parr: 1548, f.Cviiib.

82. A comparison of Catherine Parr's 1546 speech of submission to her husband, as quoted by Foxe, with Katherina of Padua's c.1594 speech of submission to her husband in Shakespeare's *The Taming of the Shrew* makes an interesting study. There are a number of parallels in imagery and word usage in the two speeches and it is fascinating to speculate that perhaps Shakespeare had read Foxe's work which was likely enough and used both Catherine's name and her grand submission as elements in his play. The tone, of course, with Shakespeare was one of comedy; for the queen, it came very close to becoming the tragedy of her life.

83. J. Foxe: 1866, V, 559–60.

84. L&P, 21, ii, no. 769, for the queen's movements.

85. L&P, 21, ii, no. 347.

86. L&P, 21, ii, no. 686. Catherine seems to have had several of these double portrait miniatures made for she also presented one to Prince Edward (BL: Cott. MS Nero C.x, f.8).

87. L&P, 21, i, no. 1383(96) and L&P, 21, ii, nos 476(56), 476(90), 476(94).

Chapter 14

1. L&P, 21, i, no. 1058.

2. *Privy Purse Expenses*: 1831, 186, for Mary's jewels, and HMC: Salisbury, I, 1306–1571, no. 242, a letter from Sir Thomas Seymour to the Princess Mary, 17 December 1548, regarding the jewels Henry had had made for the queen 'at the coming of the French admiral'. Although not individually listed, the jewels given to Catherine make up part of the list of items in her jewel coffer, inventoried in 1550 (BL: Addit. MS 46,348, ff.167b–71b.).

3. L&P, 21, ii, no. 769.

4. L&P, 21, i, no. 785.

5. Edward Hall, *Henry VIII*, vol. II, London, 1904 edition, 359.

6. L&P, 21, i, no. 1384.

7. E. Hall: 1904, 359.

8. E. Hall: 1904, 359.

9. For a detailed discussion, see J. Scarisbrick: 1968, 472–73.

10. J. Gairdner: 1908, 463–64.

11. J.Scarisbrick: 1968, 467.

12. E. Hall: 1904, 360.

13. NA: E36/237, 925 and S. Thurley: 1993, 65.

14. NA: E101/424/12, ff.98, 170, 181, 182.

15. NA: E101/424/12, f.189.

16. *The Legend*: 1874, no. 33, p.9.

17. S. Thurley: 1993, 63.

18. L&P, 21, ii, no. 769, p.402.

19. L&P, 21, ii, no. 605.

20. L&P, 21, ii, nos 605, 606.

21. L&P, 21, ii, no. 684.

22. L&P, 21, ii, no. 606.

23. L&P, 21, ii, no. 684.

24. Constance Jordan, 'Feminism and the Humanists: The Case of Sir Thomas Elyot's 'Defence of Good Women'', *Renaissance Quarterly*, 36, no. 2 (Summer 1983) 181–201.

25. Sir Thomas Elyot, *The Defence of Good Women*, London, 1540, f.Eii.

26. T. Elyot: 1540, f.Ev.

27. Sir Thomas Elyot, *The Defence of Good Women*, quoted in Hilda L. Smith, 'Humanist education and the Renaissance concept of woman', in *Women and Literature in Britain*, 1500-1700, Helen Wilcox (ed.), Cambridge, 1996, 19.

28. N. Udall: 1847.

29. NA: E101/426/3, ff.6, 23.

30. J. Scarisbrick: 1968, 488–96.

31. D. Starkey: 1985, 146–65.

32. L&P, 21, ii, no. 713.

33. For a discussion on this subject, see Lacey Baldwin Smith, 'The Last Will and Testament of Henry VIII: A Question of Perspective', *Journal of British Studies*, II (1962), 20ff, and M. Levine, 'The Last Will and Testament of Henry VIII: A Reappraisal Reappraised', *Historian*, XXVI, no. 4 (4 August 1964), 471–85.

34. In the two years that followed Henry's death, £20,000 of the Crown's annual landed income passed from the Crown into private hands, nearly half of that as outright gifts. By 1551 after Warwick's coup, this amount ballooned to £40,000 (G. R. Elton: 1977, 335).

35. *A Collection of State Papers Relating to Affairs in the Reigns of King Henry VIII... Left by William Cecill, Lord Burghley*, Samuel Haynes (ed.), London, 1740, 104.

36. L&P, 21, ii, no. 356.

37. CSP: Spanish, IX, 6–7.

38. Samuel Rhea Gammon, *Statesman and Schemer: William, 1st Lord Paget, Tudor Minister*, Hamden, CT, 1973, 122.

39. G. Cokayne: 1929, X, 277, note j.

40. BL: Addit. MS 46,348, ff.205b–207a.

41. For early accounts of Henry's obsequies, see Charles Wriothesley, *A Chronicle of England*, William Douglas Hamilton (ed.), Camden Society, NS.XI, 1875-1877, i, 181; *Rymer's Foedera*, VI, London, 1741 (republished 1967), 142–45.

42. Maurice Bond, *The Romance of St. George's Chapel, Windsor Castle*, Windsor, 1987, 34.

43. Edward VI's coronation took place five days later, on Saturday, 19 February. Edward left the Tower at 1.00 pm, and rode in procession with one of the Scottish ambassadors. The young king, dressed all in silver and white, with pearls, diamonds and rubies sewn to his cap and clothing, rode on a horse caparisoned in crimson through the streets of the city as ordnance was fired from the Tower. Pageants and musical interludes and speeches were performed along the route to entertain the king and a conduit ran with 'fair sweet wine'. The boy king grew impatient and some speakers were by-passed 'for lack of time ... his Grace made such speed.' Near St. Paul's, an Aragonese acrobat slid down a cable strung from the steeple of the cathedral to an anchor near the gate of the Dean's house, 'as if he had been an arrow from a bow'. Landing on the ground, the acrobat kissed the king's foot and ran halfway back up the cable to perform a variety of death-defying tricks. The fascinated boy king 'detained him for a good space of time', and then proceeded past Temple Bar and eight French trumpeters and so to Westminster Abbey. *London Pageants*, J. G. Nichols (ed.), London, 1837, 42–50.

Chapter 15

1. BL: Sloane MS 1523, f.37b.

2. C. Parr: 1548, f.Bvia.

3. *Narratives*: 1859, 295.

4. W. Seymour: 1972, 66.

5. 'Anecdotes and Character of Archbishop Cranmer by Ralph Morice, his Secretary', in *Narratives of the Days of the Reformation*, J. G. Nichols (ed.), Camden Society, 77, London, 1859, 260–63, for this and quotes in the following paragraph.

6. NA: SP10/4/31, 62.

7. *The Arundel Harington Manuscript of Tudor Poetry*, Ruth Hughey (ed.), Columbus, OH, 1960, I:79, II:5.

8. L. Stone: 1965, 346.

9. *A Collection ... Henry VIII*: 1740, 61-109 for transcripts of testimonies at Seymour's trial.

10. L&P, 19, ii, no. 501.

11. L&P, 19, ii, no. 501.

12. L&P, 21, i, nos 785, 971.

13. C. Parr: 1548, f.Bva.

14. C. Parr: 1548, f.Cviib.

15. J. Strype: 1922, II, i, 197.

16. Dent-Brocklehurst MS, Sudeley Castle.

17. NA: SP 10/1/41.

18. Bodleian: Rawlinson MS D.1070.4.

19. Present whereabouts unknown.

20. Bodleian: Rawlinson MS D.1070.4.

21. Dent-Brocklehurst MS, Sudeley Castle.

22. *King's Works*: 1982, IV, 64.

23. NA: E315/340, f.20a.

24. Hanworth, together with Chelsea and Mortlake, were Catherine's dower manors. She spent little time at Mortlake but as queen dowager divided most of her time between Chelsea and Hanworth. During the first week of June 1547, Catherine had archery butts set up for her amusement at Hanworth. NA: E101/424/12, ff.11, 14. Besides being an area of outdoor recreation, the gardens at Hanworth were known for the excellence of their strawberries. *King's Works*: 1982, IV, 148.

25. NA: E101/424/12, f.162.

26. NA: SP10/1, f. 41 (p.128).

27. Bodleian: Rawlinson MS D.1070.4.

28. Present whereabouts unknown.

29. Bodleian: Ashmolean MS 1729, p.4.

30. Present whereabouts unknown.

31. NA: SP10/1/41.

32. Bodleian: Rawlinson MS D.1070.4.

33. NA: SP 10/1, f.41 (p.128).

34. NA: SP 10/1/43.

35. CSP: Edward VI, no. 198, p. 92.

36. NA: E101/424/12, f.135.

37. NA: E101/424/12, ff. 5, 12, 26.

38. Bodleian: Rawlinson MS D.1070.4.

39. *A Collection ... Henry VIII*: 1740, 106.

40. HMC: Salisbury, I, 1306-1571, no. 220, p.51.

41. CSP: Domestic, Edward VI, no. 185 (p.85). For a list of plate left to the queen by Henry VIII, BL: Addit. MS no. 5751, Pt. 2, and for warrants of money disbursed to the queen by the Privy Council, in fulfillment of the king's will, see APC: II, 120, 137, 218. For the text of Henry's will, *Rymer's Foedera*: 1726-35, XV, 112- 14.

42. BL: Addit. MS 46,348, f.67b.

43. This shortage of funds led Somerset to order an inventory of the royal plate, jewels and other valuables, completed in 1550. BL: Addit. MS 46, 348.

44. NA: PROB11/24; Image Reference 149/110. If her mother's gift was a piece of jewellery, it would have been one of the few that Catherine salvaged from the sack of Snape Castle in 1536 and would therefore have had all the more value for her.

45. NA: E101/426/3. This file, from the first six months of Edward VI's reign, is a severely damaged collection of documents, many concerning Catherine's difficulties getting her estate servants to obey her commands.

46. HMC: Salisbury, I, 1306–1571, no. 220, p.50. Somerset had as many difficulties with the recalcitrant Sir Henry Longe as the queen. Having leased Fausterne to Longe as a method of securing the park for himself, Somerset then tried to remove Longe from the place without notable success. (HMC: Salisbury, I, 1306–1571).

47. Cecil MS, Hatfield House. Also printed in *A Collection ... Henry VIII*: 61. For Seymour's advice to the queen regarding this dispute, NA: SP10/1/43.

48. Sir Thomas Seymour at his trial for treason swore that he had had one of his servants 'move the king if he could be his governor as (Sir Michael) Stanhope was (NA: SP10/6/27)'. Stanhope was 'Governor of the King's Highness' in August 1547, when he was addressed as such in a letter to him from the Privy Council (BL: Addit. MS 29, 597, f.8a).

49. CSP: Spanish, IX, 1547–1549, 429.

50. C. Jordan: 1983, 181–201.

51. NA: SP10/6, f.28–29.

52. W. Seymour: 1972, 222.

53. J. Hayward: 1630, 197-98.

54. *A Collection ... Henry VIII*: 1740, 61.

55. A. L. Rowse, *Shakespeare, The Man*, London, 1988, 80.

56. In testimony against Seymour, given by his former servant, William Wrightman, Wrightman mentions the grudge, 'borne towards him by my Lady of Somerset ... ' *A Collection ... Henry VIII*: 1740, 68.

57. Bodleian: Rawlinson MS D1070.4.

58. Bodleian: Ashmolean MS 1729, f.4.

59. BL: Lansdowne MS 1236, f. 26.

60. NA: E101/424/12, ff. 2, 23, 27.

61. CSP: Spanish, IX, 104.

62. CSP: Edward VI, no. 185 (p.84).

63. Handwritten note in the Huntington Library's copy (140887) of *Literary Remains*: 1857, 44.

64. BL: Cott. MS Faustina E.III, and *Sylloge Epistolarum*: 1716, 211.

65. C. Levin: 1986, 121.

66. St. Jerome, 'Against jovinianus', in *Library of Nicene and Post-Nicene Fathers*, 6:367, quoted in K. Henderson & B. McManus: 1985, 43, note 11.

67. CSP: Edward VI, no. 186 (p.86).

68. HMC: Ancaster, 454-56. The duchess later gave the horses as presents to Lady Lisle.

69. On 4 June, a submitted bill records an order by the queen for a large selection of presentation copies from Thomas Berthelet, one of the *Psalms or Prayers* in white and gilt on leather, twenty-four copies of *Prayers or Meditations*, two bound in white satin, sixteen written on vellum, and one, almost certainly a gift for Edward VI, 'printed in fine vellum with a great letter' (NA: E101/424/12, f.15; F. Rose-Troup: 1911, and Bodleian 2581.d.73(4), 3.) Apparently the queen was conducting her own public relations campaign and using these sumptuous copies of her works as gifts to create a more positive climate of support among her well-wishers.

70. *The Chronicle and Political Papers of King Edward VI*, W. K. Jordan (ed.), Ithaca, New York, 1966, 6.

Chapter 16

1. *Nicholas Throckmorton*: 1874, 17.

2. *A Collection ... Henry VIII*: 1740, 77–78.

3. NA: SP1/195, ff.177a-b, 179a, and L&P, 19, ii, no. 688.

4. NA: E315/340, ff.24a, 25b, 28b, 29a-b, 30a.

5. *A Collection ... Henry VIII*: 1740, 96.

6. *A Collection ... Henry VIII*: 1740, 99–102.

7. *A Collection ... Henry VIII*: 1740, 102.

8. CSP: Edward VI, no. 195 (p.91).

9. *A Collection ... Henry VIII*: 1740, 98.

10. *A Collection ... Henry VIII*: 1740, 99–102.

11. *A Collection ... Henry VIII*: 1740, 96.

12. *A Collection ... Henry VIII*: 1740, 77–81.

13. *A Collection ... Henry VIII*: 1740, 96.

14. CSP: Edward VI, no. 198 (p.92).

15. CSP: Edward VI, no. 181 (p.82).

16. *A Collection ... Henry VIII*: 1740, 96.

17. *A Collection ... Henry VIII*: 1740, 96.

18. The bearer of this message was Seymour's illegitimate half-brother, John Seymour. *A Collection ... Henry VIII*: 1740, 100.

19. *A Collection ... Henry VIII*: 1740, 99.

20. *The Sermons of Hugh Latimer*, John Watkins (ed.), London, 1926, I, 207 (the seventh sermon preached before Edward VI on 19 April 1549).

21. *A Collection ... Henry VIII*: 1740, 99–100.

22. NA: SP10/2, f.25 (p.84c).

23. BL: Addit. MS 46,348, ff.206a, 207a.

24. *A Collection ... Henry VIII*: 1740, 96-97.

25. M. Hatch: 1948, 280.
26. M. Hatch: 1948, 283-86.
27. NA: SP 10/2, f.25 (p.84c).
28. NA: SP 10/5, f.5 (p.8b).

Chapter 17

1. The members of the commission were Cranmer, Tunstall, Bishop Holbeach of Rochester, William May, Dean of St. Paul's, Simon Keynes, Dean of Exeter, Dr. John Redman, Nicholas Ridley, and John Joseph. The generally conservative character of the commission, despite the presence of Ridley, more or less ensured that Northampton would not be granted a divorce.

2. L&P, 19, i, no. 141(65); A. R. Winnett, *Divorce and Re-Marriage in Anglicanism*, London & New York, 1958, 40-41; T. E. Rogers, *Records of Yarlington*, London, 1890, 20–22. Although Strype estimates the annual worth of the manor at £30 (T. Rogers: 1890, 22), thus placing Smith's purchase price at a ten-year income, there is no proof that Smith ever actually paid Northampton a penny. The timing of the sale lends credence to its interpretation as a gift for goodwill in the marquess' very tricky divorce case.

3. Evidence of the date of the marriage exists in an enfeoffment of his northern estates which Northampton made in Elisabeth's name. CPR: Edward VI, 1547–1553, i, 210. In March 1558, Queen Mary commanded Sir Edward Waldegrave and others 'to compound with Elizabeth Cobham [*sic*] for lands held by her, parcel of the estate of the late [i.e. forfeited] Marquess of Northampton.' CSP: Domestic, 1547–1580, 100.

4. C. Cooper & T. Cooper: 1858, I, 297.
5. CSP: Spanish, IX, 253-254.
6. *A Collection ... Henry VIII*: 1740, 62.

7. Wendy Wall quotes a statistic taken from L. Stone: 1965, 590, that 'one out of every four women died in the early years of marriage,' ostensibly in childbirth. In W. Wall: 1993, 283–85.

8. *A Collection ... Henry VIII*: 1740, 62.
9. NA: SP 10/4, f.14 (p.35).
10. CSP: Edward VI, no. 188 (p.87).
11. CSP: Edward VI, no. 184 (p.84).
12. *A Collection ... Henry VIII*: 1740, 62.
13. NA: SP 10/4, f.14 (p.35).
14. *Literary Remains*: 1857, 54, note.
15. CSP: Edward VI, no. 185 (p.85).
16. CSP: Henry VIII, Part II, 1530–1547, 896; *Letter Book*: 1974-75, 22, note 18.
17. CSP: Edward VI, no. 141 (p.60).
18. CSP: Edward VI, no. 150 (p.63).
19. *A Collection ... Henry VIII*: 1740, 104.
20. *Sylloge Epistolarum*: 1716, 151–55.
21. *Sylloge Epistolarum*: 1716, 165–66.
22. NA: SP 10/5, f.2 (p.3).
23. *A Collection ... Henry VIII*: 1740, 103–04.
24. *A Collection ... Henry VIII*: 1740, 103–04.
25. College of Arms MS: RR 21/C, f.98a.
26. BL: Lansdowne MS 1236, f.9.

27. The queen's verbal will is dated 5 September, (NA: PROB 11/32; Image Reference 284/201.) The will was probated 6 December (not September, as has often been claimed) 1548, with Lord Seymour as chief executor. Intriguingly, the recorded text in the NA is a palimpsest, having been written, partially erased and rewritten a second time. It would be of immense interest to know what the original text said.

28. College of Arms MS: RR 21/C, ff.98-99 and MS: R.20 (a later copy).
29. Catherine's memorial today is a modern marble effigy in the chapel of Sudeley Castle.
30. *A Collection ... Henry VIII*: 1740, 77.
31. CSP: Edward VI, no. 195 (p.91).
32. CSP: Edward VI, no. 187 (p.87).
33. J. Strype: 1822, II, i, 188.

34. CSP: Edward VI, no. 189 (p.88). In addition to the 'valuable specialty', to which Northampton refers in his deposition, probably a sum of money, Seymour may have also presented him with the walking cane

or staff decorated with silver and gilt, 'with astronomy upon it and two rules of silver and gilt in it and a little shipman's compass on the top', which was confiscated from the marquess during his attainder for the attempted Lady Jane Grey coup in 1553. This cane may originally have been Seymour's and connected with his office as Lord Admiral, as the mariner's devices on it indicate. The cane was stored at Westminster during the reign of Mary I and returned to Northampton on the accession of Elizabeth I. BL: Addit. MS 5751, f.300 (p.292).

35. CSP: Edward VI, no. 184 (p.84).

36. CSP: Edward VI, no. 191 (p.89).

37. CSP: Edward VI, no. 203 (p.94).

38. CSP: Edward VI, no. 188 (p.87). It has been suggested (G. Elton: 1977, 333) that Warwick was the instigator of the quarrel between the Seymour brothers. While Warwick reaped the benefit some years later, the evidence points to a family quarrel whose roots may go back to before Henry VIII's death and which had no need of an outside agitator to encourage it to grow to such desperate proportions. The high-handed behavior of the Somersets when combined with Sir Thomas' hasty temper was a recipe for disaster.

39. *A Collection ... Henry VIII*: 1740, 104.

40. CSP: Edward VI, no. 186 (p.86).

41. CSP: Edward VI, no. 183 (p.84).

42. CSP: Edward VI, no. 192 (p.90).

43. Patrick Fraser Tytler, *England Under the Reigns of Edward VI and Mary I*, 2 vols, London, 1839, 149.

44. CSP: Edward VI, no. 203 (p.94).

45. *A Collection ... Henry VIII*: 1740, 82.

46. C. Parr: 1548, f.Bvia.

47. For the transcripts of testimony against Seymour, CSP: Domestic, Edward VI, nos 178–205.

48. J. Strype: 1822, II, i, 199.

49. *Sermons ... Latimer*: 1926, I, 162, note.

50. J. Strype: 1822, II, i, 199.

51. *Sermons ... Latimer*: 1926, I, 162, note.

52. J. Strype: 1822, II, i, 198.

53. *Sir Nicholas Throckmorton*: 1874, no. 74, p.19.

54. APC: II, 411.

55. CSP: Domestic (1547-1580), 21.

56. J. Strype: 1822, II, i, 202.

Bibliography

It has become customary for historians publishing books of research to expand the bibliography to cumbersome lengths, exploring and listing archives of arcana and plumbing the heights and depths of unpublished theses in the belief that a massive bibliography validates the scholarship of the text. There is not, however, an absolute correlation between the quality of the research and the length of the bibliography. Sometimes, unfortunately, the reverse is true. In the list of abbreviations that I have used, most of the standard references for the period appear. Any historian of the sixteenth century is familiar with them and I believe it to be unnecessary to repeat them once more in this bibliography. The bulk of the material which appears in the text is culled from primary source manuscripts and materials, the preponderance of which are on deposit at the National Archives, London. The records of the Exchequer contain most of Catherine Parr's chamber accounts (with a few exceptions) and the references for these can be found in the footnotes to the various chapters. I refer the reader to the footnotes as well for references to Catherine Parr's own works. What remains is a bibliography of printed works that have proven useful to me on more than one occasion and will, I hope, lead the reader to further information on those particular points in which he or she is interested.

A Collection of State Papers Relating to Affairs in the Reigns of King Henry VIII...Left by William Cecill, Lord Burghley, Samuel Haynes (ed.), London, 1740.

Allegations for Marriage Licences issued by the Bishop of London (1520-1610), I, Harleian Society, XXV, London, 1887.

Althaus, Paul, *The Theology of Martin Luther,* translated by Robert C. Schultz, Philadelphia, 1966.

Anstruther, Godfrey, *Vaux of Harrowden,* Newport, Mon., 1953.

Arnold, Janet, *Queen Elizabeth's Wardrobe Unlock'd,* Leeds, 1988,

The Arundel Harington Manuscript of Tudor Poetry, Ruth Hughey (ed.), Columbus, Ohio, 1960.

Ascham, Roger, *The Whole Works,* Dr. Giles (ed.), 3 volumes, London, 1864.

Ascu, Edward, *A Historie contayning the Warres & Etc.,* London, 1607.

Ashbee, Andrew, *Records of English Court Music, VII (1485-1558),* VII, London, 1993.

Auerbach, Erna, *Tudor Artists,* London & New York, 1954.

Baker, George, *History and Antiquities of the County of Northamptonshire,* ii, 1822- 1841.

Bale, John, *Illustrium Majoris Britanniae Scriptorum,* Wesel, 1548.

Beer, Barrett L., *Northumberland: The Political Career of John Dudley, Earl of Warwick and Duke of Northumberland,* Kent, Ohio, 1973.

Beilin, Elaine V., *Redeeming Eve,* Princeton, 1987.

Bell, H. E., *An Introduction to the History and Records of the Court of Wards and Liveries,* 1953.

Bindoff, S. T., 'Ket's Rebellion', *Historical Association Publications,* G12, 1949.

The Black Book of Warwick, Thomas Kemp (ed.), Warwick, 1898.

Bond, Maurice, *The Romance of St. George's Chapel, Windsor Castle,* Windsor, 1987.

Bradford, Charles A., *Helena, Marchioness of Northampton,* London, 1936.

Bridges, John, *History and Antiquities of Northamptonshire,* London, 1791.

Brigden, Susan, *London and the Reformation,* Oxford, 1989.

Brooks, F. W., 'The Council of the North', *Historical Association Publications,* G25, 1966.

Burnet, Gilbert, *The History of the Reformation of the Church of England,* London, 1839.

Bush, M. L., 'The Problem of the Far North, A Study of the Crisis of 1537 and Its Consequences', *Northern History,* IV, 1971, 50–52.

Bush, M. L., *The Government Policy of Protector Somerset,* London, 1975.

Camden, William, *Annals of Elizabeth,* London, 1625.

Catalogue of the Library of Henry Huth, 1880.

The Chronicle and Political Papers of King Edward VI, W. K. Jordan (ed.), Ithaca, New York, 1966.

Clark, Duncan W., 'College of Halstead or Bourchier's Chantry', *Transactions of the Essex Archaeological Society,* New Series, XIV, 1918.

Cokayne, G. E. C., *The Complete Peerage,* London, 1929.

Cooper, Charles Henry, *Annals of Cambridge,* 5 volumes, Cambridge, 1842–56.

Cooper, Charles Henry, *Memoir of Margaret, Countess of Richmond and Derby*, Cambridge, 1874.

Cooper, Charles Henry and Thompson Cooper, *Athenae Cantabrigienses*, II, Cambridge, 1858.

The Coronation of Richard III: the Extant Documents, Anne F. Sutton and P. W. Hammond (eds), Gloucester and New York, 1983.

The Correspondence of Sir Thomas More, Elizabeth Frances Rogers (ed.), Princeton, 1947.

Craster, H.H. E., *A History of Northumberland*, IX & X, 1893-1940.

Crawford, Patricia, *Women and Religion in England, 1500-1720*, London and New York, 1993.

Davies, Gerald S., *Charterhouse in London*, London, 1922.

Deacon, Richard, *John Dee*, 1968.

Dent, Emma, *Annals of Winchcombe and Sudeley*, London, 1877.

Devereux, E. J., 'The Publication of the English Paraphrases', BJRL, 51 (1968–69).

The Diary of Henry Machyn, Citizen and Merchant-Taylor of London from 1550–1563, J. G. Nichols (ed.), Camden Society, 1848.

Dibdin, Sir Lewis and Sir Charles Healey, *English Church Law and Divorce*, London, 1951.

Dictionary of National Biography, Sir Leslie Stephen and Sir Sidney Lee (eds), London, 1917.

Dodds, M. H., and R. Dodds, *The Pilgrimage of Grace, 1536–37, and the Exeter Conspiracy, 1538,* 2 volumes, Cambridge, 1915.

Dowling, Maria, 'The Gospel and the Court: Reform under Henry VIII', in *Protestantism and the National Church in the Sixteenth Century*, Peter Lake and Maria Dowling (eds.), New York & Sydney, 1987.

Dowling, Maria, 'Anne Boleyn and Reform', *Journal of Ecclesiastical History*, XXXV, 1 (January 1984).

Dowling, Maria, *Humanism in the Age of Henry VIII*, London, 1986.

Dowling, Maria, 'Anne Boleyn and Reform', *Journal of Ecclesiastical History*, XXXV, No. 1, January 1984.

Dugdale, William, *History of St. Paul's Cathedral*, London, 1716.

Eales, Richard, *Chess, The History of a Game*, London, 1985.

Echard, Lawrence, *The History of England*, London, 1707.

Elton, G. R., *Reform and Reformation England, 1509-1558,* London, 1977.

Elton, G.R., *England Under the Tudors*, Cambridge, 1962.

Elyot, Sir Thomas, *The Defence of Good Women*, London, 1540.

Emmison, F. G., *Tudor Secretary: Sir William Petre at Court and Home*, Cambridge, MA, 1961.

Erasmus, Desiderius, *The 1st Tome or Volume of the Paraphrases upon the New Testament*, London, 31 January 1548.

Farrer, William, *Records Relating to the Barony of Kendal*, 2 volumes, Kendal, 1923–1926.

Fisher, John, Bishop of Rochester, 'A Morning Remembrance, a Sermon on the Death of Margaret, Countess of Richmond', in Charles Henry Cooper, *Memoir of Margaret, Countess of Richmond and Derby*, Cambridge, 1874.

Finch, Mary E., *The Wealth of Five Northamptonshire Families, 1540-1640*, Oxford, 1956.

Fowler, R. C., 'Essex Chapels', *Transactions of the Essex Archaeological Society*, N.S. 16 (1923).

Foxe, John, *Acts and Monuments*, S.R. Cattley (ed.), V, London, 1866 edition.

Fuller, Thomas, *The History of the Worthies of England*, II, London, 1660.

Gairdner, James, *Lollardy and the Reformation in England*, II, London, 1908.

Gammon, Samuel Rhea, *Statesman and Schemer: William, 1st Lord Paget, Tudor Minister*, Hamden, Connecticut, 1973.

Ganz, Paul, *Les Dessins de Hans Holbein le Jeune*, Geneva, 1939.

Giles, J. A., *Six Old English Chronicles*, London, 1848.

Grafton, Richard, *A Chronicle at Large*, 2 volumes, London, 1569.

Guevara, Antonio, *A Dispraise of the Life of a Courier, and a Commendation of the Life of the Labouring Man*, Sir Francis Bryan (trans.), London, 1548.

Hall, Edward, *Henry VIII*, volume II, London, 1904 edition.

Hall's Chronicle: Containing the History of England (1548–1550), H. Ellis (ed.), London, 1809 edition.

The Hamilton Papers: Letters and Papers Illustrating the Political Relation of England and Scotland in the XVIth Century, Joseph Bain (ed.), 2 volumes, Edinburgh, 1890–92.

Hamilton, Dakota Lee, *The Household of Queen Katherine Parr*, unpublished D.Phil., Oxford (1992).

Harris, Ann Sutherland and Linda Nochlin, *Women Artists: 1550–1950*, New York, 1976.

Harrison, Barbara E., *The Bassanos, Italian Musicians at the English Court, 1531–1664*, privately published, 1991.

Hatch, Maurice Addison, *The Ascham Letters: An Annotated Translation of the Latin Correspondence*, unpublished Ph.D. thesis, Cornell University, New York, 1948.

Haugaard, William P., 'Katherine Parr: the Religious Convictions of a Renaissance Queen', *Renaissance Quarterly*, 22, 1969.

Hayward, Sir John, *The Life and Reign of King Edward VI,* London, 1630.

Hearne, Thomas, *Sylloge Epistolarum,* London, 1716.

Henderson, Katherine Usher and Barbara F. McManus, *Half Humankind: Contexts and Texts of the Controversy About Women in England,* 1540–1640, Urbana and Chicago, 1985.

The History of the King's Works, H. M. Colvin (ed.), IV, 1485–1660 (Part II), London, 1982.

Hoak, Dale, *The King's Council in the Reign of Edward VI,* Cambridge, 1976.

Hoby, Sir Thomas, *The Travels and Life of Sir Thomas Hoby, Knight,* Camden Miscellany, X, 3rd Series, 1902.

Hodgson, John Crawford, *A History of Northumberland,* V, Newcastle-on-Tyne & London, 1820–58.

Hoffman, C. Fenno, Jr., 'Catherine Parr as a Woman of Letters', *Huntington Library Quarterly,* 23, 1959.

Hogrefe, Pearl, 'Anne Cooke, Lady Bacon', in *Women of Action in Tudor England,* Ames, Iowa, 1977.

Holinshed, Raphael and William Harrison, *Chronicles,* iii, London, 1807–8.

Horae ad Usum Sarum, Cambridge University Library [Inc., 4.J.1.2 (3570)].

Howard, Leonard, *A Collection of Letters from the Original Manuscripts,* London, 1753.

Hughes, Philip, *The Reformation in England,* II, London 1954.

Hurstfield, J., 'Political Corruption in Modern England', *History,* LII (1967), pp. 16–34.

Ives, E. W., *Anne Boleyn,* Oxford, 1986.

James, M. E., 'Obedience and Dissent in Henrician England: The Lincolnshire Rebellion, 1536', *Past and Present,* 48 (August 1970), 3–78.

James, Susan E., 'A Tudor Divorce: The Marital History of William Parr, Marquess of Northampton', *CW2,* XC (1990), pp. 199-204.

James, Susan E., 'Parr Memorials in Kendal Parish Church', *CW2,* XCII (1992), pp.99- 103.

James, Susan E., 'Sir William Parr of Kendal: Part I, 1434–1471', *CW2,* XCIII (1993), pp. 100–114.

James, Susan E., 'Nicholas Lanier, Part I (1588–1612), *Journal of the Greenwich Historical Society,* I, 2 (1993), pp. 536.

James, Susan E., 'Sir William Parr of Kendal: Part II, 1471–1483', *CW2,* XCIV (1994), pp. 105–120

James, Susan E., 'Lady Jane Grey or Queen Kateryn Parr?', *The Burlington Magazine,* Volume CXXXVIII, Number 1114 (January 1996), pp. 20–24.

James, Susan E., 'Two Holbein Miniatures', *Apollo,* May 1998, pp. 15–20.

James, Susan E., 'Henry VII and the Prerogativa Regis: The Case of Mabel Dacre', *CW2,* XCIX (1999), 1777–84.

James, Susan E., 'A New Source for Shakespeare's *The Taming of the Shrew*', *Bulletin of the John Rylands University Library of Manchester* (Spring 1999), 49–62.

Jordan, Constance, 'Feminism and the Humanists: The Case of Sir Thomas Elyot's 'Defence of Good Women'', *Renaissance Quarterly,* 36, no.2 (Summer 1983).

Jordan, W. K., *Edward VI: The Threshold of Power,* Cambridge, Mass., 1970.

Kelso, Ruth, *Doctrine for the Lady of the Renaissance,* Urbana, 1956.

Kelso, Ruth, 'The Doctrine of the English Gentleman in the Sixteenth Century', *University of Illinois Studies in Languages and Literature,* XIV, Urbana, 1929.

Kerridge, Eric, 'Agrarian Problems in the Sixteenth Century and After', *Historical Problems: Studies and Documents,* VI, 1969.

Kerridge, Eric, 'The Movement of the Rent', *Economic History Review,* 2nd Series, VI, 1953.

King, H. W., 'Inventories of Church Goods, 6 Edward VI', *Transactions of the Essex Archaeological Society,* Volume V, 1873.

King, John N., 'Patronage and Piety: The Influence of Catherine Parr', in *Silent But for the Word: Tudor Women as Patrons, Translators and Writers of Religious Works,* Margaret Patterson Hannay (ed.), Kent, Ohio, 1985.

King, Margaret L., *Women of the Renaissance,* Chicago and London, 1991.

Kurz, Otto, 'An Architectural Design for Henry VIII', *The Burlington Magazine,* LXXXII (1943).

Lea, Rowland, *Chronicle of Queen Jane and of Two Years of Queen Mary,* J.G. Nichols (ed.), Camden Society #48, London, 1850.

The Legend of Sir Nicholas Throckmorton, John Gough Nichols (ed.), Roxburghe Club, V, London, 1874.

The Letter Book of John Parkhurst, R.A. Houlbrooke (ed.), Norfolk Record Society, Volume 43, Norwich, 1874-75.

The Letters of King Henry VIII, Muriel St. Clare Byrne (ed.), London, 1968.

The Letters of Queen Elizabeth, G. B. Harrison (ed.), London, 1968.

The Letters of Richard Scudamore to Sir Philip Hoby, September 1549-March 1555, Susan Brigden (ed.), Camden Miscellany, XXX, 4th Series, London, 1990.

The Letters of Stephen Gardiner, James Arthur Muller (ed.), Cambridge, 1933.

Levin, Carole, 'John Foxe and the Responsibilities of Queenship', in *Women in the Middle Ages and the*

Renaissance: Literary and Historical Perspectives, Mary Beth Rose (ed.), Syracuse, 1986, pp. 113–133.

Levine, M., 'The Last Will and Testament of Henry VIII: A Reappraisal Reappraised', *Historian,* 1964.

The Lisle Letters, Muriel St. Clare Byrne (ed.), 4, Chicago, 1981.

The Literary Remains of Edward VI, J. G. Nichols (ed.), London, 1857.

Lloyd, David, *State Worthies,* London, 1670.

Loades, David M., *Mary Tudor: A Life,* Oxford, 1989.

Loades, David M., *Two Tudor Conspiracies,* Cambridge, 1965.

London Pageants, J. G. Nichols (ed.), London, 1837.

MacCulloch, Diarmaid, *Thomas Cranmer, A Life,* New Haven & London, 1996.

Martienssen, Anthony, *Queen Katherine Parr,* London, 1973.

McConica, James K., *English Humanists and Reformation Politics under Henry VIII and Edward VI,* Oxford, 1965.

Mellows, W.T., 'The Last Days of Peterborough Monastery', *Publications of the Northamptonshire Record Society,* 12, 1947.

Miller, Helen, 'Early Tudor Peerage, 1485-1547', *BIHR,* XXIV, 1951.

Mueller, Janel, 'A Tudor Queen Finds Her Voice: Katherine Parr's 'Lamentation of a Sinner', *The Historical Renaissance: New Essays on Tudor and Stuart Literature and Culture,* Heather Dubrow and Richard Strier (eds.), Chicago, 1988.

Mueller, Janel, 'Devotion as Difference: Intertextuality in Queen Katherine Parr's 'Prayers or Meditations '(1545)', Huntington Library Quarterly, 53, 1988.

Muller, James Arthur, *Stephen Gardiner and the Tudor Reaction,* New York, 1926.

'Narrative of the Visit of the Duke of Najera', *Archaeologia,* XXIII (1831), pp. 348–357.

'Narratives of the Days of the Reformation, John Gough Nichols (ed.), Camden Society Papers, 77, London, 1859.

Nash, Reverend Treadway, 'Observations on the Time of Death and Place of Burial of Queen Katharine Parr', *Archaeologia,* IX (1789).

Nicholas, Sir Harris, *Proceedings and Ordinances of the Privy Council of England,* VII (1540–1542).

Nicolson, Cornelius, *The Annals of Kendal,* 1835.

Nicolson, Joseph and Richard Burn, *The History and Antiquities of the Counties of Westmorland and Cumberland,* London, 1777.

Original Letters Illustrative of English History, H. Ellis (ed.), 11 volumes, London, 1824–46.

Pantzer, Katharine F., *Short Title Catalogue,* London, 1919.

Pease, Howard, *The Lord Wardens of the Marches of England and Scotland,* New York, 1913.

Persons, Robert, *A Treatise of Three Conversions of England,* volume 2, London, 1976.

Pettegree, Andrew, *Foreign Protestant Communities in Sixteenth Century London,* Oxford, 1986.

Plowden, Alison, *Tudor Women: Queens and Commoners,* New York, 1979.

Potter, D. L., 'Diplomacy in the Mid-Sixteenth Century: England and France, 1536–1550', unpublished Ph.D. dissertation, Cambridge, 1973.

Prescott, Anne Lake, 'The Pearl of the Valois and Elizabeth I', in *Silent But for the Word: Tudor Women as Patrons, Translators and Writers of Religious Works,* Margaret Patterson Hannay (ed.), Kent, Ohio, 1985.

The Privy Purse Expenses of Princess Mary, Frederick Madden (ed.), London, 1831.

Quarto, Abbot Hall Art Gallery, vol. V, no. 4, January 1968; vol. VI, no. 4, January 1969; vol. VII, no. 4, January 1970; vol. X, no. 1, April 1972.

Read, Evelyn, *Catherine Willoughby, Duchess of Suffolk,* London, 1962.

Redworth, Glyn, *In Defence of the Catholic Church,* Oxford, 1990.

Reese, M.M., *Master of the Horse,* London, 1976.

The Renaissance Englishwoman in Print: Counterbalancing the Canon, Anne M. Haselkorn and Betty S. Travitsky (eds.), Amherst, 1990.

Return of Aliens in the City and Suburbs of London from Henry VIII to James I, R. E. G. Kirk and E. F. Kirk (eds), London, 1900–07, volume 10, parts i and iii.

Ridley, Jasper, *Thomas Cranmer,* London, 1962.

Rogers, T. E., *Records of Yarlington,* 1890.

Rose-Troup, Frances B., 'Two Book Bills of Katherine Parr', *The Library,* January 1911.

Ross, Charles, *Edward IV,* London, 1974.

Rowse, A. L., *Shakespeare, the Man,* London, 1988.

Russell, F. W., *Kett's Rebellion,* London, 1859.

Rymer's Foedera, VI, London, 1741 (republished 1967).

Scarisbrick, Diane, *Tudor and Jacobean Jewellery,* London, 1995.

Scarisbrick, J. J., *Henry VIII*, Berkeley and Los Angeles, 1968.

Scheurweghs, G., *Materials for the Study of the Old English Drama*, Volume 16, Louvain, 1939.

Scott, Daniel, *The Stricklands of Sizergh Castle*, Kendal, 1908.

The Second Book of the Travels of Nicander Nucius of Corcyra, Rev. J.A. Cramer (ed.), Camden Society, Volume 17, London, 1841, pp. 8–18

The Sermons of Hugh Latimer, John Watkins (ed.), London, 1926.

Seymour, William, *Ordeal by Ambition*, New York, 1972.

Shrewsbury, J.F.D., 'Henry VIII: A Medical Study', *Journal of the History of Medicine*, VIII, 1952, 55–106.

Simon, Joan, *Education and Society in Tudor England*, Cambridge, 1967.

Six Pamphlets on the History of Books, Bodleian 2581.d.73(4).

Slavin, A. J., *Politics and Profit: A Study of Sir Ralph Sadler, 1507–1547*, Cambridge, 1966

Smith, H. Maynard, *Henry VIII and the Reformation*, London, 1948.

Smith, Hilda L., 'Humanist education and the Renaissance concept of woman', in *Women and Literature in Britain, 1500–1700*, Helen Wilcox (ed.), Cambridge, 1996.

Smith, Lacey Baldwin, 'The Last Will and Testament of Henry VIII: A Question of Perspective', *Journal of British Studies*, ii (1962).

Smith, Lacey Baldwin, *Tudor Prelates and Politics, 1536–58*, Princeton, 1953.

Smith, Lacey Baldwin, *A Tudor Tragedy*, London, 1961.

Smith, R.B., *Land and Politics in the England of Henry VIII*, Oxford, 1970.

Starkey, David, *The Reign of Henry VIII, Personalities and Politics*, London, 1985.

State Papers and Letters of Sir Ralph Sadler, A. Clifford (ed.), 2 volumes, Edinburgh, 1809.

Stevens, David McCluer, 'The Royal Grammar School of Guildford', *The Surrey Archaeological Society Collection*, X, 1891.

Stone, Lawrence, *Family and Fortune*, Oxford, 1973.

Stone, Lawrence, *The Crisis of the Aristocracy*, Oxford, 1965.

Storey, R. L., 'The Chantries of Cumberland and Westmorland, 1546', *CW2*, LXII, 1962.

Strickland, Agnes, *Lives of the Queens of England*, III, London, 1851.

Strong, Roy, *The English Renaissance Miniature*, London, 1983 (revised edition 1984).

Strype, John, *Annals of the Reformation*, Volume II, Part ii, Oxford, 1824.

Strype, John, *Ecclesiastical Memorials of Henry VIII, Edward VI, and Mary I*, 3 volumes, London, 1822.

Strype, John, *Memorials of Thomas Cranmer*, London, 1694.

Sturge, Charles, *Cuthbert Tunstal*, London, New York & Toronto, 1938.

Swain, Margaret H., 'A New Year's Gift from the Princess Elizabeth', *The Connoisseur* (August 1973)

Thurley, Simon, 'Henry VIII and the building of Hampton Court: A reconstruction of the Tudor Palace', *Architectural History*, 31 (1988).

Thurley, Simon, *The Royal Palaces of Tudor England*, New Haven and London, 1993.

Travitsky, Betty S., 'The possibilities of prose', in *Women and Literature in Britain, 1500–1700*, Helen Wilcox, (ed.), Cambridge, 1996.

Trill, Suzanne, 'Religion and the construction of femininity', in *Women and Literature in Britain, 1500–1700*, Helen Wilcox (ed.), Cambridge, 1996.

Trill, Suzanne, 'Sixteenth-century women's writing: Mary Sidney's Psalmes and the 'femininity' of translation', in *Writing and the English Renaissance*, William Zunder and Suzanne Trill (ed.), London and New York, 1996.

Tudor Royal Proclamations: Volume I: The Early Tudors (1485–1553), Paul L. Hughes and James F. Larkin (eds.), New Haven and London, 1964.

Tuer, William, *The History of the Horn Book*, Volume 1, London, 1896.

Tytler, Patrick Fraser, *England Under the Reigns of Edward VI and Mary I*, 2 volumes, London, 1839.

Udall, Nicholas, *Ralph Roister Doister*, William Durrant Cooper (ed.), Printed for the Shakespeare Society, London, 1847.

Venn, John and J. K. Venn, *Alumni Cantabrigienses*, Part I, Volumes I & III, Cambridge, 1927.

Wall, Wendy, *The Imprint of Gender: Authorship and Publication in the English Renaissance*, Ithaca and London, 1993.

Warnicke, Retha M., *The Rise and Fall of Anne Boleyn: Family Politics at the Court of Henry VIII*, Cambridge, 1989

Warnicke, Retha M., *Women of the English Renaissance and Reformation*, Westport, 1983.

Weever, John, *Antient Funeral Monuments*, London, 1631.

Willen, Diane, 'Women and Religion in Early Modern Europe: Public and Private Worlds', in *Women in Reformation and Counter-Reformation Europe*, Sherrin Marshall (ed.), Bloomington and Indianapolis, 1989.

Williams, Neville, *Thomas Howard, Fourth Duke of Norfolk,* New York, 1964.

Williamson, George C., *The Royal Grammar School of Guildford,* 1509: *a Record and Review*, Guildford, 1929.

Wilson, Derek, *Hans Holbein, Portrait of an Unknown Man,* London, 1996.

Winnett, A. R., *Divorce and Re-Marriage in Anglicanism*, London, 1958.

Wolffe, B. P., *The Crown Lands,* 1461–1536, London, 1970.

Wolffe, B. P., 'Henry VII's Land Revenues and Chamber Finance', *EHR*, LXXIX, 1964, pp. 225–254.

Wolsey Correspondence, Camden Miscellany, III, 78.

Wriothesley, Charles, *A Chronicle of England*, William Douglas Hamilton (ed.), Camden Society, NS.XI, 1875-1877.

York Civic Records, A. Raine (ed.), III, in *The Yorkshire Archaeological Society Record Series*, CVI, 2 volumes, 1942.

Acknowledgements

Without the continuous encouragement of my family, my parents, Barbara and Royal Harrison, and my sister, Linda Franco, this book would never have reached completion. I also owe a profound debt to the kindness and generosity of Sir Geoffrey Elton, who read several early versions of the manuscript and never failed to offer unstinting support and constructive advice. To Bess Brewer Lyon, Gertrude Stadtmiller, Cynthia Berne, Rosemary Lonergan and Elizabeth Herrick, I owe a lifetime of thanks for giving me a broader vision of history and the world than I might ever have found for myself, and to my father, William James, my love and gratitude for pointing me in the right direction. Lastly, I would like to thank all the readers of the many incarnations through which this book has passed, most of them unknown to me. Those who took the time and trouble to offer helpful suggestions challenged me to write a better book. I hope that in some measure, this fulfills their expectations.

List of Illustrations

1 Drawing of the tomb of Sir Thomas and Maud Parr. (The British Library, Add 45,131, fo.109b)

2 Plan and southern elevation of Rye House. (Courtesy of the Hertfordshire County Council)

3 Horae ad Usum Sarum, CUL: Inc 4.J.1.2 (3570), fo.107a. (By permission of the Syndics of Cambridge University Library)

4 Horae ad Usum Sarum, CUL: Inc 4.J.1.2 (3570), fo.20a. (By permission of the Syndics of Cambridge University Library)

5 Horae ad Usum Sarum, CUL: Inc 4.J.1.2 (3570), fo.20b. (By permission of the Syndics of Cambridge University Library)

6 Portrait of Cuthbert Tunstall. (Burton Constable, coll. John Chichester-Constable. Photograph: Courtauld Institute of Art)

7 Horae ad Usum Sarum, CUL: Inc 4.J.1.2 (3570), fo.116a. (By permission of the Syndics of Cambridge University Library)

8 Holbein drawing of Elizabeth Cheyney. (By gracious permission of Her Majesty Queen Elizabeth II)

9 Horae ad Usum Sarum, CUL: Inc 4.J.1.2 (3570), fo.72a. (By permission of the Syndics of Cambridge University Library)

10 Portrait of Catherine Parr at Lambeth Palace. (By permission of His Grace the Archbishop of Canterbury)

11 Drawing of Gainsborough Old Hall, Lincolnshire. (Courtesy of John Bangay, MA)

12 Holbein drawing of William Parr (By gracious permission of Her Majesty Queen Elizabeth II)

13 Photograph of Snape Castle. (Courtesy of A. F. Kersting, London)

14 Holbein drawing of Anne Parr(?) (By gracious permission of Her Majesty Queen Elizabeth II)

15 Holbein miniature of Sir Thomas Seymour. (Yale Center for British Art/Paul Mellon Collection)

16 Catherine Parr's signature on the title-page of a sermon of St. John Chrysostome (Dent-Brocklehurst Collection, Sudeley Castle)

17 Holbein drawing of Edward Seymour, Duke of Somerset(?). (By gracious permission of Her Majesty Queen Elizabeth II)

18 Holbein drawing of John Dudley, Duke of Northumberland(?). (By gracious permission of Her Majesty Queen Elizabeth II)

19 Portrait of Sir William Paget. (By courtesy of the National Portrait Gallery, London)

20 Holbein drawing of Sir Richard Rich. (By gracious permission of Her Majesty Queen Elizabeth II)

21 Portrait of Catherine Parr. (Present whereabouts unknown. Photograph courtesy of the National Portrait Gallery, London)

22 Portrait of Sir William Petre. (Courtesy of the National Portrait Gallery, London)

23 Effigy of Sir William Parr of Horton. (Courtesy of Royal G. Harrison)

24 Portrait of Catherine Parr. (Courtesy of the National Portrait Gallery, London)

25 Portrait of Katherine Willoughby, Duchess of Suffolk. (By permission of the Earl of Devon. Photograph courtesy of the Courtauld Institute)

26 Effigy of Mary Salisbury, Lady Parr of Horton. (Courtesy of Royal G. Harrison)

27 Holographic poem by Sir Thomas Seymour. (Dent-Brocklehurst Collection, Sudeley Castle)

28 Holographic homilies by Catherine Parr. (Dent-Brocklehurst Collection, Sudeley Castle)

29 Hanworth Palace from an old print. (Bess B. Lyon Photographic Collection)

30 Design for a Presence Chamber. (Present whereabouts unknown.)

31 Portrait medals of the Marquess and Marchioness of Northampton by Stephen van Herwijck. (Present whereabouts unknown)

32 Catherine Parr's royal great seal. (Bess B. Lyon Photographic Collection)

33 Treadway Nash's drawing of Catherine Parr's coffin. (Archaeologia, IX [1789]. By permission of the Syndics of Cambridge University Library)

Index

TEMPUS – REVEALING HISTORY

Britannia's Empire
A Short History of the British Empire
BILL NASSON

'Crisp, economical and witty' *TLS*
'An excellent introduction the subject' *THES*

£12.99   0 7524 3808 5

Born to be Gay
A History of Homosexuality
WILLIAM NAPHY

'Fascinating' *The Financial Times*
'Excellent' *Gay Times*

£9.99   0 7524 3694 5

Madmen
A Social History of Madhouses,
Mad-Doctors & Lunatics
ROY PORTER

'Fascinating'
The Observer

£12.99   0 7524 3730 5

William II
Rufus, the Red King
EMMA MASON

'A thoroughly new reappraisal of a much
maligned king. The dramatic story of his life is
told with great pace and insight'
John Gillingham

£25   0 7524 3528 0

To Kill Rasputin
The Life and Death of Grigori Rasputin
ANDREW COOK

'Andrew Cook is a brilliant investigative historian'
Andrew Roberts
'Astonishing' *The Daily Mail*

£9.99   0 7524 3906 5

Private 12768
Memoir of a Tommy
JOHN JACKSON
FOREWORD BY HEW STRACHAN

'A refreshing new perspective' *The Sunday Times*
'At last we have John Jackson's intensely
personal and heartfelt little book to remind us
there was a view of the Great War other than
Wilfred Owen's' *The Daily Mail*

£9.99   0 7524 3531 0

The Unwritten Order
Hitler's Role in the Final Solution
PETER LONGERICH

'Compelling' *Richard Evans*
'The finest account to date of the many twists
and turns in Adolf Hitler's anti-semitic obsession'
Richard Overy

£12.99   0 7524 3328 8

The Vikings
MAGNUS MAGNUSSON

'Serious, engaging history'
BBC History Magazine

£9.99   0 7524 2699 0

If you are interested in purchasing other books published by Tempus, or in case you have difficulty finding any
Tempus books in your local bookshop, you can also place orders directly through our website

www.tempus-publishing.com

TEMPUS – REVEALING HISTORY

D-Day The First 72 Hours
WILLIAM F. BUCKINGHAM

'A compelling narrative' *The Observer*
A *BBC History Magazine* Book of the Year 2004

£9.99   0 7524 2842 X

The London Monster
Terror on the Streets in 1790
JAN BONDESON

'Gripping' *The Guardian*
'Excellent... monster-mania brought a reign of
terror to the ill-lit streets of the capital'
The Independent

£9.99   0 7524 3327 X

London
A Historical Companion
KENNETH PANTON

'A readable and reliable work of reference that
deserves a place on every Londoner's bookshelf'
Stephen Inwood

£20   0 7524 3434 9

M: MI5's First Spymaster
ANDREW COOK

'Serious spook history' *Andrew Roberts*
'Groundbreaking' *The Sunday Telegraph*
'Brilliantly researched' *Dame Stella Rimington*

£9.99   978 07524 3949 9

Agincourt
A New History
ANNE CURRY

'A highly distinguished and convincing account'
Christopher Hibbert
'A *tour de force*' *Alison Weir*
'*The* book on the battle' *Richard Holmes*
A *BBC History Magazine* Book of the Year 2005

£12.99   0 7524 3813 1

Battle of the Atlantic
MARC MILNER

'The most comprehensive short survey of the
U-boat battles' *Sir John Keegan*
'Some events are fortunate in their historian, none
more so than the Battle of the Atlantic. Marc
Milner is *the* historian of the Atlantic campaign... a
compelling narrative' *Andrew Lambert*

£12.99   0 7524 3332 6

The English Resistance
The Underground War Against the Normans
PETER REX

'An invaluable rehabilitation of an ignored
resistance movement' *The Sunday Times*
'Peter Rex's scholarship is remarkable'
The Sunday Express

£12.99   0 7524 3733 X

Elizabeth Wydeville: England's Slandered Queen
ARLENE OKERLUND

'A penetrating, thorough and wholly convincing
vindication of this unlucky queen'
Sarah Gristwood
'A gripping tale of lust, loss and tragedy'
Alison Weir
A *BBC History Magazine* Book of the Year 2005

£9.99   978 07524 3807 8

If you are interested in purchasing other books published by Tempus, or in case you have difficulty finding any
Tempus books in your local bookshop, you can also place orders directly through our website
www.tempus-publishing.com

TEMPUS – REVEALING HISTORY

Quacks Fakers and Charlatans in Medicine
ROY PORTER

'A delightful book' *The Daily Telegraph*
'Hugely entertaining' *BBC History Magazine*

£12.99   0 7524 2590 0

The Tudors
RICHARD REX

'Up-to-date, readable and reliable. The best
introduction to England's most important
dynasty' *David Starkey*
'Vivid, entertaining... quite simply the best short
introduction' *Eamon Duffy*
'Told with enviable narrative skill... a delight for
any reader' *THES*

£9.99   0 7524 3333 4

The Kings & Queens of England
MARK ORMROD

'Of the numerous books on the kings and
queens of England, this is the best'
Alison Weir

£9.99   0 7524 2598 6

The Covent Garden Ladies
Pimp General Jack & the Extraordinary Story of Harris's List
HALLIE RUBENHOLD

'Sex toys, porn... forget Ann Summers, Miss
Love was at it 250 years ago' *The Times*
'Compelling' *The Independent on Sunday*
'Marvellous' *Leonie Frieda*
'Filthy' *The Guardian*

£9.99   0 7524 3739 9

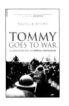

Okinawa 1945
GEORGE FEIFER

'A great book... Feifer's account of the three
sides and their experiences far surpasses most
books about war'
Stephen Ambrose

£17.99   0 7524 3324 5

Tommy Goes To War
MALCOLM BROWN

'A remarkably vivid and frank account of the
British soldier in the trenches'
Max Arthur
'The fury, fear, mud, blood, boredom and
bravery that made up life on the Western Front
are vividly presented and illustrated'
The Sunday Telegraph

£12.99   0 7524 2980 4

Ace of Spies The True Story of Sidney Reilly
ANDREW COOK

'The most definitive biography of the spying
ace yet written... both a compelling narrative
and a myth-shattering *tour de force*'
Simon Sebag Montefiore
'The absolute last word on the subject' *Nigel West*
'Makes poor 007 look like a bit of a wuss'
The Mail on Sunday

£12.99   0 7524 2959 0

Sex Crimes
From Renaissance to Enlightenment
W.M. NAPHY

'Wonderfully scandalous' *Diarmaid MacCulloch*
'A model of pin-sharp scholarship' *The Guardian*

£10.99   0 7524 2977 9

If you are interested in purchasing other books published by Tempus, or in case you have difficulty finding any
Tempus books in your local bookshop, you can also place orders directly through our website
www.tempus-publishing.com